Jewish
Buenos Aires,
1890–1930

Victor A. Mirelman

Jewish Buenos Aires, 1890–1930

In Search of an Identity

Wayne State University Press

Detroit 1990

Library of Congress Cataloging-in-Publication Data
Mirelman, Victor A.
    Jewish Buenos Aires, 1890–1930 : in search of an identity / Victor
A. Mirelman.
        p.   cm.
    Includes bibliographical references.
    ISBN 0-8143-2233-6
    1. Jews—Argentina—Buenos Aires—History. 2. Buenos Aires
(Argentina)—Ethnic relations.   I. Title.
F3001.9.J5M58 1990
982'.11—dc20   89-16739
                                               CIP

To my parents, Leon and Suzanne Mirelman

Contents

Contents

Acknowledgments

This book was envisioned quite some time ago when researching the sources dealing with the early period of Jewish life in Argentina. First presented as a doctoral dissertation at Columbia University, it is now thoroughly revised. Additional research was conducted to fully develop some chapters and to add new dimensions to the work.

I am grateful to all the Jewish institutions in Buenos Aires mentioned throughout the work for opening their archives to me. Due to the extent of their contents, the archives of the Chevra Keduscha Aschkenasi—today the Jewish Community of Buenos Aires—and the Congregación Israelita, proved to be invaluable. The various Sephardic synagogues and communities provided entrance to their records and to insightful information as well. Many libraries in Buenos Aires, Jerusalem, and New York extended deeply appreciated courtesies to me. Among them the IWO Archives, Biblioteca Nacional, Biblioteca del Congreso, and Biblioteca del Honorable Concejo Deliberante in Buenos Aires; the National and University Library, Central Zionist Archives, and archives of the Sephardic Community in Jerusalem; and the New York Public Library and YIVO archives in New York. Among the scholars who provided useful insights at different stages of the work, I wish to acknowledge Gerson D. Cohen, Zvi Ankori, Ismar Schorsch, Hebert Klein, Haim Avni, and Judith Elkin. For the location of pictures, I am indebted to the Archivos de la Nación, IWO Institute, Congregación Israelita, and Martha Wolff. In addition I wish to thank *Jewish Social Studies* for allowing the bulk of chapter 9 to be reprinted in this book, my friend John Less for designing the map, Michael Lane who edited the book for Wayne State University Press, and Anne M. G. Adamus, its managing editor.

Acknowledgments

This book owes much to my supportive family. My wife, Rose-Miriam, encouraged me to bring this work to press, and together with our daughters, Yael and Jessica, provided the necessary home atmosphere for it to be completed. Finally, to my parents, Leon and Suzanne Mirelman, who settled as immigrants and flourished in the community described, I dedicate this book in love and gratitude.

Introduction

In 1890 the only Jewish institution a newly arrived Jew could find in Buenos Aires was Congregación Israelita de la República Argentina (CIRA). It was founded by a group of Jews desirous of holding High Holy Day services in 1862. CIRA was formally organized in 1868, and after 1875 it had its permanent synagogue in Calle Artes (today Carlos Pellegrini), number 351. In 1897 it inaugurated its temple in Libertad Street, facing Plaza Lavalle, a central location in the city of Buenos Aires. At the beginning of the 1890s most members of CIRA were Jews born in Western and Central Europe—France, Germany, England, and Italy. Some Moroccan and East European Jews had arrived in Buenos Aires during the 1880s and joined CIRA. However, their numbers remained small. In fact, the whole Jewish population in the country was estimated at 1,500 souls in 1888.[1]

Though assimilated, the Jews grouped around CIRA maintained some type of Jewish identity. Services were held during the Holy Days, and attempted on Sabbaths, though most of the time without the formal quorum of ten males. A society to help the poor and ill was organized at CIRA during the early 1870s. A philanthropic committee was formed in 1881 with the purpose of raising funds for their persecuted coreligionists in Russia. Funeral services according to Jewish rites were held, and the dead were buried at the British Cemetery (Cementerio de los Disidentes). Dietary and Sabbath laws were far from being observed by most members of CIRA. Still, an Italian Jewish doctor, Aquiles Modena, circumcised the newly born males. Henry Joseph, an English businessman who had arrived in Buenos Aires during the late 1850s, officiated as rabbi after receiving a special certificate from the chief rabbi of the French Consistoire, Lazare Isidor, in 1882. Joseph, whose wife converted to Judaism when he was appointed rabbi but whose children were not raised in the Jewish faith, was the most active personality in the small Jewish community of Buenos Aires before 1890. He led religious services, officiated at weddings and other specifically religious rituals, and was always prompt to defend the interests of the Jewish immigrants.[2]

A turning point in Argentine Jewry was effected when the *Weser* anchored in the port of Buenos Aires in August 1889, bringing 824 Jewish souls from Eastern Europe. This group constituted one of the main antecedents for the creation of the Jewish Colonization Association (JCA) by Baron Maurice de Hirsch in 1891.[3] From 1890 until 1930 the arrival of Jews from Eastern Europe in Argentina was quite a common event. To the few North African Jewish families who had settled in Buenos Aires during the 1880s many more were added during the following four decades. Still, by the end of the century a new source of Jewish immigrants emerged in the form of the Ottoman Empire. Thus, Arabic-speaking Jews from Syria—mainly Damascus and Aleppo—and Ladino-speaking Jews from Izmir, Constantinople, Salonika, and Rhodes arrived during the first three decades of the twentieth century. Buenos Aires, a cosmopolitan city during this period, accordingly, became cosmopolitan also in a Jewish sense.

Eighteen ninety and 1930 are important turning points for the Jewish community in Argentina. Eighteen ninety marks the beginning, and 1930 the end, of immigration en masse to the country. During 1891 the Moroccan Jews founded their first institution, Congregación Israelita Latina, while the Russian Jews founded their first society, Poale Zedek (Sociedad Obrera Israelita). However, the influence of pre-1890 Jewish history in Buenos Aires was felt there until World War I. CIRA, especially Henry Joseph, its rabbi, and Luis H. Brie, its president, played a major role at some of the main institutions such as the Chevra Keduscha Aschkenasi (founded 1894) and Ezrah (founded 1900). This was due mainly to the fact that the West European Jews were the veterans— even if only by a generation or less—in Buenos Aires. They had a better economic situation and a more fluent command of Spanish, which was of importance when dealing with the local authorities. They thus had more free time to dedicate to institutional life, which many promptly did. On the other hand, by the end of the century—and more during the early 1900s—some Russian Jews had already secured for themselves worthy and stable economic situations, which enabled them to participate in leading positions in institutional life. Some of them entered CIRA and started occupying leading positions on its board.[4]

By 1930 the rule of the Radical party, representing by and large the interests of the middle sectors, was brought to an end by a rightist coup. Moreover, the crisis on Wall Street affected Argentina's economic stability. Furthermore, 1930 marks the end of the period of absorption of Jews in the country—with the exception of German Jews who arrived in the 1930s—when they founded most of their religious, cultural, social, educational, and philanthropic institutions, and the beginning of the most tragic period for world Jewry, with Hitler's gradual rise to power.

In this essay we shall describe the changing facade of the Jewish community in Buenos Aires during its crystallization period, up to 1930. After describing the immigration and settlement process, we shall illustrate the relations between Jews and gentiles during the period. We shall then look into the institutions the Jews created in Argentina and the interplay among these institutions—and among their constituents—which is what, in short, makes up Jewish life. An important element that developed in this period is the first generation of Argentine-born Jews. A study of their reactions to the Judaism brought by their parents from the Old World and of the roots they had developed in their country of birth will give us an understanding of the degree of assimilation, acculturation, and Argentinization of the Jews in Argentina. Finally, we shall describe the ways the various groups of immigrant Jews and their sons expressed their Judaism in Argentina.

Populationwise, Buenos Aires has always been the most important Jewish center in Argentina. In 1934 fully 131,000 Jews lived in the capital, while 12,500 lived in Rosario, and 5,300 in Córdoba. In the JCA agricultural colonies there were 30,659 Jews, counting both the urban and the rural population.[5] This essay will deal with the community of Buenos Aires. Only when it seems pertinent do we include some aspects of Jewish life in Rosario or in the JCA colonies. On the other hand, a development like agricultural settlements sponsored by JCA deserves a special and separate study.[6]

The Jewish population in Buenos Aires was cosmopolitan in itself. Jews had arrived from Poland, Russia, Roumania, Syria, Turkey, and Morocco. Their Jewishness and feelings for fellow Jews was what they had in common. But their Jewish identity was reflected in different ways, depending on their previous traditions. Ashkenazim comprised fully four-fifths of the total Jewish population. They founded tens of religious, Zionist, welfare, cultural, and educational institutions. The backbone of this sector was the Chevra Keduscha Aschkenasi, founded in 1894 as a burial society, which as years went by became the most powerful institution due to its large membership and economic prosperity. On the other hand, all four major Sephardic groups—Damascene, Aleppine, Turkish (Ladino-speaking), and Moroccan—underwent similar processes of consolidation. Each of these sectors gradually centralized most of its societies into one organization with a main synagogue, a burial society, a cemetery, and a religious school, as well as welfare institutions to provide for their ill and poor. Thus each group had the necessary institutions to constitute an independent community, and indeed contact between one Sephardic group with another was unusual.[7] In the chapters on religious life, Zionism, Jewish culture, education, and welfare we deal with each of these sectors separately. Within the Ashkenazic group CIRA is an atypical institution. Because of its unique character and its centrality in Jewish life during the period under analysis, we give it added attention.

Several visible controversial issues arose among Jews in Buenos Aires during the four decades of our concern. First, Sephardim and Ashkenazim, in spite of the attempts to join forces, went after separate goals and concerns. Even within each of these two main Jewish groups the spirit of localism determined by their communities of origin made for attachments to parochial interests. Second, religious Jews were dismayed at the growing apathy in Jewish traditional practices and the predominance of secularists in many of the institutions founded. Third, the political life, especially among Ashkenazim, was variegated and colorful, with abundant ideological argumentations. Zionists of various ideological persuasions lived side by side with non-Zionists and even with anti-Zionists; while at the same time a significant number of Jews, especially those militant in the workers' movement, were attracted to socialism, the Bund, and communism. Fourth, the established Jews active in religious, educational, and philanthropic societies were repeatedly challenged by other Jews imbued with extremist doctrines, especially the communist.

A variety of issues, most of them imported from the trans-Atlantic communities of origin, prompted these deeply felt divisions. Language was an early issue. Some Russian Jews advocated speaking Russian as a sign of enlightenment, while the vast majority of East European Jews preferred communicating in Yiddish. Later on Yiddish became a key factor in class education among leftist Jews, while small groups of Zionists propounded the use of Hebrew as a major link to the ideals of resettling Palestine. The clash between communists and the rest of the Jews was reflected in the school systems they founded, in the challenge to traditional philanthropy with fund-raising to promote self-help, and in the struggle between the Zionists and those advocating a Jewish territory in Soviet Russia. Furthermore, there were Jews who promoted specifically Jewish culture and contended with the self-styled universalists or assimilationists. Finally, the crucial fight against white slavery is described in some detail.

This work is based on primary sources heretofore never utilized. The Yiddisher Wisnshaflecher Institut (IWO) branch in Buenos Aires (founded in 1928) has preserved in its archives precious documents on the history of the Jews in Argentina, which otherwise would have disappeared. Two of the most veteran Jewish organizations in the country, the Congregación Israelita and the Chevra Keduscha Ashkenasi, have also preserved some documents of value, besides their own minutebooks. At the Central Zionist Archives in Jerusalem there is a wealth of documentation that reflects mainly on Zionist activities in Argentina. The Sephardic Community Committee (Vaad Ha'Eda HaSepharadit) Archives in Jerusalem were helpful as well. It is unfortunate, however, that many Jewish institutions in Argentina have not kept good archives of their activities during the first decades of the present century. This in itself is an historic fact of importance and throws some light on the attitude of the officials of these institutions vis-à-vis their own work in them. Still, most institutions have preserved their minutebooks. In the bibliography and notes the minutebooks of institutions consulted are listed. They have provided a perspective of Jewish life from the point of view of each of the individual institutions. Some of the annual reports of these institutions were also utilized, though unfortunately some did not preserve a complete collection of these reports. Another source of information has been the printed periodical word. The European Jewish press, especially of the 1890s and 1900s, was of value. The regular Argentine press also provided insights into the Jewish community in the country. However, the local Jewish press, in Yiddish, Spanish, and Hebrew, has proved to be of the greatest value. The several dailies, weeklies, and monthly journals with a wide range of ideologies permitted a comparison of social issues and of the views of the Jewish community of those years from different perspectives.

The bibliography provides a list of major articles and books quoted or referred to in this essay. Most of the articles describing Jewish life in Argentina appeared in the volumes in Yiddish published by the Ashkenazic community in Buenos Aires,[8] in special volumes published in honor of important anniversaries,[9] or in various issues of the *Argentiner IWO Shriftn*.[10] Though most of these articles are not the fruit of extensive research, they are important testimonies of individuals who participated to some extent in the events they describe. Their value, by and large, is that of memoirs more than that of elaborate pieces of research.

The Jewish Immigration Flow to Argentina

Argentina's Immigration Policy

Upon the unification of the Province of Buenos Aires with the Confederated Provinces in 1860, the leaders of the Argentine Republic were confronted with the responsibility of delineating new policies in order to build a progressive nation. The major idea proposed was to populate the vast extensions of land in the territory still not altogether conquered from the Indians. Adopting the motto of Juan Bautista Alberdi, who defined the duties of the heads of the country saying that "to govern is to populate" ("Gobernar es poblar"), Argentina adopted an open door policy for all immigrants. The 1853 Constitution explicitly forbade any limitations on immigrants arriving with the purpose of working the soil and developing industries, sciences, and the arts. Moreover, in 1876 the law of immigration, commonly known as Ley Avellaneda, regulated the process of absorption of immigrants in the country. The Hotel de Inmigrantes at the port of Buenos Aires was to provide shelter and meals to the newly arrived during their first days in the country; the immigrants were also to be provided with railroad tickets to their final destination in the interior of the country. With the conquest of large tracts of land from the Indians in 1880, the government and the "paternalistic oligarchy" in control of it saw fit to stimulate European immigration in order to render their newly acquired vast extentions of fertile land more profitable.[1]

The land-owning élite, with agricultural and stock-raising interests, required a large and growing labor supply and quite often preferred the immigrant worker to the native-born Argentinian. The liberal immigration policy was in consonance with their expectations that economic prosperity and growth could be accelerated by the constant flow of cheap labor. Industrialists, favoring the flow of immigrants, repeatedly demanded that the government subsidize the passage of skilled workers for their factories. The urban entrepreneurs desired immigration as well, especially of unskilled workers, in order to form a larger pool of potential strikebreakers. All these groups, though numerically small, had immense power in Argentina. The upper class assumed that the European immigrants would conform to a servile labor sector which would enhance their prosperity but would not challenge their prevailing political and economic power.

The open door policy in Argentina had the backing of the positivist social philosophy of the generation of 1880. The tendency to study social problems objectively and scientifically, stressing the practical values in life and emphasizing the importance of economic forces, flourished in Argentina at the time of the arrival of large numbers of European immigrants. Doctrines of economic liberalism, also appearing at this time, proposed that new social conditions allowing class mobility would make the nation prosper and progress. These new conditions would be promoted by an international labor force.[2]

The half-century period 1880–1930 was one of constant massive flow of immigrants from beyond the Atlantic to Argentina. The net immigration figures show that over three million immigrants settled permanently during those five decades, constituting a growing influx interrupted only by the economic crisis of 1890 and the First World War.

Jewish immigration in large numbers began in 1889, when the *Weser* anchored in the port of Buenos Aires. Over eight hundred Jews disembarked on that winter day in Argentina. From then to 1930 the arrival of immigrant Jews was a common event. According to Simón Weill's calculations the number of Jews in the country reached 10,000 in 1895, soared to 100,000 at the eve of World War I, and by the end of the 1920s had surpassed the 200,000 mark. The estimates of U. O. Schmelz and Sergio Della Pergola are slightly lower than those of Weill for the early decades. For 1930, however, they find the number of Jews living in Argentina to be considerably lower than Weill's calculation, since they estimate a larger exodus of Jews from Argentina (see Table 1).

The Jewish population was concentrated in the Jewish Colonization Association (JCA) colonies and principally in the capital city of Buenos Aires. The pace of growth of the capital, receiving an ever-soaring share of immigrants, was also reflected in the number of its Jewish inhabitants. In September 1904 a municipal census counted 6,065 Jews, or .64 percent of the total population of 950,891. Five years later, during October 1909, another census reported 16,589 Jews, or 1.35 percent of the total 1,231,698. In this latter year Rabbi Samuel Halphon collected some data on the Jewish population of most places in the country. His figure for Buenos Aires, somewhat between 30,000 and 40,000, is in discrepancy with the municipal census of the same year. The real number of Jews, most probably, was nearer to 25,000, allowing for the fact that

Table 1
Net Total Immigration and Net Jewish Immigration into Argentina

Year	Net Total Immigration[a]	Net Jewish Immigration[b]	Total Jewish[b]	Population[c]
1888	138,790	50	1,572	—
1889	220,260	1,000	—	—
1890	30,375	200	—	—
1891	− 29,835	2,850	—	—
1892	29,441	476	—	—
1893	35,624	743	—	—
1894	39,272	2,890	—	—
1895	44,169	1,763	—	—
1896	89,284	374	—	—
1897	47,686	607	—	—
1898	41,654	1,230	—	—
1899	48,842	562	—	—
1900	50,485	1,966	17,795	17,000
1901	45,700	1,885	—	—
1902	16,653	826	—	—
1903	37,895	334	—	—
1904	94,481	3,359	—	—
1905	138,850	7,516	—	—
1906	198,397	13,880	—	—
1907	119,861	4,301	—	—
1908	176,080	5,444	—	—
1909	140,640	8,865	—	—
1910	211,246	6,680	76,385	75,000
1911	109,478	6,378	—	—
1912	213,204	13,416	—	—
1913	143,288	10,860	—	—
1914	− 59,396	3,693	—	—
1915	− 64,488	606	—	—
1916	− 50,145	326	—	—
1917	− 30,977	269	—	—
1918	− 8,407	126	—	—
1919	12,170	280	—	—
1920	39,781	2,071	130,901	129,000
1921	65,753	3,908	—	—
1922	103,393	6,484	—	—
1923	160,799	13,701	—	—
1924	114,053	7,799	—	—
1925	75,277	6,920	—	—
1926	90,462	7,534	—	—
1927	111,878	5,584	—	—
1928	86,182	6,812	—	—
1929	89,221	5,986	—	—
1930	73,417	7,805	229,605	199,000

[a]*Republica Argentina, Dirección General de Estadística de la Nación*, various years. The figures include traffic to and from overseas and Montevideo. Up to 1909 only second- and third-class passengers are included. From 1910 onwards also first-class passengers are included.

[b]Simón Weill, *Población israelita en la República Argentina* (Buenos Aires, 1936), 28f.

[c]U. O. Schmelz and Sergio Della Pergola, "The Demography of Latin American Jewry," AJYB 85(1985): 65f.

many Jews preferred not to disclose their religious preference to the municipal census authorities.[3]

During the quinquennium 1910–14 large waves of immigrants arrived in Argentina, among them 41,000 Jews, most of whom remained in the capital, thus doubling its Jewish population to around 50,000.[4] During the war only a few hundred Jews arrived in Argentina, while the numbers of all emigrants exceeded that of immigrants by 213,413. Once the war was over, immigration was resumed with great impetus. During the eleven years 1920–30, 74,607 Jews entered Argentina and decided to remain there.

Weill was able to arrive at his figures of net Jewish immigration after he estimated the number of Jewish emigrants. These constituted in some periods a considerable proportion. Many Jews, not happy with their situation in Argentina, decided to return to Europe or proceed to other countries in the New World. During the 1890s, when most Jewish immigrants in Argentina went to the JCA colonies, several families left the agricultural settlements for Russia, the United States, or various urban centers in Argentina.[5] But the United States undoubtedly attracted most Jewish emigrants from Argentina. During the first decade of the century many left to try their luck there. In 1907 as many as 1,894 Jews left Argentina to go to the United States.[6] During 1908, 1,083 left Argentina, and 784 did so in 1909.[7] During the period 1920–24 about 5,000 of the Jews who entered left the country.[8] Thus, we could argue that Weill's figures may not have taken into consideration all Jewish emigrants. However, we should also bear in mind that not all those who entered declared their religion. Many Jewish freethinkers or atheists or those who felt awkward or fearful about declaring their religion were not counted as Jewish immigrants and were thus not included in the annual reports of the Immigration Department. Moreover, when obstacles were placed in front of many immigrants, some Jews—as well as nationals of most European countries—entered illegally through Brazil and Uruguay, crossing the fluvial frontiers from the cities of Salto, Concordia, or Colonia. Nevertheless, we only know about unsuccessful cases of illegal entry into Argentina, making it quite difficult to estimate the numbers of those who succeeded in their attempts.[9]

According to the municipal census of 1936 in Buenos Aires, there were in that year 120,195 Jews, constituting 5 percent of the 2,415,142 inhabitants of the Federal District. However, there is every reason to believe that among those who reported "no religion" or "religion undeclared" there were Jews, too. Ira Rosenswaike estimated their proportion to be between 8 to 12 percent of the Jews counted in the census, thus bringing the number of Jews in the capital to 130,000 or 135,000.[10] The Jews in the capital constituted therefore more than half of all Jews in the country. Up to World War I, the proportion of rural inhabitants was higher among Jews than among other large groups of immigrants such as Spanish, Italians, and French.[11] However the preference of Jews for urban settlements, especially the urban center in Buenos Aires, became evident during the 1920s. It was also reflected in the 7,858 sons of immigrants born in the provinces who had already settled in Buenos Aires by 1936 and who represented 16.8 percent of all Argentine-born Jews in Buenos Aires. There is, unfortunately, no way of establishing the number of foreign-born Jews who moved to Buenos Aires after having lived some time in the interior.

After World War I Jewish emigration from Europe resumed. The liberal laws in Argentina persuaded the Jewish emigration societies in the Old World to consider this country as a convenient place of settlement for many displaced and persecuted Jews in Eastern Europe. The leaders of Argentine Jewry, notably those in direct contact with the Alliance Israélite Universelle (AIU) and the JCA, who were, by and large, also active at the Congregación Israelita (CIRA), multiplied their efforts in order to promote Jewish immigration to Argentina and to protect the newcomers in their adoptive country by offering information about the general situation, especially in reference to work opportunities.[12]

As results of direct dealings with AIU leaders in Europe held both by Dr. Samuel Halphon and Max Glucksman, rabbi and president, respectively, of CIRA, the Sociedad de Protección a los Inmigrantes Israelitas (Soprotimis) was created on May 20, 1922, with the purpose of helping the immigrants' absorption in the land and of caring for their moral, physical, and material well-being.[13] Their activities during the twenties, and in later decades as well, were varied. Besides the conventional aid to immigrants, Soprotimis paid special attention to women immigrants arriving alone in order to prevent them from becoming the prey of white slave traffickers. Soprotimis took care of the *llamadas*, or affidavits to obtain visas for relatives of Jews already in Argentina; transferred funds to relatives in Europe; and contacted official authorities in order to ease the entrance of Jews to the country. A representative of Soprotimis, in close connection with Ezras Noschim, a society concerned with the protection of Jewish girls and women, had a special official permit granted by the Dirección de Inmigraciones to go aboard all incoming ships. The purpose of this was to advise Jewish immigrants of the existence of the society and alert them against the traffickers in human flesh and commissioners of hotels so as to prevent deceits.[14]

At this point, in 1921, Argentina's immigration policy became less liberal, and Jews in Eastern Europe were among those most seriously affected by the bureaucratic obstacles placed in front of all immigrants. In 1922 the formalities required to receive a visa for Argentina were the cause for the denial of them to most Jewish refugees. The JCA office in Argentina was able to obtain in 1922 a rule that the emigrants they recommended in Europe be accepted without some of the required documents that the refugees could not obtain.[15] This worked well for a little over a year, then the special permit was discontinued. After July 1923 Jewish refugees, unable to obtain official documentation from their places of birth, were forced to look for different horizons. Also, in mid-1923 the liberal policy of granting a *carta de llamada* for relatives who could show a guarantee of good conduct and sufficient economic means, was restricted. Soprotimis was not able to obtain the *llamadas* as liberally as before.[16] Moreover, the crucial role of Argentina at the beginning of the Roumanian evacuation was interrupted.[17] Thus, the number of Jewish immigrants, which had in 1923 surpassed the 13,000 mark, fell to 7,799 in 1924 and averaged 6,500 per year for the rest of the decade. The average of 8,100 per annum for the prewar decade 1905–14, was not reached during the 1921–30 decade, when about 7,250 Jewish immigrants entered annually into Argentina. These comparisons are even more revealing when we take into account that the United States had progressively lowered its quota for immigrants, especially from Eastern Europe, an area most Jews were fleeing. Argentina, which was the second overseas country for the period 1856–1930 not only for general but also for Jewish immigration was also closing its doors, though in a concealed way, to many potential immigrants, especially war refugees, among whom were a considerable number of Jews.[18]

Restrictions on immigration were placed as a result of the economic low ebb of the early 1920s, with the subsequent growing unemployment. No new law was passed, but Argentine consuls in Europe were instructed not to grant visas unless the candidates showed the appropriate documentation, which, in most cases, required passing through various bureaucratic stages. These documents were to come from the immigrant's country of origin, a condition practically impossible for many refugees of war. Moreover, a ministerial circular made all consuls responsible for any admissions of *undesirables*—that is, sick, mendicants, criminals, anarchists, and bolsheviks—who got visas through them. The consuls, therefore, were authorized to deny a visa without indicating their motives.[19] The selection of immigrants was enforced, though never to an extreme during the 1920s. Preference was given to specialized industrial workers and agriculturists, while other workers and professionals such as tailors, shoemakers, and barbers, as well as merchants and even intellectuals, were screened.[20]

At the end of 1924 the Departamento de Inmigración, headed by Juan P. Ramos, reached an agreement with the Paris heads of JCA, Louis and Edouard Oungre. As a result of a meeting held at the French capital on May 20, 1924, Ramos cabled JCA that this association could "take steps to attain the entrance in the Argentine Republic of immigrants who do not have the complete documentation in order, but only for those who come from European regions where the difficulties in obtaining them are unavoidable." Moreover, JCA could "only ask for the admission of agriculturists, who . . . are destined to the interior of the country, and not to the city of Buenos Aires and the towns of its surroundings." When JCA made clear that they could not be held responsible for cases in which immigrants left the interior for Buenos Aires, this restriction previously included in Ramos's resolution was omitted.[21] During the following year, however, the concession to JCA was limited to specialized agriculturists.[22]

Controls and selections of immigrants were not the only reasons for limitation of Jewish immigration to Argentina. Ticket prices to Buenos Aires had gone up 300 percent from 1923 to 1926.[23] In 1930 they were raised 25 percent. The prepaid ticket from Poland to Buenos Aires thus rose from 267 to 331 pesos.[24] Some of the emigrants from Poland, moreover, were distrustful of promises made to them about South America.[25] Furthermore, the Minister of

Poland in Argentina, Ladislaw Mazurkiewicz, wrote to his country suggesting a reduction of emigration to Argentina due to the economic crisis of 1929, first from 1,500 monthly to 500, then to 300, and finally to 150. However, he did not include Jews in the restrictions, for the latter could receive the assistance of various Jewish institutions, especially the residents associations (*landsmanschaften*).[26]

The Jewish community in Argentina organized itself in order to give refuge to larger numbers of their brethren in distress in Europe, basically in Poland. At the end of May 1928 a Congress of Immigration was held in Buenos Aires; among those present were Louis Oungre from JCA, Miron Kreinin of HICEM (HIAS, JCA, Emigdirect), Aaron Benjamin of HIAS, and delegates from all Jewish institutions in the country. The pervading spirit at this Congress was one of solidarity with the whole Jewish people, for in 1928 they believed that Argentina could become a major haven for the deteriorating communities in Eastern Europe. Moreover, the bolstering of Argentine Judaism with new additions from older Jewish communities that would fortify the local one spiritually and culturally was also contemplated.[27] All problems of immigration were discussed at these meetings, and the guest delegates received a strong impression of the hardships involved in getting a visa. However, as Benjamin reported to an HIAS board meeting two months later, it was estimated that "South America could absorb 20,000 Jewish immigrants per year, especially artisans and able-bodied people willing to settle in the land. The outlook was less favorable for merchants and intellectuals. South American industrial development also offered employment prospects."[28] We can assume that the delegates had in mind that of the above figure, Argentina would absorb fully two-thirds or more of them. Nonetheless, even before a full program of implementation of the 1928 Congress's resolution could be approved, the economic depression of 1929 produced a new situation not contemplated by the Jewish leadership. Moreover, the military forces under General José F. Uriburu took control of the government on September 6, 1930 and ordered a radical cut in the immigration policy as a means of fighting the crisis and the consequent unemployment.

Argentina As a New Home for Jews

As Table 1 indicates, over 5 percent of the immigrants who settled in Argentina during the period 1888–1930 were Jewish. They came from different areas in the world hoping to find in Argentina what they were lacking in their birthplaces. The main areas whence Jews emigrated to Argentina were Eastern Europe, North Africa, and the Ottoman Empire. Though some of the reasons for migrating were common to Jews from different parts of the world, we shall here analyze each one separately.

The population of Buenos Aires according to the census taken in 1936 can give us an estimate of the number of Jews who arrived from the above-mentioned areas (Table 2).

Table 2 shows that approximately 80 percent of the Jews in Buenos Aires in 1936 were of East European origin. They had arrived in Argentina during a span of over fifty years, starting in the early 1880s when a few individual Jews from Russia and Roumania made their way to Buenos Aires.

Table 2

Origin of the Jewish Population in Buenos Aires in 1936

Country of Birth	Jews in Buenos Aires	Percentage of Total Foreign-Born Jewish Population
Poland	31,172	
Russia	23,171	
Roumania	5,175	
Lithuania	1,056	
Latvia	202	
Total Eastern Europe	60,776	82.6
Germany	1,376	
Austria	1,092	
Hungary	499	
Czechoslovakia	203	
Total Central Europe	3,170	4.3
Syria-Lebanon	3,408	
Palestine	388	
Egypt	181	
Total Arabic-speaking Jews	3,977	5.4
Turkey	2,978	
Greece	175	
Bulgaria	164	
Total Ladino-speaking Jews	3,317	4.5
Morocco	195	
Spain	179	
Tangiers	24	
Algeria	11	
Gibraltar	5	
Portugal	4	
Tunis	2	
Total Spanish-speaking Jews	420	.6
Other foreign-born	1,946	2.7
Argentine-born	46,589	
Total	120,195	

Source: Municipalidad de la ciudad de Buenos Aires, Cuarto censo general
(Oct. 22, 1936) (Buenos Aires, 1939), vol. 3, pp. 310–23.

The Wave from Eastern Europe

In line with the Argentine government's policy of settling immigrants in the country's depopulated pampas with the purpose of making the land productive and of creating centers of distribution in the interior, an attempt was made to encourage Jewish emigration from the tsarist empire to Argentina's shores. The initiative came from José María Bustos, who, upon the first signs of pogroms and indications of new anti-Jewish measures in Russia in 1881, conceived the idea of inducing some of the would-be emigrants to consider the possibility of establishing themselves in Argentina. Bustos proposed himself as honorary agent to fulfill this task in Europe.[29]

President Julio A. Roca's administration reacted most favorably to Bustos's proposal. Catholic religious exclusivism in immigration had been terminated in 1853 when the agricultural colony of Esperanza was planned. Among the colonists in Esperanza was a considerable number of Protestants from Switzerland, Belgium, Holland, and Northern France.[30] In 1881, however, with the official appointment of Bustos as agent, the immigration policy was further liberalized to encourage non-Christian (i.e., Jewish) immigration. The second article of the decree appointing Bustos read, "The instructions which the said agent will have in the fulfillment of his commission shall be dispatched through the Comisaría General de Inmigración, . . . so that the consular agents of Argentina in Europe grant Bustos the help he might solicit from them for the better success of his mission."[31]

Argentina's open invitation to Jews to settle her country and the special appointment of an official governmental agent to attract specifically Jewish emigrants was quite remarkable. The seriousness of the Argentine policy is further attested by the involvement of the commissary of immigration in Paris, Carlos Calvo, who had initiated contacts in the same direction prior to Bustos's departure from Buenos Aires.[32] Moreover the head of the Committee of Immigration advised Calvo to contact the Alliance Israélite Universelle or the chief rabbi of Paris, Zadoc Kahn, and Ludwig Phillipson, "whose Jewish periodical [*Allgemeine Zeitung des Judentums*] was considered the best means of propaganda," and other rabbis from German localities near the Russian border.[33]

According to European Jewish newspapers, Bustos proceeded to carry out his assignment but without much success. The invitation to settle in Argentina, which was "chiefly given to the Jews in Kiev," was extended by a Mr. Nozzolini, a resident of the city.[34] Russian Jews did not consider Argentina a convenient country of migration because of the remoteness of its location, their little knowledge about conditions prevailing in this still economically underdeveloped country, and their natural aversion to a country linked to Spain with bonds of language, religion, and traditions and which might therefore—in the minds of the Russian Jews—also hold restrictive legislation for Jews. Bustos resigned in December of the same year because of his lack of success and desire to return home.[35]

Thus, this first attempt to bring large numbers of Jewish immigrants into Argentina utterly failed. It was a non-Jewish initiative, promoted by elitist, liberal-minded Catholics and aristocratic landowners seated at the head of the Argentine government. The scanty information on the issue reveals no contact with the small and still loosely organized Jewish community in Buenos Aires. On the other hand, in 1881 the Jews in Argentina were in no position of influence in governmental circles and had no strong links with Jewish organizations active in salvaging the victims of Russian antisemitism. The response of these Jews was limited to a collection in favor of the Russian Jewish victims and a strong answer to the groups in Argentina that had reacted with virulent antisemitic arguments to Roca's decree promoting Jewish immigration.[36]

Never again did an Argentine administration prompt or encourage Jewish immigration either for selfish reasons of developing its own economy and institutions or for more altruistic ones when anti-Jewish sentiments threatened the continuation of Jewish life in the Old World. Bustos's attempt, even if of no immediate positive results, had long-range consequences. Argentina, through occasional articles published in the Jewish press both in Eastern and Western Europe, began to be known in the Jewish communities of Russia as a country with possibilities for Jewish settlement. However, from now on Jews would wander to South America on an individual basis and at their own risk or at the instance of Jewish relief and emigration organizations established for that purpose in several European cities.

Argentine consuls were occasionally active in places with a considerable Jewish population, promoting emigration to their country among all dwellers without discrimination of religious belief. During the 1880s their impact among Jews was small, for the latter were quite distrustful of the consuls' asseverations and explanations of Argentine legislation and conditions. Such was the case of a young Jewish locksmith apprentice in Warsaw who in 1888 decided to consult the editors of *Hazefirah*, the influential Hebrew newspaper of that city, about the veracity of the Argentine consul's description of Argentina. *Hazefirah* attested to the credibility of the consul because "he is officially appointed by the Argentine government and behaves accordingly, without enticing people who are not permitted to leave the country to do so without a permit, . . . and he does not require any money from the people who are prepared to sail." But still their distrustfulness, which had been fed by many impostors who profited from the naïveté of the people, made them ask "our readers in America to inform us about the real situation [in Argentina], for which we shall be grateful to them."[37]

In many cities and towns of emigration, agents were making profit of the lack of knowledge of most emigrants. Many newcomers from Italy, Spain, Germany, and other European countries were deceived by these agents, who promised to take care of details of travel to and establishment in Argentina.[38] Some of the already-long-established Jews in Buenos Aires tried to put an end to these operations, at least concerning their Jewish brethren. At the end of 1889 David Hassan, an English Jew who had settled in Buenos Aires many years previously, upon learning of the miseries endured by the first mass group of Jews from Eastern Europe who were deceived by an agent in Europe, decided to ask for the cooperation of Jewish organizations in Europe that handled immigration. In a letter to the Anglo-Jewish Association (AJA) in London, Hassan urged the AJA and the Alliance Israélite Universelle in Paris to put a stop to unsystematic emigration, "particularly since such of the emigrants as have means are fleeced by self-appointed agents in Europe." This, as well as other briefings, induced the executive committee of the AJA to request the collaboration of the AIU "with a view to a stop being put to the present emigration, and to the alleged frauds practiced on Jewish emigrants."[39]

During the last third of the nineteenth century and the first decades of the twentieth century a large number of Jews from Eastern Europe crossed the Atlantic to the New World. The reasons were many, and in different regions some of these were more important than others. Two main factors, however, played a considerably important role: the progressive deterioration of the personal status of the Jews vis-à-vis the Russian government and population and the socioeconomic dislocation and eventual displacement of large numbers of Jews from the economic structure.

The pogroms of 1881, upon Alexander III's accession to the throne, were but the first of a long series of physical attacks upon Jews and their property. These outrages were at first passively tolerated and later connived at by the government, thus making the fate of the Jews even more desperate. The calculated oppression of the tsarist regime, which followed earlier attempts in the nineteenth century of enforced westernization, severely limited the rights of the Jews. The May Laws of 1882 separated the Jews from the land, banned them from rural centers, and forbade them to trade on Sundays and Christian holydays. These restrictions were an additional cause for the impoverishment of the great majority of the Jews who lacked professional or mercantile qualifications. Moreover, restrictions were also imposed against Jewish professionals, such as a *numerus clausus* for secondary schools and schools of higher learning in 1887 and special restrictions for the admission of Jewish lawyers to the bar in 1889. In a dramatic move, in addition, the government expelled the Jews from Moscow on the first day of Passover 1891.

Jews who believed that Nicholas II (1894–1917) would bring about a better future for them were totally deceived. During his reign Jews were blamed for subversive movements against the government. The pogroms in Kishinev and Gomel (1903) made a tremendous impression among Jews all over. The reaction after the First Russian Revolution of 1905, despite attempts of amelioration of the Jewish status, was even fiercer. That year a new wave of pogroms affected 660 Jewish communities in the course of a single week. This pogrom wave left 1,000 Jews dead, 7,000 to 8,000 wounded, and property losses of about 31 million dollars. Antisemitism was impressed on the Russian masses by means of books and pamphlets published and distributed under governmental sponsorship. Moreover, the *numerus clausus* for Jews was lowered, and Jews in the professions were faced with fresh restrictions.

The urbanization in Russia during the second half of the nineteenth century created an enormous demand for consumer goods. A market for ready-made garments was created by the influx of peasants into the cities, and by the needs of the armies during the Russo-Turkish War of 1877–78. The individ-

ual labor of Jewish artisans was thus progressively displaced by industrial production. Commerce on a large scale, stimulated by industrialization, bypassed
the petty local trader, usually a Jew. Furthermore, the growing railroad net-
works upset many local Jewish tradesmen and practically eliminated the functions of draymen (*balegoles*). The limiting legislation of home production and
rural distribution of liquor in the 1860s seriously affected many thousands of
petty liquor agents and innkeepers. When the monopoly in liquor trade was
reorganized by the tsar at the end of the century, forbidding Jewish participation in it, over 100,000 Jews lost their means of livelihood. Jews were thus
forced to migrate either to the cities, where they became part of the wage-
earning class in a society in process of industrialization, or overseas.

The fundamental economic problem appeared with the rapid multipli-
cation of the Jewish population in Eastern Europe during the nineteenth century. The Jewish population of 2,272,000 in Eastern Europe in 1825 rose to
7,362,000 in 1900. In the Russian Empire alone it increased from about
1,000,000 souls in 1800 to over 5,189,000 in 1897, the latter figure probably
excluding 1,000,000 emigrants and their descendants. The economic structure
of Jewish life, however, did not develop in accordance with the requirements
posed by the increasing numbers. Moreover, petty crafts and trades were becoming more obsolete with newer economic developments, thus narrowing
the areas of Jewish income.[40]

Jews left their birthplace in Russia due to the constant deterioration of
their legal status. Their economic possibilities were progressively curtailed.
Pogroms succeeded one another in several localities of the Pale of Settlement.
Due to these circumstances the United States had an almost magnetic attrac-
tion for most of them. Others moved to countries in Western Europe, to Canada, or to South Africa. Still others considered that the time had come to
return to Palestine. During the eighties, and more during the nineties, those
preparing to leave their native soil started hearing about Argentina. Letters
from the first Jewish immigrants there persuaded many other coreligionists to
make a similar trip to South America. Moreover, the JCA project of settlement
in the land and the first signs of larger groups of Jews headed to work in the
interior provinces of Argentina induced many other Russian Jews to consider
the possibility of that country as a new home not necessarily as agriculturists
but also as city dwellers.

As an aftermath of World War I Poland became independent for the first
time since the late eighteenth century. Polish Jewry, which was predominantly
urban, suffered immensely from economic insecurity in a changing society and
was adversely affected by rising legal discrimination by the Polish government
against minorities, as well as by political violence and antisemitism. Help from
abroad during and after the war alleviated only partially the plight of Polish
Jewry. Encouraged by the government, many sought better futures across the
Atlantic or in Palestine. Since the United States imposed restrictive quotas on
immigration during the 1920s, Argentina became a major country for Jews
leaving Poland. In 1922 the Polish Emigration Office issued 48,012 visas, of
which 30,981 went to Jews. Of these, 21,529 were for the United States, while

3,903 were for Argentina. Reports for the decade 1925–35 show a reversal of these figures. Out of 186,134 Jews who emigrated from Poland, Palestine received 67,242, the United States 27,755, and Argentina 31,098.[41]

Jews who were avidly looking for information about places for emigration were basically interested in the economic possibilities there, as well as in their prospective status as Jews both with respect to their legal situation and to the possibilities of carrying on their Jewish traditions. Articles in Jewish newspapers about the conditions in Argentina helped form in the mind of the eventual immigrant a picture of what awaited him. In a letter to *Hazefirah* a Jew from Lodz reported that a coreligionist from Buenos Aires who visited his town had told him about the community there. The visitor had explained that ten years earlier (i.e., in 1878) there had been only about thirty Jewish families living in Buenos Aires. Jews did not want to settle there because of the lack of synagogues, rabbis, and other necessary officials for the observance of Jewish traditions. In 1888 there were about 200 families among Ashkenazim and Sephardim, all in excellent economic situation, making profit of the developing opportunities there. He attested to the existence of two synagogues, one Ashkenazic and one Sephardic, with four Torah scrolls, a rabbi, a cantor, a ritual slaughterer, and a circumciser. The letter emphasized the economic aspects, including the possibility of working in agriculture.[42] This letter particularly appealed to the Jews in Russia because the news came from a Jew himself and because it emphasized economic opportunities in the country and the possibility of Jewish continuity there.

At the beginning of the 1890s the Jewish press in Eastern Europe as well as in Western Europe and the United States started printing news about the Jewish settlements in Argentina assiduously. Notes on the arrival and fate of the first group of over 800 Jews from Podolia who desired to pursue agricultural activities in Argentina had begun to appear in 1889. Moreover, Baron Moritz de Hirsch's final decision to found the JCA with the clear objective of colonizing Jews in several countries in the Americas, especially in Argentina, received steady coverage in the Jewish press starting in 1891.

The Jewish press in Eastern Europe was ambivalent regarding the possibilities of Jewish settlement in Argentina. Some violently opposed the idea of Jews going there, advocating that if it was imperative to migrate, the trend should be directed to Palestine. Such was the case of Alexander Zederbaum, the famed director of the influential Hebrew newspaper *Hamelitz* of Petersburg. As a supplement to no. 144 of 1893 of the newspaper, Zederbaum wrote "Four Articles," one of which was an open letter to Baron Horace Ginzburg, head of the JCA committee in Petersburg. In this article Zederbaum, who in 1878 had started a campaign in favor of settling Jews in Russia as farmers,[43] violently opposed Jewish emigration to Argentina. He asserted, based on information received from Abraham Vermont in Buenos Aires,[44] that the atmosphere in the country was not good for Jews since governmental posts were bought, bribes were freely used, and there were signs of antisemitism.[45] On the other hand, Jews already living there had opened houses of shame in Buenos Aires. There was no concern for Jewish law, synagogue, or kosher food. Their main preoccupation was amassing big fortunes. Even the rabbi there was a rich man who had his store open on the Sabbath and Jewish holy days and whose wife was a Christian.[46] Zederbaum approached Rabbi Adolf Jellinek—a distinguished preacher and scholar in Vienna and influential friend of the Baron,—and Isidore Loeb, secretary of the AIU, requesting their cooperation to try to convince Baron Hirsch to place his money in a project to settle Jews in Palestine instead of Argentina. In this Zederbaum failed, as Theodore Herzl did a few years later.[47] Finally, Zederbaum argued, Baron Hirsch wanted the Jews to assimilate and so solve the "Jewish question." For that reason the Baron had preferred that the new colonists' homes be at a distance one from another and would not make provisions for rabbis, teachers, and ritual slaughterers to sail with the colonists.[48] The *Hamelitz* editor's strong appeal was based not only on Zionist ideology but also on the belief that Argentina had too many negative factors for Jewish establishment.[49]

On the other hand, *Hazefirah* assiduously published articles about the progress in the Argentine colonies, as well as letters from a few correspondents in various colonies.[50] There were also booklets and pamphlets in Yiddish describing the country to potential Jewish emigrants. As early as 1891 Jacob Iedvabski and Isidore Hellmann published *The Trip to Argentina* in Warsaw, giving details about the history, geography and climate of the country, as well as notions about religion, legislation, and possibilities of colonization there. A few details about the recently founded JCA colonies were also added.[51] Many similar booklets continued appearing thereafter.[52] All these publications, even the articles opposed to emigration to Argentina, reveal a growing interest in opening a new place for Jewish settlement. Accordingly, Jews in Eastern Europe began making contacts for crossing the Atlantic to Buenos Aires. A large number of them got in touch with JCA committee in their areas.

When the idea of finding new settlements for Jews emigrating from Russia was first seriously considered in Europe, Jews of West European origin already established in Argentina had opposing reactions. Early in 1887, an English Jew wrote from Cordoba to the *Jewish Chronicle* concerning the future of "our brethren, the Jews of Russia," stating that "this country [Argentina] is admirably suited as a new home, being free, tolerant as regards religion, healthy and of a fruitful soil."[53] However, this extremely optimistic opinion about the Jewish future in Argentina met with the strong opposition of one of the Jewish veterans in Buenos Aires. A "resident" in the capital of the country since 1864, he quite disagreed with the above view after being in "daily contact with the Jewish emigrants who have reached these shores." After asserting that some of the Russian emigrants, to avoid starvation, had turned to Rio de Janeiro and that others, "to the daily regret of the Jewish population, are by no means a desirable addition," our correspondent concluded that "the recommendation of Russian Jewish emigration to this country in my opinion, would amount to a crime."[54] The arguments mentioned against Jews from Russia entering the country were based on the difficulty of earning a livelihood as farmers or laborers. Interestingly enough, in 1887 Argentina was undergoing a period of intense economic development, and possibilities of material progress were not scarce.[55] Evidently, among the immediate reactions of some of the well-established Jews in Buenos Aires was the consideration that their social standing vis-à-vis Argentine society might be harmed by the inflow of large quantities of poorer Russian Jews, to whom they would have to give a hand.

The initial reactions of leading members of the small Buenos Aires Jewish community to the first en masse arrival of Russian Jews was, nevertheless, favorable. They used their influence to secure lodging, kosher meat, and other indispensable needs, including necessary guarantees for new land contracts, for their Russian brethren.[56] It was only after the immigrants began to encounter difficulties that the older residents urged the cessation of large-scale Jewish immigration from Russia. Henry Joseph, the rabbi and most active member of the community, in a long and detailed letter to the *Jewish Chronicle* explained the pitiful situation of the Russian Jews recently arrived in Argentina, requesting the editor that "instead of making your valuable journal the medium of sending thousands of Jewish emigrants to these shores, you will, on the contrary, preach caution, as the Argentine Republic is quite unfit to receive such emigration as the above, and if thousands of our coreligionists are to be sent here, they must be prepared for the greatest hardships in every form."[57]

Joseph's letter, as well as David Hassan's above-mentioned request to the AJA,[58] made an impact on the latter organization. The AJA sent "warnings to the continental Hebrew Press against the emigration of other than able-bodied agriculturists and artisans possessed of means, and against dealings with unauthorized agents."[59] But the disapproval by the AJA of Jewish emigration to Argentina was not final. At such a distance from Argentina, AJA could better evaluate the conflicting reports of conditions there. Just like leaders of the AIU and other associations for the rescue of Russian Jewry and finally Baron de Hirsch, the AJA, considering Argentina a country well-adapted for Jewish emigration, reflected on how to make this migration effective.[60]

At the beginning of the last decade of the nineteenth century the members of the Congregación Israelita clearly felt that a strong wave of Russian Jewish immigrants was about to arrive in Argentina. Special meetings were called to consolidate the existing community in Buenos Aires. Rabbi Joseph, on November 22, 1891, at a general assembly of Jews in Buenos Aires, spoke of the need "to work in unity, now that we are on the eve of the arrival of thousands of new coreligionists."[61] Ironically enough, Rabbi Joseph's call to unity of the Jewish forces in Buenos Aires marked precisely the beginning of diversity and fragmentation in the Jewish community there. During that same year Jews from Morocco who had been settling in Buenos Aires—as well as in the interior of the country—for the past decade, founded the Congregación Israelita Latina, thus contesting the hegemony of CIRA as the sole Jewish institution in Argentina.[62] A few years later further immigration of Sephardic Jews coming from various sectors of the Ottoman Empire would split the Jewish community even more. The most serious challenge to the central role of CIRA in Jewish life in Buenos Aires, however, would be the continuous penetration of East European Jews into the country.[63] As we shall see, CIRA continued being a central institution in Jewish life, but only one among several; and though it retained a distinctive character, it too was progressively (and later strongly so) influenced by East European Jews and Judaism.

The First Sephardim from Morocco[64]

Parallel to the arrival of the first Russian Jews, a small group of Jews from Morocco made its way to Argentina. This emigration was firstly encouraged by the Spanish-Moroccan war of 1859–60 and the subsequent occupation of Tetouan by the Spanish for a period of nearly two years. Many of these emigrants settled in Gibraltar, while others opted for several places in East Africa and Palestine. During the 1860s the first signs of emigration to South American countries were noticed. Many of the first Jews who left settled in Brazil, where they stayed for a period of up to eight years and later either returned to Tetouan or moved to some other South American country, principally on account of the suffocating heat, yellow fever epidemics, insects, and so on.[65]

A couple of decades later, during the 1880s, the emigration movement took greater proportions. Jews leaving Morocco were recruited mainly from Tetouan, though some also from Tangiers and Larache, the latter being, nevertheless, "more or less of Tetouanese origin."[66] In other words, the emigrants were Spanish-speaking Jews who were naturally attracted by countries where their mother tongue or a very similar one was spoken. Most of them were young Jews "between the ages of twelve and thirty" who were fleeing from the compressive and sterilizing atmosphere of the *Mellah*, hoping to progress in new and free countries.[67] There were three currents of Jewish emigration from Morocco to South America. One to Venezuela; a second one to the Amazon area, including the cities of Para and Manaos in Brazil, and Iquitos in Peru; and a third one to Argentina.[68]

In 1880 the first signs of individual Jews from Morocco in Buenos Aires was evidenced when the Benjetrit family, originally from Tetouan, arrived in the Argentine capital and circumcised there their two-year-old son born in Montevideo.[69] Abraham Levy, after having lived in Gibraltar and Brazil, finally settled in Buenos Aires in the early 1880s.[70] The Moroccan Jews in the capital became quite numerous by the end of the decade, since, on January 15, 1889, José Elías Mamán, petitioned the Ministry of Justice and Religion for an authorization to establish a synagogue of the Spanish-Portuguese rite. Mamán, who entitled himself in the petition as rabbi, evidently was requesting the right to perform marriages according to the traditions of his community. Up to November 2, 1888—or ten weeks before Maman's request—when the law of civil marriage was passed, all marriages were in the hands of the church, and religious authorities of non-Catholic creeds were required a special authorization from the ministry to perform them among their coreligionists. Apparently it took some time until the civil registers started complying with the new legislation, thus prompting the Moroccan Jews to obtain a special permit. On the other hand, this move indicates a certain differentiation with, and independence from, the West European Jewish Congregation, CIRA, whose rabbi had the proper authorization since 1883.[71]

In a few years most of the Moroccan Jews in Argentina created good economic situations for themselves. Far from trying to restrict the immigration of their fellow countrymen, they made every effort possible to bring to the new latitudes families, relatives, and friends from their native cities. Usually these relatives stayed for a period of time with the first-arrived until they became acquainted with conditions in the new country. After that they would go to a city or town in the interior of Argentina and establish a branch of the main house in Buenos Aires. An eyewitness reported at the turn of the century that he knew "some Moroccan merchants established in Buenos Aires and having up to five, six, and even eight branches of their commerce disseminated in the main centers of the Republic."[72]

Another type of emigration of Moroccan Jews, more systematic, though less numerous, was promoted by the AIU and various of its alumni associations. Most of the teachers at the Jewish schools in the JCA colonies, at least at the beginning, were graduates of the schools of the AIU. In April 1895 four students from the school in Paris left for Argentina.[73] In 1899 the Association des Anciens Eleves de l'Alliance à Tanger reported it had sent five young people to Buenos Aires, two to Caracas, one to Maracaibo (Venezuela), one to Valparaiso (Chile), one to Iquitos (Peru), and two to Para (Brazil).[74] Similar efforts were made in Smyrna by an analogous association, which sent there, at its own cost, young persons formed at the AIU school "who do not always find a remunerable job in their own town."[75] By the end of the century there were twenty schools in the JCA colonies in Argentina, all directed by graduates from the AIU schools in European Turkey, Smyrna, and Morocco. In Argentina they had the advantage of a common language (Ladino and Spanish), enabling them to teach the regular program of education established by the education authorities of the country.[76]

Isaac Benchimol, who had been teaching for a number of years in the Mauricio colony, Province of Buenos Aires, wrote in 1901 that Jewish emigration to South America proved to be beneficial for the Jewish population in Tetouan itself. Letters describing economic success or visits to the city of birth after success had been attained on the other side of the Atlantic had an impact over those who never moved: "It did away with poverty, lifted the morale . . . and developed individual initiative."[77] Benchimol called the school authorities of the AIU to introduce the teachings of Spanish in the schools of the interior of Morocco, where Jews spoke Arabic. This would provide the students with an additional weapon in case they would contemplate emigrating to Latin America, for "Latin America needs hands."[78]

By 1905 there were, according to the calculations of D. S. D. Levy, director of the JCA school in Mauricio, about 3,000 Sephardim in Argentina, of whom about 750 lived in Buenos Aires. Almost all of them were Moroccan in origin, for "85 percent are Tetouanese, and the rest from Gibraltar, from Tangiers of the Moroccan coast, and Turks."[79] From the above figures, and from Rabbi Halphon's study of the Jewish population of Argentina in 1909, as well as from diverse sources of information of later periods,[80] we notice that there were always more Moroccan Jews in the interior than in the capital city, which was not the case for other Jewish immigrations to the country. Throughout the period up to 1930 there was a constant immigration—though in limited numbers compared to the numbers of East European Jews—of Jews from Tetouan and other towns in North Africa.[81]

For a few Moroccan Jews emigration to Argentina was only temporary. They came back after having achieved economic stability, in some cases after ten years but sometimes even after thirty![82] However, most did not return to their old home. They permanently established themselves in their adoptive country, with no idea of going back except for a visit. They formed communities and organized their communal Jewish life. Even among those who had gone back, many preferred to adopt Argentine citizenship before doing so, for an Argentine passport was a better protection in unstable Morocco. Thus in 1927, out of 95 Argentine citizens who depended on the Consul General of Argentina in Rabat 79 (83 percent) were born in Morocco and later naturalized.[83] Such was the case of Jacobo Bibas, vice-consul of Argentina in the Spanish Protectorate of Morocco in 1935, who was born in Tangiers and then lived in Rosario of Santa Fe, where he had been active in several local Jewish institutions.[84]

Sephardim from the Ottoman Empire

In addition to the Russian and Moroccan immigrations into Argentina, a third developed from the Ottoman Empire towards the end of the century. Already in the 1880s a movement of emigration could be observed in several parts of the Ottoman Empire. The financial debacle and bankruptcy of the empire left a strong imprint on the general population—the Jews included— all over its vast territories. Christians and Muslims, though in much smaller numbers, were the first to leave, and Jews followed by the end of the century. People from Beyrut, Aleppo, and Damascus, as well as from Istambul and Izmir, left for Egypt, Western Europe, the United States, and several Latin American republics. The underlying motive of their migration was the search for new economic horizons due to the impoverishment of the population in communities with little mineral wealth and no industrial development, constantly threatened with overpopulation.[85]

Christians and Muslims from the Ottoman Empire preceded Jews into Argentina for over a decade. Already in 1887 an English Jew living in Córdoba remarked that the country was suitable for Jewish settlement, but strictly limited to the agricultural class "because itinerant vendors have no chance here on account of the many Arabs who are to be seen ... selling Christian beads and crosses and every other article that is saleable."[86]

Jews followed suit in the 1890s, settling in the capital city of Buenos Aires. Those who came from the same city stayed together and, with the arrival of fellow immigrant townsmen, slowly formed small nuclei resembling appendixes to their home communities. At the turn of the century, Ladino-speaking Jews from Izmir, Constantinople, and other areas, settled along the streets 25 de Mayo and Reconquista, not far from the port. By 1904 they were numerous enough to found their first society, Hermandad, to help the needy among them.[87] That same year, a recently arrived Jew from Aleppo wrote to his family that he had found many acquaintances from his home town. They all dwelled in rooms in the Once precinct, where the Aleppine Jews would continue settling and where their community organizations and life have centered up to the present time.[88] Damascus Jews arrived in Buenos Aires during the same period and settled in the area of Boca and Barracas, a populous zone of predominantly Italian, especially Genoese, immigrants.[89]

There were two predominant factors that played heavily upon the economic motivation for the Jews to leave the Ottoman territories. First, letters enthusiastically describing the liberal laws and economic possibilities of the country, picturing fortunes to be made in peaceful Argentina; and second, the revolution of the Young Turks in 1908. This movement, which aimed at securing a constitutional government, in a certain sense, worked hardship for many Jews—and also Christians—by introducing compulsory military service. Until then Jews and Christians were not conscripted into the Turkish Army. Thus, escaping the draft became an impelling force for the increase of Jewish emigration from the empire because serving in the army meant an additional difficulty in supporting a family and interfered with religious observances.[90]

Not all the Jews who arrived in Argentina from the Ottoman Empire had decided that their final destination would be this South American country. Thus was the case of three Aleppine Jews who left for the United States in 1904. When a medical examination in Marseille revealed that one of them suffered from trachoma, which disabled him from entering the United States, they decided to change their route to Argentina, where they could disembark without documentation.[91] On the other hand, some emigrants preferred Argentina to the United States. Such was the case of a family that migrated at the beginning of the century from Aleppo to Cairo. From there, the head of the family left for the United States right before World War I but finally resolved due to instigations of friends in Buenos Aires to settle in the latter city.[92]

The first to arrive from Ottoman territories—young men desiring economic progress—had in mind, at the moment of departure, the clear idea of returning once they had earned enough money to live comfortably back home. The desire to reintegrate themselves into the closely knit family and community life of their first years weighed heavily upon these immigrants. Their case was not exactly identical to the *golondrina* migrations, thousands of South European, mostly Italian, laborers who came—many of them yearly for a span of several years—just for the harvest seasons in Argentina, to return to Europe afterward. Their profits were generally good, for salaries were much higher than what they could get in their native countries, where they could not always find employment, and ship fares were still inexpensive due to the immense development of trans-Atlantic traffic.[93] Turkish and Syrian Jews had in mind other ways of making a living. Back home their families, for many generations, had worked in commercial occupations, and that was the way they would also start in Argentina. They knew that the process of earning capital in this branch of trade would take a number of years. They started from the very bottom, most as peddlers in the streets of Buenos Aires, and some in other towns in the interior. With heavy loads of cloth and other types of merchandise they would make their rounds all day long. A few of them did not endure the effort and their longing for family and friends motivated them to sail home.[94] But the majority, even if they had contemplated returning, never did so. Nissim Teubal, who left Aleppo in 1906 at the age of 15 to join his brother Ezra in Buenos Aires, reports in his memoires:

> In the proximities of Buenos Aires, I made a type of covenant with myself. When I shall have earned, I said to myself, the first 300 pounds, I shall return to Aleppo, and in Aleppo I will be considered as a Croesus. . . . But when Buenos Aires was at sight, I increased the sum. Three hundred pounds was too little; I would wait until I had five hundred. That sum continued growing. I needed more and more. Mad with enthusiasm and ambition, I said to myself that I would not return to Aleppo other than with a real fortune.[95]

But Nissim never returned to settle in Aleppo. By 1910, together with Ezra, they brought their parents, brothers, and sisters to Buenos Aires, as most of the Ottoman Jews started then to do.

The revolt of the Young Turks in 1908, the subsequent legislation that touched upon the Jews—such as compulsory military service—the Balkan Wars, and finally World War I with the gradual dismemberment of the Ottoman Empire eventually produced a radical change in the mentality of the Jewish emigrant of those areas. From now on the Jews who left for the Americas had already decided they would make their new homes there. Those who went to Argentina had ample knowledge of conditions in the country. Many already had members of their families there, and those who had no direct relatives knew of former members of their own communities who had emigrated to Argentina. They were assured of jobs until they could start their own businesses.

Patterns of Settlement in Buenos Aires

The war years had in many ways interrupted communications across the Atlantic, thus forcing immigrants to make a decision to rebuild their lives in Argentina.

Jews who had arrived from the various areas in East Europe, Morocco, and the Ottoman Empire gathered to form more stable institutions. The decisions on the part of each group—Ashkenazi, Moroccan, Damascene, Aleppine, and Ladino-speaking Jews—to buy lots of land for their private cemeteries, are indicative of the fact that these Jews had already decided upon a final break with the community of their youth and had arrived at the conclusion that Argentina was the country of their permanent settlement. Parallel to these acquisitions came the consolidation, especially during the period 1914–20, of the main religious, educational, cultural, and mutual help centers of all these various communities, each one along its independent lines.

We can follow the trends of city settlement among Jews arriving in the Federal District from the three municipal censuses of 1904, 1909, and 1936. In

1904, 2,000 Jews, or one-third of the 6,065 Jews in the city, lived in the four-teenth district, located between Córdoba and Rivadavia Avenues to the east of Callao Avenue and comprising the Center of Buenos Aires. Nearly one-fourth of the Jews in the city—1,416—lived in the eleventh district, directly west of the fourteenth, encircled by Callao, Córdoba, Pueyrredón, and Rivadavia Ave-nues. Five years later, in 1909, 5,122 Jews, or 31 percent of all Jews, already lived in the eleventh district, constituting 13.2 percent of the whole district's popu-lation. The fourteenth district housed 2,776 Jews—17 percent of all Jews—who represented 4.8 percent of the district.

The next municipal census was taken twenty-seven years later, in 1936 (Table 3). However, it still reflects the way the Jewish population spread over the capital during the second and third decades of the century. The Jewish population of the fourteenth district practically did not grow. The 2,865 Jews living there represented only 2.4 percent of the Jewish population in the city, and only 3.8 percent of the district's population. The 14,550 Jews in the elev-enth district constituted now 27.5 percent of the whole population there, and 12.1 percent of all Jews. In other words, the eleventh district became more "Jewish," though a smaller proportion of the Jews in Buenos Aires lived there. Jews were settling west of the eleventh district, in the ninth, eighteenth and seventh and especially in the fifteenth district. Thus, Jews settled preferably in the Villa Crespo, Caballito, and La Paternal neighborhoods, which roughly cor-respond to the above-mentioned census districts.

The pattern of settlement of Jews in Buenos Aires was in direct relation to their daily occupations. In Villa Crespo a large number of Jewish workers settled side by side with their Jewish employers' factories or workshops (*tall-eres*). Concentrated in this neighborhood was almost the entire Jewish knitting industry, owners and workers. Many Jews there also worked in their own homes in this trade. In La Paternal an analogous process took place. Here, the Jewish wood and furniture industry was concentrated, as well as that of artificial silk or rayon. The Once neighborhood, nearer to the center of town, continued being the commercial center for Jews in Argentina and the headquarters of many main Jewish institutions. Tailors, a Jewish profession par excellence at the time, were spread over the whole city but favored Villa Crespo and La Paternal.[96]

The Jews in the Economy

Jewish immigrants arriving in Buenos Aires were eager to start support-ing themselves from the moment they stepped off ship. Many were already employed before their five days stay at the Hotel de Inmigrantes was over. However, very few among the newly arrived possessed vocational skills.[97] Still, they did manage to earn a living and contribute to the development of the economy. Before the end of the nineteenth century a Jewish oldtimer de-scribed the new situation created in Buenos Aires by the arrival of Russian Jews, who then numbered between 350 and 400 families:[98]

Table 3

Distribution of Jewish and Total Population by Districts in Buenos Aires in
1936

District	Total Population	Jewish Population	Percentage
1 V. Sarsfield	149,446	4,536	3.0
N. Chicago	67,702	876	1.3
N. Pompeya	113,834	2,994	2.6
2	88,997	1,709	1.9
3 Zone 1	41,107	468	1.1
Zone 2	62,155	1,600	2.6
4	73,631	2,072	2.8
5	123,396	6,002	4.8
6	105,837	2,542	2.4
7	78,401	6,222	7.9
8	72,634	1,929	2.6
9	84,712	12,272	14.5
10	44,262	1,521	3.4
11	51,791	14,550	27.5
12	74,950	1,425	1.9
13	81,307	1,251	1.5
14	74,809	2,865	3.8
15 S. Bernardo	145,014	23,820	16.4
V. Devoto	146,717	4,167	2.8
V. Mitre	104,638	5,972	5.7
16 Belgrano	110,313	2,395	2.2
V. Urquiza	118,646	1,950	1.6
17	115,532	2,861	2.5
18	123,047	10,672	8.6
19	99,427	2,600	2.6
20	62,837	922	1.5
All districts	2,415,142	120,195	5.0

Source: *Municipalidad de la Ciudad de Buenos Aires, Cuarto Censo Gen
eral* (1936), vol. 3, pp. 294–99.

> Though they are comparative strangers they have shown much enterprise
> and activity, and this energy is bearing fruit in the progressive improve-
> ment their condition is undergoing. Whatever Englishmen may think of the
> Russian immigrant, Argentines have every reason to be thankful for his
> presence, for in his wake there have come a number of industries abso-
> lutely new to the country, such as the manufacture of mackintoshes, em-
> broidery, laces, hats, Russian soaps, and a number of other articles which
> Argentina had previously to import from abroad. Many of these Russian
> immigrants have become metal workers, watchmakers, tailors, shoemak-
> ers, etc.

By the end of the century, however, several hundred Jews were directly
involved in buying and selling second-hand goods. This type of commerce developed mainly among newcomers without professions or skills, often known
as *luftmenschen*. Previous to this they earned a few pesos as waiters, servants, or

Percentage of Jews in Each District of Buenos Aires, 1936

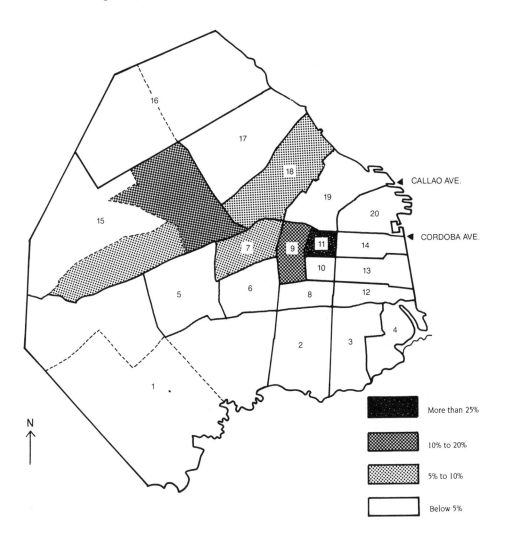

employees or were colonists who had left the colonies for the city with some savings. The expenses to get started in this branch of commerce were not high. *Patentes*, or licenses were inexpensive, thus permitting the dealer to open a shop with an expenditure of 400 to 1,000 pesos. By 1910 *cambalachero*, or second-hand dealer," had become synonymous with *Jew* even though only twenty-one such Jewish shops remained from earlier days. A contemporary commented that second-hand dealings was as much a Jewish occupation as a Bottegleria was Genoese, and most of the unskilled jobs in the streets of Buenos Aires were Neopolitan.[99]

The largest number of Jews started in a slightly different occupation. Having arrived in Argentina without skills and resources, they resorted to peddling with packages of merchandise on their shoulders in different quarters of the capital and the interior. Usually the peddler sold his goods on installments, thus introducing an important innovation in the economy of the country, especially among the lower strata who could not afford the full price of an article but could only acquire it by means of weekly payments. Every week the Jewish peddler would come to collect the quota for that period, thus acquiring the popular name of *cuentenik* or *sucuentenik*, a word formed with the Spanish *cuenta* (bill) with a Yiddish suffix. Peddling in Buenos Aires was not restricted to Ashkenazim. Among all sectors of the Sephardic population, peddling constituted a conspicuous occupation during the first decades of the twentieth century.[100]

Gradually Jews began participating in the commercial and industrial life of the city. They soon became conspicuous in the commerce of furniture, clothes, and furs, among other branches. Jews also imported goods from Europe that were either not manufactured in Argentina or were of inferior quality. Likewise, Jews entered several branches of Argentine industry and were pioneers in some of them. They were most important in the needle and furniture industry both as industrialists and as workers in workshops and factories.

By 1903 the Jews of West European origin—French, German, and English—were the best off among Jews in Buenos Aires. They either owned or represented export and import companies and were also active in special branches of commerce, such as jewelry and the like. About 20 percent of Sephardim owned houses of commerce, especially haberdasheries and imported cloths' stores. The rest were engaged in peddling. The Russian Jewish immigrants in Buenos Aires were also engaged in commerce, owning cloth and furniture shops, as well as second-hand stores. Most of them were poor and were employed as workers or became peddlers.[101] At the beginning of the century Ashkenazic Jews worked in branches of industry that were to become areas of special Jewish concern before the end of the first decade and more so during the twenties and thirties. A correspondent from Buenos Aires informed the *Jewish Chronicle* in 1905 that "a great many of the [Russian] Jewish immigrants find easy work here, especially in the tailoring, cap-making, furniture, and boot-making trades."[102]

Still in 1909 the majority of the Sephardim were poor dealers in second-hand goods, peddlers, or small merchants. Those of Turkish origin had some haberdashery stores; the Moroccan dealt in fabrics and in ready-made clothes. West European Jews were engaged in jewelry and export-import. Among Russian Jews there was a large number of workers in all types of handicrafts.[103] By 1926 fully 27 percent of the active Jewish population were employed as workers in various handicrafts and industries.[104]

Though at the beginning of the century the number of Jews active in liberal professions was small, the number of Jewish professionals by 1926 had grown, clearly indicating the continuous trend of later decades. According to data gathered in 1909 and 1926 the number of Jewish physicians in Buenos Aires grew from 26 to 135. In those years the corresponding increase for dentists was 18 to 128, for pharmacists 11 to 50, for engineers 10 to 41, for architects 7 to 13, and for lawyers 2 to 32.[105]

Jews were also conspicuous in the development of new industries in the country and by the end of the 1920s had control of large sectors of them. In 1935 Simón Weill pointed to hundreds of Jewish workshops and factories in the capital: 113 produced furs; 58, clothes; 57, furniture; 49, handbags and belts; 45, beds and springs; 39, caps and hats; 38, cloth and silk; 13, raincoats; and 12, leather goods.[106]

Most of the Jews, however, were active in commerce. During the last years of the twenties an estimate of the activities of the gainfully employed Jews in the country established that 55 percent were in commerce, 27 percent worked in the industries, 4 percent were academicians or professionals, and 14 percent were agriculturists.[107] Evidently, though these are rough estimates, the percentages of the first three categories should be somewhat raised for Buenos Aires, where no agriculturists lived. A conspicuous proportion of the Jews in commerce were ex-*cuenteniks* who established fixed stores. Many of the latter now had their own salesmen who offered their merchandise in all corners of the city and interior. The *cuenteniks* prospered during the 1920s and more so after the financial crisis around 1930. In Buenos Aires there were about four thousand of them still in 1940.[108]

The main preoccupation of the *cuenteniks* was the acquisition of merchandise. The wholesale merchants speculated with the fluctuating market and imposed their prices upon the peddlers. The latter, on the other hand, were forced to raise their prices accordingly, a fact that caused a diminution of their sales. In order to protect themselves from these situations the peddlers founded unions. During the prewar period a number of these guilds were founded, which, due to the difficulties involved in the organization of peddlers, failed after a few years or even a few months.[109]

During the crisis of the World War I years some peddler organizations were established on firmer bases. On October 24, 1915, the Unión Ambulantes Israelitas (Yiddishn Ambulantn Varain) was founded by seven peddlers as a mutual help institution that would defend their interests. Membership was limited to peddlers "who speak in Yiddish."[110] With the economic boom after the war a cooperative was appended to the union in order to furnish the members with good quality merchandise at lower prices. This cooperative underwent difficult periods due to the fight of the wholesalers against it, the lack of practical cooperativists among its members, and its unbalanced trade policy of giving credits in larger measures than its income warranted. Nonetheless, by 1920 this peddlers' union showed positive signs of prosperity.[111]

More successful, especially in its defense work against monopolies of wholesale merchants, was the peddlers' society founded on August 13, 1916, under the name Liga de Defensa Comercial Israelita y Socorros Mutuos. Its name was changed several times and was finally called Sociedad Comercial Israelita and popularly known as Primera Cooperativa. The cooperative was actually attached to the society in 1919, when shares of 100 pesos each, to be paid in ten installments, were issued. The modest economic situation of the shareholders at the time is evident from the fact that the biggest ones had bought only five shares each. This cooperative grew rapidly after 1921 when large numbers of new members joined it and sales were tripled. The cooperative moved many times into larger premises where goods were stored, until in 1928 it moved into its own large new building in Victoria Street (now Hipólito Yrigoyen), number 2221–51, which cost at the time 1,043,000 pesos (over 400,000 dollars). To the furniture and domestic articles sections were added cloths, menswear, tailoring, furs, and shoes sections. By the end of the decade this cooperative had reached a position of steady economic progress and had become a pillar in philanthropy within the Jewish community.

The postwar arrival of new *luftmenschen*, or unqualified workers, who became *cuenteniks* in Buenos Aires quickly brought additional members to the Sociedad Comercial Israelita. However, it preferred to limit its membership. Therefore, a number of Jewish peddlers, unable to enter, founded a new cooperative during 1923, Cooperativa Comercial Israelita (later Corporación Commercial Israelita), known as La Segunda Cooperativa, with identical motivations.

During the 1920s Jews in various branches of commerce in Buenos Aires formed mutual societies intended to further their economic progress. A third peddler cooperative was founded in 1928; tailors united in 1922; furriers in 1923; painters in 1923; remitters for auctions in 1924. Smaller cooperatives sprouted in Buenos Aires during the late 1920s. Retail merchants in specific clothing items founded their separate associations, as did retail grocers, furriers, and the like.[112]

Towards the end of World War I, especially during the 1920s, Jewish commerce and small industries were promoted by the establishment of banks. They were founded by small groups of Jewish workers and artisans as credit chests that provided loans. In short periods of time they developed and grew stronger, thus changing their functions into those of a bank. The first Jewish bank was the Banco Industrial, founded in 1917 by eight workers and small industrialists, with a capital of 120 pesos. In 1930, in spite of the crisis, the Banco Industrial gave credits for a total of 724,441 pesos (about 270,000 dollars). Of more rapid growth was the Banco Popular Israelita (Yiddishe Folks Bank), founded in 1921 with 90 members and 1,805 pesos. Nine years later, in 1930, it issued loans for a value of 5,351,938.81 pesos (nearly 2,000,000 dollars). During that year the Banco Israelita Argentino issued loans for 2,240,000 pesos, and the Banco Israelita Polaco for 615,590 pesos. Other banks were still undergoing their formative period at the end of the third decade of the century. Their importance in Jewish commerce and industry grew in later decades. The popular character of the banks, with literally thousands of shareholders, gave them a positive role in the development of Jewish institutions in the country. The banks were Jewish not only in name or in their management but also because of their concern with Jewish life and needs. They contributed considerable sums to most Jewish concerns both in Argentina and outside of it.[113]

Simultaneous with the development of their economic life, the immigrant Jews in Argentina established their Jewish institutional lives on firmer foundations. Starting as peddlers, many Jews established retail stores, some wholesale commerces, enterprises for the importation of goods from European countries, and finally entered industry—mainly textile and furniture—thus becoming a more active element in the economic life of their adoptive country. At the same time they founded their main Jewish societies and purchased plots of land for permanent cemeteries. These factors—the consolidation on a much more permanent basis of both their Jewish life by means of their various institutions and their economic life—were parallel developments, each influencing the other and both making for the adaptation of the Jewish immigrant to his new home in Argentina.

Jew and Gentile in Argentina

Jews manifest their identity through a wide range of activities and associations. Some accentuate the religious character of this identity, while others emphasize one of several currents of Jewish nationalism or Zionism. Still others view their Jewishness along ethnic lines, preferring to participate in Jewish mutual help societies or associations dedicated to protect the immigrants newly arrived from lands in which their situation had gradually deteriorated. Finally, there are Jews who consider their ties with other Jews as essentially cultural, which might be expressed in centers such as libraries, Yiddish theaters, or through the Jewish press and journalism. There is, however, another crucial factor in the identity of the Jews, namely, the fact that they are considered as such by their non-Jewish neighbors and society. Nathan Glazer and Daniel P. Moynihan have asserted that "two wills make a group—the self-will that creates unity, and the will of others that imposes a unity where hardly any is felt."[1] Conceivably this will of others had an effect on Jews in Argentina, for after the 1880s antisemitism has played a role in the country, though its virulence and even its practical results in the Jewish community have not been uniform throughout the last hundred years.

It has been asserted that antisemitism in Argentina became a strong element in various sectors of society in the 1930s when the same sentiment was rampant in many Western countries. Both Moisés Goldman and Silvia Schenkolewsky have asserted that before 1930 there were only sporadic outbursts of anti-Jewish feelings, with no great inner coherence or ideological

basis. Four reasons adduced for the nonexistence of strong antisemitic sentiments were (1) that the country was very cosmopolitan, with a heterogenous
population of varied races and religions living together, leaving no room for
rivalries; (2) that since the country was undergoing a process of development,
there was no real competition between Jews and non-Jews in areas such as
agriculture, industry, and science; (3) that the mass of immigrants from Southern Europe—Italians, Spaniards, and to a large extent also Frenchmen—knew
little about Jews from experience and had only a literary-theological conception of them; and (4) that Jews were not individualized as Jews but as Russians,
Roumanians, Germans, and so on.[2]

Indeed, anti-Jewish demonstrations before 1930 only sporadically attained the vehemence, fury, and consistency they showed in later periods.
Even if sporadic during the period that ended in 1930, expressions against
Jews produced an impact on the Jewish community of Argentina. We shall see
that antisemitic expressions appeared constantly, thus disproving the view
that antisemitism was not a factor in the life of the Jewish community. However, we must bear in mind that the antisemitic attitudes before 1930 and
those of the period immediately after were different not only in intensity but
also in quality. After 1930 antisemitism in Argentina was a consistent ideology
among more or less influential nationalist groups, which was not the case, by
and large, before that time.

This chapter will not focus on the causes of antisemitism in different
periods in the history of Argentina. We shall concern ourselves with the different areas in which this sentiment was made manifest and the assiduity with
which it recurred, dedicating special attention to the reaction it produced
among Jews living in the country. Finally, we shall gauge from the data thus
obtained the role antisemitism played in strengthening Jewish identity. Still, it
should be noted that the four reasons given above for the lack of strong antisemitic manifestations before 1930 do not stand criticism. Through our analysis we shall show that each one of them is untrue. In the first case, the cosmopolitan character of the country in the period was the main factor for the rise
of a forceful movement to Argentinize the country, thus provoking xenophobic
sentiments. This xenophobia had strong notes of antisemitism, for Jews were
the Foreigners by antonomasia. Against the second reason we shall note signs
of discrimination against Jews in the universities—both students and profes-
sors—and in the workers' movements, as well as arguments against the participation of Jews in certain branches of commerce. Third, with respect to the
immigrants from Southern Europe who knew about the Jews mainly from literature and Catholic teachings, it will be pointed out that they were precisely
the most susceptible to the teachings of Catholic groups that disseminated
hatred of the Jews based on their belief that the latter were descendants of
deicides. The fourth reason is not altogether correct even if during the last
years of the nineteenth century some Jews preferred to be singled out by their
country of origin instead of by their religion. Most Jews did not deny their
origin. Moreover, the general population, especially in the big cities, was used
to reading about *israelitas* and even about *judíos* in newspapers, magazines, and

books. On the other hand, the causes of the anti-Jewish uprisings during the period should be looked for in the rising nationalist feeling that developed in Argentina from the first years of the present century, in the fear the dominant elite had of the workers' movements that might plant socialist, communist, or anarchist ideas among the population and in the teachings of certain clerical groups.

Anti-Jewish Sentiments before 1905

The first signs of antisemitism in the country appeared in 1881 as a consequence of the decree that opened the doors of the country to the Jews of Russia.[3] Active opposition to the government's policy to appoint an immigration agent in Europe to encourage immigration of Jews who were suffering pogroms and other restrictions in Russia was led by the Buenos Aires French newspaper, *L'Union Française*. Its editorial of August 22, 1881, included an extremely deprecatory description of the Jews and warned against the disastrous consequences of their mass immigration. The arguments were basically economic, with an undercurrent of racism: "We do not know what people would ever have the idea of sending an agent outside to gather noxious insects, powerful parasites; we do not fully understand a physician who having to treat a growing body which is in need of daily renewed blood, does not know better than to inject leeches instead."[4]

La Nación, the reputable daily founded by Bartolomé Mitre, carried an interesting editorial on the appointment of José María Bustos, the government's agent. While milder in tone than its French counterpart, it also denounced the administration's policy, arguing that the Jews would encounter enormous difficulties in assimilating themselves to their new environment. The editor concluded that bringing "this race of men to our soil, with its eccentric constitution of race and beliefs as well as habits, is to generate a kernel of population without relationship, without incorporation, and without adherence to the national society."[5]

On the other hand, one sector of the Argentine press, *El Nacional*, founded by Domingo F. Sarmiento, was more sympathetic to the Jews and denounced *L'Union Française*, asserting that "the slanderous and insulting words against the Israelites . . . indicate the moral level of the editor."[6]

The reaction of the few Jews residing in 1881 in Buenos Aires to these events is indicative of their identification as Jews. These West European Jews seized the opportunity to demonstrate their concern for Jewish rights. Members of the Congregación Israelita protested against the slanderous attacks of the French newspaper and even challenged the editor to a duel. This was the first time that the Jews of Buenos Aires had to defend themselves against attacks by the press. They responded immediately and forcefully and learned that they had some support in the gentile community. Moreover, the attacks provided an opportunity to call for the unity of all Jews in the city. Thus the persecutions of Jews in Russia and the negative response of some sectors in

Argentina to Jewish immigration to its shores, strengthened the Jewish identity of the few Jews living there.[7]

For the Jews, especially those who had emigrated from countries where they had personally experienced antisemitic attacks, the possibility of causing the anger of the general population against them was something they forever tried to avoid. The fear of antisemitic uprisings was more in their minds than in those of potential antisemites. This is understandable from the point of view of the long history of pogroms, forced migrations, and special legislation the Jews had undergone.

In 1895 Rabbi Joseph, who had been in the country for over thirty years, warned the members of the Chevra Keduscha that the Moroccan Jews in Buenos Aires, "when they bury a coreligionist, hold ridiculous ceremonies in public which attract the attention of the populace, and could provoke a conflict with the [general] population and authorities, who already tolerate us in this country and do not make any impediments for us to keep our cult. . . . We must try not to encourage antisemitism in this hospitable land."[8]

In the last years of the nineteenth century reports attest to the fact that some Jews did not want to be considered as such. Pinie Katz observed that when the first Jewish periodicals appeared in Buenos Aires, in 1898, "many subscribers requested that the newspaper be sent in an envelope or completely wrapped in paper, so that nobody would see the Hebrew letters."[9]

Because Jews were called "Rusos" in the country, some preferred to declare themselves Germans, or, if accepting their Russian origin, a few added that they were *real* Russian and not Jews. Furthermore, some closed their shops on the High Holy Days but placed signs in the windows announcing, "Closed because of family mourning" or "Closed for stocktaking."[10] In 1901 Simon Ostwald, who had been active in various Jewish societies and who was also one of the richest Jews in Buenos Aires at the turn of the century, spoke of this attitude in a speech he gave at a celebration in Buenos Aires of the Fifth Zionist Congress in Basle. He asserted that "nowhere is there less reason to hide one's origin or creed than in this Argentine land, where antisemitism is an exotic plant that will never prosper."[11]

There were Jews who forever tried to hide their origin in fear of antisemitic provocations. However, in Argentina such Jews were more conspicuous in the 1890s and first years of the twentieth century. Interestingly enough, those were years of calmness with respect to instigations against them. In later decades (before 1930), when antisemitic writings were more widespread and when physical attacks against Jews had taken place, the tendency to conceal their identity was not so noticeable among Jews. The fear of antisemitism, which indeed did not decrease, took a different form among active Jews. Along with the rise of nationalism in Argentina, especially in the programs of education at all levels of instruction, some Jews feared opposing this nationalism with Zionist activities. Testimonies to this attitude are obviously scarce, but the documentation found clearly attests to the existence of apprehension in some sectors of the Jewish population. At a board meeting of CIRA in 1927

Jacobo Edelberg was "opposed to CIRA's participation in Zionist affairs, because it could be charged of propagating an antinationalist Argentine spirit and produce antisemitism."[12]

Once some antisemitic activities had shaken the Jewish population in Argentina, the attempt to cover their Jewishness was a much less common event. It was not merely the natural reaction to antisemitism that made Jews more conscious of their particularities as such but also their realization that they could be assured of the sympathy of larger sectors of the Argentine population when such attacks erupted. The arrival of larger numbers of Jewish immigrants during the decade before World War I worked both as a cause of antisemitism (the élite saw in the Jewish, as well as in other foreign workers, the peril of leftist infiltration) and as a balsam to the fear of revealing their origin among Jews, who felt more comfortable among larger numbers of their coreligionists.

A large number of false notions are transmitted through what sociologists call stereotype. In this way physical traits or cultural and social characteristics of individuals of a group are attributed to the group in general. People are judged not according to their own personalities but according to what they are supposed to conform to as members of a particular group. Stereotypes of Jews appeared in Argentine literature for the first time in 1891 when José María Miró (nom de plume, Julián Martel) began publishing his novel *La Bolsa* in the newspaper *La Nación*.

A vivid description of the activities in and around the stock exchange in Buenos Aires is given in this novel, as well as detailed portrayals of both the place and the people who frequented it. The plot of the novel is built around the economic boom that took place in Argentina during the 1880 decade with the consequent abundance of currency that made for a favorable climate for business deals. Thus the stock exchange became the scene of feverish activity.[13] This speculative fever was the cause of economic cataclysms that followed. The state, as well as many private individuals, "suffered grave losses, which, of course, had an impact on the entire economy."[14]

The opinion Miró had of the Jews is of interest:

> The one that spoke swallowing the French words with German teeth, and not the purest ones, indeed, was a pale, blonde, lymphatic man, of medium height, in whose disagreeable and effeminate face one could see the expression of hypocritical humility that a long period of servility has made the typical seal of the Jewish race. He had small eyes, striated with red filaments, that betray the descendants of Zebulun, and the nose bent typical of the tribe of Ephraim. He dressed with the bad tasted luxury of the Jews, who can never acquire the noble distinction that characterizes a man of the Aryan race, his antagonist. He was called Filiberto Mackser and had the title of Barcn which he had bought in Germany, thinking that in this way he could give importance to his obscure name. He was with a young man, a compatriot of the same religion, who practiced commerce with women, supplying the *porteño* brothels with the beauties of the German and Oriental markets.[15]

Martel could not have been a witness to many situations involving Jews, although he described several in detail. At the time there were practically no instances of overt racial prejudices in Argentina. However, there was in existence, and circulating in Buenos Aires, some literature of an antisemitic character that had arrived from Europe, mainly from France. To understand a work like La Bolsa, therefore, it is necessary to comprehend the attitude of the people in Buenos Aires, especially the oligarchy, with respect to Europe. For the political leaders, "To govern meant to Europeanize."[16] The same was true of the literary activities of this oligarchy. The élite "assailed the traditional way of thinking. They preferred the French authors to the Spanish ones, and some, the Anglo-Saxon to the French."[17] Doubtless, in the atmosphere of the literary salons of the city—in the milieu of the oligarchy that had its eyes more upon Europe than upon its own country,[18]—where European authors were discussed, books, magazines, and newspaper articles with antisemitic propaganda, were discussed as well. Just as in Europe some authors blamed the Jews for the economic failures and depressions produced as a result of the Industrial Revolution, Martel blamed the immigrants, especially the Jews, for the economic crisis of 1889. The Argentine society, which had relatively few Jews, showed that it, too, could give rise to antisemitic expressions.[19]

[margin handwriting: Economic society Failure]

The influence of Edouard Drumont is evident in Martel's work. The former is mentioned in a dialogue, and several lines are taken verbatim from his La France Juive.[20] The racist sentiment, which had earlier roots in Count Gobineau's Essai sur l'inegalité des races humaines and had influenced Richard Wagner and Drumont, among others, weighed heavily in Martel's prejudice. "You do not realize the sad role you would be playing [Glow explained to Granulillo] if it were known that you are part of a trust of German Jews, since associating with them means going against the country, against the race, against everything good and honest in the world. . . . They, they are the ones who are unwilling to become part of a race that has proclaimed to all the universe that all men are equal."[21]

Martel also denounced the financial feudalism of the Jews, an accusation that had been spread in France for almost half a century before. The Jews inspired fear in one of the characters of La Bolsa because they begin by invading silently, and "will end monopolizing everything."[22] The Alliance Israélite Universelle is accused of being one of the most powerful secret organizations in the world, silently awaiting the moment of Jewish revenge, and of having "branches everywhere in the world where there is a means of profiting at the expense of the Aryan."[23] Baron Mackser is Rothschild's envoy, "who has been sent to Buenos Aires to exert pressure on the market, and to control and monopolize, with the help of a strong Jewish trust, . . . the main sources of production of the country."[24] Rothschild himself is an excellent example of a Jew who has no roots in the country in which he lives and makes his money. He has doubled his capital to the damage of France.[25]

Martel's antisemitism did not have an immediate influence in the society of his time. A young man just twenty-three years old, he finished writing La

Bolsa on December 30, 1890, and died six years later. His main concern was that of denouncing and slandering not the Jews but, in general, all immigrants speculating in the stock exchange. His antisemitism was coupled with xenophobia. It did not lead to exclusion laws or to riots and pogroms. We have gone some length into describing La Bolsa because stereotype accusations against Jews did reappear in Argentina a few years later, and Martel's work represents the first attempt to spread this type of concept in the country. The success of the novel among the Argentine population of the time, as well as in later generations, testifies to the fact that there was a considerable sector of the population absorbing stereotyped concepts denigrating the Jews. This characterization of the Jews remained latent in their minds but was liable to come out in a more active form of aggressiveness once the general atmosphere in the country demanded a scapegoat for its problems or a justification of repressive measures by the government.

Few anti-Jewish sentiments, nevertheless, were manifest in Argentina before 1905. Two of them, however, deserve some consideration because of the importance of the circles in which they originated. The first one concerned Juan Alsina, for almost twenty years the government's director of immigration. Alsina repeatedly warned the governor of Entre Ríos, where the largest JCA settlements were located, to beware of the Jews because they did not mix with others. Alsina asserted that on account of their high birthrate Jews threaten to grow into a separate power that would never adopt Argentine culture.[26] In other instances Alsina deviated from the law by making differences between Jewish and non-Jewish immigrants. He refused to a group of Jewish immigrants the usual right they had upon arrival to be harbored in the Hotel de Inmigrantes and to obtain free tickets to travel into the interior of the republic to their places of settlement. The minister of agriculture censured Alsina and advised him to be guided by the principle of law that permits no distinction of race, religion, or nationality to be made among immigrants.[27] However, Alsina, who wrote repeatedly against the formation in Argentina of foreign communities with a strong inner cohesion that would prevent the total assimilation of the immigrants,[28] did much to turn Argentine opinion against the Jews by means of reports on the state of immigration.[29]

The second serious instance of antisemitism before 1905 appeared in Revista Nacional in 1902. Arturo Reynal O'Connor, describing the life and problems of the various agricultural colonies constituted in their majority by foreigners of diverse origin, also had something to say about the Jewish ones. The Jewish colonists, according to Reynal O'Connor, were not like the rest of the Russian colonists who "adapt themselves more than any other immigrants to the nature of our country." Jews are not capable of agricultural work, nor do they want to be agriculturists: "The Jew is a merchant, and his business is usury." After a description of their small bric-a-brac businesses in several towns near the colonies and a derogatory picture of their outer appearance, the author added a few final remarks that reveal his prejudice against Jews: "Dirty and disheveled; the aquiline profile and long beard predominate; and most of them have yellow faces that look as if they really were two thousand years old. You would think they are the same who crucified Christ; morally, they are Shylocks; and from the social point of view, they turn up in the villages like a pest."[30]

Revista Nacional was one of the few literary magazines of the time. Both its contributors and readers belonged to the educated upper class, the only class that had a say in official policy in the country. Alsina was also a member of this class. Both he and Reynal O'Connor were prejudiced against the Jews. Alsina thought the latter would not assimilate to the country's mores; Reynal O'Connor saw a deicide and a usurer in every Jew. However, the time was not yet ripe for a limitation of Jewish immigration nor for violent attacks against Jews. The governing elite still promoted the immigration of large numbers of immigrants to populate the country and serve its own economic needs. Furthermore, warnings against the peril of losing the Argentine character of the country to a growing cosmopolitan population had not yet been voiced.

Rise of Nationalism and Its Effects upon the Jews

After the economic crisis of 1890–91 immigration into Argentina was resumed. From 1892 up to World War I the net immigration into the country surpassed the 2,000,000 mark. Large proportions of the newcomers remained in the port city of Buenos Aires, which throughout the quarter of a century before the war had 50 percent of its population composed of foreigners. Moreover, foreigners constituted more than 72 percent of the total population over twenty years old.[31] They thus constituted a very noticeable element among the urban militant workers determined to improve their economic situation and represented a threat to the Argentine ruling classes long accustomed to servile laborers.

The working classes became active during the last decade of the nineteenth century, especially by means of general strikes. Between 1885 and 1889 Enrico Malatesta visited the Río de la Plata, and in 1898 Pedro Gori did the same, both prominent leaders of the European anarchist movement. Both these activists urged anarchist workers to organize into syndicates in order to unite their forces when necessary. Anarchists reached the working masses mainly by means of two newspapers, *L'Avenire* in Italian and *La Protesta Humana* in Spanish. At the same time the socialist movement began mustering forces. In 1882 German socialists formed the Club Vorwarts. In 1894 *La Vanguardia* began appearing as the organ of the socialist group, which was formed into a political party under the leadership of Juan B. Justo two years later.[32]

Strikes were organized by both socialist and anarchist groups, though they were not often in agreement. In the eyes of the upper class both movements were harmful to the security and progress of the country. As a consequence of a huge anarchist-led general strike in November 1902 in which dock workers and draymen joined most other unskilled workers, President Julio A. Roca called both chambers of Congress into a special session. A state of siege was immediately declared to put an end to the strike, and after a short debate the Residence Law was enacted. Since most problems within the workers' movements were believed to be caused by foreign agitators who launched the workers into conflicts against their own best interests, the Residence Law of 1902 emerged as Argentina's first legislation designed specifically to discriminate against the foreign-born. The principal provision of this law enabled the executive to expel any foreigner because of civil crimes or one whose conduct "compromises national security or disturbs the public order." The Residence Law became a controversial issue; many voices—among them the editors of La Nación and La Prensa, as well as Socialist congressman Alfredo L. Palacios—argued that it might discredit the country among prospective agricultural immigrants in Europe, who were urgently needed in Argentina.[33]

Because of the support the Residence Law had among the governing class, the movement to repeal it failed.[34] Nevertheless, agitation continued, and the number of strikes grew.[35] Accordingly, police repression became harsher. At the same time, the anarchists were consolidating their strength in the Federación Obrera Argentina, which they dominated in 1905.[36] In May 1909 violent incidents took place when 200,000 workers in Buenos Aires struck in protest of the violent manner in which the police had dispersed a May Day anarchist march, leaving 8 dead and 105 wounded. Violence reached its peak when a young Russian Jewish anarchist, Simon Radowitzky, assassinated Chief of Police Ramón L. Falcón, on November 14, 1909, thus avenging most workers, who hated Falcón for his fierce repression of strikes and demonstrations.[37]

Antiforeign sentiments were thus accentuated. Even the important newspapers that had advocated repealing the Residence Law a few years before now called for more repressive legislation and for the investigation of new immigrants to avoid potential agitators.[38] The government had, moreover, additional preoccupations in this area. It was preparing elaborate celebrations of the first centenary of the May 25, 1810, revolution, to which were invited foreign dignitaries, including President Montt of Chile and Princess Isabella of Spain. The anarchists, on the other hand, had already announced their plans for a general strike during the celebrations. However, the government was determined to celebrate the centennial peacefully and applied all necessary repression to subdue the nonconformist agitators. On May 14, while Congress was voting on another state of siege, conspicuous members of the exclusive Sociedad Sportiva Argentina, and other members of the wealthy class, under the permissive eye of the police, organized assaults on key workers' institutions. That evening, they completely destroyed and burned the premises, furniture, and printing presses of La Protesta and La Vanguardia, while the police arrested several hundred working class leaders, including the head of the Socialist party, Juan B. Justo. Several workers' locales were assaulted and destroyed. One column of the demonstrators further indulged in a series of outrages in the Jewish quarter of Barrio Once. In the corner of Lavalle and Andes (today, José E. Uriburu) they plundered a grocery store, destroying it afterwards. Not satisfied with this, they also violated women.[39] Jews were also among the foreigners deported right after these raids; among them was Zalman (Salomón) Sorkin, the Labor Zionist leader of the first years in Buenos Aires.[40]

On June 27 of the same year another law was rapidly passed by both Houses of Congress. It came as a response to the explosion of a bomb under a seat at the Colón Opera House during a performance. Romanoff, a Russian anarchist, was accused by the police of being responsible for the act of terrorism, though he was probably innocent.[41] But the oligarchy in power became even more distrustful of foreigners and requested stricter legislation against anarchists. The Ley de Defensa Social, which was passed immediately by Congress, prohibited the entry to the country of anarchists, foreigners who had committed civil crimes, or anyone who advocated the use of force or violence against public functionaries, governments, or institutions. It further prohibited meetings and demonstrations of anarchists and established fines against all those indirectly involved in bringing anarchists into the country or helping them in any of their activities.[42]

The generally hostile attitude of the ruling class towards foreigners also made an imprint among the Jews living there. In 1910, even before the events of May 14th and the final adoption of the Ley de Defensa Social, Jews were voicing their disappointment with the direction affairs were taking in the country. The Labor Zionist organ *Broit un Ehre* indicated the need for unity of all Jews in the country with the main purpose of "protecting themselves from external attacks which are becoming stronger every day here." Being realistic, though not without disillusionment, the editor added,

> To defend oneself from the outside! Only a few years ago we could speak about Argentina as a new "Eretz Israel," a land that opened generously its doors for us, where we enjoyed the same freedom the Republic gives all its inhabitants, without distinction of nationalities or beliefs. And now? The whole atmosphere around us is filled with hatred of Jews; eyes hostile to Jews are staring from all corners; they lie in wait in all directions, awaiting an opportunity to attack. The word "Ruso" has become a shameful one among official elements, meaning a white slave dealer, a *cambalachero* (dealer in old stuffs), a person who has dark dealings; and among reactionaries: a revolutionary, an anarchist. All are against us.... And this is not simply hatred of Jews; it is a sign of a future movement, which is long known under the name of antisemitism.[43]

In a letter dated May 5, 1910, Jacobo Joselevich reported to *Haolam*, which was then published in Vilna, that antisemitism had been developing at a fast pace in Argentina. He went as far as stating that "if Baron Hirsch would rise from his grave, he would recognize his error, because of the growth of antisemitism in Argentina."[44]

In those days anti-Jewish activities were mainly directed against Jewish workers' organizations. Jews were quite conspicuous among the victims of the "patriotic" bands of 1910. When the latter entered the Jewish quarters during the sad evening of May 15, they also destroyed the locale of Biblioteca Rusa, a Jewish proletarian and socialist cultural center. Besides being the most important Russian and Yiddish library at the time, Biblioteca Rusa was also a cultural center where discussions on international social problems were held. Biblioteca Rusa was active as well in gathering contributions for the Jewish victims of the pogroms in Russia, for the deportees in Siberia, for the deputies of the Duma who were arrested, for the revolutionary movement in Russia in general, and for the striking workers in Argentina. It also sponsored theater shows in Russian and Yiddish and other social activities for the Jewish workers. The end of this organization came abruptly when the patriotic mobs burnt most of its books in a bonfire in Plaza Congreso.[45]

The growing antiforeign sentiment in Argentina manifested itself against the Jews in other areas besides workers' movements. Jews were accused of spreading anti-Argentine sentiments to their children in their private schools. The first reports concerned the schools in the JCA colonies in the province of Entre Ríos, though their repercussions were felt not only there but also in the capital city. Ernesto A. Bavio, who had been director general of education in Entre Ríos during the 1890s wrote in the November 1908 issue of *El Monitor de la Educación Común* a report, "Foreign Schools in Entre Ríos," concentrating on the Russo-German and Jewish ones. His report was in no way pleasing to the developing national sentiment in the country: "The schools in the Russo-German villages transmit an instruction exclusively foreign in letter and spirit. . . . What takes place in the Jewish villages is even worse because the colonists are more closed and exclusive. There, all instruction in the schools, absolutely all, is in Hebrew, and there is no reading book other than the Bible." After confirming that most of the Jewish schools in the province received a subsidy from the provincial government, Bavio asserted that neither the Spanish language nor Argentine geography and history were taught there. Finally, Bavio concluded that the Russian and Jewish schools were a threat to the nation.[46]

The report raised an issue in high circles. The main newspapers in the capital reported assiduously during the following months about the situation in the schools of Entre Ríos, always based on Bavio's conclusions. However, Manuel P. Antequeda, at the time occupying Bavio's former post of director general of education in Entre Ríos, immediately published an updated report, denying most of his predecessor's asseverations. Antequeda stated that "Bavio has never visited the schools in the Jewish villages; he does not even know the location of even one of the twenty-three JCA schools in the Departments of Villaguay, Uruguay, and Colón." Furthermore, the only person who visited the Jewish schools was the subinspector of the Consejo Nacional de Educación, who arrived there on a Saturday evening, and returned on Sunday.[47] Antequeda, moreover, deplored the position taken by Bavio because it provoked "the unfortunately long latent question of antisemitism."[48]

In Antequeda's report there are a series of documents clarifying the situation in the Jewish schools at the time, all confirming that they were fulfilling at least the minimum requirements of the provincial school system. In any case the reaction in various circles, especially among the upper class in Buenos Aires, to the report is indicative of a strong xenophobic feeling. Both *La Nación* and *La Prensa* kept their readers well informed on the issue. Both availed themselves of the opportunity of criticizing what apparently seemed an antipatriotic attitude of the Jews and added a few other concepts that in no way made for a just evaluation of Jews among their readers. *La Nación*, in effect, blamed the Jews for the stagnant situation of regional industries and other small-scale industrial activities because they monopolized the land for material gain, not agreeing to its subdivision.[49] With respect to the schools, *La Nación* appealed to the "energetic intervention of the government, called to put into practice the most noble and patriotic of its duties."[50] *La Prensa* as well repeatedly advocated taking strong action against the anti-Argentine schools. It recommended that if the Entre Ríos government did not proceed with the urgency that the gravity of the case required, the national government should order the immediate Argentinization of the schools or close them in case of disobedience: "This is a supreme patriotic duty."[51]

Among those who accepted Bavio's reports was Ricardo Rojas, whose *La restauración nacionalista* (1909) repeated the inspector's charges. This was Rojas's first major work, consisting of a sharp attack on the cultural impact of the cosmopolitan population of the country. Rojas soon became the most influential intellectual figure of the generation that advocated a complete revision of the educational programs in the country to protect the creole cultural heritage against the alleged corrupting influences of immigration. In particular, the danger posed by the Hebrew schools, according to Rojas, was that "when they bring their fanaticisms, they also bring us a Semitic question which did not exist here because there were no Jews, but which will exist as soon as the creole son of the Semite immigrant prefers being Jewish, instead of being Argentine in complete union with the people and the soil in which he was born."[52] Another disadvantage of the Jewish school was that "it creates the Jewish family, whose religious patriarchate will prevent it from fusing itself with the families of the country, and assimilate to our sociableness."[53] But Rojas was prejudiced enough to believe that "a foreign association of Jewish bankers legislates over our country and mocks its laws."[54] Though others accused European governments of similar interference, Rojas preferred to ground his attack on a financially powerful alliance of Jews who did not respect national boundaries when the issue concerned the furtherance of Jewish values.

Before the celebration of the independence centennial in Argentina the concepts about the Jews spread by Bavio and repeated by authors of influence such as Rojas, created similar situations vis-à-vis Jewish schools in different areas where Jews lived. Complaints about the anti-Argentine education in Jewish schools in the provinces of Buenos Aires and Santa Fe and finally in the city of Buenos Aires ended with the temporary closing of some of them for the same reasons.[55] Among the motivations given for closing the Talmud Torahs (Jewish religious schools) in the capital by the Consejo Nacional de Educación was the accusation that not all the students received the minimum required in subjects such as Argentine history and geography and civic instruction and that the education did not have an eminently national character.[56] Actually, these were only Jewish religious schools, and the students who received their religious education there also attended the national schools. On the other hand, Jewish leaders concerned with the low level of Jewish education in the

Talmud Torahs, complained that the strong assimilationist education of the Argentine schools was estranging the Jewish children from any Jewish atmosphere.[57]

The wave of protests against the Jewish schools subsided shortly after the celebrations of the centennial. By that time the Ley de Defensa Social had also become effective, and the war against anarchists had calmed some of the nationalists. But the attacks prompted a response from various sectors of the Jewish population in the country. From the available documentation we can assert that the strongest responses came from some of the small Jewish workers' parties and Zionist movements. These organizations were the most violently attacked by the reactionary elements in Argentina and had some of their more active leaders deported as a result of the Ley de Residencia and Ley de Defensa Social.[58] The workers' organizations were assailed not only because of their Jewishness, but also because of their participation in strikes and demonstrations along with the general workers' movement. The Bundist group Avangard revealed its solidarity with the general Jewish community when it wrote, "We are no admirers of the Talmud Torahs, we are against their [study] program, and also against whatever is taught there, because when the children come out of the Talmud Torah they know almost nothing about Jewish [i.e., Yiddish] language, history and literature; but no one has the right to take oppressive measures against the Talmud Torahs, which have rights according to the Constitution." Avangard further tried to awaken the Jewish population to think about the near future: "We must protest sharply against the injustice that the government is making, and we hope that our voice will not be lost in the desert of Jewish unconcern."[59] The Zionist workers' party, Poale Zion, had called, by means of their short-lived biweekly *Broit un Ehre*, for the union of all Jewish institutions and individuals in order to defend the community "against the attacks of the press and in society, as well as from the government." But the union, in their view, had also to include cultural, economic, and mutual help committees to serve all Jews inhabiting Argentina.[60] The "General Zionists," or Zionists active in societies directly connected with the Zionist Organization in Europe, wrote assiduously in their journal *Di Yiddishe Hofnung* against assimilation and concentrated on the improvement of Jewish education, through which, they hoped, Zionist ideals might also be taught.[61]

Institutions representing the most established part of the Ashkenazi community in Buenos Aires were during this period (1908–10) grouped around the Federación Israelita Argentina. This sector of the Jewish community endured the attacks of the press against the Jews in general but probably sided with many of the government's measures against workers' strikes. The Federación sent flowers to Falcón's funeral and decided not to take any action with respect to Jews in prison.[62] Rabbi Halphon, "the soul of the Federation," wrote to the JCA headquarters in Paris about antisemitism in Argentina and pointed out the need for improving the situation of the working class Jews in Argentina by offering them more courses in the Spanish language and in Jewish history and also for "improving the Jewish immigration" coming into the country, in order to avoid new uprisings against them.[63] Doubtless, Jews active in societies

attached to the Federación considered Jewish activists in the workers' movements to be the cause of antisemitic responses in various sectors of the population and thought that if the latter's immigration were reduced, normalcy
could be restored.

In preparation for the centennial many articles were written on the general state of affairs in the country. Many of them were devoted to studies on
the population and the influence of different groups of immigrants in Argentine life. There were many who praised the Russo-Jewish newcomers along
with other foreign immigrants. Both Leopoldo Lugones in his *Odas Seculares*
and Rubén Darío in his *Canto a la Argentina* praised the contribution of Jewish
colonists to the development of agriculture in the country.[64] On the other
hand, Jews praised the freedom they had found in Argentina and expressed the
willingness with which many of their coreligionists were adapting to their new
country's mores and developing a strong sense of patriotism. Outstanding
among the latter was Russian-born Alberto Gerchunoff, who in 1908 published
in *La Nación* stories about the Jewish agricultural colonies, which two years
later he edited and presented as homage to the country's centennial under the
title *Los gauchos judíos.* In these short episodes Gerchunoff expressed his convic-
tion that the Jewish colonists, while keeping a few of their Jewish traditions,
were gradually adopting ways of life typical to their surrounding neighbors,
the gauchos. Gerchunoff thought, as did many other Jewish colonists in the
country, "that Argentina is Palestine for the Israelite, because the Promised
Land, in the strict sense of Scripture, is the land of freedom." Furthermore, in
Gerchunoff's eyes, "the sons of the Israelites, residing in the cities or in the
Argentine country, are almost chauvinists, and even the older ones, those born
in Odessa or Warsaw, are highly patriotic, deeply and sincerely Argentine."[65]
Los gauchos judíos, which obtained almost unanimous praise by Argentine men
of letters—including Martiniano Leguizamón, the "father of Entre Ríos's writers," who wrote the prologue—also found some resistance, not for its style but
for the message it conveyed. Benjamín García Tores considered Gerchunoff's
work an apology for the Jewish colonists and asserted that Jews and Creoles
could never harmonize due to essential characteristics of the Jews that did not
allow them to mix freely with gentiles.[66] This was not the only time that Jews
would be criticized in Argentina by an ardent nationalist who, when confronted
with evidence disproving his basic convictions, dismissed it by branding it as
apologetic.

During the second decade of the twentieth century Jewish immigration
continued to be criticized by the main newspapers in the capital. During that
period the problems raised by Rojas and a whole generation of nationalist
authors became a major concern for the upper class in Argentina. Editorials in
the main newspapers and in the literary magazines of greater prestige among
Argentina's educated high society presented different opinions about the
types of immigration the country should encourage and those it should reject.
The Jews were usually among the undesirable ones for different reasons,
though their difficulty in assimilating to the country's way of life and customs
was a constant argument.

The colonists of Palacios and Moisesville in Santa Fe were accused by *La Nación* of forming a state within a state because most municipal posts in these towns were filled by Jews. A long article describing the strong bonds between these Jews—bonds that prevented them from fusing with the general population of the country—concluded that "to mock the 'foreign' law is a program that one might think is the obligation of every Jewish colonist; they think that this constitutes a form of religious consequence to history and to the law of the race."[67] An apparent deviation of the law that was often mentioned with respect to the Jews was that even among those born in the country only a small percentage fulfilled the military service requirements. A strong denial was made by Coronel Ricardo Solá in a letter to *La Nación* in 1914, but the argument continued being voiced.[68]

The frequency with which articles criticizing Jewish immigration appeared, along with new aspects of Argentine law against all foreigners, alarmed the Jewish community in the country. When the first Argentine Jewish Congress was convened in Buenos Aires on February 26–29, 1916 with the purpose of deciding about conditions a Jewish delegation should demand at the eventual peace conference once the war ended, internal problems of Argentine Jewry were also discussed. The delegate from Moisesville, Noe Cociovich, in his address, "The Organization of Argentine Jewry," proposed the creation of a central body representing the whole Jewish community in the country. The main reason for this he explained quite clearly: "We cannot remain optimistic when confronted with frequent and unjust attacks against Jewry in this country. We must struggle so that the Argentine atmosphere does not become polluted with antisemitism. . . . Jews should not suffer from regulations that limit their rights. . . . [this legislation] which is passed under the category of 'extranjeros' is due to the fancy of the executive power or propaganda by the press. . . . The word 'extranjeros' frightens us, . . . it has the same connotation as the word *zhid* in Russia."[69]

Cociovich also mentioned a few of the antisemitic attacks that had taken place in Argentina to which Jews had not responded effectively and suggested that the formation of a Jewish representative body could prevent more attacks. A provisional committee was elected at the Congress, but it never convened.[70]

Some Jewish officials answered the attacks made against the Jewish community by means of explanatory articles. Though apologetic, these articles fulfilled the purpose of not letting defamatory concepts go by unchallenged. Such was the case when Francisco Stach published an article in the *Boletín Mensual del Museo Social Argentino* in 1916 in which he reviewed the accomplishments of several groups of immigrants, denigrating the Jewish ones. Manuel Bronstein, active in Juventud Israelita Argentina, answered with an elaborate article in the same journal, and Natan Gesang did likewise, publishing in the *Revista Argentina de Ciencias Políticas*.[71] Stach had asserted that the most unfitting element for the country was the Russian-Jewish one, because among them "there are many dangerous elements, anarchists, caftens [white slave dealers], and prostitutes capable of criminal acts." Moreover he wrote that Jews did not succeed in Argentina either in agriculture or as artisans. They were mainly in commerce and controlled the cereal market not only in the country but also in the international market. Furthermore, Stach suggested that the rise in the number of fraudulent bankruptcies during the previous years was due to the participation of the Jews. Finally, "besides the religious, economic, and moral reasons, which would be sufficient for not fomenting but flatly rejecting Jewish immigration, there is also a physiological reason, because there is no other race in Europe as degenerate as the Jewish one. We have today in the insane asylums in the Capital a large number of degenerate and idiotic children of Jewish origin."[72]

Bronstein defended the Jewish immigration, first by making a clear difference between the Jewish *caftens* and prostitutes and the rest of the Jewish community, which had no real contact with the other in daily life. Second, Bronstein showed that the Jewish immigration fulfilled what he considered were the three most important conditions for a good assimilation to the country, namely, the habit for work, good morale in their customs, and physical health. Furthermore, Bronstein emphasized the contributions Jews had made to Argentine economic progress and to the country's culture.[73] Gesang, a Zionist leader, answered along the same lines, dwelling upon the contributions of the Jewish people to civilization in general, as well as to the Argentine people.[74]

The immigration question continued being debated in official circles. The events in Europe during the last part of World War I, especially the Bolshevik Revolution in Russia, made a strong imprint in these circles. The growing restlessness among workers that caused an increase in the number of strikes in the last years of the 1910s[75] further alerted the upper class against the possibility of a communist takeover in Argentina. Indeed, the Bolshevik example gave new strength to the labor movement in the country, and the Argentine elite reacted against the immigration of labor leaders who would spread their doctrine among the local proletariat. In particular, Jewish proletarians were considered by many a revolutionary stock because they were identified as Russians due to their country of origin. Thus world events, magnified by the fear that most reactinary elements in Argentina had of their possible consequences in their own country, set the stage for what is considered the first pogrom in Argentina.

La Semana Trágica

The metallurgic factory of Pedro Vasena, in Buenos Aires, by the end of World War I employed about 2,500 persons, workers and employees. The workers were on strike since the first day of December 1918, demanding the reduction of the working day from eleven to eight hours, a gradual increase in salaries, the enforcement of Sunday rest, and the reinstatement of the workers' delegates fired at the beginning of the conflicts when on January 7, 1919, the police accompanied a group of strikebreakers to the premises of the factory. The clash between strikers and strikebreakers was inevitable. The police intervened in favor of the latter killing a few workers and wounding many others.

These events caused the greatest general strike in Argentina up to that time and gave rise to a confrontation between the forces of order—police and army, backed by many upper class persons and the Radical government—and the workers. The former saw in the latter an anarchist, foreign-dominated force that had to be abated in order to save the country and its institutions. Jews—specifically Ashkenazi, or "Russian" Jews—were considered to be an important part of the "maximalist" movement by the forces of order. The week that started on January 7 was called La Semana Trágica in the history of the Argentine workers' movement. It was no less tragic in the history of the Jews in Argentina.[76]

At the time the workers were divided into several ideological currents. Up until 1905 there had been two ideologies within the working class: anarchist and socialist. Towards the end of the first decade of the twentieth century a third current began having influence among the proletarian masses in Argentina. This was called syndicalism (or unionism), which started among adherents of the Socialist party, who criticized its essentially parliamentary struggle. They considered parliamentary activities only auxiliary to the union struggle, along the lines of Georges Sorel's ideas of revolutionary unionism. Anarchists and syndicalists, in spite of having a common enemy within the workers' movement, namely, the Socialist party, were divided into two different organizations. Anarchists constituted the Federación Obrera Regional Argentina (FORA) del V° Congreso along the lines of their fifth Congress of 1905, while the syndicalists, who were the strongest in 1919, constituted the FORA del IX° Congreso (of 1915). There were, in particular, Jews active in all branches of the workers' movement, in both FORAs and in the Socialist party.[77]

When the general strike paralyzed the country's commerce, industries, and transportation, the army was called in to help the police restore order. A civilian group called Guardia Blanca, integrated by members of the Argentine elite, decided that they too should actively participate in the defense of the national institutions. They launched physical attacks against anarchists, including principally foreign workers who "looked" maximalist or "Russian."

Other groups under the general name of Defensores del Orden were rapidly organized by leaders of the elite clan. The most important group formed in the midst of the disturbances of January 1919 was the Liga Patriótica Argentina. Its leader was the Radical congressman Manuel Carlés, who, like many liberals of the time, was rapidly turning conservative. Moreover, the Liga Patriótica was sponsored by other strongly nationalist organizations, notably Asociación del Trabajo and Comité Nacional de la Juventud. The latter sent a note to the chief of police offering the collaboration of its members with the police forces because "civil backing is necessary to counteract subversive action." The young men of the Comité Nacional de la Juventud did not lose time: "In its midst there were liberals, oligarchic nationalists, and clericals, but all acted in unison organizing pogroms against the Jews, shooting against workers, and assaulting union and party locales. This they did on January 10, 11, and 12."[78]

The Jewish quarters during the tragic week were attacked mainly by the civilian groups under the permissive presence of policemen and soldiers. Juan E. Carulla, a nationalist, gave a personal account of one of the "missions" of the Defensores del Orden:

> A phalanx of enthusiastic Argentines, later to be called Liga Patriótica Argentina, was grouped around him [Carlés]. . . . I heard that they were burning the Jewish quarter, and there I directed my steps. I walked on Junín, Uriburu, and Azcuénaga streets, at first finding no manifest signs of disturbances. There were only groups of men, women, and children in expectant attitude at doors and street corners. Only when I reached Viamonte [street], opposite the School of Medicine, was I able to witness what could be called the first pogrom in Argentina. Piles of books and old furniture were burning in the middle of the street. One could recognize among them chairs, tables, and other domestic chattels. The flames sadly illuminated the night, making prominent with reddish glare the faces of a gesticulating and shaking multitude. I made my way through the crowd and saw fighting in and around buildings nearby. I was told that a Jewish merchant was accused of making communist propaganda. I thought, nevertheless, that other Hebrew homes were suffering from this cruel punishment. There was noise of furniture and cases violently thrown into the street mixed with voices screaming "death to the Jews, death to the maximalists." Every now and then long bearded old men and dishevelled women passed by me. I shall never forget the livid face and supplicant look of one of them who was being dragged by a couple of youngsters; or that of a crying child who held fast to the old black coat, already torn, of another of those poor devils. Not without repugnance, I could not but see similar pictures wherever I set my eyes, because the disturbances provoked by the attacks to the Hebrew stores and homes had spread to various blocks around us.[79]

Juan José de Soiza Reilly, a journalist, described what he called the "martyrdom of the innocent," who were attacked by gangs carrying the Argentine banner: "I saw innocent old men whose beards were uprooted . . . ; an old man lifted his undershirt to show us two ribs. They came out of his skin like two needles, bleeding. . . . A woman was forced to eat her own excrement, . . . poor girls of fourteen or fifteen . . . [were] raped."[80]

The precincts of the Bundist association Avangard and of Poale Zion were assaulted by the mobs and burned. Books from the Moses Hess library (Poale Zion center) and archives from all these institutions, went up in flames in bonfires kindled by the Guardia Blanca. Pedro Wald, active leader of Avangard, was arrested in the streets by the police. He was tortured in order to "confess" the Bolshevik plan in Argentina since he was supposed to be the president of the future Argentine Soviet.[81] His fiancée, Rosa Weinstein, was arrested together with Wald. The charges against her, according to different sources, were being the fiancée of the future president of the soviet, having too many books, and being Russian.[82]

The Jewish quarters returned to normal when the general strike was finally terminated after a series of negotiations between FORA del IX°, government officials, and industrialists.

As part of the general reaction against foreign agitators in the workers' movement, Jews were attacked. The elite was prejudiced against all Russian immigrants—of whom about 80 percent were Jewish[83]—and considered that they were the source of all the major uprisings and disturbances in the working class. The Russian Revolution, in the opinion of the upper class, had affected the mental health of a large part of the Russian urban population. Horacio Beccar Varela argued that "it is undeniable that the brain of those who were Nicholas' subjects can be considered sick. It is a type of collective insanity, which we should avoid. I exclude the agriculturists and prefer the illiterate, because the agriculturist lost in the country is a minor danger, and the illiterate, in Russia, is an uncontaminated being, who will easily adapt himself to our atmosphere of freedom and order."[84] Tomás Amadeo affirmed along the same lines that "[Russia] is at present sick, and most of those who emigrate from that country suffer from that sickness, thus spreading all over the world a perturbing current."[85]

The upper class remained convinced that the strike had been planned outside of the country's borders. Carlos Ibarguren, who was later to become one of the theoreticians of nationalism in Argentina, clearly stated this in his memoires: "The 'Semana Trágica' in Buenos Aires was undoubtedly prompted by Russian agitators, revolutionary agents of the Soviet, who profited from the climate of workers' malaise among us for that uprising. Public opinion and the government accused the 'Russian anarchists' or 'maximalists' of being the main promotors of the rebellion, and, in effect, the police imprisoned the so-called 'Dictator,' named Pedro Wald, and the appointed Chief of Police in case of triumph, a Slav called Juan Selestuk or Macario Ziazin, both foreigners of dangerous antecedents."[86] The daily press described Wald's antecedents in detail, including his participation in the Russian Bund and, from 1906, in Avangard in Buenos Aires.[87] Ibarguren, however, repeated the charges against Wald in spite of the clearly socialist, anti-Zionist, and antianarchist platform of these organizations.

Frederick Jessup Stimson, United States ambassador in Argentina during World War I and up to 1921, was convinced that the workers had been terrorized into striking under Bolshevist or German orders. The early official figures received at the embassy were that 1,500 had been killed and 4,000 wounded, "mostly Russians and generally Jews." When the strike was settled, Stimson met one of the commanders of the military repression, who proudly told him that at the arsenal there were 193 corpses of workers who had been identified: "Fourteen were Catalans—the other 179 were Russian Jews." Stimson maintained twelve years later in his memoirs that a Bolshevist revolution was avoided by the services of the military police, "and there was discovered the whole plan of their government, with the names of their president, secretaries of state, military leaders, the whole proposed Bolshevist regime."[88] Moreover, Stimson claims to have received secret knowledge that the strike in Buenos Aires was part of an international communist movement to strike in 1918–19 in the five principal seaports of the world most important to the Allies—Stockholm, Rotterdam, Liverpool, New York, and Buenos Aires—and that he had received the names and addresses of the ringleaders: "The names were in great part Jewish, the addresses always in slums near the ports."

It has been impossible to confirm Stimson's recollections. On the contrary, all reports seem to contradict his assertion that so-called Jewish conspirators like Wald or even Selestuk, were really part of a Bolshevist plan. They were in fact freed after a few days. Nevertheless, Stimson's testimony indicates quite vividly the confusion and fear of communism in Argentina toward the end of World War I. Katherine S. Dreier, a U.S. citizen visiting Argentina for a period of five months coinciding with the Semana Tragica, offers supporting evidence for the atmosphere of a "red scare" and its implications for the Jewish community of Buenos Aires: "Feeling ran so high, and so great was the confusion which existed in the minds of the people between Russians and Jews, that many Jews were attacked as they were mistaken for Russians, and all Russians were classed as Bolshevists. Already several firms had dismissed all their Russian and Jewish employees."[89]

At the time, antisemitic groups were found in various schools of the University of Buenos Aires, notably at the School of Medicine, situated on the borders of the Jewish quarter. Jewish students were repeatedly confronted by attacks of other students, most of them sons of the *porteño* elite. A witness told us about some cases that took place before the Semana Trágica, in which Jewish students were insulted because of their accent and their origin.[90]

A second important cause of the onslaught upon Jews in 1919 was the continuous antisemitic propaganda and education sponsored by some Catholic groups in Argentina. Already in 1908, when the Jewish schools in Entre Ríos were accused of being anti-Argentine, some defenders of the Jewish colonists observed the influence of Jesuit hatred, spread especially from the city of Córdoba to all corners of the country.[91] A few years later, in 1917, the publishers Hermanos de las Escuelas Cristianas put out two books, *La Tierra* and *La Argentina*, that were utilized as textbooks in elementary and high schools in the country. These books contained several deprecatory statements of Jews in general and the Jews in Argentina specifically. They accused the Jews of being almost exclusively moneylenders and usurers and the wave of migration to the country promoted by Baron Hirsch—"that modern Moses with a dresscoat, monocle, and white tie"—of attempting to create a new Palestine in Argentina. Rabbi Halphon, representing CIRA, approached Dr. Francisco Beiró, president of the Municipal Council (Concejo Deliberante), requesting the suppression of these books from the school program. Halphon mentioned the case to President Yrigoyen when a delegation of Jewish officials visited him during the aftermath of the Semana Trágica, but still the texts continued being used. The colonists in Clara, Entre Ríos, made similar requests in 1926![92]

For years before the events of 1919 the Catholic church in Argentina had been a most reactionary institution and actively denounced the activities of maximalists within the working class. Prominent among the clergymen who fought against anarchism, socialism, and finally against communism, was Monseñor Miguel de Andrea. In 1912 de Andrea was appointed spiritual director of the Círculos Católicos de Obreros, which were started twenty years before with the purpose of helping workers by means of social works and of protecting them from the liberal philosophy of other workers' organizations.[93] While in this post, Andrea put into practice his initiative of popular conferences by the clergy in the streets to counter the propaganda made in similar way by "agitators" in the anarchist and socialist movements. A contemporary admirer of the Monseñor described the situation as follows: "The city [Buenos Aires] seemed seized by the rostrum of the enemies of God and his Church; in front of the factories and in the places most frequented by the people, in the streets, plazas and walks, the socialist stage was placed, while the Catholic circles circumscribed their propaganda and their popular action to the pulpit in the churches."[94]

Sponsored by the Círculos Católicos de Obreros, many priests spoke on streetcorners against anarchists and socialists. In their harangues they quite often attacked the Jews, which they did even in the Jewish neighborhoods. Monseñor Dionisio Napal, "the apostle of this crusade," around the time of the Catholic festivities of Christmas and New Year delivered strong lectures against socialists and Jews in different sections of the city. On December 22, 1918, he spoke at the corner of Junín and Corrientes, the heart of Once, the most important Jewish quarter in Buenos Aires, attacking the Jews in the country as being traitors and the only ones guilty for local scarcity. On another occasion he asserted that socialism was a Jewish malady and that Jews were bloodsuckers who had been thrown out from all countries.[95]

The priests were also active in the antisemitic indoctrination of their parishioners in the very churches. Augusto Bunge witnessed in the streets "and in certain churches a no less infamous libel, seeking to import into Argentina that shame of civilization called antisemitism, combat banner of the European clerical parties that followed the influence of the Jesuits."[96] José Ingenieros, one of the most original thinkers in Argentina at the time, blamed a "semi-secret student society, alumni of the Jesuit schools and directed by some priests," of leading a militant clerical political life at the service of the conservative classes. The latter had promoted antisemitic agitations against Jews at the universities.[97] Still others decried the Jesuit press, especially *Los Principios*, directed by the disciples of Loyola in Córdoba, which made frequent antisemitic attacks.[98]

There was still a third element, which, though not a main cause of persecution of Jews, was of major importance in making these attacks more fierce. This was the plunder and pillage of Jewish property and money. Several sources attest to this type of activity by many policemen, who made a poor living from their salaries and were used to accepting bribes for infractions that were not reported. The daily *Crítica* reported that "the poor policemen took what they could in three days of antisemitic riots. In the assault of calle Victoria 300 pesos were lost, as well as many pieces of jewelry." Among the sons of the elite there were many who thought that together with the Jews "some disturbing promissory notes could also fall, and the honest and patriotic grocers inferred that by killing all of them [the Jews] they would free themselves from many competitors."[99] Many an assailant, besides defending his country from dangerous foreign elements, did not lay aside the opportunity of indulging in personal gain.

Jews and the Socialists

The growing nationalism in Argentina during the 1900s and 1910s was not limited to the conservative and upper sectors of the society. The Socialist party likewise advocated a rapid adaptation of all foreign elements to the culture and norms of the country. The views of some of the most conspicuous Socialist leaders on Jewish particularism is of special interest.

The Socialist party in Argentina was organized in 1896 at a Constituent Congress attended by delegates of nineteen socialist centers and fifteen workers' unions, all from the capital city. At this Congress, led by Dr. Juan B. Justo, the basic program of the party was approved. In Justo's words, "The Socialist Party is, above all, the party of the workers, of the proletarians, of those who have but their working power; the doors of the party are nevertheless wide open to those individuals of other classes who want to enter subordinating their interests to those of the proletarian class." Cognizant of the large numbers of recent immigrants, Justo added that "the milieu in which we act forces us to assume a well-defined attitude with respect to foreigners, whom we must admit into the party, with propaganda goals, even if they have no political rights."[100] The Socialist party throughout this period was composed of a large number of foreigners. In their attempt to capture the leadership of the urban working classes with proposals of better working conditions the socialists propagandized in workers' circles of different and foreign origin.

Many Russian Jews upon arriving in Buenos Aires were attracted by the Socialist party, which conformed the most to their ideological background. As a result of the wave of immigration from Russia after 1905, Jewish workers' societies were formed in Buenos Aires. Jews expressed their socialist ideology by means of membership either in the Socialist party, in Avangard (founded in 1907 along the lines of the East European Bund), or in the Zionist Socialist workers' party, Poale Zion (founded in 1906). The latter two organizations advised their members and sympathizers who were empowered to vote in presidential and congressional elections in Argentina to do so in favor of the Socialist party. Other Jewish societies, notably Juventud Israelita Argentina (founded in 1908, a cultural society composed mainly of Jews of Russian origin educated in Argentina), though not specifically involved in politics, sympathized as well with the socialists.

The Socialist party from its inception considered as a basic and fundamental principle the absolute assimilation of the immigrants to the mores of the country. After a short period it dissolved the national centers—Italian, French, and German—out of which the party had been founded. Linguistic groups, however, continued operating, and socialist leaders permitted them among workers who had not yet mastered the Spanish language. Along the same lines, the Socialist party led a strong campaign for the naturalization of immigrants, its goal being to incorporate them into the political life of the country, thus stressing its national character. The proletarian struggle, accordingly, had to be fought by parties representing the labor forces within national boundaries. It was this last concept which put the Jewish people in an ambiguous position vis-à-vis the Socialist party.

Relations between the Socialist party and the Jewish socialist organizations were cordial. Actually, Avangard was recognized as a linguistic group with the specific function of propagandizing among the Yiddish-speaking immigrants. However, Avangard managed to remain quite independent from the Socialist party in its activities in Jewish circles. The monthly *Der Avangard* was published exclusively through the effort of the Bundist society. It remained autonomous in its organizational structure and in the arrangement of cultural activities such as meetings and demonstrations in the streets.[101]

Poale Zion, on the other hand, had little contact with the Socialists before the Balfour Declaration. The society itself had not been too active between 1910 and 1917 due to the expulsion of some of its most active leaders during the 1909–10 repression against workers' agitators. The Balfour Declaration and the arrival of the Poale Zionist *sheliach* (emissary) Marcos Regalsky shortly thereafter gave new strength to the organization. At the time, Enrique Dickmann, a Russian-born Jew who had arrived in Argentina in 1891, a leading figure of the Socialist party, and congressman since 1914, wrote a short article entitled "Zionism and Socialism." Writing exclusively as an Argentine socialist, Dickmann hailed the Balfour Declaration for what it represented for the Jewish people, maintaining that the Socialist party "even before the war accepted and upheld the principle of nationalities as one of the postulates of international socialism."[102] Furthermore, the Socialist party sent an official note of sympathy to the Poale Zion center in Buenos Aires on the occasion of the first anniversary of the Balfour Declaration, encouraging the attainment of the aspirations of Labor Zionism.[103] On several occasions during the following decade Enrique Dickmann and his brother Adolfo, also a militant socialist and congressman, spoke at Poale Zionist meetings.[104]

Relations were also good between Poale Zion and the Partido Socialista Argentino, which was formed after a schism had taken place in the Socialist party in 1915. It was led by Alfredo L. Palacios, the first socialist to occupy a chair in Congress (1904) and a close friend of the Jewish community in Argentina.[105] During the Semana Trágica the Partido Socialista Argentino issued a declaration denouncing the "excesses committed against the Jews, contributors to our progress, respectful of our laws, who arrived in the country fleeing brutal European antisemitism and seeking the shelter of our wise and humane constitution."[106] This declaration, as it was formally expressed, was formulated after direct contacts with the Partido Socialista Sionista (Poale Zion).

Not all the leaders of the socialist movement in Argentina were sympathetic to the Jews. Its founder and mentor of a generation of socialist leaders in Argentine politics, Juan B. Justo, manifested in many opportunities his strong prejudices against the Jews as a people and against Judaism as a religion. The first of Justo's antisemitic remarks appeared in the Yiddish monthly *Shtraln* in 1913 when the editors of that periodical submitted to various distinguished Argentine personalities a questionnaire about the (Menachem Mendel) Beilis case.[107] All the other persons who responded to the questionnaire—including the socialists Palacios and Enrique del Valle Iberlucea—denounced in strong terms the antisemitic accusations of ritual murder against Beilis in Kiev and forcefully denied that Jews ever engaged in this type of ritual. Justo, on the other hand, in line with his well-known antipathy to all religions, answered that "in questions of religion and superstition I consider everything possible . . . [and] if the Jews are capable of practicing circumcisions, they might observe other blood rituals as well."[108]

Justo represented the Socialist party of Argentina at the International Socialist Conference of Amsterdam in April 1919, at which a special resolution on Jewish rights was adopted. Besides the demands for equal civil rights, freedom of immigration and settlement in all countries, national autonomy, and representation of the Jewish people in the League of Nations, the resolution contained a clause demanding "recognition of the right of the Jewish people to build their National Home in Palestine." Justo was opposed to this resolution, maintaining that an independent Jewish state might be a good idea but had no relation with the International. With respect to the Jewish problem, he added that "the Jews do not differ at all from the non-Jews and can therefore merge with the non-Jewish population. In this way we shall be freed once and for all of the Jewish problem." The president of the plenary session in Amsterdam responded in a way that may well explain some of Justo's motivations or lack of them. Henderson, of England, said that "Dr. Justo comes from far away countries and is not therefore at home with European conditions."[109] Indeed, in the Latin American countries the question of minority rights had never been raised. The Jewish problem, as Justo had experienced it in Argentina, had a relatively easy solution. Having the same rights and the same education as the general population, Jews would assimilate to the majority in each country.

Finally in 1923, when the editors of *Vida Nuestra* prevailed upon Justo to write an article for their periodical, the latter entitled it "Why I Do Not Like To Write for a Journal That Calls Itself Jewish." Here Justo explained not only what the title suggests but also why he disliked the Jews. Justo, who was married to a Russian-born Jewish woman, differentiated between Jews as individuals and Jews as a group: "Separately, or mixed with the rabble of peoples, I admire some and esteem many human specimens labelled as Jews. Together, instead, they become immediately suspicious and enigmatic to me." Moreover, he utterly opposed Jewish racial, religious, and national particularisms. The preservation of a Jewish race in Argentina was contrary to the process of racial mixture taking place in the country. Justo found the Jewish religion dogmatic and exclusive and full of myths that prevented its followers from freely developing their individuality. Practices such as the "dirty and bloody rite" of circumcision, the special slaughtering laws, their separatedness in questions of burials, the "dogma" against the consumption of pork, and other "sectarian preoccupations" are some of the many manifestations of "a spirit that will contribute nothing to the national unity and energy." With respect to Jews as a nation, Justo saw little sense "in the national ideas of people scattered all over the world, under all governments and flags, without a living language or an autonomous government in any country of the world." Only Zionism found sympathy in Justo's eyes but solely if "it did not bother too much other peoples already established in Palestine." Zionism had, moreover, an additional positive factor: "No established nation would complain if the Jewish crusade to Zion purifies it from heteroclite and unassimilable elements." Justo's final recommendation to the Jews was "Abdicate, as Jews, from all secret pride, and thus the word 'Jew' will faster loose its present offensive connotation."[110]

The Socialist members of the Municipal Council of the capital showed a similar attitude with respect to Jewish particularism in a long-fought issue over the opening of a Jewish cemetery within the city limits during the 1920s. On December 31, 1921, the Municipal Council authorized the Chevra Keduscha to build a cemetery in their plot in Punta Arenas street. During 1923 the Chevra Keduscha initiated the building of offices and other appropriate chambers, which were completed in 1925. In the meantime the Sociedad de Beneficencia—which had bought a neighboring lot, though after the 1921 authorization to the Chevra Keduscha, for the purpose of building an orphan asylum for girls—as well as some residents of the area, appealed for the repeal of the permit granted to the Jewish institution. The Municipal Council discussed the issue in various lengthy sessions during the period 1924–27. Its Socialist members were the more strongly opposed to the authorization and finally succeeded in outvoting the faction leaning to grant the Chevra Keduscha the permit for a private cemetery, in the session of May 11, 1926. Throughout the debates the Socialist members of the council—notably Angel Giménez and Américo Ghioldi—emphasized the existence of municipal cemeteries for the interment of the dead of all religious and national communities and the danger of proliferation of burial grounds if all religious groups demanded the authorization of a private area for their dead. With this argument socialists desired to avert all possibility of retarding the effects of the Argentine "melting pot" among the immigrants' descendants.[111]

Repeatedly the Socialist representatives at the Municipal Council manifested their acquaintance with many individual Jews and the multitude of socialists the world over of Jewish origin. However, their assimilationist desires, mixed with a forcible impatience with religious "prejudices" can be discerned in their speeches, which include subtle attacks against Jewish particularism.[112] Giménez, when stressing the contributions of Jews to socialism, pointed out that "we have in Parliament two congressmen [Adolfo and Enrique Dickmann] of Jewish origin, fortunately redeemed Jews, who honor the Argentine Parliament."[113]

The Jewish press in the country denounced what they considered an antisemitic attitude of the Socialist representatives at the Municipal Council. The Chevra Keduscha appealed to the good services of Rabbi Halphon to attain a hearing with President Marcelo T. de Alvear in order to try to influence a favorable decision of the council.[114] However, all these efforts were of no avail, and the Chevra Keduscha had no alternative but to sell its plot in the capital and buy another one outside the city limits. Interestingly enough the Municipal Council passed an ordinance on December 16, 1925, prohibiting the establishment of private cemeteries in the city of Buenos Aires, which, because it was passed after the first authorization to the Chevra Keduscha in 1921, did not facilitate the latter's final repeal in 1926.[115] This prohibition, however, obviated all further conflicts regarding Jewish cemeteries within the capital city limits. The cemetery incident further made clear to the Jews in Argentina that they were viewed with good eyes by the socialists as long as they conformed to the general population's customs. However, all particularistic deviations were scorned and contested.

Aftermath of La Semana Trágica

The Semana Trágica had important consequences for the inner structure of the Jewish community in Argentina. Jews realized at the time that many of their rights could also be vulnerable in Argentina. This came as a shock to many who considered the country as their Promised Land, where they would enjoy full freedom and tranquillity. It was now evident to them that they should not take those things for granted, and many sought to find a way through which their lives would not be endangered.

The Comité de la Colectividad was the main organization formed at the time to protect the Jewish population. It carried out varied activities within the Jewish community. Almost immediately, delegations were sent to various cities in the interior and even to Montevideo to intervene in favor of several Jews imprisoned as consequence of the uprisings in these cities.[116] Funds were immediately raised to help the victims of the riots, and to care for the final recovery of the wounded.[117]

The *comité*, which was formed by officials of the Federación Sionista Argentina, the Congregación Israelita, Juventud Israelita Argentina, and leaders of other Jewish organizations, made several important achievements. In a strong and bold memorandum submitted to the government, which was entered in full into the minutes of the lower chamber of the Argentine Congress, the *comité* denounced the police and Guardia Blanca, petitioning the government to investigate the matter, to individualize the guilty, and to carry out justice.[118] During the month of May of the same year—May being traditionally a month of disorders and workers' agitation due to May Day and May 25th, when workers tried to boycott celebrations of the anniversary of the 1810 revolution—representatives of the main institutions of the Jewish community in Buenos Aires gathered together in order to avoid possible repetition of the January disturbances. A delegation visited President Yrigoyen, who assured them of his administration's intentions of keeping order and protecting every inhabitant of the country.[119]

Nevertheless, the Jewish community, as soon as the atmosphere seemed calm, returned to its petty quarrels for representation.[120] A central body was not formed, and the *comité* slowly dissolved. In July of that year a new attempt to create a Comité de la Colectividad with no political or trade union attributions but purely for the defense and protection of Judaism and Jewry in Argentina failed. Among the reasons for the formation of this type of body was the fact that some individuals and organizations had tried, sometimes with political or particular motivations in mind, to represent and speak in the name of the whole Jewish community. The preparatory meetings of this new *comité* took several months and were attended by representatives of up to forty-two Jewish societies of the capital. When the moment came to choose a board for the *comité*, personal ambitions produced all sorts of fragmentations and disunity (see ch. 5). The united voice of the Jews went down with this project.

What bothered the Jewish officials was the formation of the Partido Israelita Argentino right after the January events. This was led by Jews who utilized the name of the whole community for political activities and self-gain. This Jewish party, of short existence, had the purpose of "organizing the [Argentine] citizens of Jewish origin in the social and political level in order to defend the security of the Jews in the future and support its millenarian culture for the good of the country."[121]

The Partido Israelita Argentino supported candidates of the Demócrata Progresista and Socialist parties for the congressional elections of March 1919. Among the main points of its platform was a liberalization of the naturalization laws for foreigners, and suppression of antisemitic textbooks, and the introduction of divorce laws and laws in defense of workers. During the three years that the Radical party had been in power it had not improved the situation in those areas. Thus the Partido Israelita Argentino launched a campaign in the Jewish quarters by means of pamphlets and signs both in Spanish and in Yiddish, inducing the Jewish population that had the right to vote to do so against the official party, elements of which captained "the barbarian hordes . . . who satiated their perverse instincts in the defenseless members of the Jewish community."[122] Jews, however, voted for different parties. Indeed, many apparently voted Socialist, but still many continued to vote for the Radical party.[123] In any case, most Jews—except those active in Avangard (Bund) and Poale Zion, who openly favored the Socialist party—were opposed to the creation of a Jewish political party or to the proclamation of specific candidates emphasizing the benefits they would give to the Jewish community in the country.[124]

A small group of Jews, however, decided to try to establish good relations with the reactionary groups that were formed as a consequence of the January disturbances. As we have mentioned above, the main organization that took upon itself the role of "keeper of Argentine patriotism [*Argentinidad*]" was the Liga Patriótica Argentina, founded by elitist members of the armed forces, government, church, and the Ladies of the Argentine society, with the motto *Fatherland and Order* (*Patria y Orden*).[125] Most of the Jews willing to collaborate with the Liga were not involved in Jewish communal life. They were active in the stock exchange and in contact with members of the Argentine upper class. When they finally formed the Liga Israelita Pro-Argentinidad and adhered to the Liga Patriótica Argentina, they met with the general repudiation of those Jews who cared to take notice of them. Their membership was limited to twenty or so members, and this *liga* only lasted for some months.[126]

The bulk of the Jewish population in Argentina responded to the attacks of the forces of order—for which they were totally unprepared—with appeals to the government and came to the rescue of the victims quite promptly. Except for some marginal Jews who attempted to gain political power or who sought the approval of the country's upper and reactionary class, Jewish officials in Buenos Aires put personal and ideological differences aside and united in the Comité de la Colectividad to deal with the emergency. When the emergency had subsided, however, these personal and ideological differences became paramount once more. The impact of the assault on the Jewish quarters was only momentary. During the 1920s the Semana Trágica was mentioned only sporadically by Jewish publications, in spite of a few other cases of antisemitic expressions—though in a lesser scale of gravity—that took place. On the other hand, it was a decade in which Jewish institutions were consolidated, Jews prospered economically, and the community grew in numbers. Antisemitism played a small role during a decade in which Jews enjoyed extremely good relations with government authorities. The few antisemitic sentiments came from groups of limited influence in the country, thus producing in Jewish officials a reassuring feeling of trust in the country's institutions vis-à-vis their own coreligionists. This confidence was the central motive for the failure of all attempts to create a representative board of the Jewish community that could speak in the name of all Jewish societies. Only as a result of the systematic antisemitism of the 1930s would this board be formed. The Semana Trágica was only an isolated major antisemitic issue and thus did not constitute a strong enough incentive to the centralization of the Jewish community.[127]

The Late 1920s

Anti-Jewish feelings and prejudices that were manifest for almost five decades in Argentina, with more or less virulence according to the occasion and the source, had an effect on various sectors of the population of the country. During the last years of the third decade of the twentieth century there was a recrudescence of these prejudices and sentiments, harbingers of a more systematic antisemitism during the 1930s. The main sources of antisemitism in Argentine society—politics and the Catholic church—had a growing effect on similarly conservative elements of the more popular classes of the country's population.

Parallel to these antisemitic feelings was the growing discontent and dissatisfaction of the oligarchy with the Radical party, which was in power from 1916 until a military coup dethroned it in 1930. Such was the position of Lucas Ayarragaray, a conservative congressman and writer of influence since the dawn of the century. Ayarragaray perceived that since 1916 Jews had been more active in left-wing parties in the country, and that by 1930 their numbers had waxed to more than 300,000. He saw a danger for his country, because Jews were constituting a separate society, with synagogues, periodicals, and political committees of their own. Their chief rabbi was even received by President

Yrigoyen! The solution, according to Ayarragaray, could only be found in apply-
ing a proportional quota system of immigration to limit the growth of a community that would not take proper roots in the country's institutions.[128]

Ayarragaray, who had often written about Sephardim in the colonial and
early independent periods in the Río de la Plata area, always showing the good
influence that Jewish blood had had upon important personalities in the first
decades of Argentine history, had somewhat changed his views by 1930. Actually, the Sephardim he was referring to were *conversos* who had penetrated into
the Spanish colonies in America and had mixed with the aristocracy of the
time. Ayarragaray admired the fact that those *conversos* fully integrated with the
rest of the population and that their descendants were now proud Catholics,
some even members of the Argentine high society. The new Sephardic immigration, alas, was not the same as the old one in his eyes: "The wave of Jew[ish
immigration]: Syrians, Turks, Greeks, Lebanese, Moroccans, Arabs, Russians,
. . . we should filter with a selective and restrictive sieve."[129] Ayarragaray was
one of the few people in Argentina who noted that Sephardim were just as
Jewish as Ashkenazim and that the restrictive measures suggested for the latter immigration should also be enforced against the former.

During the late twenties Catholic elements started to write antisemitic
articles with renewed vigor. *Criterio*, the most representative weekly of the Catholic establishment in the country systematically published charges against the
Jews. It introduced antisemitism even into articles in their theater section.
When Henri Bernstein's *Israel* was first performed in Buenos Aires, the critic
sided with Dreyfus's accusers in France, adding that "as Catholics we cannot
here [in Argentina] but understand the antisemitic movement of those times,
and justify it, recognizing, as we do, that it had some excesses."[130]

Jews were consistently accused in *Criterio* of being deicides. The present
generation was also guilty in their eyes because "it incurs in the same fault
committed by their parents and makes common cause with it." Jews were further criticized for not accepting the New Testament because "their greediness,
lust, vengeance, and racial and personal or national pride dim the spirit [and
prevent them from] . . . seeing the truth and disable them for faith and piety."
Furthermore, Jewish hatred of Jesus and the church was stressed in *Criterio*. But
what most bothered the editors of the weekly was the Jewish obstinacy not to
accept the Catholic faith: "Skeptics and heretics see that in the Church is
found the human Right, Moral, Culture, Intelligence and Piety; that only she
solves with comforting and pacifying solutions the problems of social peace,
of human injustice, of pain, of death, and of the unknown beyond the grave;
that outside of her there is barbarity, corruption, cruelty, and in spite of it they
reject it, they slander it and they persecute it like the Jews with the Christ."[131]
Articles such as the above-quoted one could not but form in the minds of the
naive Catholic believers a monstrous picture of the Jews.

Restrictions to immigration, advocated by Ayarragaray and other conservative political leaders, were put into practice after the September 1930
revolution ousted the middle-class regime of Hipólito Yrigoyen. Potential immigrants, especially Jews fleeing Europe due to the developments there during

the 1930s, were confronted with obstacles when trying to enter the country in a much higher degree than their predecessors. On the other hand, the church started attacking the Jews in Argentina for theological reasons at the end of the period. To the main traits of Catholic antisemitism in the country in earlier periods—antianarchism and anticommunism, with a strong dose of xenophobia especially directed against Jews—was now added the belief that the Jews were deicides and obstinate nonbelievers in Jesus' gospel. Parallel to these developments, a growing interference by the military—influenced by German training missions, modern weapons, and esprit de corps—and the strengthening during the 1930s of European fascism, which had many emulators and sympathizers in Argentina, shaped a picture of a country not-too-friendly to Jewish settlement.

We have seen that antisemitism was not lacking during the period before 1930. This was not a sentiment that expressed itself in violent antisemitic activities by and large, though there were occasions in which force was used, property damaged and stolen, and Jews injured and even killed. During the period, antisemitism was not systematic. No organization had a policy of attacking Jews and their institutions. However, fear of foreign and leftist ideas created an atmosphere of intolerance to Jewish workers who were considered Foreigners by antonomasia. Though unsystematic, antisemitism was growing in the minds of several groups in Argentina. There was a rising dislike for the foreigner, for the unassimilable, and later for the God-killer. Prejudice and lack of significant contact with actual Jewish customs were creating problems for Jews in places such as hospitals, universities, and to some extent even within workers' unions.[132]

The Jews maintained, however, excellent contacts with the Radical party leaders. Numerous delegations of diverse Jewish sectors were received by Yrigoyen during his first period in office (1916–22). Most of the Jewish institutions participated in a demonstration to both Yrigoyen and Alvear before the presidency was passed from the former to the latter. Rabbi Halphon and Max Glucksmann, president of CIRA and Soprotimis, had direct and personal contact with Alvear during his period as president (1922–28). Outwardly, the life of the Jews in the country seemed not to be affected by Jew hatred. When difficulties arose, such as in the Semana Trágica, most institutions united to solve the emergency. Some of the written attacks, moreover, did not remain unchallenged. However, little could be done to counter the growing feeling of dislike for the Jews in many circles of the population. Jews had realized upon arriving in the country that it was not free from antisemitism, but they still considered that this sentiment would not grow into dangerous proportions. Even if they responded whenever threatened, they were not moved to create a special committee to check all uprisings and to combat antisemitic manifestations at their very inception. Nonetheless, all the attacks on Jews were felt by them even if they did not grant them sufficient importance. They reminded them of their Jewishness and stood as an important factor in keeping Jews linked to their people.

Religious
Institutions and
Observances

During the 1870s and 1880s the Congregación Israelita (CIRA) had been providing religious services during the Jewish Holy Days and had arranged for circumcisions and funeral and burial services for the small Jewish community in Buenos Aires. But during those decades the religious needs of the Jews in Buenos Aires remained limited to those offered at CIRA. With the arrival of Jews from North Africa and Eastern Europe starting in the 1880s, and from the Ottoman Empire starting in the early 1900s, the religious needs became more diversified. Religious Jews were confronted with the need of adapting themselves to new situations in Argentina. They had to create institutions that would allow their religious observances, institutions that had existed for many generations in their home towns and that were taken for granted there. Among the major areas of preoccupation were the availability of religious functionaries, such as a rabbi to solve legal questions and to speak to Jews gathered at the synagogues, a ritual slaughterer (*shochet*) who would provide them with kosher meat, and a cantor (*hazan*) for the Jewish holy days. Furthermore, Jews in Buenos Aires lacked a Talmud Torah (religious school) for their children, a *mikveh* (ritual immersion pool) for their wives, and a Jewish cemetery for their dead.

In 1891 the Moroccan Jews founded the synagogue Congregación Israelita Latina (CIL) in the Barrio Sud section of Buenos Aires. The East European Jews, on the other hand, had first settled in the Centro area, especially in the Lavalle and Talcahuano streets, near CIRA. Jewish white slave dealers of East European origin had settled in the same neighborhood (see ch. 9). Early in the nineties East European synagogues were founded in this section of Buenos

Aires. The first one, Sociedad Obrera Israelita (Poale Zedek), was established in 1891. According to one of its founders, the inclusion of the word *obrera* (worker) in the name of the society had the purpose of differentiating its members from the white slave dealers.[1]

Late in 1892 a second synagogue was founded by East European Jews of the neighborhood. Isaac Presser, Joseph Gotlieb, and others who were not in full agreement with the priorities adopted by Soly Borok and Miguel Kuperman, leaders of Poale Zedek, formed Machzikei Emunah.[2] According to A. L. Schusheim the disagreement had a religious foundation. Poale Zedek considered it the top priority to start a religious school for the children, while Machzikei Emunah wanted to build a *mikveh* before anything else.[3] This reason seems legitimate, though it probably was not the main one. Indeed, Poale Zedek issued a circular both in Spanish and in German (at the time there were no printing types in Yiddish, the language they would probably have written in)[4] calling attention to the lack of Hebrew and religious education for Jewish children and announcing that the association would found an institution where such instruction would be given. Furthermore, several of the members volunteered to teach various topics gratuitously.[5] Apparently they succeeded in founding the school, for in the minutes of CIRA it is mentioned that it took under its protection "the Jewish school recently founded in Buenos Aires."[6] On the other hand, *mikvaot* were inaugurated in the area around the same time, the first one in Victoria Street, and others in Viamonte.[7]

However, the reason for the creation of two separate synagogues of Russian Jews in Buenos Aires in 1892, when they probably did not number more than a few dozen families, does not seem to rest only on a theological controversy (*Maḥloket leshem shamaim*). They could have accomplished both the *mikveh* and the school better united than separately. More likely the motive was one of personal ambitions, which made for a situation where there were fewer leading roles to fulfill than people willing to perform them, thus making a severance inevitable. Four years later, in 1896, and also the following year, a visitor in Buenos Aires from the agricultural colonies described in letters to *Hazefirah* in Warsaw the growing number of synagogues founded in the Russian Jewish quarter of the capital. Jews there were "dispersed and scattered in small communities . . . each one having a pulpit of its own."[8] In 1898 a correspondent of the *Jewish Chronicle* reported along the same lines: "The usual squabbles prevail. They divide and subdivide themselves just because 'So and So' has been elected, with the result that more 'congregations' are formed than are required, and with naturally unsatisfactory results, from a financial point of view, for everybody concerned."[9] In 1901 the same correspondent further informed that the Jewish population of about 8,000 souls gathered for the High Holy Days in twenty-three different congregations, four belonging to the different Sephardic groups, and nineteen to the Ashkenazim.[10]

From the very beginning of Jewish immigration en masse to Argentina the clash of personalities, forever nurtured on individual jealousies and aspirations, was an important factor in organizational life. This factor will become even more prevalent in religious institutions, especially when there is an economic component appended to it. Such will be the case, as we shall see, among such religious functionaries as rabbis, *shochtim*, and bakers of *matzot* (sing., *matza*, or unleavened bread).

First Priority: The Cemetery

The young Jewish community in Buenos Aires was soon confronted with a situation that demanded its immediate attention. Whether religious or secular, almost all Jews during this period wanted their dead buried in a Jewish burial site and funerals according to their particular rites. During the 1870s and 1880s the members of CIRA had made all the arrangements necessary for Jewish burials, which took place at the Cementerio de los Disidentes in Buenos Aires. In 1892 this Cementerio de los Disidentes was definitely closed. When in 1919 the Concejo Deliberante (Municipal Council) of the capital decided to exchange that location for another in the Cementerio del Oeste (Chacarita), the cadavers were moved to the new place. However, not all the corpses were claimed, including some Jewish ones, and due to the depth in which some were buried it was considered inconvenient to recover them. They remain many meters under today's Plaza Primero de Mayo.[11]

The influx of larger numbers of Jewish immigrants into the city called for a wider organization for funeral rites and for necessary procedures of burials. But various sectors of the Jewish population in Buenos Aires had great difficulties reaching an agreement over who should run the organization and how. The Chevra Keduscha (Burial Society) was founded on February 11, 1894. The minutes of the founding meeting illustrate that compromises were made by the delegates of some of the Jewish societies there represented. Rabbi Henry Joseph was elected honorary president, and the board was formed by four officials from CIRA, four from the Moroccan Jewish Congregación Israelita Latina (CIL), three from Poale Zedek, and two from Machzikei Emunah. Furthermore, "at Mr. Achille Levy's suggestion, [Soly] Borok, M. Lazarus, and [Miguel] Kuperman were nominated initiating members."[12] Levy was at the time president of CIRA.

Indeed, the initiative to form the Chevra Keduscha had come from these leading members of Poale Zedek, who had called a general assembly of their institution on September 26, 1893, for that purpose. However, there was also a definite desire to constitute the society independently of CIRA. Kuperman arrogantly stated at this assembly that "until now no one had thought of taking the initiative of creating a Burial Corporation, in order to give the dead of mosaic religion their last honors,"[13] knowing well enough that Rabbi Joseph and other officials at CIRA had been filling precisely those functions up to the present. At a second meeting held on October 3, 1893, Poale Zedek invited Joseph to become the rabbi of the new society, totally disregarding CIRA.[14]

This attitude was probably due to personal misunderstandings between Borok and Kuperman and the members of CIRA. Borok, besides presiding over Poale Zedek, was a member of the board of CIRA. On September 4, 1893, he resigned because he disagreed with a resolution taken by the board and sent an insulting letter to its members. The issue was explained, and Borok reintegrated the board of CIRA. However, a few days later, on September 17, at the annual general assembly, Borok was not reelected to the board of CIRA.[15] Even after the Chevra Keduscha was created, Borok, Kuperman, and Lazarus continued being at odds with the members of CIRA. In September 1894 they launched a lampoon against the board, which ended in the expulsion of the first two from CIRA. The incident provoked antagonisms between Jews of East and West European origin. One of CIRA's members said, "Only a Russian Jew like him [Borok] could be the author of such a lampoon."[16]

When Rabbi Joseph announced to the board of CIRA that he had been invited by Poale Zedek to represent their burial society, the response was violently negative. President A. Levy retorted that "the present board [of CIRA] has been elected by the Jews of Buenos Aires, and being officially recognized, these coreligionists [Poale Zedek] have the duty to inform us of their project."[17]

Rabbi Joseph was the go-between. He evidently convinced the Poale Zedek people that he could not represent their burial society if CIRA was not among the sponsors. Joseph, furthermore, acted as a conciliatory figure, sponsoring the meeting of representatives of Jewish societies in Buenos Aires to form the Chevra Keduscha on February 11, 1894. Poale Zedek only agreed, apparently, when assured of being given credit for the initiative to form the society.[18] Antagonisms between East and West European Jews in Buenos Aires were overcome thanks to the good services of Rabbi Joseph. However, as we already mentioned, they arose again a few months later, and would reappear sporadically.

The Moroccan Jews did not get involved in this power struggle between the two major Ashkenazic groups. Their essential concern was to keep the particular traditions they brought from their North African communities and not to become diluted in the much more numerous Ashkenazic community. A large number of the members of the Chevra Keduscha during its first three years was of Moroccan origin. Not only those living in Buenos Aires joined the institution but also some who had settled in places where Jews were so few that they could not afford buying substantial pieces of land for a separate cemetery. Thus in 1895 we find Moroccan Jews living in Río Cuarto, Province of Córdoba and even in distant Tucumán joining the Chevra Keduscha.[19] Soon, however, they formed a separate burial society and in 1900 bought land in Barracas al Sud for their own cemetery. The discrepancies within the Chevra Keduscha that motivated this secession were the different burial customs, which bothered both groups, and, especially, the impossibility of reaching a financial agreement.

Already in 1895 Rabbi Joseph complained "that the members of CIL, . . . when they bury a coreligionist, hold ridiculous ceremonies in public that attract the attention of the populace, and could provoke a conflict with the [general] population and authorities." Furthermore, at the same meeting, Rodolfo Ornstein protested against the claims of the members of CIL, who "pretend that the Chevra Keduscha pay for nurse services for their sick, something which is against our constitution, . . . and likewise demand that the chamoschim [*sic*, meaning the attendant of the burial society] be obligated in some cases to make two night watches for the same price [as one]."[20]

These differences in ritual and pretensions that were not justified by their Ashkenazic coreligionists constituted the weightiest considerations among the Moroccan Jewish community to form a separate burial society, Gemilut Hassadim, at the beginning of 1897.[21] Thus, two burial societies were active in Buenos Aires by that year. In addition, the Jewish white slave dealers also formed a similar organization.[22] Nevertheless, none had an independent cemetery, and all buried their dead at the Cementerio de los Disidentes.

The acquisition of a permanent burial place was much more complicated than forming a society to take care of the ritual arrangements of the interment. The former required a head investment that was beyond the means of the still young Jewish community. It was necessary, furthermore, to obtain municipal permits that wold enable them to utilize an extension of land as a burial place. Technical problems, such as complaints of neighbors against having a cemetery in their own vicinity, complicated the issue. Efforts were made as early as 1874 to acquire a permanent field for Jewish burials by the first Jewish residents in Buenos Aires.[23] Indeed, the minutes of the CIRA continuously deal with the problems they were having in finding suitable conditions for a private cemetery.[24] Jewish burials, as mentioned previously, took place at the Dissidents' Cemetery before 1892, and at the British Cemetery in Chacarita after that date.

The number of Jewish burials increased with the years. There were twenty-three in 1895, and thirty-six in 1896.[25] On September 24, 1897 the authorities of the British Cemetery communicated to the Chevra Keduscha that they could not accommodate more Jewish dead in their premises. The Chevra Keduscha obtained from the former a year's extension for Jewish burials, but the necessity of a new site remained extremely acute.[26] Immediately, all possibilities were studied very carefully, including an offer by the Municipality of Buenos Aires of extensions of land for 300 or 600 graves at a price of 10,000 and 20,000 pesos respectively, half to be paid in cash with a discount of 20 percent, and the rest in installments during three years' time. To this the Chevra Keduscha had to add 9,000 pesos to close the fence and other expenses. Evidently, with only 4,000 pesos in reserve and few members, it was out of the question. It seems that the Chevra Keduscha, nevertheless, got an extension at the British Cemetery until 1900.[27] After that the only solution was to rent graves at the Municipal Cemetery of Flores, thus having to pay a yearly sum.[28] Only in 1910, when the Chevra Keduscha bought its own cemetery in Liniers, were these graves transferred there.

In 1898 the Chevra Keduscha tried to buy a permanent piece of land for burials and attempted a joint venture with the newly formed Gemilut Hassadim of the Moroccan Jews. The first approach took place at the general assembly of the former, on March 20, when the president R. Ornstein asked the Sephardim present to "decide if they would consider cooperating with us." Soli Cohen thought that they could not deny their cooperation and proposed that the Chevra Keduscha invite them formally, specifying the conditions under which they could cooperate. When it was suggested that both groups, Sephardim and Ashkenazim, would have equal representation on the board, Cohen replied that "we Sephardim want to contribute only one-fourth of the amount needed and have, therefore, the right to ask for the conditions." The Ashkenazim did not want to make separate conditions. Ornstein as president declared at a subsequent meeting that "there cannot be special conditions for the Sephardim" and that he would be opposed to them "even in the case that other members of the board were inclined to grant them."[29]

The issue was basically financial. The Ashkenazic population was much larger than the Sephardic. However, the former insisted on equal representation, which meant, equal shares in the expenses. On the other hand, the Sephardim wanted to provide for only one-fourth of the expenses, considering this share more in accordance with their relative numbers. Furthermore, they insisted on having the freedom to establish the rate for the burials of their members independently from the Chevra Keduscha. Finally, on June 12, 1898 the Ashkenazim decided that they too would prefer to run their society without the interference of the Sephardim. They proposed to Gemilut Hassadim that their members cooperate individually with the Chevra Keduscha either as members or as contributors to a fund for the cemetery. Conversations continued for the rest of the year, but to no avail.[30]

A fourth party was also interested in a private Jewish burial site. They were the Jews who dealt with human flesh. The *tmeyim* (Yiddish "impure"; in Argentina it applied to the Jewish white slave dealers) had organized their synagogue with cantors and religious authorities[31] and were anxious to have a foot in some of the "clean" Jewish institutions. Due to their commerce in "expensive" merchandise, many of them had acquired a prominent economic situation. This encouraged them to attempt to buy their way into general Jewish institutions. Thus when the Chevra Keduscha tried to bring together different sectors of the Jewish population in Buenos Aires for a cemetery, the *tmeyim* availed themselves of the opportunity to join forces. On May 4, 1898, Ornstein informed the board that a group of Jews offered to contribute a substantial amount of money for the purchase of a cemetery without becoming members of the institution.[32] Evidently, this offer came from the white slave dealers, who realized they would not be accepted as members but considered that a substantial donation would at least allow Jewish funerals for their dead.[33] The Chevra Keduscha did not consider the offer. Shortly thereafter the white slave dealers acquired land for a cemetery in Barracas al Sud (later on called Avellaneda, a suburb of Buenos Aires). The Moroccan Jews bought from the latter a section of their land for their own burial site. While the Ashkenazic Jews remained firm in their total exclusion of the *tmeyim*, some type of accommodation was effected by the Moroccan group. In any case, no condemnation of the latter was found in the available documentation at the Chevra Keduscha and CIRA. The small group of Moroccan Jews, who could not agree with the Ashkenazim regarding a joint cemetery, thus solved their burial need[34] (for more on this see ch. 9).

These voices of condemnation against those willing to compromise and accept contributions of *tmeyim* were the first signs of a growing sense of responsibility among Jewish leaders in Buenos Aires vis-à-vis their relation to the impure sector in their midst. The cemetery question was the first one that tempted the Jewish community in the capital to accept collaboration from those elements because of the financial implications. The result was a complete separation in this area. But it was not mere coincidence that the cemetery question became a major issue between sectors of the Jewish population in Buenos Aires. It really was the first major enterprise of the community since the building of the first synagogue of CIRA in 1897. Notwithstanding the disagreements motivated by differences in ritual and in views over financial participation, the issue of a Jewish burial ground brought all Jews together in order to find a solution. During the last years of the nineteenth century all Jews in the city, Sephardim and Ashkenazim, religious or secular, pure or impure concerned themselves with the question of burial according to Jewish rites and practices. In spite of the fact that the actual interment constituted a religious act, even secular Jews acknowledged the supremacy of an independent cemetery for their people. From the very outset, burial in a Jewish necropolis comprised a leading factor in Jewish identity in Buenos Aires.

It was not until 1910 that the Chevra Keduscha was permitted to transform its property in Liniers into a cemetery. The Sephardic communities that were formed during the first years of the twentieth century also acquired their own cemeteries, though for some periods they concluded agreements with the Chevra Keduscha, which enabled them to utilize the latter's cemetery. The Damascene Jews officially opened their private grounds in Lomas de Zamora in 1915. The Aleppine Jews did likewise at the end of the 1920s with a field in Ciudadela. Part of this field was sold to the Ladino-speaking Jews, while still another to the Chevra Keduscha itself, which had gone through great difficulties obtaining a municipal permit to transform its grounds in Chacarita into a cemetery, which was finally denied (Cf. ch. 2).

Religious Observances

It is difficult to measure the religious observances and practices of the immigrant Jews in their new environment because those who followed a routine of observance in their homes and in their *hebrot* did not leave records of it. Although tens of *hebrot* began functioning in the Jewish quarters of Buenos Aires, their names indicative of a strong attachment to the Jewish faith, such as Hebra Tehilim (Psalms Society), Hebra Mishnaies Shomrei Shabbes (Mishna and Sabbath Observers' Society), and Hebra Shas DeAnshei Polin (Talmud Society of Polish Jews), we have no way of knowing what the actual participation of its membership was in daily, weekly, or yearly services in the synagogue. Was membership in one of these *hebrot* indicative of observance of other religious precepts as well, or did the new immigrants select, keeping specific areas of their heritage and abandoning others? How did the general attitude towards religious life in Buenos Aires affect the Jews? Were the observant immigrants successful in transmitting their faith and practices to the new generation born in Argentina? Documentation about these issues is scanty and sparse.

In our attempt to draw a picture of the religious identity of the Jews in Buenos Aires during the period up to 1930 we shall first look into their religious attachment at the moment of migration. Another source will be descriptions of religious practices by Jewish residents and visitors in Argentina. Moreover, the religious authorities and leaders who came to the country and the response of individuals to their work are indicative of the actual state of affairs. Finally, from testimonies of the "old" generation and those born or at least educated in Argentina, we shall describe the process of this identity.

As early as 1898 a correspondent of the *Jewish Chronicle* describing the way Christians fraternized with Jews in Buenos Aires, wrote sarcastically:[35] "They join in sorrow as well as in pleasure, due principally to the liberal tendencies of both, for "Tephillin" are at a large discount in Buenos Ayres." On the other hand, East European Jews formed many small congregations where they met for praying. According to the same correspondent, in 1901 there were nineteen of these places open for the High Holy Days.[36] The number of these congregations grew during the following decades. In 1925, for example, the *Yiddishe Zeitung* was filled, starting over a month before Rosh Hashana, with advertisements of more than forty different societies organizing services for the Holy Days. However, these *casas de oraciones* (praying houses), as they were called by *El Sionista*, in 1905 were not open all year around: "The Holy Days have passed, and with them, the doors of all salons, temples, and synagogues have been closed."[37] Another description of these improvised houses of prayer was offered by *Di Yiddishe Hofnung* in 1912;[38] "Very soon, in two or three weeks, one will be able to see in the streets of Buenos Aires how Jews run into the synagogues to pray three days a year, the Days of Awe. Where is that synagogue?, you might ask. That, however, would be a naive question. Better ask where is there no synagogue in Buenos Aires during the three Days of Awe."

Religious heritage among the Jews who arrived from Russia was not monolithic. Even if many were devout in the observance of traditional laws and customs of the Jewish people, the majority of the newcomers were already advanced in a process of secularization or, as many would later refer to it. modernization, which meant a gradual if not total relaxation of religious customs. The impact of *haskalah* (Jewish enlightenment) had been felt in many Jewish homes in Russia, promoting a release from the ghetto and an alienation from religious life. Most of those who came directly to Buenos Aires had already abandoned many religious practices in Europe. Whatever they had read or heard about Jewish life in the Argentine capital before departing did not, for sure, include a description of orthodox practices there. Moreover, the existence of Jewish white slave dealers in noticeable numbers did not encourage observant Jews to move there, in spite of the fact that the former were known for their concern with religious practices.

Among the first colonizers of the JCA project in Argentina were a good number of nonobservant Jews even if some of these were learned in Jewish texts. An early settler of the Mauricio colony described the scene of the first meal his group received in the country, at the Hotel de Inmigrantes:[39] "'Waiters' of dark, almost copper-colored complexions, served us white rolls, and gave each one of us a can with meat. Many of us ate it (it was very tasty) but the more religious did not even touch it." Furthermore, Mordechai Alpersohn mentioned that in the same colony the settlers were divided in several groups. Among those who were appointed to the Alicia section were the nonobservant, the "nonkosher fellows" (*treifener hebre*).[40] The same was true in other colonies in Santa Fe and Entre Ríos. We can say so a fortiori of the Jewish population in the cities since in the colonies Jews lived near each other, thus facilitating a continuation of organized Jewish life. In the city the new immigrant could choose whether to live in the Jewish quarters or not. And even if he did dwell there, it was fairly easy for him, if he so wanted, to remain aloof from the religious manifestations of his fellow Jews.

The different Sephardic communities in Buenos Aires preserved stronger links with religious practices. Quite naturally there were differences among the various communities, which were a direct reflection of their Jewish background beyond the Atlantic. The Arabic-speaking Jews were the most religiously inclined. In Damascus and Aleppo the role of the *hacham* was one of supreme weight within the community. Cases in which an individual Jew challenged the *hacham*'s dictum were very infrequent, as were deviations from strict orthodoxy in the observance of religious precepts and communal discipline. Before World War I the rabbis had issued an order of excommunication against a violator of the Sabbath and had issued a proclamation of warning to the community. It was only after the war that communal discipline weakened because of the departure of many of the rabbis and the wealthy.[41] In Buenos Aires they continued a strict observance of the commandments. The vanguard of Syrian Jews in Argentina, almost all making a living as peddlers during the first years, did not go out to their clients on the Sabbath, preferring to congregate in their synagogues. Likewise, it was customary among them to meet early in the morning for their daily prayers before initiating their workday. In later years and up to 1930, when many had become retail or wholesale merchants and importers with shops in the quarters of Boca-Barracas, Once, and Flores, most of their businesses remained closed on the Sabbath. Some opened on Sunday morning instead, and then made transactions with non-Jewish wholesale merchants.[42] In all the respective Talmud Torah schools the students were not allowed to go to their classes at the national schools on Saturdays, on pain of expulsion from the Talmud Torah.[43] The numerous complaints by teachers at the Syrian Talmud Torahs indicate that many parents were actually sending their children to the state schools on Saturdays because the children might be expelled for reiterated absences. Officials of the Unión Israelita Sefaradit Or Torah of Damascean Jews in Barracas approached some members of the Consejo Escolar in order to obtain an exemption for their students. The result was a semiofficial success. Two members of the Consejo Escolar, at the beginning of the school year, 1923, ordered the directors of the schools of the area not to compel the Jewish students to attend school on Saturdays.[44] Similarly, through the insistence of members of Yesod Hadath of the Aleppine community in Once, as well as pressures made by Rabbi Halphon and Israel magazine, the Consejo Nacional de Educación resolved on October 28, 1925 that it was not possible to "compel those students, sons of Jews, to attend classes on Saturday if they do not do so for religious reasons."[45]

The Ladino-speaking community, though orthodox, was "not as staunchly observant as . . . the Arabic-speaking [one]"[46] in their home towns. When in Buenos Aires, their knowledge of the Spanish language made their adaptation to the mores and customs of the country much easier. In spite of living in specific neighborhoods, notably Villa Crespo and its vicinities, they did not encircle themselves as closely as their Arabic-speaking coreligionists.

The Jews of Morocco underwent the most rapid assimilation to the country. The first generation of immigrants were very observant and preserved almost all the traditions of their native communities, not only religious customs but in some cases also social and economic ones.[47] However, they were dispersed in many communities throughout the country, and in the capital they comprised only a few hundred families during the 1920s. At this time there was a grown-up generation of Argentine-born Jews from the Moroccan community that was much more liberal in religion. A contemporary described this community in 1921 as religious but not overzealous, opening their stores on the Sabbath and Jewish Holy Days.[48] Five years later another contemporary wrote that "the elders are extremist believers in the Messiah on a white horse, . . . while the young are completely assimilated."[49] In 1929 a member of the Congregación Israelita Latina protested against the appointment of Rabbi Shabbetai Djaen—originally from Monastir and belonging to the Ladino-speaking community—as chief rabbi jointly of the Moroccans and Ladino-speaking Jews in Argentina. He wrote that the Moroccan Jews do not need Rabbi Djaen "to correct them of all these errors we commit voluntarily."[50] In the list of "errors" he included opening business and smoking on Saturdays, not going to the synagogue on the Sabbath and Holy Days, organizing banquets to celebrate religious ceremonies (weddings, circumcisions, Bar Mitzvahs) without fulfilling the prescribed Jewish dietary laws, and so on.

The attitude to religious observance by Jews in Buenos Aires during the first years of their settlement there was a reflection of their experience in their home towns. Many Ashkenazic Jews had been exposed not only to the haskalah in Eastern Europe but also to the growing influence of socialism, anarchism, and other radical workers' movements in Russia, which their Sephardic counterparts had never heard of. But the general situation in their new environment very soon had its effect upon the religious life of the immigrant Jew. Due to compelling circumstances many otherwise observant Jews—with the exception of Arabic and Ladino-speaking Jews—found themselves working on the Sabbath, something unthinkable to most of them before crossing the Atlantic. Labor circumstances did not permit them to do otherwise, especially for those employed as workers and apprentices in workshops and factories owned by Christians. However, an index of the little observance of the Sabbath among Ashkenazim can be obtained from the fact that even when there were enough

Jewish patrons of workshops and mills to employ large numbers of Jewish workers, all, to the best of our knowledge, opened on Saturdays. Moreover, this was the payday of the week.[51] An orthodox visitor of the community in 1907 wrote the following description of the situation:[52] "Practically every Jewish shop opens on Sabbath, even the butchers' shops kept by rabbis. The offices of the JCA there only close at two o'clock on Saturdays."

Although there was growing indifference and laxity, few immigrants showed resentment or rejection of their religious heritage, except in radical antireligious circles. Notably, among the first generation of Ashkenazim educated in Argentina, who had gathered around Juventud Israelita Argentina since 1908, a strong sentiment of scorn and contempt for religion was manifest. They not only had been "long divorced from the affairs in heaven"[53] and advocated the "religion of the future," which is that of "human Justice, Science, Equality, and Fraternity"[54] but they also fought bravely against permitting the Federación Israelita Argentina which was being envisaged in 1914, to promote religious initiatives.[55] Members of a similar group applauded when *Di Presse*, a Yiddish daily, decided to appear also on Saturdays against the protests of a few orthodox voices and criticized de Levy, the Sephardic editor of *Israel*, for observing the Sabbath and other Jewish customs.[56]

The Rabbis

In Eastern Europe and in the Sephardic communities the rabbi was the central figure in Jewish communal life. He was the authority that adjudicated judicial cases and was in control of marital affairs. Due to either his personality or his investiture, he commanded the respect of a large part of his community. For these reasons, an investigation of the rabbinical situation will help us understand the religious attachment of the various communities transplanted to Buenos Aires. How many rabbis arrived in Argentina and from where? How did they fare there? What was the response to their work among their respective coreligionists?

Among observant Jewry in Buenos Aires the lack of rabbis was very noticeable. Indeed, the number of rabbis in Argentina remained very small, and those who had a scholarly preparation that enabled them to influence the local community by means of legal Responsa that carried weight were even less. Among the latter we can but name Hacham Shaul Setton Dabbah of the Aleppine community in Buenos Aires, Rabbis Aharon Goldman, active in Moisesville, and Joseph Taran in Colonia Zonnenfeld, Province of Entre Ríos.

Rabbis Goldman and Taran engaged in a scholarly polemic regarding the *kashrut* of wild ducks common in Argentina with such famous rabbinic authorities in Europe and Jerusalem as Rabbis Haim Berlin and Samuel Salant. After long discussions, the latter two confirmed the verdict of the rabbis in the Argentine colonies that permitted consumption of wild ducks. They also engaged in religious and legal problems of the Jewish community in Argentina, especially regarding mixed marriages and conversions to Judaism.[57] Rabbi Goldman also corresponded with Chief Rabbi Hermann (Naphtali) Adler of

England, Chief Rabbi Zadoc Kahn of France, and Rabbi Isaac Elḥanan Spektor of Kovno on different legal issues and contributed to scholarly publications in Europe and Jerusalem.[58] However, except for some legal consultations from the communities near the colonies where these rabbis lived, their influence in religious life in Argentina was limited to the groups of colonists that were in close contact with them.[59]

Some of the groups that left Eastern Europe to settle in the JCA colonies in Argentina departed their home towns with their necessary religious ministrants. In that manner Rabbis Taran and Goldman arrived in Entre Ríos and Santa Fe, respectively.[60] In 1894 a group leaving Grodno to settle in Moisesville took with them two *melammedim* [teachers of religious subjects for children], "and one *shochet*, . . . Rabbi Mordechai Reuben Sinai, whom the Central Committee of JCA had appointed as leader and counsellor for the colonists for their religious needs, . . . left with the same group."[61]

Rabbi Sinai did not stay long in Moisesville. In 1896 he spent the Tishre festivities (Rosh Hashana, Yom Kippur, and Sukkot) in Buenos Aires, where he preached and lectured on ten different occasions. Rabbi Sinai's visit had great impact as it stirred memories of the *maggid* (popular preacher) who would come and preach in the Jews' home towns in Eastern Europe. During Yom Kippur 1896 Sinai preached three times in synagogues at the Jewish quarter, on each occasion for over two hours. Some Jews followed him from one synagogue to the other, and even a few members of CIRA came to listen to his words.[62] The following year, 1897, Rabbi Sinai moved permanently to Buenos Aires.[63]

The role of the *hazan* (cantor) was much more important than that of the rabbi. A good cantor not only evoked in his audience pleasant memories of his old home synagogue and life-style but also contributed in inducing them to prayer. Occasionally, though quite seldom in Buenos Aires, Jews had an opportunity of listening to a *maggid* like Sinai.[64] The leaders of *hebrot* and Talmud Torahs, knowing that attendance for the High Holy Day services would be greater than on other days of the year, rented a salon or prepared larger rooms to accommodate them. Advertisements in the newspapers and magazines set in large letters the name of the cantor hired to perform and indicated the number of participants in a specially trained choir, usually directed by the cantor himself.

The role of the rabbi was altogether secondary. The poverty of the *hebrot* and the nonexistence of a central rabbinical body in Argentina made for the sad situation of the few East European rabbis who arrived in Buenos Aires. Actually, the latter's duties were not pastoral but legal. He would decide upon appointments of *shochtim* and supervise the *kashrut* of meat and *matzot* and wine for Passover and was arbiter in family and commercial cases, as well as teacher of the most learned Jews. As we shall see below, even in these aspects, the few rabbis in Buenos Aires during the first three decades of the twentieth century did not enjoy the respect of the community.

A unique case in this respect was CIRA. Being a synagogue that operated along the lines of the German and French congregations that had undergone a process of modernization during the nineteenth century, CIRA needed a religious leader who would perform pastoral duties and would represent the Jewish community to the general population. As a legal authority, his functions were to be only minor. However, even if CIRA was the only organization that could afford the services of a rabbi, it did not engage in such an expense easily.

Henry Joseph had been performing these functions on a voluntary basis without salary, empowered by a certificate extended by Lazare Isidor, the chief rabbi of the French Consistory, in 1882.[65] When in 1894 Joseph's daughter was married in a church to a Catholic, a great commotion took place at CIRA. Most of the board members considered asking Joseph for his resignation, while others, including president Achille Levy, did not believe that the daughter's intermarriage disqualified Joseph from his rabbinical duties. When the General Assembly specifically called to discuss this contingency decided to accept Joseph's resignation, Levy likewise resigned.[66] Solomon Liebeschutz filled the post as temporary rabbi with an annual salary of 600 pesos. However, divergencies with some of the members caused his resignation in November 1895.[67] In the meantime efforts were made to attain the services of a rabbi, and numerous personal and epistolar contacts were made in Europe, especially with the French Consistory.[68]

For a full decade CIRA was officially without a rabbi. Joseph, however, continued serving and was sometimes consulted about religious practices. However, on questions of rabbinic jurisprudence it was preferred to obtain the opinion of authorities in Europe.[69] In 1903, when Rabbi Amsel Hoffmann arrived in Buenos Aires and applied for the job at CIRA, the latter was forced to clarify the situation. When CIRA discussed the problem, the economic advantage of the current arrangement was noted immediately. Most of those present considered that Joseph was already filling the post and was doing so without pay, which was quite advantageous; thus they decided that no rabbi was needed.[70]

Nevertheless, a few months later the board realized "that CIRA, for its prosperity, needs a rabbi," and new approaches were made to the French Consistory. They received a promise from its rabbinic head, Zadoc Kahn, to cooperate in their efforts.[71] The rabbi for CIRA, however, was already in Argentina. On April 1904 Rabbi Samuel Halphon, originally from Russia and a recent graduate of the Ecole Rabbinique de France, arrived with the mission of strengthening religious life in the JCA colonies. This was the first rabbinical mission sponsored by JCA in the country. Halphon traveled through the colonies and organized various religious institutions there. He also had contact with the colonists, to whom he delivered sermons on "diverse subjects dealing with the moral and material situation of his flock, on religious questions, on man's duties, etc."[72] Before the High Holy Days in 1905 Halphon arranged to deliver a sermon on Yom Kippur at CIRA. After this "brilliant speech" CIRA offered Halphon the post, which the latter accepted after consultations with JCA authorities in Paris. Halphon continued, in addition to his duties at CIRA, his pastoral tours of the colonies.[73]

From 1906 until 1930, when he returned to Paris because of a severe heart condition, Halphon was one of the most influential and active Jews in Argentina. His activities were not circumscribed to his rabbinical functions at the Temple or his tours of the colonies. Halphon was the force behind the first attempt of a Kehilla (representative Jewish body) in Buenos Aires (1908–10), the director of a network of religious schools in the whole country sponsored to a large extent by JCA, an active member in Ezras Noschim, the Argentine branch of the Jewish Association for the Protection of Girls and Women with headquarters in London, and one of the initiators of Soprotimis. Halphon's personal acquaintance of Marcelo T. de Alvear, president of the country for the period 1922–28, facilitated hearings of representatives of Jewish institutions with the chief executive, though it did not always guarantee positive results.[74]

Halphon became the religious leader representing CIRA and institutions led by its conspicuous members. In addition to these institutions, Rabbi Halphon advised the Sociedad de Damas Israelitas, which was constituted by the women of CIRA and which founded and sponsored the Asilo de Huérfanas (Jewish Orphanage for Girls). In spite of the fact that these organizations were created for the protection of new immigrants, mainly from Eastern Europe, the Jews of this origin never accepted Halphon's leadership. In their eyes, Halphon belonged to the Temple Jews, the rich, the more assimilated Yahudim who lived downtown of Callao Avenue.[75]

Halphon was a unique figure in Argentine Jewry up to 1930. No other rabbi with West European instruction came to the country in that period, except for Amsel Hoffmann. Hoffmann's case, tragic as it was, is indicative of the religious situation in Buenos Aires. A duly certified Austrian rabbi, aged twenty-seven, Dr. Hoffmann arrived in Buenos Aires early in 1903, where he came in contact with Simon Ostwald, a German Jewish millionaire who tried to guide his first steps in the city. Most probably Ostwald proposed Hoffmann to CIRA. CIRA did not consider his candidacy, due to either his age or the fact that they preferred a rabbi with French rather than German background. Hoffmann, again probably at Ostwald's suggestion, became active in the Zionist movement.[76] In 1904 Hoffmann published articles in El Sionista[77] and participated in the propaganda committee of the first Federación Sionista Argentina, traveling throughout the Jewish colonies and cities in the interior in order to unite the Zionist groups, an activity he pursued until his death in 1908.[78] In spite of his varied occupations, Hoffmann did not succeed in attaining a secure economic position.[79] Finally, in 1907, officials at CIRA lead a campaign to rid the community of Hoffmann's presence, claiming the latter was responsible for defrauding colonists in a travel agency he had started. References about Hoffmann were solicited from the chief rabbi in Hamburg, M. Hirsch, who claimed that Hoffmann had worked in a Christian mission there.[80] CIRA resolved "to do everything possible so that this gentleman leaves without delay."[81]

Hoffmann was found dead in June 1908, and after careful investigations by the federal police in the capital it was concluded that he had committed suicide.[82] There are contradictory arguments as to the reason Hoffmann took this determinate action. Hoffmann was learned in Jewish texts and had written on Biblical criticism.[83] On the other hand he had become uncongenial to many Jews active in the community, which contributed to his economic impoverishment.[84] The accusations of dishonesty in his commercial relations were not confirmed by the investigations, and the accusations were made exclusively by CIRA. In a suicide letter Hoffmann asserted that "the Jewish community in Argentina had not contributed to it" and named the main persons responsible, though their names were not printed in the press.[85]

Hoffmann's case was that of a learned man completely incompetent of solving his economic poverty. After failing to get the job at CIRA, over which, according to one contemporary, there had been some tension between Hoffmann and Halphon,[86] he held minor jobs in which he barely survived. His embarrassment in this respect, only increased by the accusations of dishonesty, constituted no small cause for his tragic decision. On the other hand, the Jewish community in Buenos Aires could not make room for another religious functionary of the category of a rabbi, in spite of the fact that there were none besides Halphon and Sinai.

The East European rabbis who arrived in Argentina before 1930 found great difficulties not only in promoting observance and learning but even in sheer survival. Some of them threw away their rabbinic garb and occupied themselves in different branches of commerce. Those active in the community had to struggle with some *shochtim* who, noticing the lack of rabbinic authorities, had appointed themselves as supervisors of the ritual purity of various foodstuffs and as arbiters in family relations. Soon it did not matter whether they were ordained rabbis or merely *shochtim* performing rabbinic functions. Furthermore, personal rivalries between the few rabbis, caused by professional antagonisms or by sheer competitive factors in a limited market, brought additional disunity on the religious front. This, too, was reflected in the attitude of the general Jewish population towards them.

Some of these rabbis formed small synagogues in the city, of which they were the leaders, teaching courses in rabbinic texts on Sabbaths and other special occasions. However, they did not derive much profit from these functions. At times they even had to concern themselves with obtaining money for the rent of the room they used as synagogue. Thus in 1930 Rabbi Israel Ehrlich solicited a loan from the Chevra Keduscha "in order to spare the [Jewish] community the shame that a *schil* [synagogue] be evicted for owing two months' rent."[87]

An important part of most rabbis' income came from their arbitration functions. Of these, divorces were the most common. Rabbi David Maler, for example, during the period 1924–30, arbitrated in over one hundred cases of divorce, most of which consisted of wives left in Europe and husbands wanting to remarry in Argentina.[88] At the end of the 1920s the number of divorces grew to enormous proportions. An informant of a meeting of several representatives of Jewish organizations convened to deal with the situation, narrated "alarming facts with respect to divorces and weddings among the immigrants, because the majority of them leave their wives in Europe, and send them from here the divorce in order to remarry. He deplores that the institution he represents [Soprotimis] has not been able to do anything for the more serious cases, but he is convinced that the Chevra Keduscha is the only one that can have control over the rabbis, who have direct contact with the petitioners of divorces."[89] In 1931 Ezras Noschim called a meeting of all Jewish institutions in Buenos Aires to deal with the problem, and in the presence of delegates of thirty-eight such organizations it was resolved that "no rabbi will have the right to grant a Get [divorce] without the respective authorization of Ezras Noschim," and in case he did grant a divorce, he could be "expelled from the Jewish community of Buenos Aires."[90] In other words, the lay officials of the community were imposing restrictive measures upon the rabbis, even in situations demanding the consideration and intervention of someone deeply versed in rabbinic law. The lay leaders feared the rabbis would grant divorces with ease in order to profit by it without taking into consideration the extremely miserable situation of wives and children still in Europe. This attitude is a telling example of the poor esteem in which the rabbis were held, be it due to their generally not-so-outstanding scholarship or to their economic dependence on communal functions. It also denotes a tendency to give precedence to a secular leader's discernment concerning social problems even if there is a religious element involved.

A similar confrontation took place regarding members who were expelled because of their involvement in white slavery. When some of these *tmeyim* died the Chevra Keduscha was asked to bury them. Some members of the board proposed sending the matter to the religious committee, but they were outvoted by those who "did not recognize it to intervene in the case of the expelled members."[91] Thus in an issue concerning ritual burial, the opinion of those members who would have based their verdict upon rabbinic sources was excluded, and the policy to follow was formulated by lay officials.

There were no permanent rabbis in the hinterland with the exception of some JCA colonies. The communities there approached the rabbis in Buenos Aires and the colonies when some question concerning religious law or procedure arose. Thus the Asociación Israelita de Beneficencia (AIB), the main Ashkenazic association in Rosario, repeatedly consulted with Rabbis Aharon Goldman of Moisesville and Aharon Waisman in Buenos Aires.[92] The only attempt to maintain a permanent rabbi in Rosario did not last long due to economic problems that arose as consequence of the general indifference of the Jewish population to this type of functionary. In 1926 a group of the more observant Jews in the city invited Rabbi Isaac Gottlieb, at the time in Buenos Aires, to settle there, assuring him a salary, which they gathered from among themselves, and the participation of AIB. Rabbi Gottlieb was to be in charge of all rabbinic functions, especially the surveillance of ritual slaughtering. After eighteen months, however, the members of the committee that sponsored the rabbi was reduced, and AIB refused to subsidize the project any more. Rabbi Gottlieb, after a sad experience regarding his payments, returned to Buenos Aires.[93] Other rabbis had contacts in several Jewish communities of the interior and even in neighboring countries. David Glasserman traveled repeatedly even to Asunción, Paraguay, while Raphael Kitaygorodsky traveled to Montevideo, Uruguay.[94]

After the establishment of the first *hebrot* of East European Jews in Buenos Aires early in the 1890s, one of the major preoccupations was the availability of kosher meat. In 1892 a *shochet*, David Hurwitz, was sponsored by the newly formed *hebra* Machzikei Emuna.[95] Through the years many more ritual slaughterers started to practice in Buenos Aires, most of them ex-colonists who moved to the capital.[96] Indeed, conflicts soon arose concerning the appropriate supervision of the slaughtering and the retail sale of kosher meat.

In 1903 Gustavo Glaser, president of CIRA, noted that some Jews "wanted to have the monopoly, or something similar, over the sale of kosher meat, and therefore asked the Board's intervention to avoid such abuses." After long deliberations they decided that "CIRA shall issue permits to sell kosher meat to qualified persons who merit their confidence."[97] Interestingly enough, CIRA arrogated this function to itself without having the slightest idea of the laws governing ritual slaughtering. However, convinced that CIRA was the *Jefe de la Kehila* (chief institution of the Jewish community), Glaser considered that they should intervene for the sake of the whole Jewish population in the city.

But the problem was not solved, and abuses continued. Aaron Vecht, an orthodox manufacturer visiting the country in 1907, was horrified at the situation and attempted to form a "Board of Shechita which enjoyed Sabbath closing."[98] However, Vecht was too optimistic. The selling of kosher meat represented a profitable gain for those controlling it, and many of these were not scrupulous enough to adhere to Jewish ritual law.

By the end of 1908 orthodox officials in Buenos Aires were extremely disturbed at this state of affairs. Ephraim Rosenzwit, president of the Talmud Torah Harischono, tried to put a stop to it. He contacted La Negra packinghouse, where evidently most *shochtim* slaughtered, and solicited for his institution the control over Jewish slaughterers. When La Negra responded that they were willing to deal only with a larger representation of the Jewish community, Rosenzwit appealed to the most established institutions in the city, namely, CIRA, Chevra Keduscha, Ezrah, and Bikur Joilim. From these contacts the Federación Israelita Argentina was born.[99]

After many preliminary sessions, the FIA began operating in August 1909 with four representatives of each of the federated institutions under the presidency of Gustavo Weil of CIRA. Part of their program was that the FIA would take upon itself the expenditure of kosher meat, ensuring an appropriate surveillance of each and every step. The FIA officials further considered that this activity would create a source of income for the community's needs.[100]

During the same month negotiations for the export of kosher meat to London were started. Hermann Adler, the chief rabbi of England, informed La Negra that he was sending two inspectors to supervise the meat that would be exported to London. The FIA felt the necessity to cable back to Adler requesting him not to send the inspectors because the newly formed FIA, together with Rabbi Halphon, would have complete control.[101] Adler, indeed, did not heed this request. His priorities were to his own community and the reaction it would have to importing kosher meat from Argentina. There were protests in London's East End against importing frozen and chilled meat from abroad on the grounds that there were possibilities that this product might be contaminated but mainly because of suspicions about its *kashrut*. The chief rabbi repeatedly assured the Jewish population in London that "every proper care would be taken by the London *Schochtim* before they left the Argentine that the meat there was killed by expert *schochtim* who enjoyed their complete confidence."[102] Evidently Rabbi Adler did not have full confidence in the Argentine community's way of regulating kosher slaughtering and distribution. He was not mistaken.

For local consumption FIA reached an agreement with La Negra that no *shochet* without their authorization would be admitted to the abattoirs. For a short period most *shochtim* and kosher butchers adhered to the FIA's stipulations.[103] But Halphon soon realized that they were doing so to temporize and appease the FIA. The situation was still deplorable, since "there are Jewish butchers who buy from their gentile neighbors the front parts of their beasts at more or less .15 pesos per kilogram, to sell it afterwards as kosher for .35 pesos, and this will be impossible to avoid, given the desire for gain that dominates them."[104]

Shochtim and butchers finally defeated the FIA. They could easily convince their clients that FIA involvement would cause a rise in the price of meat. A major factor in the final collapse of the FIA in October 1910 was the Jewish population's indifference to Jewish dietary laws and, among those who consumed kosher meat, indifference to the way it reached their hands.[105]

Several attempts were made in the following years to remedy this situation. Even after World War I, when a few rabbis of East European origin were in Buenos Aires, things did not improve. Some of the rabbis, together with officials of many orthodox *hebrot*, started on June 30, 1925 a Committee for Kashrut with hopes of controlling religious affairs and founding unions of rabbis and *shochtim* respectively.[106] The initiators observed that "there are now a number of Jews who do not buy kosher meat arguing that it is really not kosher. With the practical regulations of the Committee for Kashrut it will be assured in the whole city."[107] Hacham Shaul Setton also actively participated in this endeavor. CIRA was also approached, but even if Rabbi Halphon promised to help, he did not take an active role.[108] More than twenty different synagogues and Talmud Torahs adhered to this Committee for Kashrut. By December the goal of forming a rabbinical union duly authorized to give licenses to *shochtim* and bakers of *matzot* was almost achieved, but due to internal strifes and opposition of some groups among the latter, the project failed.[109]

When Rabbi Raphael Kitaygorodsky arrived in Buenos Aries early in 1927, orthodox officials were optimistic once more. Rabbi Kitaygorodsky studied in famous *yeshivot* in Eastern Europe and received his ordination from noted authorities, including Rabbi Haim Berlin.[110] Orthodox Jews, especially Isidro Masel and Gershon Ginzberg, immediately founded a new society, Machzikei HaDath (Upholders of the Religion), with Kitaygorodsky as spiritual leader, with the purpose of "solving the anarchy and licentiousness rampant in the Jewish street."[111] Therefore they wanted to found a Rabbinical Committee or Beit Din and put an end to competition between rabbis and between *shochtim* in Argentina. However, before they could organize the Rabbinical Committee, three of the older rabbis in town—Waisman, Maler, and Abraham David Kamiker—in a parallel initiative founded a Permanent Beit Din.[112] Machzikei HaDath, which already was representing eighteen *hebrot* and more than 400 undersigned, warned the Jewish population against the Permanent Beit Din, qualifying it as "absolutely fraudulent," without the backing of an organized community, and the fancy of Rabbi Waisman, "who wants to crown himself with the title of Gaon and Av Beit Din [Learned and Presiding Judge], which is too big for him."[113]

Both groups tried to get more sympathizers to their respective movements, thus widening the breach between them.[114] The new organization of Machzikei HaDath did not succeed in unifying the rabbinic functions in the city. The lack of support from rabbis, *shochtim*, and other religious officials, weakened its basis. Rabbi Kitaygorodsky already in July 1927 accepted a rabbinical position in Montevideo.[115]

In Buenos Aires each rabbi operated individually and "did what seemed good in his eyes." Glasserman had his own rabbinic office. The Agudat Israel group, on the other hand, supervised kosher slaughtering themselves. This was violently opposed by the Permanent Beit Din, which in some cases approved the *shechita* that Agudat Israel had declared deficient, thus creating more confusion for observant Jews.[116] Enmity continued between rabbis, and some did not refrain from utilizing base means to defame their colleagues. A note signed by Waisman appeared in *Unzer Lebn* of Montevideo claiming that Kitaygorodsky had false papers and therefore was not an ordained rabbi. After the intervention of the Chevra Keduscha and numerous petitions of orthodox Jews in Buenos Aires, Waisman assured them that he had not sent the letter, the contents of which were false, and wrote to *Unzer Lebn* clearing himself from all responsibility in the issue. But the harm had already been done, and Kitaygorodsky returned to Buenos Aires.[117] Apparently this was also the cause for the dissolution of the Permanent Beit Din in November 1927 when Waisman's two colleagues announced that they were no more "responsible for what is done in the name of the Beit Din."[118]

The few religious elements in the city, however, did not slacken in their attempts to form a central body that would regulate religious affairs for the Jewish community. During the first week of 1928 a meeting was convened at the precincts of the Chevra Keduscha with the participation of representatives of the most important institutions. A provisional committee for a new "Religious Organization" was elected, under the presidency of Abraham Elias Wainer.[119] This Religious Organization was able to unite the seven East European rabbis then active in Buenos Aires with respect to giving rabbinical authorization to *shochtim*. All rabbis agreed not to do so separately but only with the approval of their organization. Furthermore, an agreement was reached with the *matza* bakers, who also adhered to the Religious Organization. The same was true for a large number of the *shochtim*. However, soon some of the *matza* bakers dissociated themselves, arguing that "until the Religious Organization is recognized by some more |Jewish| societies, and thus able to impose a special taxation for *matzot* in the city, we cannot initiate dealings with them."[120] The real reason, however, was that the bakers were not prepared to pay the two-cent taxation per kilogram of *matza* (which they sold at forty-seven cents), arguing that they sold up to 60 percent of their produce to the Jews in the provinces. To no avail the Religious Organization appealed to those communities to back their project of organizing a central religious body and not to approve the move of the bakers.[121] Moreover, the lack of unity shown by the latter was followed by a final break among the rabbis. Four of them left the rabbinical committee of the Religious Organization, because of "moral motives."[122] Again, it was an attack directed mainly against Rabbi Kitaygorodsky and those who recognized his superior qualifications compared to those of his colleagues. Only Rabbis Kitaygorodsky and Gottlieb remained when Glaserman resigned because of his numerous trips to the interior. Rabbinic unity again failed, and the goal of reaching a centralization of the rabbis' functions was postponed once more.

The Chevra Keduscha was the major Jewish institution in the city, not only because of the number of its members but also due to its sound economy. When there was no representative body for Argentine Jewry, some individuals—though not without opposition—proposed that the Chevra Keduscha change its statutes and become the Kehilla of Buenos Aires.[123] Under the sponsorship of such a body a union of the religious leadership could have been imposed. The *hebrot* that sponsored the various committees and unions in the 1920s were small in membership and without a solid monetary basis. Even together they could not have supported a rabbinic committee. Furthermore, a centralized religious body, in their eyes, would produce, through taxation of the different services—supervision of meat and *matzot*, granting wedding and divorce bills, and arbitrations—sufficient income to provide the rabbinic committee an honorable existence and to subsidize Jewish education in the city.[124] They never got past the first stages of such an organization because the different groups involved—*shochtim*, bakers, butchers, and rabbis—were not in a position to make concessions. Such rabbinic organizations, at least during the initial periods would diminish the personal profits of the rabbis. In a society that was more and more oblivious to religious observances the religious functionaries, who, with few exceptions, did not have the will to promote an atmosphere for the continuance of such values, saw fit to protect their own personal interests. The Jewish community—to a large extent indifferent in religious matters—supported neither the religious functionaries nor their work. The reaction of the Jewish population to the rupture of solidarity among the rabbis was along the lines of the following remarks of *Mundo Israelita*:[125] "This disunion does not afflict us, for it does not affect in any way the stability of our collective life. We see in this a sign of the lack of interest for these types of religious associations, that have no place here. For the indispensable ritual services every one will go to the rabbi of his choice, as he used to do before. On the other hand, the rabbis' disunion makes evident their lack of moral authority over the community. . . . There is none [among them] capable of exerting it."

A rabbinic authority had more weight in the life of the Sephardim in Buenos Aires than among their Ashkenazic brethren. Moreover, we notice significant differences in the attitudes towards religious leaders among Sephardim.

Among the Moroccan and Ladino-speaking Jews no ordained rabbi served before the late 1920s. However, their respect for such an authority is reflected in their attitude to rabbis in their original communities and to those who visited Argentina. When rabbis of their home towns passed away, memorial services were held in their honor in Buenos Aires. Such was the case when, among others, Rabbis Mordechai Bengis of Tangiers, Moses Benaim of Gibraltar, and Samuel Israel of Tetouan died.[126] Rabbi Hizkia Shabetay, upon his visit to the Comunidad Israelita Sefaradí in 1922, was received with all honors, and his opinions at a General Assembly of the institution were accepted unanimously.[127]

The Moroccan synagogues were directed in all details by their respective boards because there was no rabbi. This procedure did not seem effective at CIL, their most important institution. In 1901 a *parnás* was nominated "with the obligation of attending the Sabbath and Holy Days prayers, collecting dues and paying debts, and having ample authority to do and undo in the synagogue."[128] This system proved inadequate after two years, and it was decided to return to the previous one. The basic guidelines at the Ladino-speaking Comunidad Israelita Sefaradí were also drawn by the lay officials. Samuel Buchuk was occasionally called *Rabino* because he was in charge of officiating at weddings and circumcisions and taught at their Talmud Torah. However, the latter was far from being a religious authority. On the contrary, he was merely a functionary of the community who performed some ceremonies, though always under the strict control of the board.[129] In questions of Jewish law or practice the members of this Turkish community preferred to address themselves to Rabbi Halphon at CIRA. Their Talmud Torah received directives from Halphon's Central Committee for Jewish Education in Argentina. Moreover, Halphon was made honorary president of the Comunidad Israelita Sefaradí for his cooperation in different opportunities.[130] It is interesting to notice that both these communities, when confronted with situations that demanded contact with other Jewish organizations in the city outside their own, directed themselves to CIRA. They rarely contacted the Damascene or Aleppine communities, which were much more observant of Jewish law.

The most orthodox elements of both these groups repeatedly tried to attract a rabbi from their original communities to become their religious authority in Buenos Aires. In 1923 several members of these communities, together with a few from the Syrian ones, assembled with the idea of forming a Sephardic Union that would not only unite all Sephardim in the country but also would "constitute a representative committee before the public powers, and would nominate a rabbi for religious affairs."[131] This attempt failed because of the lack of a unifying rabbinic personality.

When Rabbi Shabbetai Djaen, representing the Confederation Universelle des Juifs Sepharadim arrived in Buenos Aires in 1927, the officials of many of the representative organizations of the Moroccan and Turkish Jews in the city invited him to stay there as their chief rabbi.[132] Djaen immediately declined the offer, adducing that he had a three-year contract with his community in Monastir. Contacts with officials of the Confederation des Juifs Sepharadim in Jerusalem succeeded in convincing Rabbi Djaen to return to Buenos Aires one year later.[133]

At the end of 1928 Rabbi Djaen was installed as chief rabbi of the Moroccan and Ladino-speaking Jews. He stated that the rabbinate, "an institution that never existed before here ... includes contrasts of several worlds, great fanatics, modern religious, opponents to religion, and many assimilated."[134] With such a variety of people, coupled with the differences in ritual practices between the two main communities sponsoring it, it is no surprise that the new institution would very soon encounter serious opposition.

Djaen sent a circular calling all the Sephardic communities to unite. In it he stressed the importance of a rabbinate to "guide the religious, spiritual, and cultural destinies of our community, which are dispersed and incoherent" and to assure the future of the "race" against the assimilationist spirit.[135] He also visited some of the communities in the interior and tried to organize a file of vital statistics among the Jews. In some cases, he was also approached with questions concerning Jewish practices.[136] In Buenos Aires he divided his time between the two main synagogues of Moroccan and Turkish Jews respectively. The beginnings of the rabbinate were full of grand projects that promised active work among the Sephardic population. However, different factors were already operating within the communities that caused the final folding of the institution and Djaen's departure after less than two years.[137]

It did not take much time for the Moroccan Jews to protest the nomination of Djaen, who belonged to the Ladino-speaking community. The board at CIL, noticing "the disrespect for Gran Rabino Djaen in the Temple," decided to place notice there "reminding [the members] that the Gran Rabino is invested with authority in religious affairs in agreement with the Board as decided by the General Assembly."[138] This was answered by a sixteen-page pamphlet full of arguments against the nomination of Djaen, and criticizing the Rabbi for his haughty personality and his insistence on trying to impose his own customs among the Moroccan Jews. This pamphlet, written by Benjamín Benzaquén, caused great turmoil at CIL. At first most were against Benzaquén, and it was decided to form a committee to judge him. However, it was impossible to gather the individuals to form such a committee, and the issue was postponed many times until it was finally dropped. In the meantime, Djaen requested vindication. CIL was ready to make it, but they were also tired of the issue, and the only vindication they made was sending Djaen a letter notifying him that CIL did not make common cause with Benzaquén's pamphlet. In December

1929 the issue was brought to the General Assembly of CIL, which decided to keep the rabbi, though the vote casting (eighteen in favor, nine against, two undecided) showed a noticeable amount of dissatisfaction.[139]

The Turkish Jews followed the lead of CIL when the latter decided that the rabbinate was a useless expense. The rabbinate committee on July 10, 1930, decided to terminate Rabbi Djaen's mission since it was considered ineffective. Moreover, the economic crisis might very well have prompted this resolution. There were some institutions that could not pay their respective allotments to the rabbinate, and the others did not consider that it was their duty to increase their own shares, especially during the crisis period. Furthermore, Djaen was a rabbi with modern education and interests; he wrote drama and essays for popular Jewish journals; he had deep Zionist sentiments and wanted to change the Talmud Torahs into modern schools. These factors doubtlessly angered the most orthodox elements among the Sephardim sponsoring the rabbinate, and made for the cancellation of Djaen's contract.[140]

The Syrian Jews had an attitude vis-à-vis their *hacham* radically different from all the other sectors of the Jewish population in Buenos Aires. Hacham Shaul Setton Dabbah moved to Buenos Aires from his native Aleppo in 1912. From then until his death in 1930 he exerted strong influence in the Aleppine community in Buenos Aires and to a large extent also among the Damascene coreligionists. Hacham Setton was rigid in religious affairs, and his departure from Aleppo was due, among other reasons, to disagreements with other members of the Rabbinic Bet Din of that city. Furthermore, his influence in the life of his community was also a consequence of the positive attitude of most of the Syrian Jews to religious practices. Many of them, according to some of the oldtimers of this community, "were superstitious with respect to religion."[141] Moreover, Setton was active in the formation of institutions that strengthened the religious and communal feelings of his community. He promoted the creation of the Talmud Torah Yesod Hadath and the society Hesed Schel Emeth Sefaradit of the Aleppine Jews in Buenos Aires.

The respect of the community for their rabbi is reflected in policy discussions with officials of the various institutions. Jacobo Setton (president of Yesod Hadath, no relation with the *hacham*) and the board of Yesod Hadath decided to change the old system of learning at the Talmud Torah—which consisted in translating texts into Arabic, thus not giving the students the possibility of learning the Hebrew language and grammar—and brought for that purpose a teacher from Jerusalem who would stress the teaching of Hebrew. Hacham Shaul was violently opposed to this, prohibited the teaching of Hebrew, and asked that the teacher be fired. The board immediately acquiesced and President Setton resigned. Though some members present at the General Assembly protested against this action by the officials, the policy at the school was not changed during Hacham Setton's lifetime. Jacobo Setton, who had been president for eight years, since the foundation of Yesod Hadath, and who had modern ideas about Jewish education, fought strongly to sway the general opinion of the community to his side but to no avail. Even if many showed a preference for the teaching of Hebrew, their conservative attitude and their devotion to the Hacham's dictum prevented them from openly supporting such a change in the curriculum. Jacobo Setton finally used offensive language against other members of the board, who then decided to expel him from the institution.[142]

The Damascene community had no rabbi until the end of the 1920s and thus used the services of Hacham Shaul Setton in cases of legal decisions. In 1928 their main synagogue and Talmud Torah, Or Torah, made arrangements with Hacham Jacobo Mizrahi to serve their community. It was difficult to reach an agreement because of the various offers Mizrahi had had from Beyruth, other cities in the Middle East, and the Syrian Jewish community in Rio de Janeiro. Nevertheless, Or Torah conceded to Mizrahi's demands in order not to be deprived of a rabbinical authority.[143]

The Syrian Jewish communities in Argentina preserved a strong attachment to religious values. Their respective Talmud Torahs emphasized the teaching of religious observances and customs. Hacham Setton, moreover, was a renowned scholar in a city that was not known for its rabbinic scholarship. The Syrian group that arrived in Argentina with a stronger religious identification also had in its midst a recognized authority in Jewish law who was respected even in Aleppo, his home community, and had the support of the chief rabbis of Palestine for his legal Responsa.[144] In other words, the most observant Jewish group in Buenos Aires, at the time of its arrival, also made arrangements to have the services of a religious official who would help them continue their religious practices in their new environment and assist them in transmitting this heritage to their descendants.[145]

Decreasing Influence of the Synagogue

The Jews who were uprooted from their native communities underwent a rapid process of adaptation to their new environment in Argentina. There was a decreasing influence of the synagogue in organized Jewish life in Argentina throughout the period ending in 1930. The main reasons for this are to be found in the general social and political developments taking place in the country's institutions, especially in reference to the Catholic church.

Although there had been full religious freedom in Argentina after 1860, the Catholic church had a privileged position in the public and social life of the country until the 1880s. A fundamental institutional change took place during the first administration of Julio A. Roca (1880–86) and that of Miguel Juárez Celman (1886–90). The impact of the liberal ideas of that decade reduced the previously strong Catholic influence in social and cultural institutions in Argentina. Congress passed, after long-debated controversies between clericals and liberals, a series of laws that stripped the church from many of its prerogatives. In 1884 the Ley de Educación Común made religious education no longer compulsory, relegated it to parental option, and limited instruction to before or after the class hours in all public schools of the country. That same year the Civil Registration Law took away from the parishes the duty of registering births, marriages, and deaths. Finally in 1888 civil marriage was made compulsory.[146]

Debates about these laws—and their aftermath—produced two antithetical political spheres: the socioreligious one, supported by the Catholic church and clerical groups, and the liberal secularist one, which advocated the relegation of the church from its position of public influence to a less powerful one. Thus, the Argentine Catholic community was divided between a clerical segment and an anticlerical one. The Jews were placed by the clericals—among whom were the strongest antisemites—in the liberal group. Indeed, the Jews themselves sided with the anticlericals or non-Catholic group quite naturally, due to the exclusivist ideas of the clericals. Thus they agreed with the position held by the liberal secular group of the nominally "Catholic" community, which regarded all religious adherence as outmoded. This was particularly true of the Argentine-born Jews, whose education had been essentially secular and who closely followed the internal social developments in the country.[147]

The liberal ideas of the "generation of [18]80" had a strong effect upon the following generations as well. The church became a conservative body struggling to preserve vestiges of its former glory. However, the masses, even if they continued supporting the church, were loosing their religious zeal and abnegation. Joaquín Adúriz, S. J., depicted Catholic life in Argentina before 1930 as follows: "Being a hereditary Catholicism, hardly balanced because of a deficient education in personal faith, it appeared in mainly affective forms, and was incapable of assimilating the cultural evolution of society. The Christian living content was hardly recognizable in attitudes transmitted almost conventionally from generation to generation. Seen from outside, Catholic religious life was presented as bordering on superstition among the more popular strata, and formalist among the more evolved."[148]

Religious fervor was comparatively small. The majority of the *porteño* Catholic population may be characterized by Fichter's expression of "marginal Catholics" because of their low mass attendance, their only occasional paschal reception of the sacraments of Communion and Penance, and their little concern for religious education of their children. In big cities, such as Buenos Aires, church-goers were mainly women, a characteristic of most Latin countries. Hence, Catholic passivity in religious affairs was reflected in the Jewish community—especially Catholic male apathy, which left an imprint among Jews, who were taught that in Judaism the male role was dominant.[149]

Liberal religious movements did not take root in Argentina as they did in North American Jewry. This was due to the fact that Argentina was a country where Catholicism remained practically uncontested. Protestant denominations did not pose a challenge to the church. The more liberal movements in Judaism were born in Germany, following the example of religious diversity there, and later passed to the United States. The overwhelming majority of Argentine Jewry had come either from Eastern Europe or from Sephardic communities and thus had never experienced this religious ferment in nineteenth-century West European Jewish communities. The only example in Buenos

Aires of a modern Temple was CIRA, which was looked upon with reservations by the majority of Russian and Polish Jews. Moreover, there was no religious leadership available to present Judaism in a more liberal fashion, already successful in Anglo-Saxon countries. Hence, when confronted with modernity in the form of universal culture and higher education in the national universities, the Argentine-born Jew had basically two alternatives: either orthodoxy in religious practices or secularism. Most chose the latter.

Mixed Marriages

The individual Jew can identify with the Jewish group in various ways, be it by means of religious, cultural, or ethnic links. Likewise, there are several patterns to measure assimilation and acculturation to the majority group in the adopted country. A crucial index of assimilation, however, is the phenomenon of mixed marriages, when a Jew decides to form a family with a non-Jew. Moreover, the response of the leadership of the organized Jewish community to this phenomenon indicates the degree of group assimilation within this particular community.

During the first period of Argentine Jewry, 1860–90, mixed marriages were a frequent event. Due to the scarcity of Jewish women many of the first settlers in Buenos Aires married gentiles. During that period, and up to World War I being intermarried was not an impediment to being an active member at CIRA. Luis H. Brie, for example, was its president during 1904–14. However, this may be seen as an extension of the situation rampant before 1890, when many members of CIRA were intermarried. In any case, almost all descendants from a mixed marriage, where there had been no conversion of either partner to the faith of the other, had no participation in Jewish life in the country.

From 1880 to 1930 immigration of Jews to Argentina was a continuous event interrupted only by World War I. As a consequence of this immigration there was a surplus of Jewish young men with respect to Jewish women, thus causing many men to find their partners outside Jewish circles. This was particularly true in towns in the interior of the country. Being few in numbers, the

Jews naturally constituted a limited social group, and therefore were more inclined to having daily contacts with gentiles. Furthermore, for religious practices as well as for Jewish cultural and national activities, the Jews in the small towns depended upon envoys from the larger Jewish communities in the vicinity, which, on their part, greatly depended on the community in Buenos Aires. But these contacts were sporadic, thus promoting their gradual relaxation of Jewish customs and traditions, as well as of their Jewish identity, much more rapidly than in larger Jewish concentrations.

Even in Rosario, the second-largest city in Argentina, with the second-largest Jewish population, mixed marriages were taking place in large enough proportions to worry the officials of the Asociación Israelita de Beneficencia (AIB). At a board meeting of this institution it was proposed that "the propaganda committee investigate if the wives of the Sephardim who inscribe themselves as members of our community are Jewish, because many Sephardim marry non-Jewesses, and in that case it would not be convenient to accept them as members since it might result that non-Jews would be buried in our cemetery." This proposal was accepted after it was observed that a similar type of investigation was needed for the Ashkenazim![1]

It is practically impossible to find statistics about the rate of intermarriage in Argentina during this period. However, from the frequency with which this problem is mentioned by the Jewish leadership and from their concern with the situation thus caused, we shall be able to draw a picture.

Jewish officials were concerned about the large exodus from the Jewish community. In 1921 Nachman Gesang warned his coreligionists about the ever-growing numbers of conversions from Judaism and of mixed marriages in Argentina. Both these phenomena were debilitating the community and reducing the number of participants in common causes.[2] During the 1920s these cases became even more frequent. Samuel Rollansky, writing in Di Yiddishe Zeitung, was scandalized at the "innumerable cases among Jews of family tragedies caused by mixed marriages."[3]

The marital decision represented a reliable indication of the individual's commitment to or disaffiliation from his community or tradition. It is important, indeed, to emphasize the difference between intermarriage—where one of the partners adopts the faith of the other in the hope of achieving religious unity in the family—and mixed marriage—where both partners remain in their respective faiths without regarding this as an obstacle in raising a family.[4] In the former case, pressure from one partner or family demanding conversion of the other is indicative of a stronger affiliation to the group. In the latter case, mostly involving nonbelievers in organized religion, ties to the group are weaker. Finally, the bonds are even more feeble in the person that decides to convert out of his faith. Our documentation, quite naturally, is based on cases preserved in many of the Jewish institutions in Buenos Aires and the Argentine hinterland. The immense majority of the few documented cases found deal with mixed marriages and concern the situation of the Jewish partner and the children born to the couple vis-à-vis the Jewish institution. Some cases also deal with the attitude of Jewish officials regarding conversions to Judaism.

Many Jews, in spite of having non-Jewish partners, wanted to be buried in the cemetery belonging to their original community. Thus, the Chevra Keduscha, besides being the largest Jewish institution, was also the one most confronted with questions of what to do in cases of mixed marriages. This institution set the tone for the policy in most Jewish societies in the country. The Chevra Keduscha, which was organized on a family membership basis, officially maintained the position of not admitting mixed families as members.[5] The Jewish member, ordinarily, was not denied Jewish burial privileges, though there were exceptions even to this rule.[6] Apparently, with regard to burials of intermarried Jews the policy was unclear. During the first decade that the Chevra Keduscha had its own cemetery (1910–20) Jews married to gentile women were buried there. However, during the early 1920s the Chevra Keduscha considered that "the Cemetery is designed for Jewish members" to the exclusion of Jews married outside the faith.[7] In 1926 an agreement could still not be reached among officials of the institution with regard to persons married to Christians, and it was decided "to treat each case separately after consultation with some members of the Board."[8]

The issue was reopened in 1930, when some officials of the Chevra Keduscha considered that their policy should be reexamined. It was proposed to consult various rabbis, and above all "to take into consideration the century in which we live, an era of tolerance, . . . so that no hatred will infiltrate between our sons and brothers, because they have been placed outside of the community." The orthodox members of the board reacted immediately. Quoting religious fundamentals and previous rulings of the institution, they vehemently argued that the only way one could be accepted as a member was by having a religious wedding ceremony.[9] The orthodox faction won, but still the discussion indicates the existence of a growing tendency among Jews in Argentina to consider themselves an ethnic group more than a religious one.

The Sephardic communities were not exempt from cases of mixed marriages. There is documentation dealing with situations in which the mixed couple or their children wanted to become active in their respective Jewish circles. However, a larger number of Jews completely left their community once they married out of it.[10]

There were also many cases in which the non-Jewish partners—by and large women—converted to Judaism. During the 1880s there were a few cases at CIRA. Rabbi Joseph presided over short ceremonies in which the concerned person abjured from a previous faith and adopted the Jewish one.[11] During Rabbi Halphon's ministration at CIRA (1906–30) converts were accepted if they submitted a letter indicating that they had decided upon the conversion of their own free will and if they promised to educate their children in the Jewish faith. However, even if conversions were occasionally practiced at CIRA, some of its officers were categorically opposed to them, maintaining that they were not sincere acts since there were personal interests involved. The majority, nevertheless, argued that the country granted absolute religious freedom and thus that the will of the individual was enough.[12]

In a community where the religious and spiritual values of Judaism were becoming more and more obsolete many Jews still were willing to maintain ethnic ties with the Jewish people. Thus it proved sufficient to many wanting to marry gentile women and form a Jewish home to arrange private and simple ceremonies of conversion that had no rabbinical sanction. This caused great confusion regarding the status of the children of these couples. Furthermore, it denoted a relaxation of essential precepts in Jewish law that was disturbing to both secular and religious leaders in the community. For the former it meant a deviation from the ethnic particularism of the Jewish people, while for the latter these "pseudoconversions" meant a religious legalization of mixed marriages under a haphazard ritual disguise. There was nothing secularists could do to cope with the situation of mixed marriages from a legal point of view because Argentina guaranteed full freedom of association and had instituted compulsory civil marriage in 1888. On the other hand, the religious leadership could attempt to enforce Jewish religious legislation upon the Jewish community in order to prevent the situation from deteriorating even more.

Rabbi Shaul Setton of the Aleppine community in Buenos Aires, after consultations with Rabbi Aharon Goldman of Moisesville, issued a *herem*, or ban, on all proselytism in Argentina in the mid-1920s. The exchange of letters between these two religious authorities in the country, as well as words of approval of their action by other rabbis, were printed in Setton's *Dibber Shaul*. Besides announcing their ban on proselytization in the country "forever," Setton and Goldman gave honest descriptions of what, in their eyes, was a deep religious crisis among Jews in Argentina. In the words of Goldman:[13]

I received your fervent and impassioned words, reflecting the glow of the fiery law. I was stunned and shocked by the dreadful report on the state of affairs in the land, the shameful situation of those men who have thrown off the yoke of Heaven. They have taken to themselves foreign wives and have begotten with them children. Then, to cover up their hasty actions, they wish to have them accepted by the community as converts to Judaism so that they may be included in the Congregation of Israel. Regarding your description I became excited and frightened. I was previously consulted on a similar state of affairs in Paraguay, Entre Ríos and elsewhere. I responded to them at length. Heaven forbid we do such things which are forbidden by the teachings of our holy Torah.

From the references to the halakhic sources which we presented on the question in point it will be that . . . in consequence of their trespasses they put themselves outside of the community and attach themselves to something akin to idolatry. . . . Who will be so gullible as to trust their motives, since all their gestures and demands of conversion are nothing but an attempt of whitewashing and irresponsibility, in order to obtain religious sanction? . . .

In summing up all the arguments we issue a strict warning to these uncontrolled persons lest they think that by simply pronouncing the marriage formula "Be thou betrothed unto me in keeping with the traditions of Moses and Israel," over an alien woman, or by just removing the preputial stigma from their alien children they have introduced and initiated them into the covenant of Israel. . . . However, if the gentile adult or these children, when they grow up, will come before us, and in complete sincerity and out of their own free will seek admission to Judaism without any ulterior motive, and only after each case has been properly investigated by a duly qualified rabbinical court, we shall not reject them.

These unprincipled offenders, however, call for stern measures; we are impelled to restrict them all around, to reinforce the fence within and without, to keep them at a distance from us and from our sacred institutions. Neither they nor their like shall constitute the Congregation of Jacob.

Hacham Setton added,[14]

> Life in this city [Buenos Aires] is exceedingly unrestrained, and everyone does what he pleases; there is no rabbinical authority to be minded and respected, neither a governmentally appointed rabbi nor a rabbi maintained by the Jewish community itself. Hence, anyone who so desires takes an alien woman for his wife without her being converted; or he chooses individuals at random [to serve as witnesses] and "converts" her in their presence. And they have children who do not qualify [as Jews], though their natural Jewish fathers claim that they were converted. If anyone asks them: in whose presence did this conversion take place? they counter brazenly: who has appointed you [as judge over us]? . . . He keeps his alien wife, begets children whose status is like their mother's, to be absorbed by the Gentiles.
>
> I prepared a ruling and forwarded it together with the cited opinion of Rabbi Aharon Halevi [Goldman] to Rabbi Joseph Yadid Halevi, president of the Aleppo community Rabbinical Court in Jerusalem. The latter endorsed our judgment. . . . I disseminated announcements that it is forever forbidden to accept converts in Argentina, for the various reasons endorsed by the three of us. . . . Whoever wishes to be converted may travel to Jerusalem; perhaps the court there will accept the applicant.

The ban was published with the written consent of both the Sephardi and Ashkenazi chief rabbis of Palestine—Jacob Meir and Abraham Isaac Kook respectively—and Rabbi Judah Leib Zirelson of Kishinev, a founder of Agudat Israel. In spite of the backing of these renowned Jewish authorities, the ban had an effect only in those reduced and limited circles that were under the surveillance of a rabbinical leader. Furthermore, it is impossible to measure the preventive role this ban played in the large Jewish population of Buenos Aires in the years immediately after it was issued.

The ban's major influence was exerted in the Aleppine Jewish institutions in Buenos Aires. This is confirmed by the changes made in their Statutes. Before the ban was promulgated all members were required to be Sephardic Jews not younger than eighteen years and of good reputation, while after the ban the requirements included having Jewish parents.[15]

The Comunidad Israelita Sefaradí of Turkish Jews signed an agreement with Hesed Schel Emeth Sefaradit in 1930, by which the latter sold part of their cemetery in Ciudadela to the former. The Aleppine Jews required from their Turkish coreligionists to submit all cases of Jews in their community married to gentiles to a Bet Din (Religious Court) of the Aleppine community that would judge "according with a book edited by Rabbi Shaul Setton Dabbah."[16] The status of these mixed marriages, as well as the status of the children born to them and who were circumcised, remained unclear. In 1932 concerned officials at the Comunidad Israelita Sefaradí demanded the formation of a Bet Din to solve "the cases of weddings and circumcisions of the mixed families in our community formed many years ago."[17]

The Aleppine and the Turkish communities—and it stands to reason also the Damascene one,—in Buenos Aires officially rejected proselytism in the country. The only way open for a Jew of these communities who desired to marry a gentile was either to form a mixed family and thus be excluded from his community or to convert out of Judaism. Due to the ban, a conversion by a rabbi or at a private ceremony would still not open the doors for the couple in the community of the Jewish-born partner. The knowledge of this communal reaction may have exerted weighty pressure on many young Jews and dissuaded them from making the move that would mark their separation from their community. But the ban did not succeed in preventing mixed marriages; it only guaranteed that the mixed families would not become part of the Jewish people. Moreover, the peremptory character of the ban did not consider particular cases in which a conversion ceremony would solve enormous personal problems in many families; this needed a more humane approach, not a ban that did not admit exceptions.

Persistent opposition to Rabbi Setton's dictum continued even among the Syrian Jews in Buenos Aires. The issue was formally reopened in 1937 upon the return trip of Rabbi Hiskia Shabetay to Argentina. Rabbi Shabetay, who had presided over the community of Aleppo for eighteen years (1909–27) and was now a leader of the Sephardic Rabbinate in Jerusalem, studied the matter and wrote long Responsa analyzing the legality of the ban. He also consulted with Rabbi Isaac Herzog, chief rabbi of Palestine, and Rabbi Tzvi Pesah Frank, chief rabbi of Jerusalem, regarding the legality of declaring void even the conversions practiced before the ban was issued and regarding the circumcision and Jewish instruction of children born of such marriages. While these rabbis sought to find a fair and plausible solution to these questions, their major conclusion took into consideration the special situation rampant among Jews in Buenos Aires. They recommended to maintain the prohibition, even retroactively. In those cases Rabbi Shabetay proposed a reconversion ceremony in Buenos Aires under the surveillance of a special envoy from the rabbinical courts in Jerusalem, while Rabbi Frank insisted on the need of those who wanted to "legalize" their conversion to do so in Jerusalem, as stated earlier in Rabbi Setton's original declaration. Moreover, the children born of these unions should not be deprived of a Jewish education. In a communication to the whole Jewish community of Buenos Aires in 1938 Rabbi Shabetay declared that "it is forbidden to estrange these children; even more, it is a commandment [*mitzvah*] to bring them under the wings of the Divine Presence."[18]

These influential rabbinic endorsements of Rabbi Setton's decree encouraged the leadership of the Aleppine community in Buenos Aires to make another major effort to bring the situation under control and to exert stronger influence over rabbis and individuals who did not observe the ban. In 1938 they published a booklet with the *halachic* (legal) opinions of the chief rabbis of Palestine and the heads of the rabbinical courts of the Sephardi, Ashkenazi, and Aleppine communities in Jerusalem, as well as the heads of the rabbinical court of the city of Aleppo.[19] Neither the original ban nor the fresh endorsements put an end to mixed marriages or stopped conversions to Judaism in Buenos Aires. On the contrary, the efforts of certain sectors in various of the local Jewish groups to enforce the ban indicate that unions between Jews and non-Jews continued being a reality.

The Moroccan Jewish community in Buenos Aires did not accept Hacham Shaul Setton's legislation for the whole Jewish population in Argentina. During the first half of the 1930s conversions and wedding ceremonies in which one of the partners was a convert were performed at CIL.

In January 1936, as a reaction to this situation, a group of sixty-seven of the most concerned members of CIL presented to the board the following petition:[20]

> The undersigned, reckoning the extraordinary importance that the problem of assimilation is obtaining daily among the members of the community, and, considering, that even not taking into account religious precepts, which prohibit and confine within narrow limits the conversion of persons of other beliefs, there are secular bases [for it] such as:
> 1. Vehement doubts arise immediately about the firmness of the convictions of those who abjure from the beliefs their parents impressed upon them, and
> 2. That in the present hour the recrudescence of the antisemitic persecutions compel us to maintain the community united, without defections of any type.

They accordingly proposed

> i. That from this date on it is positively prohibited to the First Sexton [Oficiante], or any other employee of the Society, being liable to be fired in case of non-compliance, to perform conversions or bless marriages of converted persons.
> ii. Hereafter any member who officiates at conversions or who gives his consent to a marriage with a converted person or belonging to a different religion will be declared source of dishonor for the Society, and thus be passible to the extremes of Article 12 of our Statutes [expulsions]. The head of the family shall be regarded as a consenting person.

The petition was accepted by a General Assembly of the institution. It should be emphasized that the petition itself was not prompted by a concern with religious practices. Religious prohibitions to mixed marriages are mentioned en passant in the exposition of the problem. It stressed, however, secular reasons such as difficulties adapting to Jewish values by the converts and the need to unite the Jewish people when antisemitism was the sign of the time not only on the international scene but also in Argentina. The attitude of the Moroccan Jewish community in Buenos Aires can clearly be extended to larger sectors of the Jewish population in the country: a ban with a definite religious character, which was issued to prevent religious transgressions, was seriously considered only by a limited group and was redressed in a secular frame and accepted by wider circles when the continuity of the people was menaced. A religious dictum obtained additional relevance when it applied to an ethnic issue, thus making it manifest that Jewish identity was being expressed more along ethnic rather than religious lines.

Mixed marriages and conversions were a growing problem in the Jewish community during the 1920s. The leadership noticed it, but only a few of the religious authorities of weight could and did try to remedy the situation. They sought and attained endorsements of higher authorities overseas, but locally their influence was confined to reduced groups, notably the Syrian communities, and limited elements of other sectors of the Jewish population. Moreover, the unclear policy in many institutions regarding mixed families evinces that the religious aspects of the situation were only secondary to the ethnic aspects.

First synagogue of Congregacion Israelita, built in 1897.

Congressman Enrique Dickmann speaking. Seated, with moustache, is Alfredo Palacios, also a Socialist congressman and leader.

Interior of Congregacion Israelita's first synagogue.

Cigarette vendor, early 1900.

Rabbi Henry Joseph (left) and Rabbi Samuel Halphon.

Sociedad "La Union-Obrera-Israelita"

Movimiento de la Sociedad
desde 1° de Noviembre de 1897 hasta 1° de Mayo 1898.

En la Sociedad se encuentra actualmente 48 socios activos y 6 Protectores, que abonan $ 50 mensualmente.

La Sociedad tiene una Colegio nocturno donde se educaron desde el 18 de Abril con año 7 hombres, la lengua Castellana etc.

La biblioteca tiene ahora 159 libros comprados, 6 donados de la "Gruppa Proletariat" de New-York, por S.º I. Liachovitzky — 16 libros por I. Liachovitzky 2 por I. Koriman 8 por A. Diamond, en total 194 libros.

12 diarios mandados periódicamente por diferentes redaciones por la recom. de S.º Liachovitzky 1 por S.º I. Juritz 2 por S.º I. Poverene 2 por D.º I. Liachovitzky, en total 17 diarios y periódicos.

Desde el 16 de Marzo de corr. año hayan llevado libros á la casa 19 lectores, en el salon de la Socieda leeron 138 lectores.

Para la biblioteca como 12½ % de la entrada $ 87-39. Total de la Reserva — $ 100,–00.

Buenos-Aires 1 de Mayo de 1898.
Presidente — I. Koriman
Secretario — I. Zoiling

Report of La Union Obrera Israelita for the six-month period from November 1, 1897, to May 1, 1898.

Cover of the humorous journal Penimer un Penimlach of March 26, 1924. The large caricature is of writer Alberto Gerchunoff.

Max Glucksmann.

During the Semana Trágica.

scar Wengrevich.

Máximo Grosman.

Samuel L. Siffles.

Rosa Ch. Urserbbo.

Cina A. de Mittelchtein.

Esther Kohn, la millonaria.

e las salas de la sociedad alle Córdoba donde se reunían los tenebrosos.

Achill Mastofsky.

Mauricio Steinberg.

Miguel Klaiman.

Amalia Lichtenfeld.

Sinagoga que servía para la simulación de los casamientos ordenados por los dirigentes.

é Rouman.

Mauricio Lachman.

Max Cysman.

Salomón José Korn.

Isaac Bentlimol.

Salley Brin.

Arrest of individuals involved in white slave traffic. From Caras y Caretas, June 7, 1930.

Leaders of the Jewish Community visit retiring Director of Immigration Juan A. Alsina on December 18, 1910. (Left to right, front) M. Sigal, David Elkin, Alsina, Rabbi Joseph, and Dr. Alejandro Zabotinsky. (Back) Naum Enquin, Jacobo Joselevich, Arnoldo Elkin.

A Jewish furniture workshop, Tulipan, 1927.

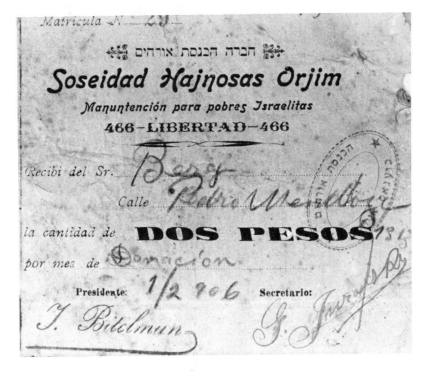

Member card in the union of furniture workers.

SINDICATO UNICO DE OBREROS EN MADERA Y ANEXOS

Secretaría: RIVADAVIA 3965
U. T. 62, MITRE 6438
LOCALES DE BARRIO
Av. PARRAL 1400 y ALVARADO 1965

N⁰ 1014

El compañero _NIVARCSKIN JOSÉ_

Está en condiciones para trabajar en el taller de

Calle _Sadi Carnot 320_

UBLICACION

Receipt from Hachnosas Orchim, 1920s.

National and Political Challenges

The Beginnings of the Zionist Parties

On November 2, 1917, the Balfour Declaration, viewing with favor the establishment of a Jewish National Home in Palestine, produced a great impact among Argentine Jewry. Various sectors of the community—at the time far from the national aspirations of the Jewish people— were shaken by the announcement. Even the then small community of Jews who had arrived from Syria—both Damascus and Aleppo—which a few months before the Declaration had started a periodical in Arabic with news about their institutions and other short articles felt the necessity of devoting an issue almost completely to the developments in Palestine. Thus several articles on Palestine and the Jews appeared; others on General Allenby, Theodore Herzl, agriculture among the Jews, and even the pogroms of 1881 in Russia completed the issue.[1] Even if the impact of the Balfour Declaration was short-lived among the Arab-speaking Jews in Buenos Aires—they were still quite far from playing a role in local Zionism—the event served to keep their Zionist sentiments awake.

Dr. Enrique Dickmann, a Russian-born Jew who rose to prominence as one of the main leaders of the Socialist party in Argentina, was affected by the Balfour Declaration on quite a different level. Dickmann at the time had almost forgotten his boyhood yearnings for Zion.[2] However, he was induced to write an article entitled "Zionism and Socialism," first printed in *Vida Nuestra* in October 1918. Writing exclusively as a socialist identified with Argentina, Dickmann maintained that his party had already accepted the principle of nationalities as one of the postulates of international socialism. He thus viewed Zionism with sympathetic eyes.[3]

The Balfour Declaration did not constitute the first impulse for Zionist work in Argentina. Organized Zionist activities had been going on there for already twenty years. On August 12, 1897, when news arrived from Europe announcing the impending meeting of a Zionist Congress in Basle, a few Jews in Buenos Aires decided to found a Hovevei Zion group.

During the first twenty years (1897–1917) the Zionist movement in Argentina remained a limited one. Far from being a popular cause, it could be portrayed as the pastime of a few idealistic Jews with some Jewish knowledge. However, in spite of the many internal strifes between leaders of the different groups and organizations that were being founded and, many times, closed after a short span, the ideas behind Zionist propaganda began to attract the attention of more and more Jews both in the capital city of Buenos Aires and in the provinces.

The Federación Sionista Argentina (FSA) of 1913 was founded after a hard-fought battle for recognition by Zionist headquarters in Europe between two different groups in Buenos Aires, the Liga Dr. Herzl and Tiferet Zion.[4] Jacobo Liachovitzky, who headed the former, had been with one of the Hovevei Zion groups that in 1891 had attempted to establish themselves in Palestine. This group was stopped at the doors of Constantinople and through the services of the Jewish Colonization Association, recently founded by Baron Maurice de Hirsch, was diverted to the Jewish colonies in the Entre Ríos province in Argentina. Analogously, Jacobo Joselevich, leader of Tiferet Zion, was an ardent and passionate Hovev Zion from Lithuania, who had later moved to Odessa and Warsaw before establishing himself permanently in Buenos Aires. He was influenced by Leib Lilienblum and especially Ahad Ha'Am. The membership in these two Zionist organizations was of similar stock. Tiferet Zion, being constituted by more liberal and active forces, was recognized in 1909 as representative of Argentine Zionism by the Zionist Organization in Europe, and formed the FSA at a congress of all Zionist groups in 1913. The activities of the FSA were also limited. Up to World War I its main concerns were organizing propaganda meetings to spread Zionist goals, collecting funds, and founding new Zionist groups.

A new wave of immigrants from Russia, imbued with the liberal ideas rampant among wider groups of Jews, arrived after the abortive revolution of 1905. They founded Zionist groups with the ideals they had imported with them from their home countries. Thus already in 1906 a Poale Zionist (Labor Zionist) society was established in Buenos Aires. Their activities, in what for years remained a small group, were limited to raising money for the organization of libraries in the capital and later in some provincial cities and colonies where Jewish workers met and discussed topics related to their ideology. They also fought against the Jewish white slave dealers in Argentina and finally, under the initiative of Leon Chazanovich, attempted to defend the interests of the Jewish colonists in the JCA colonies against the abuses of the administration. A publication, *Broit un Ehre* (*Bread and Honor*), was published in 1910, of which only a few numbers appeared. In that same year, however, the Poale Zionists were deprived of the participation and active leadership of both Chazanovich and Zalman Sorkin, who were expelled from the country in a "depuration" effected by the Argentine government of workers' ringleaders who might blur the celebrations of the country's first centenary.[5]

World War I almost completely stopped the Atlantic migrations for four years. In particular, it interrupted the flow of Jewish immigrants who were leaving Eastern Europe searching for a haven in the Americas.[6] The Jewish community in the country was still relatively young and in constant need of new blood from the old country. This was due to the lack of inner cohesiveness in the Jewish community and to the failure of the Jewish leadership, so far as it existed, to establish conditions within the community that would induce the Jewish immigrants to participate in the building of institutional life within the Jewish sphere and not elsewhere. The war also touched directly upon Zionist institutions in Argentina because the organizations became isolated from the centers of world Zionism in Europe, a fact that "demoralized the limited numbers of Zionists" in Argentina.[7] Furthermore, the Russian Jewish immigrants usually brought added strength to the Jewish national movement because they had been in contact with and also worked for Zionism before migrating. The war deprived the ranks of Argentine Zionism of this new addition.

During the first years of the war the FSA busied itself with two quite important enterprises: (1) It organized, together with other Jewish officials in the community, the Comité Central to help Jewish war victims—throughout the country funds were collected and sent through Jewish international organizations to those in need of aid in the countries at war (cf. ch. 8); (2) The FSA was responsible for the First Argentine Jewish Congress, which met in Buenos Aires on February 26–29, 1916.[8] Both these activities were strongly related to Zionism. Of course, help to persecuted and homeless Jews did not end with the signing of peace. It continued being an argument in favor of the endeavors of Zionists.

The First Argentine Jewish Congress, on the other hand, had greater political importance. It constituted the response of the Jews in Argentina to the idea of Luigi Luzzatti, ex-minister of finance and prime minister in Italy, who already during the first stages of the war contemplated the possibility of a Jewish representation at the eventual Peace Conference. At that opportunity the Jewish delegation should have the backing of as many Jewish communities as possible, in order to give validity to their claims.[9] The Argentine Jews, called by the FSA, were among the first to take heed of Luzzatti's general call, and decided upon the following resolutions:[10] (1) Jews should have equal rights with other citizens in the countries where they live; (2) where Jews constitute the majority of the population they should enjoy recognized national rights; and (3) those Jews who want to settle in Palestine should be given broad and unlimited rights to migrate and occupy land autonomously, with power to govern. On May 23, 1919, on the occasion of the Paris Peace Treaty, the FSA sent telegrams to the Committee of Jewish Delegations there, as well as to Georges Clemenceau and Woodrow Wilson, in support of the 1916 Congress's resolutions.[11]

A period of fundamental Zionist activities in Argentina was inaugurated in 1917. During the first weeks of the year the FSA asked the Zionist Organization in the United States to send a propagandist to awaken the Jewish population in the country to the national Jewish aspirations. The leaders of the FSA considered, nearly one year before the Balfour Declaration, that the time was ripe for tighter organization and that there were good possibilities of spreading the "idea" among wider circles of the Jewish population in all corners of the country, even in neighboring republics. It is to the credit of the FSA that it was decided to invite Dr. Baer Epstein from the United States to tour the Jewish communities in Argentina as a Zionist envoy. The efforts and achievements of Epstein on behalf of Zionism were substantial, from his arrival in March 1917 until his departure early in 1919. The number of branches affiliated to the FSA rose, as did the amount of money collected and the people working for the cause. Epstein's stay added prestige to the FSA among the rest of the Jews in the country.[12]

The Balfour Declaration and England's involvement in the Palestine area during the latter part of World War I produced a realignment of the relations between Jews all over the world and His Majesty's government. The FSA, accordingly, made immediate contacts with the British embassy in Buenos Aires and received a favorable reply from Sir Reginald Tower, the British minister in Argentina. During his stay in Buenos Aires Tower maintained good relations with the Jews and on several occasions visited different Jewish organizations in various localities throughout the country. However, as we shall see below, this special situation of the British minister vis-à-vis the Jews widened the conflicts between different sectors of the Jewish community, particularly in reference to leadership in and representation of the Jewish community.[13]

For the period starting in 1917 up to 1930, leadership in Zionist activities in Argentina was held, by and large, by Jews born in Eastern Europe. Many of the initial founders of the FSA in 1913 continued at its head during the 1920s. It was during this decade, furthermore, that some young Jews, including professionals, held leading positions within the FSA. The majority of the latter were foreign-born, though they had studied at the universities in Argentina and had received a strong Hebrew and Zionist education both in their old home and in their new homes across the Atlantic. But overweighing the few physicians and lawyers, Zionist leadership was held by successful manufacturers and merchants. The East European background of these Jews is evident from the enormous proportions of letters written in Yiddish. On the other hand, the Zionist atmosphere they had been trained in emanates from the Hebrew correspondence with the centers in Jerusalem and Europe. Though small in number, it was this nucleus of educated and enthusiastic Zionists that was responsible for gaining the support for national ideals, in accordance with the Basle program and the Zionist Organization directives, among Jews in Argentina, as well as in some of the neighboring countries.

The Poale Zion group, or Zionists with a socialist ideology, had been operating in a reduced way after 1910. It underwent a sudden revival in 1918, due mainly to the Balfour Declaration, which enforced its national leanings, and to the international events during the last stages of the war, especially the new political developments in Austria and Germany and the Russian Revolution.[14] In addition to these factors we must emphasize the effect of the work of Marcos (Mordechai) Regalsky, the Poale Zionist delegate who arrived in Argentina in 1918. Regalsky was responsible for many of the achievements of this group, which, in addition to its followers in Buenos Aires and major cities in the provinces, was able to enroll in its ranks young Jews from the colonies.

At the end of 1919 the first assembly of Poale Zion delegates was held. This convention, to which delegates from all important centers attended, laid down the groundwork for the founding of the Jewish Socialist Workers' Party Poale Zion in Argentina with a sociopolitical and national platform. Already at their second meeting in 1921, the Poale Zionists in Argentina were divided along the same lines as the World Union of Poale Zion movement. The latter had split in 1920 over the issue of joining the Third (Communist) International. The resolution in Argentina favored remaining with the rightist world association of Poale Zion by a vote of 238 against 153, with two abstentions. With the departure of the leftist Poale Zionists, the movement was deprived of many active forces. The division weakened the movement, which during the previous three years had been very active. The two popular schools created by Poale Zion in Buenos Aires—Folks Shul in Villa Crespo and Ber Borochov in the center of town—remained in the hands of the leftists after the division.[15]

The rightist Poale Zion, as its name indicates, was a Zionist socialist workers' organization. In their struggle for socialist ideals these Jewish workers believed that the way to a socialist society was different for Jews than for others. Only a people living independently in its own land could form a healthy proletariat. In particular, the Jewish proletariat could only be strengthened within its independent boundaries. Their special political aspirations, geared to form a socialist society in Palestine, were made clear even prior to the 1921 split. When the Peace Conference after World War I was to receive a Jewish delegation, Poale Zion made an appeal to all Jewish workers in Argentina for an independent representation of Poale Zion at the conference.[16] Moreover, their practical aim, when spreading their ideology among the Jewish proletariat in Argentina, was the collection of money for the Palestinian Workers' Fund (PAF). Within the context of the world Poale Zion movement, the collections in Argentina were of major importance. For the period April 1924–January 1926 the sums collected for PAF in Argentina were second only to those assembled in the United States and surpassed those of England, France, and Eastern Galicia.[17] After 1923 the PAF campaigns were strengthened by visits of delegates from the Palestinian Histadrut (Labor Federation).[18]

The rightist Poale Zionists in Argentina were concerned with the improvement of the situation of all workers, and their periodical *Di Neie Zeit* (started 1918) contained constant references to the progress of workers' movements all over the world, in Argentina and Palestine in particular. In this respect they were in close ties with the Socialist party in the country and openly supported the Socialist candidates in all elections in Argentina.[19]

In line with their Labor Zionist position, the rightist Poale Zion platform for the Fifteenth Zionist Congress of 1927 included demands for active support of Jewish colonization and help by creating jobs for the unemployed in Palestine. The Zionist budget had to give preferential consideration to these aspects. Furthermore, national funds should not help private enterprises in any way. Cultural projects, not religious ones, were to be emphasized.[20]

Early in 1919 a group of dissenting Zionists seceded from the FSA and formed an independent branch of Zeire Zion. Most of the founders of Zeire Zion had been active in Tiferet Zion, which was composed of younger Zionists, including many workers, who were interested in a more active organization with more radical goals, including *aliyah* (immigration to Palestine) and conquest of labor in Palestine.[21] Already during the Fourth Zionist Land Conference held in Buenos Aires during February 23–26, 1918, the Tiferet Zion members were strongly opposed to the direction given by the FSA to the last Emergency Campaign for the Jews in Palestine (1917). At a certain point the representatives of Tiferet Zion left the Conference, though they did not sever their affiliation with the Zionist Organization. On May 1, 1918 a proclamation was launched, announcing the formation of a new branch of Zeire Zion. The founders themselves had only a vague idea of what it meant to be part of the Zeire Zion movement, for the war years had cut the Argentine Jewish community from much news of Europe, in particular with respect to social and political directions of the Zionist movement. The forty-three persons who signed this proclamation concurred that the Balfour Declaration had opened a new era for the Jews. They foresaw an epoch of more democratic work in Jewish institutions, in particular among Zionists. The era of dependence on the Rothschilds, the JCA, and the like was over; Jews should rely more on the masses. At present the leaders were removed from the Jewish masses; the folk was forgotten: "The leaders in the Zionist movement know how to ask the masses to *give* for our high purpose, but never ask them to *do* as well."[22]

The basic intentions of this new group were not separatist. They accepted the basis of the Basle program, recognized the World Zionist Congresses and their resolutions, especially the Jewish National Fund, but opposed autocracy in the movement, mainly from the rich elements in Jewry. Their motto was to defend the democratic spirit in the Zionist Organization, and their purpose was to give the Zionist movement a popular character and to democratize the institutions in Palestine.[23]

They formulated their program in the following eleven points:

1. Propagandize among the Jewish masses the necessity of immediate and direct work for Palestine, of founding a Pioneers' Fund and Pioneers' Groups, and of organizing industrial cooperatives, etc. . . .

2. Create in Argentina a special information bureau for opportunities in Eretz Israel.

3. Systematize the collections for Zionist funds.

4. Help organize here [Argentina] the Jewish communal institutions.

5. Democratize and modernize the already existing ones.

6. Propagandize among the Jewish population the necessity of taking an active part in the political life of the country.

7. Propagandize for the founding of loans and saving chests, mutual credit, and insurance companies against unemployment, sickness and death.

8. Strengthen the organization of the Jewish population with professions and employments.

9. Agitate in favor of the use of the Hebrew language in daily life.

10. Spread and support Hebrew literature.

11. Help found Hebrew libraries, kindergartens, and schools.

In spite of all the glamour that the proclamation seemed to throw into the Zionist camp in Argentina, the Zeire Zion faction did not do too much in the way of adding new blood to the movement.[24] It did not spread out of Buenos Aires, except for a group formed in Basavilbaso, Entre Ríos. Precisely this factor helps us understand the formation of Zeire Zion. First, it is evident that it rose against the establishment in the Zionist movement, the FSA. The fact that it did not take roots in places without a numerous Jewish, and in particular Zionist, population shows that ideological differences were not fundamental in the split, at least not as fundamental as the will to oppose the present leaders and inject new life into the Zionist movement. Second, Zeire Zion did not have a separatist position in Zionist affairs, as Poale Zion had. This prevented them from presenting a novel platform, except for the fact that they considered themselves more capable than the FSA people to do practically the same things.

The reaction at FSA was strong, both as a response to the challenge and as an attempt to minimize the new organization's importance. At the very beginning Joselevich, the FSA president, could not understand their complaints and called for unity.[25] In letters to the Zionist Organization in Europe FSA wrote that the new faction of Zeire Zion "does not really know what to do . . . , [however], we see a peril for our movement, because it has brought anarchy, less discipline, and disorder."[26] Though they ridiculed Zeire Zion, they saw in it a threat. This threat became stronger when the Zionist Organization in Copenhagen responded that it recognized the new faction. FSA was thus forced to protest to Copenhagen, mentioning that this official recognition by the Zionist Organization of the Zeire Zion "will produce more divisions and factions."[27]

During the first few years, however, Zeire Zion was not extremely active. Its main Zionist activities of that period were the initiative of organizing a group of legionaries to fight with the Allied armies in Palestine and the resolution to collect 100,000 pesos for a cooperative colony in Palestine to colonize Argentine Jews. Among those who left with the legionaries were a few Zeire Zion leaders, thus restricting the movement. Moreover, the campaign for the colony in Palestine, which was launched on the first anniversary of the Balfour Declaration, on November 2, 1918, was not successful. According to Zeire Zion's own version, besides the grippe epidemic at the time, the main reason for only collecting 10,000 pesos in place of 100,000 was the opposition of the FSA to such an independent initiative.[28] But we should also look for the causes of the failure of this campaign in the Zeire Zion organization itself. The FSA might have made a vacuum around the project, but Zeire Zion lacked an important element in that their own goals were unclear in their differences with the FSA. Moreover, settling in Palestine was not in the minds of more than a few Zionists in Argentina, even of those who had moved there with the ultimate intention of migrating later to Palestine.

On the other hand, antisemitic manifestations in Argentina had been quite sporadic. Only two months after this issue, during the Semana Trágica of January 1919, Jews, in somewhat larger numbers, inquired at the FSA's offices about opportunities and economic conditions in Palestine.[29]

The failure, quite immediately after, of colonizing most of the volunteers to the Jewish Legion from the Americas, was a confirmation of the fact that settling the Biblical Land was still something for the future for the majority of the Jews.[30] Thus the colonization fund did not sufficiently attract the Jews in Argentina, especially, when sponsored, as it was, by an organization competing with FSA, on which they relied.

When Poale Zion in Argentina invited Zeire Zion to join their committee to decide about their demands to both the Peace Conference and the Socialist International, the latter, consistent with its nonseparatist position, answered strongly in the negative. Zeire Zion's refusal to separate demands was based on the following reasons: (1) Jews should be united in one group at Versailles; (2) the Argentine Jewish Congress of 1916 had made the attempt to unite all Jews in the country, and had decided about the action to be taken once the war was over; (3) as part of the Zionist Organization, Zeire Zion did not feel free to make any political move without its approval. Moreover, they deemed sending Poale Zion's demands to the Peace Conference as injurious because it could deprive the Zionist Organization of its role as a unique representative of Jewry. On the other hand, sending demands to the Socialist International was impossible because not all sectors of Jewry recognized the International.[31] The exchange of letters with Poale Zion, as well as the formal declaration of their position regarding the Jewish postures at the Peace Conference, are telling arguments for the vague position Zeire Zion had, at least during the first years, among Zionists in Argentina. Poale Zionists saw in it a group with proletarian leanings that might approach their own position. On the other hand, FSA saw in it a group without real principles, leading a personal fight. At the Fifth Land Conference (November 1–6, 1919) FSA resolved that there was no reason for the faction and that Zeire Zion had no justified existence. They demanded that Zeire Zion stay within the Zionist Organization.[32]

Only in 1922, with the influx of new immigrants from Eastern Europe, who instilled new energies into the local organization, did Zeire Zion become more active. At this time they started contacts with the same movement in Europe. Deliberations were held over the question whether to become formal members of the Zeire Zion movement in Eastern Europe. For most of the first members of Zeire Zion in Argentina the European Organization was too far to the left. This caused, by the end of 1922, the rupture between rightist and leftist Zeire Zion. The latter, after a short independent existence, joined the rightist Poale Zion. On the other hand, with the departure of the leftist elements, the Zeire Zion organization associated itself with the world Hitachdut movement.[33]

After World War I new immigrants brought new ideas to Zeire Zion in Argentina. Among them was the organization of *halutzim* (Heb., "pioneers") and their training for *aliyah*. With this intention Zeire Zion founded a Hechalutz group in 1924. Most of its members lived around Berisso, an industrial town near Buenos Aires. In January 1925 nine certificates were received by Hechalutz, thus prompting the departure to Palestine of nine of its members. Shortly thereafter it dissolved because of its reduced numbers and few chances in Berisso of organizing larger Jewish groups. This branch that had been formed in Buenos Aires thus became central.[34]

Signs of a rapprochement between Poale Zion (right) and Zeire Zion were already evident in 1929, when a group formed by members of both parties and also of a Hug Eretzisraeli (Eretz Israel Group) joined forces to promote among the young the ideals of Hechalutz. Furthermore, Poale Zion and Zeire Zion, in the same year, under the initiative of Eliahu Golomb, delegate of the Palestine Histadrut, worked jointly in the recently formed League for Palestine Workers. It was in 1932 when finally both groups joined into the Jewish Socialist Party Poale Zion–Zeire Zion.[35]

Towards the end of the 1920s the FSA and the main parties—Poale Zion and Zeire Zion (Hitachdut)—formed a local committee (Vaad Artzi) for joint work on behalf of the Jewish National Fund (JNF) and for placement of *shekalim*. In spite of this committee, the results obtained by the parties were quite unsatisfactory.[36] But while both parties were able to compromise with the FSA for the formation of a joint board for JNF work, they could not accept the conditions offered by FSA for identical work on behalf of Keren Hayesod (Palestine Foundation Fund). At the end of 1928 the FSA had sent an invitation to the parties to join in the work for Keren Hayesod. Zeire Zion answered that in a plenary session they decided not to join the FSA in this enterprise because (1) they did not believe in the usefulness of a mixed committee for practical work in Eretz Israel; (2) an interparty committee should be completely independent from all parties, like the one of JNF (FSA had proposed the formation of a Keren Hayesod Board dependent mainly on the General Zionists, or FSA, and thus it would be ruled by them as it had been previously); and (3) according to the proposal of FSA the new board would have no autonomy, since the budget would be administered by FSA, while the parties would only help in taking the responsibilities of the budget.[37] On the other hand, Poale Zion did not even bother to answer FSA's letters. When Solomon Pazi, envoy of Keren Hayesod, arrived in Argentina in 1929, one of his main goals was to get the parties to join the FSA in an autonomous board for Keren Hayesod. He had many long discussions with members of Zeire Zion but to no avail. The latter again demanded direct elections for the Keren Hayesod Board by individual donors and were opposed to the appointment of members directly by the FSA. Furthermore, they resisted the financing of the budget of the FSA with Keren Hayesod's money. The root of the conflict appeared to be in the Labor Zionist parties' opposition to the financing of FSA's local budget with monies from the Keren Hayesod campaign. They would only enter a joint board for Keren Hayesod when they would be guaranteed a voice in it proportionate to their strength.[38]

The Poale Zion sector had a growing influence on Jewish life in Argentina, not only in its capital city but also in the interior and in the agricultural colonies. The Zionist Organization in London felt the effects of Poale Zionist work in Argentina and advised Jacob (Akiva) Ettinger, envoy of Keren Hayesod, upon his arrival in Buenos Aires in 1928, about the structure of Zionist work in the country, emphasizing the importance of Poale Zion, a comparatively small, but militant group.

The different ideologies of the various Zionist groups working simultaneously in Argentina were clearly delineated when Jacob Zerubavel visited the country in 1927. Zerubavel, a leader of Poale Zion (left) in Warsaw, came to South America to gather support for the Yiddish Schools in Poland. He received the unconditional backing of the leftist Poale Zionists, while FSA and even Zeire Zion (Hitachdut), made war on them, arguing that Hebrew should take precedence to Yiddish in Jewish education.[39] The rightist Poale Zion did not oppose Zerubavel's endeavors but advised its members and sympathizers to help this action only after having finished the work for PAF.[40] The struggle between Yiddishists and Hebraists, rampant in Eastern Europe, did not spread to Argentina, so far as we can verify it, with the same virulence. There were some advocates for Hebrew among FSA leaders, especially in Zeire Zion, who organized a few Hebrew-speaking groups, and whose leaders published, though irregularly, some Hebrew periodicals. The vast majority of Zionists, however, utilized Yiddish more than Hebrew; and the official organs of all the Zionist organizations—FSA, Zeire Zion (Hitachdut), Poale Zion (right), and Poale Zion (left)—were in Yiddish.[41]

After having traced the main ideologies within the Zionist camp in Argentina, an evaluation of the role that Zionists and the separate Zionist ideologies played within the Jewish community in Argentina and the role that Argentine Zionism played within the World Zionist movement seems pertinent. In order to assess the role of Zionism within Argentine Jewry we shall analyze the different forces active in two events that shook the Jewish community: the formation of a Jewish Legion to fight with the British armies on the Palestinian front in 1918 and the different reactions of the various sectors of Argentine Jewry to the Semana Trágica in 1919. We shall then proceed to describe the interaction of Zionists with other groups of Jews in Argentina, for instance, the communists, the Sephardim, and the assimilationists. Furthermore, the political weight of Argentine Zionism, its ties with the Zionist Organization, and the way it was seen by the leaders of the movement in Europe and Palestine will be analyzed. Finally, we shall evaluate the practical work for Zionism done in Argentina, namely, monetary contributions, Zionist education of the masses, and commerce with Palestine.

The Jewish Legion

During the first months of 1918 several young Jews in Argentina decided to emulate the movement that was officially authorized in England in August 1917 and had stirred many Zionists in the United States a few months afterwards to constitute a Jewish Legion to fight on the side of the British on the Palestine front. Official communiqués reached the British Ministry of Information reporting that young men in Moisesville, as well as in other Jewish colonies and in Buenos Aires proper, were organizing a group of volunteers to go to the Palestine front.[42] Individual Jews and the FSA approached Ambassador Tower for information about the procedure of the matter. Tower, due to the unprecedented character of the request, consulted the Foreign Office in London before giving a definite reply. The FSA made contacts with the Zionist Organization in London, which took up matters with the British government. Nahum Sokolow conveyed the offer of the Jewish community in Argentina to provide volunteers for the British Army in Palestine to Mark Sykes. The answer, originating from Balfour, and in the form of a letter from R. Graham, at the Foreign Office, to Sokolow, mentioned that "the British Military Attaché at His Majesty's Legation at Buenos Aires has been informed by telegraph that these volunteers will be accepted provided adequate credentials are forthcoming and that they understand that the right is reserved to send these recruits elsewhere in the event of any individual being found on arrival to be unsuitable for a Jewish unit."[43]

The group of legionaries were not that rapidly organized. Vladimir German, a twenty-five-year-old Jew who had migrated six years earlier to Argentina, was the initiator of the Jewish Legion in the country. Early in 1918 he had been very active in Tiferet Zion. In March he approached the English minister in Buenos Aires, who on April 2 suggested that German and his followers resort to the Zionist Federation in London. Later, it was agreed to meet with the president of FSA, Jacobo Joselevich. Relations were not too good between the leaders of the FSA and the group of volunteers. First, the volunteers did not resort to the FSA at the beginning and were later hesitant to contact them. Furthermore, FSA did not, apparently, respond enthusiastically to the project and only at a later stage of the deliberations fully supported the legionaries.[44] This passivity of the FSA was violently attacked by *Vida Nuestra*, a Jewish monthly in Spanish with assimilationist tendencies but that had reacted very favorably to the Balfour Declaration. This publication accused FSA of Germanophilia due to the obstacles it placed in the way of the volunteers. When the volunteers finally were able to arrange for their departure to the front, FSA made difficulties until credit was given to it for the enterprise.[45]

Germanophilia, it appears, was not really the main issue for the initial passivity of FSA. The problem was basically a financial one. The British embassy was not interested in sponsoring the trip of the Jewish legionaries. FSA did not offer to do it either. Finally, a committee was formed with the participation of fifteen Jewish organizations from Buenos Aires and two from the agricultural settlements of Clara and Basavilbaso in the Province of Entre Ríos to help finance the endeavor of the volunteers, most of them modest artisans or students. The central role of this committee was played by the Congregación Israelita de la República Argentina (CIRA). Some of their more conspicuous members were active in raising funds for the project and contributed the lion's share. For better or for worse, their coming into the picture angered FSA and ushered in a long period of tense relations between both institutions and between most of their leading members.[46]

CIRA had taken the lead in May 1917 as a result of a communication from Europe regarding the situation of the Jews in Palestine during the war. Max Nordau and Professor Abraham S. Yahuda were active in Madrid trying to induce Spain to negotiate in favor of the Jews in Palestine. Nordau was in good relations with the Argentine ambassador in Madrid, Marco M. Avellaneda. The latter assured Nordau of his cooperation and his readiness to speak about the matter with the Argentine minister of foreign relations. He also recommended that the Jews make contacts with government officials in Argentina. At this point Nordau cabled Rabbi Halphon of CIRA to organize such a movement among Argentine Jews. Nordau's contact with Halphon and not with the FSA gave CIRA an additional mark of prestige in the eyes of the Jews there. Halphon, therefore, presided over the delegation that spoke with Dr. Francisco Beiró, a congressman belonging to the Radical party in power at the time, and on June 4, 1917, spoke with Hipólito Yrigoyen, the president of the nation. Later the minister of foreign relations notified the delegation that the Yrigoyen administration had agreed to the petition of the Jews and had advised the ambassador in Madrid to support Spain's negotiations in favor of the Jews in Palestine.[47]

Again in 1918 members of the board of CIRA came in contact with the legionaries and upon learning of the financial problems of the group, succeeded in having the treasury of CIRA authorize the sum of 3,950 pesos and 50 British pounds for expenses. In the meantime Rabbi Halphon started to work in favor of Zionist ideals, especially at public functions concerning the Jewish Legion being formed in the country.[48] What is more, through the services of Halphon, and due to the good name CIRA enjoyed in the Jewish communities of France and England,[49] it was finally achieved from the British embassy that Halphon, and only he, could extend the official identity certificates to the legionaries, by stamping the rabbinate's seal on them. CIRA also organized a farewell ceremony for the legionaries at the Coliseo Theater, in which in the presence of all diplomatic representatives from the allied countries and with major repercussions in the Argentine press, a Zionist flag was given to "the Jewish legionaries who are leaving, offering their lives. . . . The first flag to wave in the battlefields side by side with the glorious colors of the allied armies. . . ."[50]

The first contingent of fifty volunteers left Buenos Aires on October 4,

1918. There were about one hundred more volunteers ready to leave for England and Palestine when the armistice made their participation unnecessary. In the booklet issued in commemoration of their departure we find short biographical details of the first group. All of them were born in Eastern Europe and most were between twenty and thirty years old. They had been in the country from four to ten years in 1918. In other words, they had left Russia between the revolt of 1905 and World War I. Some belonged to the lower-middle-class Zionist societies in Buenos Aires—Tiferet Zion and the recently constituted Zeire Zion—and even more were active in Poale Zion and other workers' circles.[51] Just as the larger groups in the United States and Canada, the legionaries movement in Argentina had a Zionist and popular character. It was inspired by a strong belief in Zionism on the part of the East European youth. Furthermore, even if Argentina remained neutral throughout the war—both during the administration of Victorino de la Plaza (1914–16) and the first term of the Radical leader Yrigoyen (1916–22)—the country was divided between *neutralistas* and *rupturistas* vis-à-vis the European conflagration. The Jews, by and large, favored the Allies. With the fall of tsarism in Russia, the Russian Jews in Argentina could more freely side with the "Entente" powers, thus removing all doubts in the minds of ardent Zionists about fighting on the Palestinian front.[52]

The episode of the Jewish Legion revealed that many groups were open to Zionist ideals, including the members of CIRA, usually depicted by the East European Jews as the Temple of the rich, the elite among the Jews, who were considered assimilationists. In matters of religion they certainly were not among the most observant Jews, and the Zionist idea did not especially appeal to them, though they never discouraged it. For these reasons, the East European Jews, among them the Zionists, preferred to refer to them as *Yahudim*, the same way German and other West European Jews were referred to by their East European coreligionists in the Old World.[53] CIRA became involved in the issue of the legionaries, thus demonstrating that they could be concerned with Zionist endeavors. However, FSA saw a threat in the way CIRA was gaining prestige in Zionist circles abroad. The whole episode throws light on some of the concerns of FSA, which repeatedly requested from the Zionist Organization in London not to grant so much prestige to CIRA at the expense of FSA.[54] Through the ministration of the Zionist Organization, FSA finally was recognized by the British government as the representative of all Zionists in South America, by means of a letter from the minister of foreign relations, dated June 7, 1919, London.[55]

There were two main issues related to FSA's prestige and ascendancy that bothered its leadership. On the one hand they were in constant competition for hegemony in the local Jewish community, while on the other hand, they were forever trying to attract more attention from the Zionist World Headquarters, an attention that, as we shall see, was mainly based on the financial worth of the community. The above-mentioned British recognition had the effect of a momentary balm for their complaints. It conceded the FSA some political power, bestowed upon them by the nation that was now in control of

Palestine; and it proved that the Zionist leadership in Europe considered the FSA to be sufficiently important to try and get them the representation of South American Zionism. However, it solved neither of the issues. The British recognition referred to Zionists in South America and made no mention of "Jews" in Argentina, for there was obviously no connection between the Jews and the British government. Locally the FSA would have to continue striving for hegemony. Furthermore, we shall see that the Zionist Organization did not always utilize the FSA in political issues developing in South America, preferring to rely on its own envoys.

Zionists during La Semana Trágica

Several issues arose during this period that demanded a response from Zionists, regardless of the fact that they were not directly related to Zionists' activities but concerned the entire Jewish population of Argentina. We have already noted that the FSA had been the initiator of the First Argentine Jewish Congress, where the formation of a central body of Argentine Jewry was suggested. However, the 1916 congress did not have an effective influence in Jewish life in the country. It did, nonetheless, attain its basic goal of presenting the requests of Argentine Jewry vis-à-vis Palestine and Zionist aspirations that were later, in 1919, forwarded to the Peace Conference in Versailles.

In 1919 Zionists played an important role in affairs of the local community. The issue started with a succession of workers' strikes at Pedro Vasena's metallurgic factory in Buenos Aires. On January 7, 1919 the armed forces fired against the workers concentrated at the factory. Many were wounded and a few killed. It was this incident that started the Semana Trágica.[56]

Among the Jews, the first to react was Rabbi Halphon. On January 12 he informed the Jewish population of his visit to Francisco Laguarda, inspector general of the police, who, in the name of Elpidio González, chief of police, had assured him that all necessary measures had been taken to protect the Jewish community from all future types of disorders. This announcement was not published by the Yiddish daily press until the fifteenth.[57] The FSA presented its argument soon afterwards. They argued that "the Jewish community of Buenos Aires, just as those in the provinces, has no relation with the last deplorable events. . . . We peremptorily deny the insinuation that the Jewish community is responsible for the sad events that came to pass. Unfortunately there are in our community some hot-headed elements, such as there are in other communities. We are, however, sure of the honesty of the great Argentine people, who shall not confuse these hot-headed individuals with the great and pacific Jewish community of the country."[58]

This response by the FSA, the apologetic character of which coincided with a reply given later by other sectors of the Jewish population to the undiscriminate attacks against Jews, merely constituted a negation of the maximalist character of the Jewish population in Argentina. The hotheads were limited in number and did not represent in any manner the whole Jewish community. It seems as if the FSA with this declaration was brushing off an accusation made by some reactionary sectors in Argentina against the Jews in general, and diverting the blame to a fairly reduced part of the Jewish population. On the other hand, there is no plea for justice; there is no mention of the possibility that the riots and assaults carried on by the police, the army, and some civilian reactionary groups, were altogether out of place or that justice should be administered.

A letter sent by a leader of Poale Zion appeared in some of the Buenos Aires newspapers. Marcos Paryseusky protested against the massacre of Jews that had taken place in Buenos Aires, "the only reason being that they are Jews, and confused unfortunately with lawless elements and Moscovite Russians." Paryseusky wrote that civilian groups under the surveillance of the police had destroyed books and archives, as well as injured many members at these places. Furthermore, he affirmed that their organization did not accept the internationalism and cosmopolitanism of the maximalists, being a cultural society that spreads nationalist doctrines among the Jewish proletariat.[59] The reaction of Poale Zion left much to be desired. Their published protests were weak and apologetic. On the other hand, they denounced the aggression together with other workers' organizations, but not so much through Jewish conduits.

CIRA, leading eighteen other Jewish organizations, by means of a pamphlet in Spanish that was posted in the streets of Buenos Aires and published in the country's press, came out with a somewhat more vigorous publication. The pamphlet, entitled 150.000 *Israelitas al Pueblo de la República* (150,000 *Jews to the People of the Republic*), regardless of a somewhat angry tone, maintained a tenor of an undoubted apologetic makeup.[60] "ARGENTINES: 150,000 honest men from all conditions, affiliated to all political parties, are speaking to you through us, so that you come to prevent the consummation of an unatonable crime. . . . Let the justice you are preparing to do with the malefactors, whom we repudiate, be inexorable and severe, but corresponding to the faith that we deposited in you." FSA was among those institutions that signed the document. Evidently the Jewish community was unprepared for an attack of that sort. It had never successfully organized itself into a unified body to respond to an outside assault. In the midst of the onslaught the leading figures of the main institutions tried to respond. Rabbi Halphon, due to his position of dignity and his ability in representing the Jews before the governmental authorities, had first tried to make profit of his accessibility to these authorities and attempted to secure protection and assurances of well-being for the Jews. Later, the FSA, of growing prestige during the last two years, and CIRA, as the most veteran and reputable institution, tried to create a representative body of the community.

Nonetheless, the role of FSA became more energetic. Under the FSA leadership, the Comité de la Colectividad convened in its precincts. The idea that the Jewish community had to take action for its own protection and for the enforcement of its legal rights had slowly presented itself in the minds of the Jewish officials. The *comité* declared itself in permanent session. It immediately assigned different commissions; one in charge of mutual aid, which had to care for the situation of the imprisoned; a juridical committee that included the socialist Alfredo L. Palacios; a third in charge of medical assistance for the wounded; and a political committee. FSA heads, its president Joselevich, its first vice-president Gesang, and the director of JNF Solomon Liebeschütz were, together with Rabbi Halphon, the main organizers of the *comité*. It was not without unmerited pride that FSA reported to the Zionist Organization in Copenhagen about the forceful role the FSA took in the events. For a moment all other Jewish institutions followed the leadership of FSA. Even the proud CIRA, seeing the central position of its rabbi in the *comité*, accepted FSA directives in the contingency.[61]

Zionism among Sephardim

With the purpose of involving the growing Sephardic communities around the world in Zionist work, the World Zionist Organization considered it convenient to propagandize among their circles. Therefore Dr. Ariel Bension traveled throughout Latin America in the latter part of 1926 and the beginnings of the following year. His main interests were in Argentina, where a considerable Sephardic population had settled. Before Bension's trip various Sephardic groups in Buenos Aires had initiated some Zionist activities; however, most of these accomplished little.

By the turn of the century a few Moroccan Jews had achieved financial stability and even wealth. Thus, not surprisingly, the emerging Zionist leadership tried to involve them in national work. The Argentine Zionist Congress convened in Buenos Aires on April 16–18, 1904 was also sponsored by Congregación Israelita Latina, and Hebra Gemilut Hassadim of the Moroccan community. In practical terms the role of the Moroccan Jews at the congress was minor when compared to that of the Ashkenazic Jews. Nonetheless, some of the Moroccans were appointed to positions of leadership, doubtless with the intent of ensuring their support for Zionist ideals. Thus Isaac Benzaquén was appointed vice-president of the congress, and Abraham Benchetrit was a member of the committee.[62]

As a result of the congress, a Federación Sionista Argentina (not to be confused with the federation of the same name founded in 1913) came into being. Two prominent leaders of Congregación Israelita Latina, Mair Cohen, its president, and Yona Migueres, a past secretary, were elected vice-president and secretary, respectively, of the Federación Sionista Argentina. Moreover, in line with a recommendation by the Argentine Zionist Congress, a biweekly Zionist magazine in Spanish was created in order to reach those Jews who did not understand Yiddish, especially the Sephardim. Isaac Bentata, an active leader of the Moroccan Jews, helped in the editing of El *Sionista* during its early stages.[63]

Two years later, in 1906, Adolfo Crenovich of the Federación Sionista Argentina reiterated in a letter to the Zionist Action Committee in Cologne, Germany that the two Moroccan synagogues in Buenos Aires, Congregación Israelita Latina and Ez Hayim, continued to sympathize with Zionism.[64] In

March 1907 in a long report to Cologne describing the overall Jewish situation in Argentina, the country's Zionist leaders mentioned the formation of two small Zionist groups by Moroccan Jews in the interior, one in Villa Mercedes, Province of San Luis, and the other in Margarita, Province of Santa Fe. However, toward the end of the report the correspondents asserted that among the Spanish (i.e., Moroccan) Jews, "some are religious fanatics, who see in Zionism a blasphemy of the Messianic idea."[65] This last statement clearly reflects the existence among Moroccan Jews of a strong religious undercurrent militating against the adoption of a positive political posture with regard to Jewish national goals. This attitude would appear even more strongly among the Ladino-speaking Jews from the Balkans and the Arabic-speaking Jews from Syria (both Aleppo and Damascus), who settled in Argentina in much larger numbers than their Moroccan brethren around the turn of the century and thereafter.

The impact of the Balfour Declaration, however, was reflected positively at the Congregación Israelita Latina. A few days before the celebration of the first anniversary of the declaration, the congregational board resolved "to adhere to the celebrations programmed for next November 2 [1918], by buying a box for the performance that FSA is sponsoring at the Opera Theater; participating in the public manifestation on Nov. 3; celebrating a special ceremony during the morning services of Saturday, Nov. 2; sending circular letters to all members to adhere to the celebrations by closing their businesses and displaying flags in front of their houses."[66]

The Moroccan community, however, remained cool to the Jewish national aspirations. Some sparks of activity were evinced during Herzl's lifetime but subsided shortly after his death. Again, at the moment of Jewish pride and renewed hopes in Zion as a consequence of the Balfour Declaration, support was given to the efforts of the Federación Sionista Argentina, but when the enthusiasm gave way to more realistic analyses in the political sphere, support of the national cause also decreased. During the Keren Hayesod campaign of 1924, the FSA sent a long letter to the Congregación Israelita Latina asking for a contribution, but the congregation's board answered "that this society is strictly religious, and they are not authorized [to approve expenditures] to this end."[67]

Some initiatives also took place among Ladino- and Arabic-speaking Jews before 1926. Jews from Turkey and the island of Rhodes founded Bené Sión in 1914 for Zionist work. After the Balfour Declaration its membership increased somewhat, but shortly afterwards it was discontinued.[68] Another group of Arabic-speaking Sephardic Jews, originally from Eretz Israel and Syria, founded Geulat Sion in 1916 and participated in the popular demonstration of 1917 together with the rest of the Zionists. Geulat Sion sent three of its most prominent members to the Fifth Land Conference of Argentine Zionists in 1919. Hacham Shaul Setton Dabbah, serving the Jewish community of Aleppine origin, was invited to the conference as a special guest, but due to the fact that the majority of the speakers insisted on expressing their views in Yiddish, the Sephardic participants left the gathering. In 1921 due principally to the language problem, both Spanish- and Arabic-speaking Sephardim decided to establish a Zionist federation independent of the FSA.[69] The formation of the Centro Sionista Sefaradí did not take place until 1925, however. It initiated some small-scale activities in the capital and some of the cities of the interior and during Bension's visit served as an instrument for his educational program and for his efforts to organize a network of Sephardic Zionist clusters. Nonetheless, throughout the 1920s the great majority of the country's Sephardim remained far removed from the Zionist ideal.

Argentina's Zionists leaders, aware of the need to enlist more of the Sephardim in Zionist activities, repeatedly tried to broaden the FSA's sphere of influence. The Sephardic question came up again and again at land conferences and during special campaigns, and in most instances the delegates adopted resolutions encouraging a more positive approach to the Sephardim. As early as 1921 the FSA asked the World Zionist Organization in London to send a Sephardic delegate to work with the Argentine Sephardic communities. The Sephardim, it was felt, would more readily listen to the Zionist message from one of their own, basically because of their localism and parochialism but also because in the eyes of many Sephardim Zionism was a secular ideology, opposed to the traditional Messianic conception. Moreover, since the Sephardim mistrusted the world Zionist leadership, which in effect was East European, they needed assurance that the movement would benefit Sephardim in the Land of Israel and also in their communities of origin. These assurances, quite naturally, would be better conveyed by delegates who shared their roots, concerns, culture, and traditions.[70]

In 1924, Sephardic leaders in Europe and the Middle East founded a World Union of Sephardic Jews (WUSJ), claiming the support of such Zionist leaders as Chaim Weizmann, Nahum Sokolow, Menahem Ussishkin, and Vladimir (Ze'ev) Jabotinsky. At the time Sephardim constituted nearly a third of the Jews in Palestine, and the founders of WUSJ claimed they were not receiving, upon their arrival in Palestine, the same guidance and help as was given the Askkenazic Jews from Russia and Poland. In light of this, the WUSJ intended to advise potential Sephardic emigrants from the Middle East, North Africa, and the Balkans before their departure from their communities of origin, in order to facilitate their settlement in Palestine. WUSJ also launched a campaign against Keren Hayesod for failing to keep its promises to Sephardic *olim* and for pursuing policies that favored the Ashkenazim.[71]

When Bension arrived in Mendoza after having visited the Jewish community in Chile, he learned that the WUSJ had begun propagandizing in Buenos Aires against Keren Hayesod. Sephardim who met Bension in Buenos Aires told him that they would only contribute to Zionist causes if the money went to WUSJ for the Sephardim in Jerusalem. Jacobo Karmona, president of the Centro Sionista Sefaradí, further argued that unless all the money collected in Bension's campaign was sent to the WUSJ, they would not officially recognize his delegation. Moreover, despite Bension's objections, the Sephardim insisted on complete autonomy, including the authority to deal directly with London, since they felt it was impossible for them to work with the FSA.[72]

Although the WUSJ tried to prevent him from founding a Sephardic branch of the World Zionist Organization, Bension was able to achieve some temporary success. On October 23, 1926, after a month-long mobilization of Sephardic Zionists led by Bension, the Order Bene Kedem was founded at a large public gathering in Buenos Aires, in the presence of Dr. Isaac Nissensohn, president of the FSA. Bene Kedem was established as an independent organization, with no formal ties with the FSA. Its first president was Jacobo Benarroch, an honored member of CIL, of Moroccan origin. Branches of Bene Kedem were immediately started, under the auspices and activation of Bension, in Rosario, Córdoba, Río Cuarto, Tucumán, Mendoza, and Santa Fe. Contacts were made with the Sephardic communities in Montevideo, Uruguay, and Rio de Janeiro, Brazil.[73]

In addition to external factors impeding his work, Bension found in Buenos Aires a Sephardic community divided along origin lines. Jews from Morocco, Ladino-speaking Jews from Turkey, Salonika, and Rhodes, and the two Arabic-speaking Jewish groups from Aleppo and Damascus formed the four main Sephardic communities in the city. At the time there was little contact among these groups. The Moroccan Jews constituted the smallest—about 200 families—but also the richest group. The Turkish community was larger but much poorer. The Aleppine Jews, except for a few individuals, were also poor, while the Damascene ones constituted the largest Sephardic community, with a few rich men. In most organizations Bension visited he received the impression that most Sephardim in Buenos Aires were extremely indifferent to Zionist efforts. The older elements of the Moroccan community were "extremist believers in the Messiah on a white horse, . . . while the young are completely assimilated." At the Damascene community, Bension was badly received by its president, Moisés Schoua, who insulted his whole committee with the allegation "that all the Zionist leaders and delegates were working on a commission basis" and refused to contribute. The rabbi of the Aleppine community, Hacham Shaul Setton Dabbah, the chief representative among Sephardim in Argentina of Agudat Israel, was anti-Zionist on religious grounds. In his sermons he forbade his congregation to contribute to Keren Hayesod. Hacham Setton's negative attitude to modern Zionism is reflected in some of his Responsa. His views regarding education at the Aleppine Talmus Torah confirmed his anti-Zionist position, for he obstinately refused to permit the teaching of Hebrew as a language. Bension contacted Setton, and after a long debate the latter promised that he would no longer actively interfere in the former's efforts but that he would not help in any way.[74]

Poor results obtained by Keren Hayesod in the campaign among Ashkenazic Jews did not help inspire Zionist ideals among Sephardim. Yiddish, spoken by most Ashkenazic Zionist officials in Buenos Aires, was incomprehensible to the Sephardim. Finally, the fact that most of the World Zionist leadership was Ashkenazic and that most of the immigrants to Palestine came from Eastern Europe, created in the minds of these Sephardic Jews, who, after all, had migrated from regions near Palestine, the idea that Zionism was mainly an enterprise of Ashkenazim. Bension's labors opened the door to na-

tional work for the Sephardim in Argentina, but even if there were cordial relations between Bene Kedem and the FSA, the former being in direct connection with London, a major collaboration between Sephardim and Ashkenazim
was not effected via Zionism.

Meanwhile the WUSJ sent Shabbetai Djaen, rabbi in Monastir and one
of the founders of WUSJ, as delegate to South and North America. He arrived
in Buenos Aires in April 1927, just before Passover, and during his stay in Argentina visited Rosario, Mendoza, and other centers with Sephardic populations.[75] Djaen soon aroused suspicion among Zionist leaders in Argentina, including leaders of Bene Kedem. Dr. Moisés Cadoche, at the time secretary of
Bene Kedem, mentioned on several occasions that Djaen was playing a double
role: on the one hand he spoke highly about Zionism as an ideal, and on the
other he spoke against the Zionist Organization and its personnel, demanding
that the Sephardim send their contributions only to the WUSJ.[76]

In 1928 Cadoche became president of Bene Kedem and in an interview
in London with Zionist leaders asserted that "the WUSJ ... in spite of its pre-
tended Zionist tendencies, only created obstacles for us and made our Zionist
work much more difficult ... trying to convince us to change our allegiance."[77]
In a campaign to discredit the Zionist Organization in the eyes of Sephardic
communities all over the world, the WUSJ published some of its attacks in an
independent Sephardic publication that had a large following among Sephardim all over South and Central America and in Morocco. These articles argued
that the Zionist Organization did not help Sephardim in Palestine and did not
appoint Sephardim to posts in its bureaucratic hierarchy. The WUSJ would do
a better job.[78]

At the end of 1928, Rabbi Djaen returned from the United States to Argentina, where, with the help of some leaders of the Moroccan Jews (CIL) and
Jews from Turkey (Comunidad Israelita Sefaradí) he formed a Consistorio Rabínico to deal with rabbinical questions among Sephardic Jews. He also became Gran Rabino of the Moroccan and Turkish Jews. Meanwhile, the central
offices of Keren Hayesod in Jerusalem approved a proposal suggested by their
delegate in Argentina, Akiva Ettinger, to ask Djaen to spend four months working among Sephardim in their fund-raising campaign across the country. The
first three thousand pounds collected would go to Keren Hayesod; 30 percent
of anything over that amount would be given to WUSJ. For some time Djaen
handled this work, though without great success. He was again approached by
Keren Hayesod on the eve of the enlargement of the Jewish Agency, to allow
his name to be included, along with the names of chief rabbis and teachers in
every country, in a circular sponsoring Keren Hayesod's work as provider for
the Jewish Agency. In spite of these recognitions, Djaen was already complain-
ing about his personal situation in Buenos Aires. In June 1930 the Consistorio
Rabínico was permanently closed, having accomplished little. Soon thereafter
Djaen left the country for Europe.[79]

Bene Kedem initiated its Zionist activities with energy and enthusiasm,
but, as often happens, once its founder—in this case Ariel Bension—left and
contacts with him became more diluted, the organization languished. Bene

Kedem published a booklet containing "Call to Sephardim" by Bension; salutations by Wiezmann, Sokolow, Sir Alfred Mond (president of Keren Hayesod in England), and Isaac Nissensohn from the FSA. The goals of Zionism, and the functions of each of its institutions and funds were explained in this publication, emphasizing the particular interests of Sephardim.[80] The organization was chiefly involved in financial affairs, promoting a *shekel* campaign. During the first two and a half years of activities, until May 1929, Bene Kedem did poorly even in the distribution of *shekalim*. Ettinger in 1928, and Pazi, as Keren Hayesod delegate in 1929, believed there was no hope of effective action among Sephardim. Pazi wrote, just before the Jerusalem riots of 1929, that Djaen could help with the *shekel* campaign, although he was convinced that "for Keren Hayesod it is impossible to do something among Sephardim."[81]

Bension's efforts, and the continuation of his work by the leaders of Bene Kedem, finally had positive results in the aftermath of the anti-Jewish riots that swept Palestine in 1929. Argentine Jewry, seriously concerned about the safety of the Palestinian Jewish community, immediately proclaimed an Emergency Campaign at a meeting attended by Jews from all sectors, Ashkenazim and Sephardim, Zionists and non-Zionists. The grandiose goal of raising 1,000,000 pesos by September 30, 1929, was not achieved. However, although the harvest in the Jewish agricultural colonies had been poor and the country was experiencing a monetary crisis, Argentina's Jews contributed 313,000 pesos to the emergency fund. More than 50,000 pesos were collected by and among Sephardim. In Buenos Aires alone, where a total of 194,399.69 pesos was raised, fully 35,661 pesos were contributed by Sephardim. These figures make it evident that Bension and Bene Kedem had succeeded in influencing wider circles of the various Sephardic communities.[82]

The localism of the Sephardim, however, remained strong. The Emergency Campaign was intended to aid Palestinian Jewry, but the Aleppine community in Buenos Aires, for example, decided to allocate only half of the money it raised to Zionists in Palestine and to divide the other half among institutions in Aleppo, Sephardim in Palestine, and the Ahavat Zedek society, which helped Aleppine widows, orphans, and poor people in Buenos Aires. Thus only half of the proceeds were turned over to the Federación Sionista Argentina.[83]

The leadership of the FSA enthusiastically welcomed the participation of the Sephardim in this campaign. Dr. Isaac Nissensohn, its president, wrote to Chaim Weizmann in London that "the Sephardim, who had hardly contributed to the upbuilding of Palestine, are now contributing to the Emergency Fund with a liberal hand."[84] Bension had brought the Zionist message to the Sephardim in Argentina in a language they understood. As a result, they were now somewhat more conscious of the Zionist program and recognized the importance of working for and contributing to its fulfillment. They had also begun to realize that the Sephardim already in Palestine and potential Sephardic immigrants were benefiting from the building of the Jewish National Homeland.[85]

Despite these accomplishments, however, Zionism made little progress among the Sephardim of Argentina in the years that followed. Although some of the Sephardic leaders had begun warming up to the Zionist program and had worked together with Ashkenazim in an effort to propagate the Zionist idea among the country's Jews, the Sephardic rank and file continued to distrust the Ashkenazic leadership. Strongly linked to their communities of origin and imbued with intense localist feelings, Argentina's Sephardim required much more in the way of explanation and reassurance if they were to overcome their suspicions and doubts. In the 1930s, however, both the Zionists and world Jewry as a whole were preoccupied with other issues that took precedence over the work of reassuring the Sephardim. Thus the necessary effort was not forthcoming, and the attempt to win over the Sephardim was dropped before it ever attained substantial results. In part because of this unfortunate inconsistency in the approach to Argentina's Sephardim, a segment of the community was permanently alienated from Zionism.

The Zionist movement failed to win the cooperation of the Sephardim during its early decades either locally in Argentina or at the international level. In later years, especially after the creation of the State of Israel and once its most urgent challenges—including the absorption of large numbers of refugees in a very short period of time—were met, the rift between these two major segments of Jewry would again be evident. Even today it continues to be a concern shared by Sephardim and Ashkenazim in Israel and the diaspora.

Political and Practical Work of Zionists

The developments in the Zionist movement in Europe after World War I had their effect upon FSA officials in Buenos Aires. In April 1920, when the Peace Conference at San Remo conferred the Mandate for Palestine upon Great Britain, tens of thousands of Jews in Buenos Aires, and more in every city and town of the interior, celebrated with joy. Again, in July 1922, with the confirmation of the Mandate in London by the Council of the League of Nations, over 30,000 Jews demonstrated in the capital of Argentina. On both occasions delegations from the FSA were received by President Yrigoyen. At the 1920 meeting Joselevich, as president of the FSA, asserted that the San Remo declaration provided Jews the world over with the possibility of becoming a nation. After explaining briefly the special situation of Jews in Argentina, he asked Yrigoyen to recognize the Jewish nation, so that Argentina should become the first republic in South America to do so. Yrigoyen complimented the Jews in the country and stated that antisemitic outbursts like the previous year's Semana Trágica would never occur again. With respect to Joselevich's request, Yrigoyen suggested the presentation of a memorandum to the cabinet. Some time later FSA presented a long memorandum describing the history of the Zionist movement and the aspirations of the Jewish people, as well as some particulars about Zionist activities in the country. It ended with the following petitions:

1. Recognition of the existence of the Jewish nationality.
2. Recognition of the Jewish flag as symbol of that nationality. . . .

3. A declaration from the government of the young and noble Argentine Republic expressing its sympathy and moral support for the Jewish Nation.[86]

This memorandum was discussed at a special meeting of the cabinet. According to Nachman Gesang's view, it had the support from Yrigoyen and some of the ministers, but the majority of the latter were opposed to it. The main reason was the Vatican's objection to the ratification of the Mandate and to the recognition of the Jews as a separate nation.[87]

Brazil's unwillingness to support the ratification of the Mandate was a further stumbling block to Zionist aspirations. Brazil's government was under strong influence from the Vatican, and as was the rule of the Allied nations, absolute unanimity was required for this question. It was at this moment that the FSA should have been instructed to petition the Brazilian government, according to the power the Zionist Organization had given the FSA in 1919. However, the executive of the Zionist Organization in London did not turn to the FSA to deal with the situation. Instead, they entrusted the mission to Dr. Judah L. Wilensky, delegate of Keren Hayesod then in South America. Wilensky was able to change Brazil's position, and the Mandate was ratified.

Nevertheless, the FSA attempted to play a political role in this issue. Once more in the name of all Jews residing in Argentina, the FSA solicited the Brazilian minister in Buenos Aires, Pedro de Toledo, to convey to his government the wishes of Argentine Jewry for a favorable vote of the Brazilian delegate at the League of Nations concerning the ratification of the Mandate. Toledo sent a cable to Río de Janeiro forwarding the request.[88] FSA cabled to the League of Nations a few days before the vote with similar petitions. In the midst of all the turmoil before the vote at the League of Nations, the FSA complained to the executive of the Zionist Organization in London that the latter did not utilize the political ties the former had with other South American countries. The answer, indeed not very encouraging for the FSA, affirmed "that Dr. Wilensky, being fully acquainted with the South American situation, would be in the best position to judge what action would be most effective and through what channels it should be taken."[89] It seems that the long distances to and from the Zionist headquarters had other effects besides delaying communications; it produced an attitude of circumspection in the minds of European leaders vis-à-vis their distant partners in the movement, especially in the most delicate situations. After all, their only contact had been through the mail. Moreover, the European officials might have considered the FSA leaders not sufficiently competent to handle international political matters.

In 1922 there was a decline in Zionist work in Argentina. Its ascent had started in 1917 with Epstein's visit and the Balfour Declaration. The consequent maturity and the substantial achievements of Zionism at San Remo and the ratification of the Mandate by the League of Nations had produced enormous enthusiasm among Jews in Argentina.[90] After the San Remo resolution Zionists in Argentina contributed to the JNF the third largest sum, after the United States and England.[91] In the same year they conducted a campaign for the Restoration Fund, assembling 380,000 pesos, a sum that gave the Zionist executive the incentive of starting the Keren Hayesod in Argentina.[92] Active leaders of Keren Hayesod in Europe and Palestine—Alexander Goldstein and Judah Wilensky—visited Argentina and the neighboring countries during the early twenties, arousing interest in others for what was happening in world politics for the sake of the Jewish nation.

However, there was something obstructing the continuous growth of the Zionist movement in the country. Jewish national education was at an extremely low level—regarding both education of the general public in Zionist ideals and the preparation of new leadership by instructing the young in the national aspirations of the Jews—and the officials of FSA did not succeed in developing resources to fill the gap. Delegates from the Keren Hayesod continued visiting the area. Leib Jaffe and Benzion Mossensohn, in 1923 and 1925 respectively, traveled to South America and again accomplished the main task of contributing to a successful campaign. However, the movement needed a day-to-day effort in educating the Jews about Zionism, not just an annual uplifting lecture pronounced by a world leader of the movement.[93]

Leib Jaffe arrived in Buenos Aires during the first week of 1923.[94] During his nine-month stay in South America Jaffe was active in Buenos Aires and in most of the Jewish centers in the interior of Argentina. He also visited Chile and Brazil. It happened to be a year of great economic crisis, especially with a decrease in the price of cattle. Some of the Jewish colonies were in an extremely impoverished situation. Jaffe pointed out the deficiencies of the Jewish community in general. There was an enormous lack of Jewish education, and religion did not play much of a role either: "The youth is not taught about the history of their people, they are not given any spiritual values, no national instruction." In his lectures Jaffe not only spoke about fund-raising for Keren Hayesod but tried to awaken the nation, the conscience of the people; he attempted to make his audiences aware of the need of national education and schools. He saw assimilation as a tremendous problem in the country. On the other hand, his success in spite of the economic crisis gave him second thoughts about the community and about the role of Zionism within it. The fact that in some of the colonies Jews were setting apart the produce of the corners of their fields as contributions to the Jewish National Fund (JNF) strengthened those thoughts, up to the point of asserting that Zionism and Eretz Israel were the only hope for the future of Argentine Jewry.

> They asked how do I see Argentina. I responded that she is in my eyes like the trees I saw in Moisesville—eaten by the locust—but they shall grow leaves and buds once more as long as there is some sap of life preserved in their roots and in the race. Eretz Israel nourishes this sap of life, she brings to Argentine Jewry spirit and content to life, as she does to the few leaves that remain from the tree of the people. Eretz Israel and Zionism plant personal pride and honor. Fifteen years ago, twenty years ago, it was difficult in Argentina to be a "Jew in public." Jews were basically a small abhorrent group, which debased the name of Israel. . . . Only in the light of Eretz Israel and Zionism did Judaism become known in Argentina.[95]

For the period 1923–28 Argentine Jewry contributed to Keren Hayesod a more or less stable annual sum. A delegate from the Zionist executive visited Argentina each year—except in 1924 and 1926—to direct the fund-raising campaign.[96] The FSA understood the importance of having a representative from Jerusalem bring a message to the Jews in South America. Zionism in Argentina needed bolstering from the outside; it had not produced leaders capable of attracting Jews to the movement in the same way a *sheliach* (emissary) of Leib Jaffe's stature could.[97] The envoys viewed the internal problems of the organization from a better perspective, thus enabling them to easily spot deficiencies and contribute to their solution. Furthermore, the cosmopolitan structure of the country during this period, especially of its capital city Buenos Aires, communicated a feeling that the "best" was always imported.[98]

At the beginning of 1926 the FSA devoted special attention to strengthening the organization. Its president Wolf Nijensohn wrote to London about the need of "an instructor whose duties should be to visit the Zionist societies in a frequent and regular manner in order to instruct them in discipline, to encourage the active members, and to increase their numbers. . . . The prevailing local conditions, however, demand that such an instructor come from abroad, and we therefore request that you propose to us a candidate for the post."[99] Jacob (Akiva) Ettinger, delegate to South America, upon returning to Jerusalem, advised sending a special director to Argentina who would devote himself full-time to Zionist and Keren Hayesod work.[100] Furthermore, after the Jerusalem riots of 1929 the FSA invited Nahum Sokolow to come and launch the 1930 campaign.[101] None of these requests materialized, yet they show the deep need felt by leaders of Zionism in Argentina for support and collaboration from the highest echelons of world Zionism. Moreover, the Poale Zion organization was since 1918 under the direction of Regalsky, who arrived in Buenos Aires after having been active in Poale Zion circles in the United States. Regalsky established himself in Buenos Aires, thus providing his movement with new strength.[102] Finally, the Zeire Zion group also recognized the need for a leader from overseas. They wrote to the Zionist Organization in London requesting a *sheliach* representing their organization who could unite and fortify it in Argentina.[103]

Zionists in Argentina did not play a central role in the ideological evolution of the Zionist movement at large during this period. Even at the Zionist congresses Argentine Jewry—both FSA and Poale Zion—was represented in most cases by proxy. Alexander Goldstein, Wilensky, Jaffe, and other leaders in world Zionism represented the FSA on different occasions while A. S. Juris took the representation of Poale Zion in Argentina. Samuel Hurwitz went from Argentina to the Twelfth Zionist Congress at Carlsbad, but he did not participate actively. Nahman Gesang brought the message of the FSA to the Fourteenth Congress in Vienna in 1925. In his speech he presented the resolutions arrived at nine months earlier at the Ninth Argentine Land Conference of Zionists: (1) to vote unconditionally for Dr. Weizmann's proposals with regard to the Jewish Agency and (2) to vote for transferring the financial and economic institutions from London to Palestine. The first point was one of deep concern and dispute between Weizmann's group and his opponents. The former wanted serious negotiations with the non-Zionists, hoping to reach an agreement for the establishment of an enlarged Jewish Agency comprising also the non-Zionists. The various groups opposing Weizmann saw in his scheme a compromise that would hamper the achievements of Herzl's program of a political struggle for obtaining statehood. FSA unconditionally supported Weizmann's plan and soon made attempts to establish a Jewish Agency in Argentina.[104]

It was right after the enlargement of the Jewish Agency at the Sixteenth Zionist Congress in Zurich, which only preceded the riots in Palestine by a few weeks, that Gesang, then president of the Keren Hayesod in Argentina, and Isaac Nissensohn, president of the FSA, insistently tried to constitute a Jewish Agency in the country. During the last three months of 1929 letters to Jaffe in Jerusalem and to Weizmann in London explained the situation of Zionism in Argentina. The time was ripe for active work—especially after the Emergency Campaign for the Jewish victims in Palestine—among Jewish circles in Argentina that had hitherto remained aloof from national work. The leaders of the FSA had in mind different sectors of Argentine Jewry, including some of the rich officials in the community who had not taken a role in Zionist endeavors, especially members of CIRA. They also considered approaching some of the Sephardic Jews—who had, in the Emergency Campaign, participated for the first time in considerable manner in the work of reconstruction of Palestine—and some well-known Jewish politicians and writers, such as Enrique Dickmann and Alberto Gerchunoff. Both Gesang and Nissensohn considered the visit of Nahum Sokolow imperative for launching the forthcoming campaign of Keren Hayesod and for starting a branch of the Jewish Agency in Argentina.[105]

Leib Jaffe stressed in letters to Sokolow, who was undecided about the profit of such a trip, the importance of the visit for Zionist propaganda and for its financial results. Sokolow, in reply to Jaffe, clearly expressed what he thought of Zionism in South America:

> For these matters [political value and Jewish Agency in Argentina] I do not have the moral right to move away from Europe for such a long time [three months] and to go to the end of the world. As a political factor, the value of Argentina and of all of South America is not too much, and spiritual help they can probably get from someone else, as is the case with respect to the foundation of the Jewish Agency. . . . But we have to make clear to Mr. Gesang without waiting for his letter, under what conditions I am prepared to travel to South America. If it is not possible to obtain the sum of 40,000 pounds sterling, there is no justification for me to make the trip now.[106]

Already at the beginning of February 1930 the economic crisis profoundly touched most sectors of the Argentine population, obviously not to the exclusion of the Jews. Moreover, Argentine Jews had only a few months earlier sent 300,000 pesos (about two thirds of the 40,000 pounds sterling sum) for the Emergency Campaign. When presenting these arguments Gesang added that Sokolow's trip might be financially useful and also might instill a new spirit in Zionist work.[107] Only in September did Sokolow agree to make the trip to South America. However, by that time important developments had occurred in Argentina. Yrigoyen's second term in office ended abruptly when the Conservative forces in the country led a successful revolution (September 6). With the toppling of the Radical party's administration a new era started for Argentina. Along with most of the Western countries, Argentina underwent a period of intense nationalism with numerous and violent antisemitic eruptions during the 1930s and throughout World War II. At that juncture, right after the September coup, leaders of the FSA, just as many other Argentines, had an expectant attitude. The new government—the military and the conservatives—knew nothing about Zionism. The extremely good relations the Jews had had with both Radical presidents—Yrigoyen and Alvear—could continue, but the issue was still an open question. Moreover, there was an economic crisis, and farmers were once more distressed by a decrease in the price of cereal. Jewish colonists, except in part those in the province of Entre Ríos, were deeply affected. The FSA, dramatically, had to cancel Sokolow's trip.[108]

Palestine had also been affected by the economic crisis and riots at the end of the 1920s. The Passfield White Paper of 1930, which echoed the view that immigration, land purchase, and settlement policies of the Zionist Organization were prejudicial to Arab interests, contended that restrictions would be imposed on the growth of the Jewish National Home. At this point, already at the beginning of 1931, the FSA was urged to accept the request of the actions committee of the Zionist Organization that Sokolow visit the South American communities. The Zionist Organization further appealed to those communities to carry out an especially energetic Keren Hayesod campaign, in spite of the difficulties.[109]

Due to the enormous pressures on the Zionist Organization, exerted mainly by the economic conditions in Palestine and the White Paper, the Zionist leadership in Europe was in need of greater sums of money to allocate to its various projects. This situation partly justifies Sokolow's financial conditions for his trip to Argentina. When the economic situation became critical, the Zionist Organization decided to encourage the trip, considering that Sokolow would induce the Jews in Argentina, in spite of their present situation, to contribute to the Palestine funds.[110] However, the argument that Sokolow's presence would stir the Jewish community and would transmit the national message through the appropriate communication and propaganda means to which the FSA would resort for the occasion, was not convincing enough. Because they had had no first-hand contact with the South American communities, the top Zionist leaders in Europe had only a vague idea of the situation there. The issue for a national education program was raised by Leib Jaffe in 1923. But Jaffe was a lonely voice that favored Sokolow's trip not only for its possible financial benefits but also for its long-range effects in educating Jewish generations.[111] The episode of Sokolow's prospective trip to Argentina illustrated the great need in the Argentine community of messengers who would inspire the Jewish population with the national and educational ideals of the Jewish people.

The riots in Palestine in 1929 proved that Argentine Jewry was seriously concerned with the situation of the Jews living in the National Home. While not all sectors of the general population in Argentina decried the riots—conspicuously enough, an important Catholic weekly wrote against the right of the Jews to settle in the land[112]—the incident created a major response among the Jews there. An Emergency Campaign was proclaimed a few days after news was received from Palestine. At a meeting held during the first days of the events in Palestine, which was attended by Jews from all sectors, Ashkenazim and Sephardim, Zionists and non-Zionists, a resolution was passed:[113]

> United Argentine Jewry declares solemnly that Palestine is a question of life and death for the Jews; it proclaims a universal campaign for the collection of one million pesos, to be handed over to the Jewish Agency, the Argentine contributing towards that universal fund one million pesos, to be raised in cash until September 30th.
> Argentinian Jewry believes in the urgent need of a World Jewish Congress to be convened by the Jewish Agency, to be held in New York, in order to eliminate any trace of doubt with regard to the realization of the Balfour Declaration, and for the purpose of demanding from the governments that they should honor their statements and agreements.

Furthermore, among the resolutions adopted at this public meeting we find the determination to assess every Jew in Buenos Aires and the interior in accordance with his ability to contribute to the Emergency Fund and to demand additional contributions from those who did not conform to their assessment (Art. 1, 2). No Jew was to be omitted from the list of contributors (Art. 5); women and children should also join the list (Art. 6); and quotas were imposed on societies and groups (Art. 3). Other American countries should be informed that Sephardim in Argentina were united with Ashkenazim for Palestine work (Art. 10).

They fell far short of the 1,000,000 pesos goal. However, in spite of its being a year of bad climate for the colonists and the monetary crisis' being already felt in the country, Argentine Jewry gathered over 313,000 pesos for the Emergency Fund.[114]

The events in Palestine also deeply touched the more assimilated groups of Argentine Jewry. In the Sociedad Hebraica Argentina (hereafter SHA)—a cultural organization that promoted intellectual activities and created bonds between the Jewish community and Argentine intellectuals, whose members were professionals, students, and Jews adapted to the language and norms of the country—a climax was reached. The SHA was formed in 1926 through the fusion of former organizations of similar character; prominent among the latter was Asociación Juventud Israelita Argentina, or Juventud. Some ardent Zionists had been members of Juventud and SHA, but the general policy of the first and to a certain degree also of the second was one of noninvolvement concerning issues of Jewish religion, race, or patriotism.[115] SHA's assimilationist tendencies were interrupted—with respect to Jewish "nationalism," at least—in 1929. It was not without discussions among its leaders that the SHA turned from a position of mere spectators to semiactive assistants.[116]

The main interests of the Zionist activists in Argentina were geared to the financial success of the campaigns for the Jewish National Home. Education was a topic brought up at every land conference in the country, but resolutions on that topic were not fully heeded. Furthermore, early attempts in the 1920s to promote trade between Argentine firms and their Israel counterparts were maintained on a low key. The economic crisis put a parenthesis around most of these operations, which were resumed some years later, and developed into heavy trade in the postwar period, especially since the establishment of the State of Israel.[117]

The roots for the inertia and apathy of the Zionist leaders concerning Hebrew and national education are to be found in the general atmosphere of a cosmopolitan country, especially in the city of Buenos Aires. Cosmopolitanism had produced a violent reaction among certain sectors of the people that resulted in particular in attacks against the Jewish schools, claiming they were of an anti-Argentine character. In 1909 Ricardo Rojas launched a sharp attack on the cultural impact of foreign immigration and reproduced the prejudiced argumentation against the Jewish schools. But Rojas was not alone in proclaiming the imperious necessity of a major restructuring of the education program. A generation of writers arose with him. Patterns of education were thus revised. National heroes were exalted; national pride became a central point in all schools in the country.[118]

Jews were not an exception to the new wave in education. Very soon Jewish children were absorbed by Argentine culture, as expected by those who proposed the change. Even the family of Jacobo Joselevich, president of FSA, who had been a member of Ahad Ha'Am's Bene Moshe, and founder of Zionism in Argentina, had a hostile reaction to Judaism. Children of Jews, as all others, were educated in a spirit of extreme love for their fatherland Argentina and its national heroes. This made Leib Jaffe remark in 1923.[119] "The children are educated with extreme love for their Argentine fatherland; the lessons in history here are nothing but passionate speeches about Argentine heroes, and about acts of heroism for their fatherland. The people of the South know very well the art of rhetoric."

Hebrew instruction, still not well developed in Argentina, was no competition. Assimilation via education was bearing its fruits. Zionists in Argentina, conscious of their failure in promoting Jewish national education among Jewish youngsters, were evidently helpless in front of the strong national revival in Argentine education. Some of the Hebraist circles blamed Zionists for their apathy in this respect.[120]

In 1929, shortly before the Palestine riots, according to the organ of the FSA only 700 of the 20,000 Jewish families in Buenos Aires contributed to the Keren Hayesod. "Where are the 19,300?" it asked. Evidently, they were not actively participating in the national movement. There were, doubtless, some who proceeded to Palestine, but the ample majority of the Jewish immigrants had decided to remain in Argentina. All the various communities built synagogues and acquired cemeteries. Furthermore, the investment in the building of two pavilions of the Hospital Israelita was a telling sign that they were there to stay. The above-mentioned enterprises, as well as the preparation for the reception of large numbers of new immigrants after the world war were, in the eyes of many active Jews, more important than the reconstruction of a Jewish Palestine. Many of the above-mentioned 700 were among those who participated in the latter projects. On the other hand, most of those engaged in the bolstering of the Jewish community in Buenos Aires, were among the 19,300.

A large number of the Jews in Argentina had been affected by years of propaganda from the Zionist circles. Their interest in Jewish survival and the sentiment of brotherhood they felt for all Jews were major factors in producing the response it did in 1929. By 1930 Zionism had already made attempts, some successful, of recruiting important individuals from among the Sephardic communities, the West European Jews of CIRA, and some Jews in Argentine political and cultural life, who had some influence among the Jews in their own circles. A branch of the WIZO, the Organización Sionista Femenina de la Argentina (OSFA), was founded, which occupied itself in establishing an agricultural school for women in Afulah (Palestine).

But Zionism was far from conquering all Jews in Argentina by 1930. Besides the nonaffiliated Jews, there was ambivalence towards Zionism among Sephardim, *Yahudim*, and other assimilationist groups of importance, such as SHA. Sephardim were rightly opposed to the Yiddish utilized by most FSA delegates, although the largest Sephardic groups by 1930 still utilized Arabic assiduously. The localism of Sephardim and their suspicions of Ashkenazim, made their collaboration in Zionist goals with the Ashkenazim difficult. On the other hand, the West European Jews of CIRA saw a serious competition in FSA because of the latter's growing prestige. Furthermore, by 1930 most of their leading members were engaged in institutions for an upbuilding of the Argentine Jewish community that had a clear non-Zionist ideology. Likewise, SHA had a non-Zionist position, opposing all types of political activity.

The political Labor Zionist parties also entered the picture in this period. Zeire Zion and Hitachdut started the Hechalutz movement, which promoted the migration of some groups of young idealists to Palestine. Poale Zion, after its division in 1922, was weakened. But by 1930 the right wing of the party was gathering strength. Upon the unification of Poale Zion with Zeire Zion in 1932, they would start a period of intense activity in Argentina.

The communist Jews were totally opposed to Zionism. Zionists were also threatened by the Procor organization's settlement of Jews in Birobidzhan and did everything possible to dissuade Jews from contributing to their campaigns and listening to their message.

The Leftist Parties

With the arrival of large numbers of Jewish workers from Russia after 1905 the areas of Jewish settlement, especially Once, became the stage for their political activities. Most of them were young people, mainly bachelors, who fled Russia in the aftermath of the abortive revolt against the tsar. Their socialist ideology was what they had in common, though they differed in particulars that during those days of ferment and protest constituted dividing walls between the factions. Socialists, Labor Zionists, Bundists, socialist territorialists, and anarchists settled in the same areas. Their activities, in contrast to what they had experienced in Russia, were now carried on openly.

We have already described those groups with a Zionist orientation, and have also mentioned some major developments in the Argentine workers' movements in previous chapters. In addition, there were Jewish groups representing the various political ideologies. Soon every group considered that the mere spreading of leaflets with party propaganda and adhering to demonstrations organized by the general socialist and anarchist workers in Buenos Aires was not enough. They thus printed their own organs of opinion with articles expounding their respective ideologies and explaining to the Jewish workers what in their eyes were abuses committed by the bourgeoisie against the working class. Most of these journals included sections on literature and poetry in an effort to raise the cultural level of the Yiddish-speaking immigrant worker.

The editors of these political periodicals were young immigrants imbued with enthusiasm for their fight for freedom, justice, and emancipation of the workers. Their circles were small, but their desire to spread higher ideals was strong. News about the workers' movements in and outside the country was also printed in these periodicals. Their Jewish character was not only evident in the language. They published poems, feuilletons, and news on Jewish themes. Local issues such as the fight against white slavery and some aspects of Jewish communal life in Argentina were of special concern. These periodicals had a positive influence among Jewish workers, for whom, in many cases, it was their major cultural source.

During the decade commencing in 1905, as mentioned, the anarchists were the dominant influence among workers in Argentina. There were various anarchist groups, with slightly different ideological emphases, though the prevailing orientation was anarchocommunist. A small number of Jewish workers, many of whom had previously lived in London, formed a society called Arbeter Freind with the purpose of spreading the anarchist views among the Jewish proletariat. Soon thereafter, in 1907, they published *Das Arbeter Lebn*, a monthly directed by A. Schapira. It lasted only a few months. In 1908, under the initiative of Pedro Sprinberg and E. Edelstein, another anarchist monthly, *Lebn un Freiheit*, was published. It also lasted only a few short months. In 1909 Jewish anarchists wrote a page in Yiddish in the otherwise Spanish-written anarchist daily *La Protesta*. This fact clearly reflects on the positive interest of the anarchist movement in the linguistic groups and the ideological binding among them, whether Jewish or not. These Yiddish publications also reveal the cooperation of the Jewish groups with local anarchists. Moreover, their anarchocommunist philosophy, coupled with forceful antiparliamentarianism, opposition to social democracy, nonrecognition of government or law, and their denial of religion and fatherland made it difficult for the Jewish anarchists to develop a working relation with other anarchist linguistic groups, especially the Spanish and Italian. Still, the fact that Yiddish was spoken to such a large extent in the immigrant Jewish neighborhoods, where the whole character and spirit of Jewish culture and life was so pervasive resulted in some joint actions between Jewish anarchists and Jewish workers of other ideological positions. Under the early influence of Poale Zion, some anarchists in Buenos Aires developed a sympathy for Labor Zionism.

During the early years of the century many Jewish immigrants in Argentina were attracted to socialism. A few even attained prominent positions in the Socialist party. Thus Enrique Dickmann, as well as his brother Adolfo, were repeatedly elected to Congress, and to the Concejo Deliberante (Municipal Council) of Buenos Aires, as candidates in the Socialist ticket. As noted above, most of the members of the Socialist party were foreigners, and their leaders saw the need to propagandize among the various linguistic groups in order eventually to strengthen the party. Thus in January 1907 a group of Jewish workers founded the Jewish social-democrat organization Avangard in Argentina. With the ideals of the East European Bund in mind, their goals were to spread the socialist principals and ideals of democracy among the Jewish workers, to awaken their international instincts, and to build bridges with the class-oriented parties of the Christian population in their struggle for economic and political rights.[121]

During the first few years there was a minority group among Jewish Bundists, consisting of the Jewish Iskravtses, who spoke Russian and had assimilatory tendencies, while the majority spoke Yiddish and fought against the cultural assimilation of the Iskravtses. The former separated themselves from Avangard and formed their society, called, almost identically, Centro Avangard. In 1910, when a state of siege was declared, all socialist activities were suspended for six months. After the lifting of the state of siege only the Yiddish-speaking Avangard survived.

The energies of the "Yiddish" Avangard were channeled in several directions. In the political field it worked in close cooperation with the Socialist party. It advocated celebrating May Day and urged the Jewish workers to participate in the demonstrations together with the rest of the working forces, but as a distinctive group. Avangard also propagandized the minimal program of the Socialist party and fought for the suppression of antilabor laws such as the Ley de Residencia and Ley de Orden Social. In the economic field Avangard rallied for the unionization of the Jewish workers, whether in totally Jewish unions, as was the case with cap makers and Jewish bakers, or in the general professional unions.[122]

In addition Avangard saw the need to concentrate on cultural issues and became a vigorous advocate of secular socialist Jewish culture, based on the Yiddish language. Libraries, literary and musical societies, evening courses in Spanish, mathematics, and social hygiene were among the varied cultural activities that Avangard organized. A key element in their cultural program was the publication *Der Avangard*. It started in August 1908 and appeared monthly until December 1909, when, as a consequence of the state of siege it was discontinued. It reappeared in February 1910 until May of that year, when another state of siege and the reaction in the country against socialists and anarchists caused its closing. It reappeared in 1916 and was issued until 1920. Edited first by S. Kaplansky and later by P. Wald, *Der Avangard* not only related to party questions, theories—Argentine socialist problems in the broad sense of the word—but also paid great attention to Yiddish belle-lettres, through which it played a significant role in the development of the Yiddish printed word. During 1911 ten issues of *Unzer Wort* appeared, under the direction of Robert Kogan, a Russian social democrat, and Pinie Wald, a Bundist.

The founders had opted for the name *Avangard* rather than Bund—as the Jewish party was known in Europe and the United States—in order to emphasize their estrangement from all Zionist claims of Jewish peoplehood and nationalism.

They also opposed Argentine nationalism, which put them at odds with the Socialist party of Juan B. Justo. On the occasion of the eightieth birthday of Mendele Mocher Sforim in 1916, Avangard sent a congratulatory message from the "triangular piece of land" (Argentina is shaped as a triangle), thus emphasizing that the organization operated within a geographic area, not a nation.[123]

Nonetheless Avangard showed concern with the fate of the Jewish community in Argentina. It was aware of the existence of antisemitism and noted with realism that the growing nationalism was curtailing the freedoms of all inhabitants, in particular of the Jews.

The Russian Revolution was deeply felt among the Jewish workers' quarters in Buenos Aires. A few weeks after the revolution, on January 1, 1918, a daily, *Di Presse*, was first issued, representing the views of the working masses inclined to secularism and to the struggle for social justice by means of socialism and communism. New centers advocating revised ideologies in accordance with developments in Europe were formed. Loyalties among leftists were divided along the lines of the Second International or the Communist International. During the 1920s many groups within the Jewish population were active in promoting various ideologies. The fact that these centers were all-Jewish, that the language spoken at meetings was Yiddish, and that their periodicals were in this language, testify to the existence of a Jewish sentiment in the midst of these fringe groups of the Jewish community. However, among the more leftist organizations the Jewish component was weaker, while the ideological component was stronger.

In 1920 Avangard was split into two separate groups, one socialist and the other communist. With the continuous flow of Polish Bundists during the 1920s, the socialist Avangard was restructured into the Algemeiner Yiddisher Arbeter Bund and later into the Yiddisher Sotsialist Farband (1929), which published *Sotzialistisher Bletter* (1930). Two small anarchist societies issued periodicals with names identical to their own: *Dos Freie Wort* (1921) and *Di Freiheit Shtime* (1923).

The Jewish communists initiated a period of multifaceted activities during the 1920s. Actually, the Jews played a distinguished role within the new-born Communist party in Argentina, whose members were primarily artisans and petty bourgeois immigrants from Eastern Europe.[124] Since the pillars of the Communist party during that decade were immigrants with sympathy for the USSR, important linguistic groups were formed that developed ample political and cultural activities, including the issuing of periodicals in various languages. The mission of these linguistic groups was to enroll the immigrants in the Communist party. The Jewish section—Yewsektsia—of the Communist party was established with the purpose of propagandizing among the Jews, especially among those dissatisfied with the Socialist party of Juan B. Justo. Indoctrination was done through a variety of publications in Yiddish and through the establishment of secular class schools for children and cultural programs for adults. Practical work concentrated mainly on gathering funds to help the indigent in Soviet Russia and on campaigning for a Jewish settlement in Birobidzhan. As was the case with the young Communist party in Argentina, the Jewish section was influenced more by directives from Moscow than by local developments and needs.[125]

The goal of the Communist periodicals was to spread the party ideals among Jewish workers. *Der Roiter Shtern*, published by the Jewish section of the Communist party in Argentina, was first issued in 1923. One of its editorials said, "The Jewish working masses here in Argentina must lead a struggle against the surrounding reaction, against the Jewish bourgeois press, which misleads the workers and feeds them with bourgeois poison. We must have a daily paper that will lead a work of enlightening within the Jewish proletarians and fight the harmful effects of the street press of every type."[126]

Likewise *Roite Hilf*, a journal published first in 1928 by the Jewish sub-committee of the International Red Relief (MOPR)—Polish subcommittee in the Argentine Section—urged its readers, "The Jewish workers must take part in the great communist manifestation under the banner of MOPR."[127]

Other Communist publications in Yiddish were *Dorem Amerika*, a literary journal (1926), and *Neiewelt* (1927), with a Marxist Revolutionary ideology, both directed by H. Blostein; *Unzer Shul*, put out by the parents committee at the Workers' Schools in 1929; and *Nodl Arbeter*, the official organ of the Union of Tailor Workers in Buenos Aires in 1922.

While the rest of the Jewish community raised funds to help the Jewish victims in Europe, the Jewish communists organized campaigns to help the Soviet Union. In mid-1921, the International Workers Relief Committee for Soviet Russia was formed in Berlin, while branches in all countries collected funds to fight hunger in Russia. The Argentine Communist party instructed the formation of a United Jewish Russian Committee to help the USSR, with the participation of the Communist Avangard, Poale Zion left, the cooperative owning the daily *Di Presse*, and several other cultural and workers' organizations.[128]

The Soviet Union, furthermore, started a project of settling Jews in agricultural colonies in Southern Russia and in Birobidzhan. The reaction of the expanding Jewish communist sector in Argentina immediately followed.[129]

An organization—Procor—consistent with the interests of Gezerd, the Organization for Settlement of Jewish Toilers on Land in Russia, was formed as early as November 1924 by delegates of the leftist Jewish groups in the country. Having had relatively little success during the first year in gathering contributions for the Russian project, Procor was restructured under individual affiliation in February 1926. Its numbers in Buenos Aires grew speedily for a period—from 71 in May 1926 to 1,194 in July 1927—and soon subcommittees were opened in twenty-three localities in the interior, with about 1,000 additional affiliated members. Procor's message found a response mainly among the Jewish proletariat not involved in Zionist activities. During its first years, Procor was also supported by *Mundo Israelita*, a weekly still in its period of struggle before fully accepting a Zionist position, and by some JCA colonists. The daily *Di Presse* was also in favor of the settlement plan in Soviet Russia, as were the various Yiddish communist publications listed above.

During a plenary session in 1927 a heated discussion took place concerning whether Procor should operate under ideological principles or not. H. Blostein, a leading Jewish communist, stressing the proletarian character of Procor, argued that the organization must be led by workers. Only the working class could appreciate the efforts of the Soviets "in favor of the unemployed Jewish masses suffering the consequences of their economic function in the old regime." Miguel Polak, at the time wavering between socialism and communism, did not see the need for an ideological basis for the work in favor of Jewish colonization in the USSR, since, in his opinion, all classes sympathized with the project. The majority opted for giving Procor a class orientation that would attract not only workers and farmers but also the petty bourgeoisie devoid of any ideological posture.[130] However, Procor continued to propagandize among all Jews. This prompted a Zionist reaction. Zionists did not believe the USSR could create a Jewish republic in Birobidzhan. It was too far away from the major areas of Jewish population; the weather and the land were not conducive to the establishment of agricultural colonies; and the sincerity of the Soviet leaders was doubtful.[131]

Procor's propaganda deeply affected some of the most idealist among the communist Jews, who committed themselves to travel to the USSR and settle in the Jewish colonies there. According to Pinie Katz—a member of the first delegation to visit the settlements in Russia—what motivated some Jews to leave Argentina for the Soviet Union was "the character of the Argentine Ishuv [community], which was composed of toilers and idealists of *land-arbeit* [agriculture]. Among those who left . . . there were city workers and colonists' sons, and also the so-called 'candidatos' or land workers who could not wait until the JCA colonized them".[132]

Two fact-finding committees of Procor were sent to Russia, especially to Birobidzhan, in 1929 and 1935 from Buenos Aires. Reciprocally, delegates from Gezerd in Russia visited Argentina to help in the work there, as well as to promote migrations of Jews from the South American continent to the new Jewish settlements in the Soviet Union. Jacob Levin visited Argentina in 1929,

Gina Medem in 1935. For a short period of time *Der Yiddisher Poier,* a monthly issued irregularly, was published in support of the activities of Procor.[133]

Partisans of Procor infiltrated the main institutions of the Jewish community in Buenos Aires, trying to convince the memberships to contribute to their collections, as well as spreading communist propaganda. At the Chevra Keduscha a great struggle took place concerning the amounts of money the institution was to contribute to the campaigns of Keren Hayesod and to Procor. On July 14, 1926, the board of the Chevra Keduscha decided to allocate 5,000 pesos to Keren Hayesod and 500 to Procor "because most of the members of the board have nationalistic sentiments." Protests from members of the institution and reports presented to the board made them double their contribution to Procor, thus reflecting the pressure of the communists in the community.[134]

Demonstrations were organized at social events of the Jewish community. At presentations of the Jewish theater, which concluded with the singing of *Hatikva,* Jewish communists made noise and whistled loudly, provoking the antagonism of the rest of the audience. Banquets were organized for the day of Yom Kippur, as well as affronts in synagogues. Zionists from all sectors, except the leftist Poale Zionists, responded with an avalanche of articles in the Jewish press and with lectures in public gatherings warning the public against contributing to Procor. They denounced Procor's virulent anti-Zionism and its inchoate communist designs. *Semanario Hebreo,* a Spanish weekly with Zionist goals, ardently fought against Procor, repeatedly cautioning that the monies Procor collected were not sent directly to Russia, but 83 percent of it was used locally for anti-Zionist propaganda. Furthermore, *Semanario Hebreo* warned the heads of the Talmud Torahs and synagogues in Buenos Aires of the deviousness of some advocates of Procor who attended High Holy Day Services, hoping to create a positive image of their religious concern.[135]

After the return of the delegation of Procor to Russia in 1929, the movement gained many new members and contributors. A full report was published in Yiddish stating its findings and impressions about the colonization project in Soviet Russia. Various newspapers and magazines published by leftist organizations, all of them in Yiddish, described with glowing words the future of the Jews in Birobidzhan. The Zionists, with the exception of the leftist Poale Zionists, reacted even more strongly against this new wave of attacks against their own ideals. They strongly denied "all the fantastic stories about that Gan Eden [Paradise], which the friends of Soviet Russia are spreading" and appealed to the hearts of the Jews with Zionist inclinations by denouncing "brutal, senseless, and sadist persecutions" against Zionists, "even against the Communist Hashomer Hazair."[136]

Contributions continued to come in, many, if not most, from Jews anxious to help fellow Jews in the Soviet Union. However, the executive leaders of Procor launched an all-out ideological campaign early in 1930. During a period of growing controversy in Jewish circles they denounced everything and everyone opposed to the USSR and communism, including English imperialism, the opposition press, and the socialist organizations and broke relations with *Di Presse*, which had till then supported them. Pressures were mounting to declare Procor officially a communist endeavor. In spite of warnings by the moderate Jewish press, a Congress of Procor in April 1930 voted for a resolution requiring, since the Colonization project was in the USSR, that all members of Procor sympathize with the Soviet regime. Donations, however, were accepted from everyone. This resolution set the record straight and clearly defined the ideological division within the Jewish community. The noncommunist groups, including *Mundo Israelita*, declined further support.[137]

After the revolution of 1930 and during the repression of Generals Uriburu and Justo, the communist Yiddish press became even more radical and attacked its opponents without scruples. *Roiter Shtern, Neiewelt, Unzer Shul*, and also *Pioner*, a monthly children's magazine, published vitriolic articles defaming not only the bourgeois Talmud Torahs but also the secular schools and the Borochov schools for not preparing the children for the battles against fascism and unemployment in Argentina. In their eyes the Borochov schools trained its students for English imperialism and a Palestinian utopia, while the workers' children should be taught to condemn the imperialist preparations of war against the proletarian fatherland, the USSR.[138] Even *Di Presse*, which during the 1920s had supported all the communist endeavors, including Procor, was now violently decried as a bitter enemy of the communist press. In fact, *Di Presse* was moving slightly toward socialism but still maintained a proletarian posture. In their zealousness in pursuing the mandates originating in the USSR, the Jewish Communist leaders pursued an anti-Zionist, antinationalist, and antisocialist line that allowed no deviations (for more on the leftist groups see chs. 6, 8).[139]

Concern for Jewish Education

Formal education is a fundamental means for transmitting specific values. Jewish immigrants have by and large been concerned with the Jewish education of their children in their new environments. However, this concern did not always reach the point of turning into an active force for promoting the teaching of Jewish subjects to the generations born overseas. The Jewish urban immigration to Argentina is an example of a group's indifference to Jewish instruction at the turn of the century.

Regarding Jewish education in Argentina, there was a difference between the needs and demands of the Jewish agricultural settlers and those who established themselves in the large cities. The colonists immediately requested the Jewish Colonization Association (JCA) authorities to help them in establishing schools so that their children could be taught Jewish religion, literature, history, and languages.[1] The city dwellers, however, were preoccupied with matters other than the Jewish education of their young.

At the turn of the century Argentina was developing a national system of education. In 1884, when the Ley de Educación Común Number 1420 was passed by Congress, education became secular, universal, and compulsory at public expense.[2] The Jewish immigrants profited from this situation that allowed their children to receive an elementary education and that permitted them to pursue their more immediate necessities of earning a living and adjusting to the ways of their adoptive country. For the vast majority of the new immigrants to the cities Jewish education was a matter that would be tackled once the Jewish population grew in numbers and resources. Moreover, the fact that the Jews who had settled in Buenos Aires before 1890 had not contem-

147

plated creating special courses in Jewish subjects for their young made the process even more difficult for those who moved to the city after that year.

Education in Argentina was not comparable to the highly developed national systems already adopted in several Central and West European countries. Nonetheless, it was far superior to what the Jewish immigrants had experienced in their native towns. Most of the Jews who arrived in Argentina had been educated in Eastern Europe in a *heder* (lit., "room")—a one-room school, usually the home of the *melammed* (schoolmaster). Here children—various ages simultaneously—were taught portions of the Hebrew Bible (Old Testament), elements of prayer, and other religious traditions, together with the rudiments of arithmetic and composition. The room was generally small and decrepit, and the *melammed* usually incompetent. Some gifted students aspired to a more intensive Talmudic preparation in a *yeshiva*.

Jews who arrived from the Ottoman Empire had a similar background, though with even less contact with Western culture. The boys learned—usually by heart—portions of the Pentateuch, the commentary of Rashi, selections from the Bible and the Talmud, and other legalistic texts in dark and somber schools. Due to poverty and a lack of teachers and appropriate didactical methods, not all the boys managed to learn how to count and write. The Alliance Israélite Universelle started, at the end of the nineteenth century, a net of schools in various parts of the area, thus also introducing the basic secular studies into many Sephardic communities. However, not all parents sent their children to these schools, sometimes due to religious prejudices but more often because of insufficient funds.[3]

Jewish education was only the concern of a few officials in Buenos Aires. The fact that most immigrants had an intense and all-pervading desire for "making America," thus devoting all their efforts to the attainment of a solid economic situation, was a cause of their unconcern for the Jewish education for their children. Moreover, those who came as young bachelors, with no family to support, were understandably not worried about educating children. Most Jewish immigrants, however, did want to give their children an education that would provide them with the knowledge and skills enabling them to pursue a professional career or allowing them to build a secure position in commerce or industry.

The urban Jewish immigrant found no obstacles to obtaining a secular education for his children since the legislation of the country had made it compulsory and free. However, the development of Jewish schools with the specific goal of imparting instruction in Jewish subjects was not mandatory. Not all Jews felt the need for such schools. A study of these schools will indicate the extent to which the Jewish immigrant population in Buenos Aires was interested in the strengthening of Jewish identity in their children and the extent to which they were prepared to make sacrifices for the furtherance of that identity.

The Jewish schools in Buenos Aires throughout the period ending in 1930 can be divided roughly in two categories: religious and secular. To the first category belong the Talmud Torahs, or schools that stressed the teaching of religious law and customs, Bible, languages such as Hebrew, and (depending on the origin of the members of the synagogue sponsoring the school) Yiddish and Arabic. The secular schools, on the other hand, were strongly based on the ideology of the party or society sponsoring them. There were, thus, Poale Zionist, Yiddishist, communist, and Worker's schools in Buenos Aires sponsored by different groups of Jews.[4]

The Religious Schools

The first type of Jewish school established in Buenos Aires was the Escuela Particular Primaria (later Talmud Torah Harischono), started by the *Hevra Poale Zedek* in 1891. This was an elementary day school, where the students followed the Argentine educational curriculum besides a series of Jewish subjects taught in Yiddish. The instruction concentrated in the Spanish program, but two hours a day were devoted to Jewish studies. It did not however, attract large numbers of Jewish students. Even the parents, including many on the board of the school itself, preferred to send their children to the state schools. Actually, the state schools were modern at the time, and the national program was taught with more competence. Furthermore the Jewish school buildings compared quite unfavorably with those of the national ones.

This Talmud Torah school functioned thanks to the efforts of a few communal officials and a small number of idealists and learned Jews. For a long period—until 1906—it was the only institution offering children a semisystematic program of Jewish studies. Only when the large stream of immigration from Eastern Europe—following the Russo-Japanese War and the abortive revolt against tsarism in 1905—reached Argentina and settled in Buenos Aires, were new efforts made to found additional Jewish schools. Thus in 1906 the Talmud Torah Dr. T. Herzl was founded, and during the same year the Zionist society Liga Dr. Herzl founded its own school. The latter had to close after a few years due to financial difficulties. In 1911 the Linat Hazedek society opened a Talmud Torah in the center of Buenos Aires. Between 1908 and 1910 three Talmud Torahs were started in the neighborhoods of Boca y Barracas, Constitución, and Caballito, where a large number of Jewish immigrant workers from Eastern Europe had settled.

Each of these Talmud Torahs was sponsored by a small synagogue formed by some of the more traditionally inclined Jews in the neighborhood. The synagogue itself provided a substantial part of the budget of the school. Thus, for example, the Talmud Torah Harischono expenses, which were always quite limited, were covered during 1899 in the following way: 28 percent from tuition paid by the students' parents; 20 percent from members' dues; 16 percent from the lease of one room; 18 percent from donations and contributions for honors at the synagogue. The rest was gathered by extraordinary means such as theater shows and High Holy Days profits.[5]

Among Ashkenazim only a small number of children of grammar school age attended the Talmud Torahs. In 1903 the Talmud Torah Harischono, which offered courses corresponding to the first four grammar school years in the state program, had a total of only 35 students.[6] By 1908 the two schools operating in the capital had at most 240 students, and by 1910 four schools gave instruction to 400 to 500 students.[7] Nonetheless, the situation of the Talmud Torahs was not secure, and there were constant difficulties in attracting new students. Talmud Torah Dr. Herzl had 140 students in 1914 but had difficulties the following year in reaching that same number.[8] In 1922, in spite of having 42 new students, total registration amounted to only 107. Two years later, out of 108 enrolled, an average of only 83 students attended regularly.[9] The following years, the total was reduced to 75 in 1925 and 78 in 1926.[10] In the meantime enrollment in the Talmud Torah Harischono school increased to 180 in 1927.[11] When in September 1927 these two Talmud Torahs decided to join forces in order to strengthen their schools and also to build a synagogue in the central Jewish section of Once, the new school thus formed had 250 students in two sections, morning and afternoon.[12]

As a consequence of a report of the general situation of the Jewish community—including the state of Jewish education—prepared by Rabbi Samuel Halphon for the JCA in 1909, the *Cursos Religiosos Israelitas* were created in 1911, with the purpose of offering courses in Judaism to the sons of immigrants throughout the country.[13] The JCA agreed to subsidize these Talmud Torahs or Cursos with the explicit desire that the pupils' parents, committees, and boards of each one of the schools contribute in increasing proportions to meet the yearly budgets. It was expected that the local school committees would progressively fully support their institutions, and that the JCA subventions would be gradually reduced.

Table 4 shows that throughout the period 1911–30 there was an increasing participation of the local committees in the expenses of the schools. While in 1911 the local contribution amounted to only 6.5 percent of the total educational budget, in 1912 it already reached 25 percent and in 1913 34 percent. For the period 1915–19 local contributions roughly equaled those coming from abroad. In 1926 they amounted to 60 percent and reached 73 percent in 1929, and 84 percent in 1930. The net contributions of Argentine Jewry to the schools were constantly increasing during the period. However, the total budget, which attained its peak of 304,864.18 pesos in 1923, decreased during the last years of the decade and reached the low mark of 238,547.04 pesos in 1930. The monetary figures clearly demonstrate that the Jews in Argentina were concerned more and more with the expenses of religious education for their young. The money coming in from European Jewish organizations did not increase during the World War I years, but after the conflagration was over till 1923 even these amounts increased to two and three times the sums received before and during the war. The local figures grew, nonetheless, in larger proportions. During the mid-1920s the JCA authorities, who had supported many educational and religious projects in Argentina, decided that the time had come for the Jewish communities in the country to organize and carry the burden of their continuity and support the cultural activities by themselves.[14] Thus the local communities, which had been increasingly assuming the re-

Table 4

Cursos Religiosos Israelitas: Number of Cursos, Students, and Teachers
and Budget for the Entire Argentine Republic

	Cursos functioning						Budget (in pesos)		
	Cities	Colonies	Towns	Total					
Year	a	b	c	d	Students	Teachers	JCA	Local	Total
1911	7	—	—	7	470	7	20,483.41	1,432.00	21,915.41
1912	15	—	—	15	1,089	17	27,939.22	9,261.90	37,201.12
1913	23	—	—	23	1,106	26	38,216.95	20,091.45	58,308.40
1914	25	—	—	25	2,102	29	40,345.65	27,568.80	67,914.45
1915	25	—	—	25	2,435	30	34,722.90	32,391.65	67,114.55
1916	28	—	—	28	2,757	33	36,380.23	34,202.25	70,582.48
1917	26	13	—	39	3,710	48	40,743.90	41,088.00	81,831.90
1918	25	17	—	42	3,842	51	49,957.90	49,619.00	99,576.90
1919	28	17	—	45	5,012	59	57,906.52	48,281.00	116,187.52
1920	32	49	—	81	5,180	96	78,356.78	84,394.60	162,751.38
1921	33	47	8	88	5,508	107	110,278.97	126,317.95	236,596.92
1922	33	54	12	99	6.087	112	129,763.15	155,531.57	285,294.72
1923	25	57	11	93	6,129	112	133,711.16	171,153.02	304,864.18
1924	29	57	13	99	5,171	109	125,686.59	167,429.65	293,116.24
1925	23	53	11	87	5,692	97	122,368.45	167,906.77	290,275.22
1926	23	52	12	87	4,985	96	116,365.50	164,931.20	281,296.70
1927	24	47	12	83	4,710	92	100,654.67	167,617.15	268,271.82
1928	22	45	12	79	4,447	94	83,760.46	186,296.05	270,056.51
1929	22	45	12	79	4,064	96	72,254.69	198,371.85	270,626.54
1930	24	40	11	75	4,331	88	37,416.97	201,130.07	238,547.04

Source: Jedidia Efrón, "La obra escolar en las colonias judías,"
in *50 años de colonización en la Argentina* (Buenos Aires, 1939), 250,
261. Also found in M. Meiern Laser *Dos Yiddishe Shulvezn in Argentina* (Buenos Aires, 1948), 59.

sponsibility for religious education, were confronted with the necessity of taking full responsibility.

Moreover, the table shows that the proportions between the numbers of schools, students, and teachers maintained certain uniformity. There is an average of about 1.2 teachers for each school and about 50 students per teacher. In most of these schools the instructor taught different groups of students in the morning and afternoon, thus the average number of students per class must have been near 30. Again, we note a strong increase in the number of students in the post-World War I period, with a maximum of 6,129 in 1923. For the balance of the decade these numbers sharply decreased, though not uniformly. In 1930 only 4,331 students were enrolled in the Cursos.

The greatest number of students, schools, and teachers, as well as the largest budget, was reached in the postwar years. This was due to the relatively large immigration of Jews into Argentina during those years. The lack of continuity in many of these schools, and the decreasing number of students attending them are telling arguments for the poor impact this type of religious education had upon the vast majority of the Jews established in Argentina. They attest once more to the secular character of Jewish identification among large numbers of Jewish immigrants and to the secularization process in Jewish life during the 1920s. This conclusion is further bolstered by the fact that most of the numbers of students and teachers are somewhat inflated. The figures given in the annual *rapports* of the JCA were always lower than those of table 4.[15]

One of the crucial causes for the weak state of Jewish education in the 1920s in Argentina was the teachers' situation. In many cases the teachers were Jewish immigrants who could not earn a living in other occupations. Due to the extremely low salaries paid to teachers at the Cursos Religiosos and Talmud Torahs, the most capable ones left the profession for more lucrative positions. In 1917 the teachers of Jewish schools in Buenos Aires formed a union called Agudat Hamorim. The main objectives of the Agudat Hamorim were to improve the moral situation at the Jewish schools in the country, to tighten the organization of these schools, to defend the economic interests of the teachers, and to promote interest among the Jewish population for Jewish education. They were opposed to the *heder* type of school and advocated modern institutions of learning.[16] They deplored the fact that within the Jewish community the most "intelligent representatives busy themselves with all national, social and communal daily questions, but never with Jewish education."[17]

In 1919 and 1920 the Agudat Hamorim went on strike for six months. Their demands were in accordance with the above-mentioned objectives of the union. Only after a long struggle with the boards of the schools were the teachers able to achieve their justified petitions. The Jewish press in the city kept the public informed of the slow dealings between teachers and school committees, but in spite of this effort those concerned with the problem were not able to awaken the Jewish population to the need of parochial education.[18] The long-fought battle between teachers and schools further attests to what priority Jewish education held among the leadership of the Buenos Aires Jewish community. On the other hand, the Jewish teachers were supported by a large part of the Jewish working force in Buenos Aires. Their solidarity was strictly founded on an identification with fellow workers in their struggle for better salaries and working conditions. In the special case of the Jewish teachers this also meant the struggle for recognition of their professional worth and indispensability within the Jewish community. The cap makers—an almost totally Jewish profession in Buenos Aires during the 1920s—supported the teachers "in the economic war they led against the school committees . . . and . . . ask[ed] the members [of their union] who have children enrolled in the [Jewish] schools, not to send them."[19]

The program of studies both at the Cursos Religiosos and at the Talmud Torahs included the study of the Hebrew and Yiddish languages, with more or less emphasis on one or the other according to the school, readings from the Siddur (Hebrew Prayer Book), blessings for various occasions, and stories and legends from the Bible. The program proposed by Rabbi Halphon, who headed the Cursos Religiosos, was divided into three levels spanning six or seven years. Probably a very small number of the students went through the whole program. In all likelihood most of them attended the Cursos for only two or three years.

The history courses strongly emphasized the Biblical and Second Commonwealth periods in Jewish history. Only in the last year of studies was the student confronted with the dispersion of the Jewish people after the destruction of the Second Temple. During that last year a survey of eighteen centuries of Jewish history was taught. Analogously, the Talmud Torahs Dr. Herzl and Harischono, upon uniting in 1927, issued a program that stressed Yiddish and Hebrew languages, traditions, prayers, and biblical history. In the last year was taught Jewish history after the destruction of the Second Temple and up to the twentieth century. In other words, the basic concept for Jewish education at the Cursos Religiosos and Talmud Torahs was that the Jews were a religious entity with roots in ancient times that deserved to be studied.[20] No major effort was made to adapt those values to the open environment of Argentine society. Furthermore, the Jewish children remained unchallenged by events in Jewish history of the nineteenth and twentieth centuries that touched their personal lives more directly. Moreover, the student's association with the Jewish community in Israel during the Second Commonwealth period remained a big question mark in his mind because of the gap of over eighteen centuries in his studies. On the other hand, lessons in Argentine history at the state school were emphatically taught, with the purpose of Argentinizing the large numbers of immigrants in the country, and these left a powerful imprint on the Jewish immigrant's child.

By 1909 many Jewish officials were alarmed at the widening abyss between parents and children in Argentina, due to the education received by the latter in the national schools, which estranged them from Judaism and the Jewish people. In many cases, due to the patriotic education in the state schools and the aspirations of the Argentine elite in power to assimilate all foreigners, the sons of Jewish immigrants were "even ashamed of Jews and of everything Jewish . . . Phrases such as 'You are Jewish, but I am Argentine,' were commonplace in family vocabulary, even in genuine Jewish homes."[21] Ricardo Rojas's *La restauración nacionalista* in 1909 advocated a strong revision of public education in the country in order to impede the alleged destruction of the Argentine cultural heritage by the massive immigration. It was a stimulus for stressing the national cultural values and condemning cosmopolitanism as the antithesis of civilization in state schools.[22] The strong nationalist character of the Argentine schools was also felt by other immigrant groups, notably the Italian, which constituted the most numerous one. Robert F. Foerster summarized the documentation in 1919 saying that "in the public schools the training of the children is intensely nationalistic—to a degree rare in other countries."[23]

The different Sephardic communities had their separate Talmud Torahs, each reflecting its own attitude toward Jewish learning. The emphasis in Jewish studies was, among the Sephardic communities in Buenos Aires, directly proportional to their attachment to religious traditions and observances. The oldest, smallest, and also the most assimilated of the Sephardic groups in the Argentine capital, that is, the Moroccan one, encountered the greatest obstacles to starting its own courses. Only in 1917 did the Congregación Israelita Latina consider initiating Hebrew courses.[24] Their Talmud Torah was only created in 1922, after five years during which the idea remained in oblivion. Courses included Hebrew language, traditions, prayers, and Bible.[25] However, the progressive estrangement of many members of this community from Jewish sources and traditions is also evident from the participation of the children in the school. While in 1925 it was functioning relatively well, giving instruction to about sixty students, three years later the numbers decreased drastically to only six. In spite of the great efforts made by the board to revive the Talmud Torah, it did not constitute a very popular activity of the Moroccan Jewish community in Buenos Aires.[26]

The Turkish- or Ladino-speaking Jews who migrated from Constantinople, Smyrna, Rhodes, and so on and settled in the Villa Crespo neighborhood in the capital had founded in 1914 the Kahal Kadosh and Talmud Torah La Hermandad Sefaradí. During the war there were about forty-five students.[27] In 1917 they started receiving a subsidy from the Cursos Religiosos.[28] This school developed during the 1920s. In 1921 it had seventy students, while in the last half of the decade there was an average of ninety students. The language of instruction was Spanish, and little Hebrew was taught.[29]

Much more intense was the instruction given at the Talmud Torahs of the Arabic-speaking Jewish communities. The Damascene and Aleppine Jews opened Talmud Torahs in Barracas and Once, respectively, as soon as there was a fair number of young to start a class. In 1920 both these communities founded their respective main schools, Or Torah and Yesod Hadath, in these same quarters. A third school, Agudat Dodim was formed simultaneously in Flores, consisting basically of Damascene Jews and some Aleppine Jews. These Talmud Torahs conducted their classes in Arabic. The students studied the prayer book, the Pentateuch with the commentary of Rashi, parts of the Mishna, and some Talmud. The Damascene Jews switched to Spanish as the language of instruction earlier than the Aleppine, mainly as a consequence of their close ties with the Cursos Religiosos. The Aleppine remained completely separate from the Cursos.

Hacham Shaul Setton Dabbah, the leader of the Aleppine community, was a zealous defender of orthodoxy and intransigent to changes in the school curriculum. He also controlled the school and taught advanced students in Talmud, with the intention of having them take courses in ritual slaughtering (*shechita*), and ordain them rabbis and cantors (*hachamim* and *hazzanim*). Moreover, Hacham Setton was strongly opposed on religious grounds to the "modernization" of the school, advocated by most of the board, who considered that the Hebrew language should be taught parallel to the children's learning of sacred texts. The *hacham* strongly adhered to the opinion that Hebrew was to be utilized only for sacred purposes and should not be taught as a language for daily and secular use. The conflict between some members of the board and the *hacham* over this issue started in 1928 and caused a big split in the community. At an assembly early in 1929 the argument got out of control and required the intervention of the local police. Nevertheless, during the lifetime of Hacham Setton (d. 1930) nothing was changed in the curriculum of the school. However, modernizing forces were there, and starting in 1930 even Yesod Hadath underwent basic modifications, including the introduction of a course in Hebrew. Eventually, the main language of instruction was changed from Arabic to Spanish.[30]

The program of studies at the schools of the Arabic-speaking Jews in Buenos Aires was thorough. Classes met daily for three to four hours depending on the season of the year, before or after the regular hours at the state schools.[31] The number of students remained very high during the 1920s. Or Torah had 220 in 1922 and 250 in 1930.[32] At Yesod Hadath the 200 students with four teachers in 1921 rose to 300 students and nine teachers in 1924 and to 450 students in 1931.[33] Agudat Dodim had 170 students in 1929.[34]

These schools were supported by voluntary contributions, by pledges of members at the synagogue, and especially by the profits of the sale of kosher meat at the meat markets sponsored by the societies. To help meet the need of the school budgets the boards of the Talmud Torahs made every possible effort to have every parent buy at their meat markets. Strong measures were repeatedly imposed on parents who did not patronize these shops, such as demanding special monthly tuition sums for the education of their children.[35] Indeed, the sale of kosher meat was one of the main sources of income for communal organization of Syrian Jewry before World War I, and the immigrants from these communities maintained this as a source of income for their schools also in Buenos Aires.[36]

With the intention of arousing enthusiasm among the Jewish population in Argentina for Jewish education and having local Jews contribute to its support, Rabbi Halphon—together with leading members of the Congregación Israelita and some other officials in Jewish education in the country—founded in 1917, the Comité Central de Educación Israelita en la República Argentina (also called Vaad Hajinuj). The founders of this Comité Central fought against the indifference of most of the Jews for Jewish education, arguing correctly that the few institutions of Jewish learning in the country were in existence thanks to "the generosity of some European Jews, who, justly alarmed by the negligent state of Hebrew education, did not hesitate to contribute enormous sums during eight consecutive years for the establishment of courses."[37] Until 1930 the Comité Central did not attain outstanding success from the financial point of view. During those thirteen years it was able to collect the sum of 130,000 pesos, which helped cover the deficits in the schools when the JCA gradually curtailed its financial support of the Cursos Religiosos.[38] Moreover, the Comité Central marked the transition from the first period, in which education was supported from abroad while Jews in Argentina remained by and large aloof to this problem to a period in which the Argentine community had to resort to its own resources.

The institutions dedicated to religious education were constantly, during our period, in a state of financial stress. Besides the Cursos Religiosos and the Comité Central, many Talmud Torahs approached the Chevra Keduscha, which already after World War I had become economically powerful, for monetary support of their work.[39] When the JCA, by means of the Cursos Religiosos, discontinued its grants to the Talmud Torahs, most of the latter suffered even more. Only few of the boards of these schools, composed mainly of students' parents, reacted positively to this curtailment and were able to make the schools prosper by means of stronger local contributions in order to prevent their closing.[40]

The Talmud Torahs, especially the Cursos Religiosos, were severely criticized by some sectors of Buenos Aires Ashkenazi Jewry. The orthodox circles considered the Cursos Religiosos too modern, deviating from strict religious teachers and cause for rampant assimilation and irreligiosity. On the other hand the atheists and secular Jews considered that these schools were too religious in their approach to Jewish education and that the concepts taught there were fanatic and backward.[41] Others considered religious instruction to be antidemocratic, and the fact that the Cursos Religiosos received subsidies from Paris (JCA) was regarded as a foreign encroachment in the life of Argentine Jewry.[42] In spite of these criticisms and in spite of their strong limitations, both financial and didactical, the Cursos Religiosos constituted until 1930 the most influential effort in Jewish education in the country.

Secular Jewish Schools

The Talmud Torahs and the Cursos Religiosos were not the only type of Jewish education envisaged by the immigrant parents. True, a large proportion of the latter remained indifferent to Jewish education. However, among those indifferent to religious instruction there were some who advocated a secular approach to Jewish studies. The progressive element along the Jewish workers in Buenos Aires was deeply affected by the events in Russia during the last stages of World War I and was immediately influenced by the movement advocating the creation of secular Jewish schools in Poland and Soviet Russia. A small group, the anarchists, on the other hand, received their inspiration from the (Francisco) Ferrer schools in Spain. It was only after the war that the Jewish secular proletariat in Argentina tackled the problem of giving their children a class education within a Jewish framework.

Since 1884 education in Argentina was officially secular. However, the values taught at the state schools were the values of the dominant class in the country, that is, the bourgeois, Catholic elite. The workers—and in our specific case, the Jewish workers—imbued in their respective political and class ideologies, advocated an instruction for their children that would present the other side of the coin: a secular and class-conscious education. During the 1920s approaches were made, with different political and social outlooks, to fill this gap among the Jewish working class in Argentina.

In 1909 the first Federación Obrera Israelita (Yiddisher Arbeter Verband) was founded—a society for mutual help, which also sponsored cultural activities—having among its objectives the creation of a non-religious school.[43] But the short-lived federation never put this into practice. Other attempts to found modern Jewish schools were made before 1920 in Rosario and in other towns near the Jewish agricultural colonies.[44]

The first phase in modernization took place as an aftermath of the strike of the Agudat Hamorim of 1919. A Folks-Shulrat (Popular School Board) was established, school committees were formed in several areas of Buenos Aires, and schools were founded with names of modern Jewish writers, such as Shalom Aleichem, I. L. Peretz, Shalom Asch, Mendele Mocher Sforim, and so on. These schools eliminated the name of Talmud Torah and were called Folks Shuln (Popular Schools); they did away with the skullcap for boys during the study of sacred texts as well as with other religious practices. The program, which was taught in Yiddish, consisted in language, history, and literature. For texts they utilized books prepared by Joel Entin, the Yiddish educator and translator in New York.[45]

These schools did not attract the mass of Jewish workers. The only school of the three founded in 1920 that still existed in 1929 was the Folks Shul Shalom Aleichem in the center of town (at Jean Juarés number 392). Others were established later—lasting only a few years—in various sections of Buenos Aires. The Shalom Aleichem school had an average of one hundred students, and there were no more than three Folks Shuln in existence simultaneously.[46] Moreover, the joint board of these schools existed only a few years. The Folk Shuln thus did not have a common program of studies, and the teachers were required to teach according to the instructions of the school committees, which did not always maintain a fixed ideology.[47]

The secular character of the Folks Shuln caused opposition from religious sectors. On the other hand, even if secular, these schools still retained a certain bourgeois character, at least in the eyes of the most progressive workers. During those stormy years of class differentiation some extremist groups remained completely separate from other leftist groups. This opposition, both from the religious and from the extreme left, was the cause for the little influence of the Folks Shuln among the Jewish working class.[48]

Poale Zion founded a net of schools under the name of Ber Borochov, the ideologist of the movement in Eastern Europe. A board of trustees (Curatorium) of the Borochov schools was formed in Buenos Aires on January 6, 1920, which administered the educational institutions. The first of these schools was opened in Villa Crespo, and soon others followed in the center of Buenos Aires and near Mercado Abasto. In accordance with the ideology of Labor Zionism, the Borochov schools taught in the first stage Yiddish language, stories from the Bible, and Jewish songs; in the second stage of studies emphasis was placed on Jewish history, literature, and folklore, together with notions about Eretz Israel; in the more advanced years Hebrew and the history of popular movements were taught. After the rift within the Poale Zion party in 1921 (ch. 5), the Borochov schools remained with the leftist Poale Zionists, and accordingly the ideology of the schools moved further to the left. There was an average of 200 students at the Borochov schools at the beginning of the 1920s. When they were closed in 1932 by the Argentine government, which accused them of being communist, the number of students had reached 300.[49]

The Jewish communists—consisting mainly of Jews associated with the Jewish socialist organization Avangard (after 1920), and members of Poale Zion (left)—founded Workers' Schools (Arbeter Shuln) in 1922.[50] Their propaganda in the Jewish neighborhoods was aggressive and fell among the workers "as a tempest."[51] They launched antireligious mottos and political manifestos promoting class-consciousness among the Jewish proletariat. The bourgeoisie was violently attacked because of the values taught in their schools, such as the superiority of private property, the fundamental principle for the development of society and the family. They believed that the worker's children were taught by the bourgeoisie to relate only to the machine. Moreover, the Argentine state schools were criticized for being chauvinistic and emphasizing patriotism. The Argentine heroes of independence had become, in the minds of the children, the heroes of humanity. On the other hand the Workers' Schools taught the proletarian students class loyalty and prepared them to battle for its liberation. The students were expected to become builders of a new socialist order, to think materialistically, and to acquire the necessary tools to fight against the bourgeois order.[52]

The difference, during the late 1920s, between the Borochov and the Workers' schools was that the latter fought against Zionism, while the former were positively Zionist. Both school systems were constantly in competition. A major polemic was built around the controversy between Yiddishism and proletarian culture in Yiddish, which was rampant in Poland and in the United States at the time. In Argentina there was no place for such a battle. As Pinie Katz asserted, this polemic was rooted in a fight for the hegemony of leadership in the Jewish working class.[53] The Workers' Schools were slightly more successful than the Borochov ones. In 1927 there were eight Workers' Schools and five Borochov schools.[54]

In 1925 a convention was organized in Buenos Aires with the objective of establishing a union of all Jewish proletarian schools. This attempt failed due to each group's wanting the united board to accept its own directives and principles. The communist contingent—indeed the largest—could not tolerate the position of the small Bundist cluster. The rationalists, or anarchists, who had a plan for a rational school, left the conference because of the general disagreement to their ideology. On the other hand, the Poale Zionists wanted the conference to adopt a more positive stand towards Jewish education. The rift between Poale Zionists and communists reached absurd proportions when the schools of the former were branded "Talmud Torahs" by the latter, and those of the communists were denominated "party parishes" by Poale Zionists.[55]

Both the Borochov and the Workers' schools had constant financial difficulties because they were not founded upon secure economic bases. Since they never had the support of the JCA because they were party schools, their income came basically from tuition of students, picnics, and cultural festivals. The repeatedly approached the Chevra Keduscha for financial support, which finally was granted. A few members of the board of Chevra Keduscha thought that the Talmud Torahs should get first priority regarding economic help. Others were against the secular schools because these did not contribute to the preservation of Judaism among the young generation. The majority, however, agreed that the Chevra Keduscha should help all types of Jewish schools, in the same way it supported institutions antagonistic to each other such as Karen Hayesod and Procor.[56] Thus the Chevra Keduscha, the largest Jewish organization in the country, formed around a burial society with clearly religious goals, had, already in the 1920s, adopted a more universalist position. In the area of Jewish education it chose to bolster and support, whenever its financial situation allowed, all Jewish schools, whether they be religious Talmud Torah or secular communist Workers' Schools. This fact also attests to the participation of the leftist and secular elements in the life of the Jewish community in Buenos Aires. They were granted support for their schools because they constituted a fairly discernable part of the membership at the Chevra Keduscha and their views were represented at the board of the institution. Moreover, the secular element outweighed the religious one at the Chevra Keduscha, thus confirming that Argentine Jewry, already during the 1920s, had a secular and ethnic character.

By 1930 there were over twenty Talmud Torahs in Buenos Aires. Most of them were in financial straits. The end of JCA subsidies and the economic crisis that had started a year earlier only worsened the situation. The natural road for these institutions to follow was the one that led to the Chevra Keduscha for assistance. A delegation of the various Talmud Torahs described the conditions under which these schools were operating. Besides their unstable financial situation there were deficiencies in instruction and programs due to the lack of qualified teachers, and students were lost every year. On the other hand, the Argentine national schools attracted the full attention of the students because of their better teaching programs and organization, their better physical environment, and because state education was the one needed in order to reach institutions of higher learning.[57] All Jewish schools had a sectarian approach to Jewish education. The secular program focused around one specific doctrine, be it Yiddishism, Marxism, or Labor Zionism, while the Talmud Torahs stressed languages and religion.

Both the religious and the secular schools in Buenos Aires lacked a real objective approach to Jewish education. They all considered that the basic needs of education were provided by the national Argentine school. Moreover, all the students at the Jewish schools had to be enrolled in the state schools. The Jewish schools could therefore not compete with the state schools. They could not provide a full program for the education of the child both in the official Argentine program and in one adequate to the particular ideology of the school. This could only be possible at a day school (*escuela integral*). Although there were various individuals advocating this type of school they were not established until later decades.[58]

The passionately patriotic education given at the state schools was not paralleled with a Jewish education of a similarly appealing character.[59] The Argentine-born generation of the first decades of the twentieth century, especially in the cities, was more inclined to following currents of Argentine nationalism than to retaining Jewish particularism by studying at the Jewish schools. In 1923 Leib Jaffe, an envoy of the Keren Hayesod, met Argentine Jews who told him about the necessity of the Jews to assimilate fully into the Argentine culture and society. An end had to be put to the active cosmopolitanism rampant in cities such as Buenos Aires. All expressions of particularism were to be made void in order that the Argentine heritage be preserved.[60]

The program in the Cursos Religiosos, as well as in most Talmud Torahs, did not stop the assimilationist trend among the Jews. Practically no Jewish literature or Jewish post–Second Commonwealth history was taught there. The students did not relate to their ancestors of ancient Palestine as they did to the heroes of the country where they lived or to Jewish literature as they did to Spanish and Latin American literature. In the program of the Cursos Religiosos one could see the "assimilationist myopia" of educators not able to understand the needs of the Jewish generation born in Argentina.[61]

In the secular schools there was also a lack of qualified teachers. The classrooms were narrow and small and in poor hygienic conditions. The main concern was the ideology of the party, not didactics. Moreover, classes were conducted in Yiddish, which was not the mother tongue of some students, who spoke Spanish much more fluently.[62]

With the exception of the Arabic-speaking Jews, a vast majority of the Jewish parents were negligent in the Jewish education of their children. The leadership of Buenos Aires' Jewry, on the other hand, did not build modern and efficient school systems during the 1920s in spite of both the numerous voices advocating them and even the different committees appointed to deal with this necessity.

In 1926 the Consejo Nacional de Educación confirmed that 13.5 percent of the general population of Buenos Aires was of school age. The Jewish population of the city was between 80,000 and 100,000 individuals. José Mendelson furthermore asserted that there were less than 1,000 Jewish children who went regularly to a Jewish school. Even granting that Mendelson did not include about 700 students at the various Sephardic Talmud Torahs in the city, the 1,000 Ashkenazi students represented between 8.7 and 11.4 percent of the school-age Ashkenazi population.[63] Thus, a generation practically illiterate in Jewish knowledge was being brought up in Buenos Aires. Jewish leadership a generation later had to be recruited from more recent waves of immigration or from certain limited number of Jewish colonies where Jewish education was more widespread.

Jewish Cultural Expressions in an Acculturating Community

The contributions of the Argentine Jewish community to Jewish culture did not have a noticeable distinction in centers in continental Europe at the turn of the century. The immigrants who arrived in Argentina were in no way rabbinic scholars. Moreover, among those who left Eastern Europe the pious and the learned were in the minority. They would rather settle in a land where the observance of religious precepts was assured. Buenos Aires, like most of Argentina, with the possible exception of some of the Jewish agricultural settlements, was far from being a place that would induce pious and knowledgeable Jews to settle permanently. Few Jewish immigrants in Argentina were influenced by *haskalah* (enlightenment), a movement that aspired to Europeanize Jewish social and cultural life. Furthermore, Jews in Buenos Aires were not associated with the Russified Jewish intelligentsia of the time.[1] The Sephardic immigrants in Argentina were even less enlightened than their Ashkenazi brethren. Deeply imbued in traditional Jewish life, the Sephardic communities in the Orient had only begun to receive the impact of the Europeanizing forces of the Alliance Israélite Universelle, through which an inkling of French culture and language was being instilled. Only a small number of the emigrating Sephardic Jews had been in contact with the Westernizing teachings of the AIU.[2]

The overall reason for emigrating and the main goal for the overwhelming majority of Jews arriving in the port of Buenos Aires was to improve their economic situation. The dream of "making America" was in their minds.[3]

Upon arriving in Argentina, the Jewish immigrant had to organize a social and cultural life. The first consideration was to be among coreligionists and conationals. This gave rise to tens of residents (*landsmanschaften*) associations, both among Ashkenazim and Sephardim. The Jewish immigrants had brought with them the culture and language of their native society. The Ashkenazim from Eastern Europe preferred and sought fellow Jews who spoke their native tongue, Yiddish, and were also eager to maintain in Buenos Aires their cultural pursuits. Similarly, the Sephardic Jews were concentrated in various centers, each one conducted in the respective mother tongue of its constituents—Arabic, Ladino, or Spanish—and with a membership composed of Jews of similar geographic origin.

It was imperative for the immigrant to learn the Spanish language, to adapt to the mores and customs of the Argentinian society, and to participate as far as possible in the social, political, and economic life of the adoptive country. This, together with the immediate acclimatization of children—whether born in Europe or in Argentina—made the process of Argentinization an inevitable one. Moreover, the Jewish immigrant had come to settle in the country and was eager to participate in the mainstream of Argentine life and take root in its fate and culture.

Rabbinic Culture

The Jewish immigrant's life before crossing the Atlantic was built around the Jewish community. Whether still adhering firmly to Biblical and Talmudic precepts or having already abandoned some or all religious practices, the Jew maintained a strong bond with the Jewish community in the home town. The basic roots of the immigrant Jews from Eastern Europe—and even more those from the centers of Sephardic Jewry in the Turkish Empire and in North Africa—were in historic rabbinic Judaism as practiced in their communities of origin. In these areas the rabbis or *hachamim*, the intellectual and religious leaders, constituted the epitome of wisdom and sanctity. Yet in Argentina these pious, learned, and wise personalities were not to be seen so frequently. The new communities formed in Buenos Aires and in other centers of Jewish settlement in the country offered a completely transformed scene, which created the background for an inexorable diminution of the religious leaders' authority, preeminence, and repute. This was especially noticeable in the immigrant communities formed in the urban centers; in the agricultural colonies the process was more slowly paced. The newly arrived immigrants felt not only uprooted geographically from their former Jewish environment in the Old World but also considered launching themselves into conquering the New World in every way possible. Rabbinic authority and religious observances stood, in many cases, in the way of the Jewish immigrant. In the new environment they both lost their former preponderance. The rabbis' authority—in the few instances of rabbis or *hachamim* attempting to exert some religious authority in the communities in Argentina—attracted little sympathy. With respect to observances, most Jews were gradually drawn into a transformed state of religious permissiveness.

The lack of concern in ritual law was a determinant factor regarding religious creativity in Argentina. There were few legal questions raised, thus rabbis were rarely challenged with new situations arising from the transformed environment of Jewish settlement. Therefore, there was no sizable body of Responsa to queries from immigrant Jews either to local rabbis or to authorities abroad. The major questions related to religious practice concentrated in common aspects such as ritual slaughtering and burial procedure. Moreover, the small number of rabbinic authorities sheds light on the need of the community for them. With the exception of rabbis Aharon Goldman in Moisesville, Joseph Taran in Colonia Zonnenfeld, and Shaul Setton in the Aleppine community in Buenos Aires, no rabbinic scholar produced a sizable body of Responsa.[4] The paucity of such Responsa by immigrant rabbis in the period ending in 1930 in Argentina is a major indication of the decline of the culture and cultural values that these scholars symbolized.

Hebrew Culture

When the enlightenment reached the Jewish communities in Europe, a Western literature was developed both in Hebrew and in Yiddish, departing radically from the tradition of exclusively rabbinic intellectualism. The role of Argentina in the flowering of Hebrew literature before 1920 was practically null. The Hebrew literary centers were in Galicia, Vilna, Warsaw, and Odessa; and only New York, in the Americas, reached an unsteady position of note in this respect. A reduced number of scholars during the period 1891–1911 did migrate to Argentina from centers in Eastern Europe, imbued with the ideals of reviving Hebrew culture and promoting Zionist propaganda. Their impact within the growing Jewish population in Argentina was not, however, of importance. Their activities were limited to letters they wrote to friends and relatives in their home towns and to a large number of letters to the Hebrew newspapers appearing in Europe.[5]

With the arrival of Dr. Zvi Ashkenazi as director of the Jewish Colonization Association's (JCA's) schools in the colonies in 1911, new impetus was given to Hebrew culture, both in the agricultural colonies and in Buenos Aires. Shortly after his arrival the first Hebrew-speaking group, Dovrei Sfat Ivri, was established in the capital, with fifty-five active members. Quite naturally, many of the most conspicuous participants in this group were also active in local Zionist activities. Dr. Ashkenazi, however, died suddenly, still a young man of thirty, in Moisesville in 1913; and the Hebrew-speaking group was deprived of its most enthusiastic promoter.[6]

The overwhelming majority of Jewish immigrants from Eastern Europe did not speak Hebrew. Even among the most passionate Zionists, Yiddish was nearer to their hearts than Hebrew. All Zionist groups and parties in Argentina, including the General Zionists and Zeire Zion, published their official periodicals in Yiddish, hoping to attract more sympathizers and to maintain a closer contact with their membership.

There were, nonetheless, attempts to promote Hebrew culture by means of periodicals during the 1920s. The editors of these journals wanted their publications to become the guardian of Hebrew language and culture in the country. However, they were confronted with numerous difficulties that resulted in the closing of all of them after more or less short periods of time. These difficulties arose from the lack of popular response to the Hebrew periodicals, resulting in serious financial and ideological obstacles. The limited response was due mainly to the unsuccessful side efforts to create long-standing Tarbut or Hebrew schools in the large centers of Jewish population. These schools failed during the early 1920s after short periods of existence. Secondly, the Federación Sionista Argentina (FSA) did not succeed in founding Hebrew schools in spite of the fact that in all the Zionist Land Conferences this point was discussed, and it was repeatedly decided to promote Jewish studies in Hebrew. Only towards the end of the decade did a reaction take place, and positive work was started in this direction.[7]

Habima Haivrit, founded in 1921 by Tuvia Oleisker and I. L. Gorelik, was the Hebrew periodical of longest duration during the 1920s. It appeared nearly monthly for two years, but then its issues were published more irrregularly. In 1925 only one number was issued. It reappeared in 1929 but was again discontinued until 1936. Gorelik, as a result of an argument with Oleisker in 1922, left *Habima Haivrit* and founded his own journal, *Hechalutz*, of which nine issues were published in 1922 before it had to close.

Both these Hebrew periodicals, as well as *Atideinu*, of which five issues appeared in 1926, had similar goals. Its editors saw that the Jewish community in Argentina was developing in all ways of life, in its economic, social, and cultural (In the broad sense) aspects but not with respect to Hebrew education, Hebrew culture, and the revival of the Hebrew language and literature. "All these concepts, and the like, are foreign words in the lexicon of our lives here, in Argentina."[8] Moreover, they saw a peril in the overwhelming drive of most Jewish immigrants to "make America," for they kept estranging themselves from the spiritual values of the Jewish people.[9]

The separateness within the Jewish population in Buenos Aires was an issue strongly utilized by the editors of the Hebrew periodicals to promote the diffussion of the Hebrew language and culture. The Sephardic element was repeatedly a theme in editorials, and various articles kept the readers informed about the progress made by these communities in the capital. The abyss between Sephardim and Ashkenazim was to be overcome by the development of a culture common to all Jews, that is, a Hebrew culture. "The Sephardic community here, in the capital, which is very important both in quantity and quality, is far away, as it is known, from our community, the Ashkenazic community. The Sephardic Jews have no contacts, dealings, nor relations with us Ashkenazim, in the way, for example, the Italians here—Neapolitans and Sicilians and the like—have. All this was caused by the language, their language of exile being different from our language of exile."[10] The Hebrew language would also encourage Zionist work among Sephardim, who were often estranged from these activities partly due to the insistence of most Ashkenazim on conducting their meetings and campaigns in Yiddish.[11]

During the early 1920s small groups of Hebrew enthusiasts were formed both in the capital and in the cities and towns in the provinces.[12] Furthermore, courses in the Hebrew language were opened in Buenos Aires and in many other centers of Jewish population in the country, such as La Plata, Médanos, Moisesville, Córdoba, San Salvador, Rosario, Carlos Casares, Mendoza, Tucumán, and Salta. Some of the latter, however, had a very erratic existence, especially in the small centers.

Nonetheless, during the 1920s Hebrew life and culture did not attain a position of importance among Jews in Argentina. The forces sponsoring these activities, even if enthusiastic, were very small. The desire to unite Sephardim and Ashkenazim was not within a good framework of probability, because the immense majority of Sephardim, as well as most Ashkenazim, did not know the Hebrew language, nor were they involved in circles that promoted its learning. Yiddish among Ashkenazic immigrants, Arabic among Syrian ones, and Spanish among Turkish and Moroccan newcomers as well as among the children of all Jewish immigrants were the languages of discourse. For some, Hebrew was utilized only at the synagogue or in Zionist correspondence, while for others it constituted a dead language. Notwithstanding, the resurgence of Hebrew in Eastern Europe made an impact in Argentina through the activities of a few immigrants. The more positive consequences of this impact were only manifest after 1930 and, even more, after the Second World War, when developments in world and Jewish history promoted a major trend from Yiddish to Hebrew education in Jewish schools in Argentina.

Yiddish Culture

While Hebrew was the language spoken by a small elite of educated Jews in Eastern Europe, mainly ardent *Hovevei Zionists* and *Maskilim*, or enlightened Jews, Yiddish was spoken by the Jewish masses. Similarly, the enlightened Jews in Russia who had undergone a process of Russification and preferred the Russian language to Yiddish (usually as a sign of superior culture) were very few. Among the Jewish immigrants in Argentina who arrived from Eastern Europe before 1930 there were very few belonging either to the Hebrew-speaking or the Russian-speaking elites. The masses of poor immigrants spoke only Yiddish, and it was quite natural for them to express themselves in this language whenever the opportunity of doing so presented itself in their new Spanish-speaking atmosphere. The bulk of cultural expressions during this period were thus conducted in the language of the Jewish masses.

The original literary production in Yiddish was not, however, of great importance before 1930 in Argentina. During the period 1910–30 about one hundred books and brochures were printed in that language in the country, including Isaac David Horowitz' short *Spanish-Yiddish Dictionary* (between 1911 and 1914), David Goldman's Di *Juden in Argentine, in der Vergangenheit un in der*

Gegenwart, in Wort un in Bild (*The Jews in Argentina, in the Past and in the Present, in Word and in Pictures*) of 1914, and Mordechai Alpersohn's three volumes, *Thirty Years in Argentina* (1922, 1926, 1928).[13]

It was difficult for a Yiddish writer to earn a livelihood from his writings. The market for Yiddish books in Argentina was reduced to the Jewish immigrants of East European origin, and the cost of printing could not always be met. Thus the poet or writer in that language had either to forsake his calling or emigrate. José Horn quotes an ad in *Der Tog* of October 2, 1914, where a benefit cultural function was announced, the profits of which would allow the young writers Moshe Pinchewsky and Abba Kliger to travel to the United States to pursue their literary goals.[14] Writers then resorted to the Yiddish press, where their poems, feuilletons, and sometimes novels or plays, were published in installments. However, even this did not represent a sufficient income for the authors.

Even if the relatively small Yiddish-speaking population in Argentina did not make notable contributions to Yiddish letters during the first three decades of the twentieth century, the interest of this same population in what was being published originally in Yiddish, or was translated from other languages abroad—mainly in Poland and New York—always remained high. Proof of this is the continuous stream of visits of Yiddish writers from centers in Europe and the United States to the Jewish communities in Buenos Aires and the interior of Argentina.[15]

A large number of cultural centers sprouted in several neighborhoods of Buenos Aires, as well as in many cities in the interior. Practically the entire membership of these centers was composed of Jewish immigrant workers who found in them a place for socializing and cultural uplifting. Most of these centers had a sociopolitical ideology that their members brought with them from Eastern Europe. Their activities consisted of weekly or periodical debates and conferences on sociopolitical, literary, artistic, and even scientific topics. Many offered courses in Spanish, Yiddish literature, and even mathematics. The goal was to raise the cultural level of the Jewish worker. Moreover, many had as their principal preoccupation the building of a library for their members and the public in general.

In 1905 a group of Russian Jews with different ideologies, such as social democrats, Bundists, and social revolutionaries, formed the biblioteca Rusa. At the beginning the language spoken there was Russian, but within a few years the Yiddish-speaking members won a hard-fought battle against the Russified minority.[16] When the Biblioteca Rusa was destroyed by the antimaximalist mobs in the wake of celebrations of the centenary of Argentina's revolt against Spain, in 1910, the library consisted of 5,000 volumes in Russian and Yiddish. By 1916 the largest Jewish cultural centers in Buenos Aires had voluminous libraries, especially the Biblioteca Progreso, the Society Dr. Herzl, Juventud Israelita de Boca y Barracas, the Center I. L. Peretz in Caballito, and Biblioteca Israelita de Villa Crespo.[17] New centers were formed and many were enlarged during the following fifteen years.[18] The impact of these centers upon the masses of the Jewish proletariat in Buenos Aires was described in 1916 in the following way:[19]

> The worker leaves his labor tools at the workshop or at the factory, and hurriedly goes, just as the employee or any other, to the warm hearth of the library, to take delight in the reading of good works; to acquire in the night school the rudimentary and indispensable knowledge that he was deprived of because of the ignorance or poverty of his parents. . . . Everything [takes place] in a familiar, pleasant, and comfortable atmosphere, which he could not find outside his own nucleus, to which he feels attracted by irresistible forces, and where he can speak his language and keep his customs.

At the end of November 1915, at the initiative of the literary society and library Max Nordau in La Plata, Province of Buenos Aires, a congress of Jewish cultural centers in the country was held in their premises. Delegates from twelve institutions, representing centers in La Plata, Colonia Dora (Santiago del Estero), Santa Fe, Rosario (Santa Fe), Tucumán, and Bernasconi (La Pampa), and six in Buenos Aires—with the backing of ten other centers that could not send delegates due to the economic crisis rampant in Argentina—founded at this congress the Federación Israelita Argentina de Cultura (FIAC). Later, other centers in the country entered FIAC.[20]

Most of the constituent members of FIAC were centers with a definite ideology, including Bundism and anarchism. The congress in La Plata provoked a negative reaction from some sectors of the more established Jewish societies in the country, notably the Zionists. Di Yiddishe Zeitung published articles against the congress, and recommended institutions not to participate in it. The issue was intensified by the proximity in time of the First Argentine Jewish Congress called for the end of February 1916. The sponsors of the Argentine Jewish Congress—Zionist leaders in Buenos Aires—had proclaimed that the platform would be the demand of effective equality of rights for Jews and other citizens in the countries where they reside and Jewish autonomy in a territory where they could lead an authentic national life. In accordance with this platform—which the sponsors of the congress would forward to Jewish leaders at the eventual Peace Conference after the war, once it was approved by the congress itself—propaganda was launched for the Argentine Jewish Congress. At this moment Avangard—a Bundist center founded in 1907 and a major force in FIAC, opposed to the second point of the platform—left the organizing committee of the congress and demonstrated against it. Avangard was followed by many other cultural societies, also members of FIAC.[21]

FIAC slowly started to develop its program. It contemplated the translation of Yiddish classics, mainly I. L. Peretz, into Spanish. The latter's death, as well as Sholem Aleichem's, were duly commemorated. Moreover, FIAC petitioned the Ministry of Education to stop the circulation of some textbooks that included clear antisemitic paragraphs.[22] This provoked the ire of the editors of Di Yiddishe Zeitung, who argued against FIAC's taking the initiative in petitioning the government. They asserted the FIAC was not the organization to petition because its representation was limited. This should be the prerogative of the officials of the more veteran Jewish institutions who considered that they were the appropriate representatives of the Jewish population vis-à-vis the government, not a federation of institutions leaning to leftist ideologies.[23]

At a second convention at the premises of Biblioteca Villa Crespo in Buenos Aires—of anarchist orientation—on March 25, 1917 the objectives of FIAC were discussed. The delegates contemplated creating secular schools and night schools for adults where the workers would learn the Spanish language and Argentine history and institutions and would have an opportunity of receiving technical instruction, with the final objective of promoting culture among the Jewish proletariat and strengthening the bonds of union and fraternity among the various federated circles.[24]

Not all the delegates had the same attitude to Jewish culture. The spirit of universalism and the negation of Jewish particularism had impressed many of them. At the second convention a group proposed to change the name of FIAC so that it would not include Jewish culture. Though the majority voted against this motion, and Jewish culture was retained as an integral part of FIAC, the spirit of acculturation to values not particularly akin to their culture of birth was evident in these circles.[25]

The heterogeneity within FIAC was a major reason for its dissolution towards the end of World War I. Indeed, the changes effected in Europe, especially with the Russian Revolution, also produced a realignment of loyalties among Jewish workers in Argentina. Some opted for a more extremist position and ceased associating with their previous circles. Moreover, the long distances between cities, the economic crisis, and the indifference of other sectors of the Jewish community accelerated the process of dismemberment.

Yiddish continued being the language of the Ashkenazi majority. In several neighborhoods in Buenos Aires, especially in Once, Villa Crespo, Caballito, and Boca-Barracas, a large proportion of commerce was carried on in Yiddish. Political parties tried to attract the relatively insignificant Jewish vote (most Jewish immigrants, like most immigrants in general, did not attain Argentine citizenship and thus did not constitute a considerable element in the elections) by posting political propaganda in Yiddish in the Jewish quarters.[26] Moreover, many Jewish workshops were located in these quarters. Furniture *talleres* (workshops), as well as tailors' and other needle industry shops were situated in their neighborhoods. The cultural centers, synagogues, mutual help societies, and other *hebrot*, had their premises side by side with Jewish grocery stores, restaurants, and travel agents.

The growing number of Yiddish-speaking Jews settling in Buenos Aires and in other centers throughout the country gave the final impulse to those Jews with literary or journalistic talents to start publishing periodicals in Yiddish. Thus the Yiddish press saw the light of day—indeed as early as 1898— and soon became a pivotal factor in Jewish cultural life in Argentina. The considerations were quite simple. Commerce and institutions were forever sprouting and developing, and the press was the best way of letting other Jews learn about those commercial enterprises and about the activities of the societies. Both commercial and institutional advertisements provided for the lion's share of the budget of the periodicals. Indeed, the Yiddish press in Argentina, in contradistinction to its counterpart in Warsaw or New York, was not as dependent on the number of its readers as it was on commercial and communal sponsorship and advertisements.[27]

The Yiddish press in Argentina,[28] had an important role in the development of Jewish life there as did later (though to a much lesser degree) the Spanish Jewish press in the country. Its influence in communal life was such that it could often decide upon the success or failure of communal enterprises, depending upon its feeling about them. It moreover was the inspiring force of many initiatives within the community.[29] This tendency could be perceived at the beginning of the Yiddish press in Buenos Aires, for the first Linotype with Yiddish characters was brought into the city for the purpose of journalism; previous needs for printing Yiddish brochures had been satisfied in printing offices in New York.[30] Literary purposes came only second to journalism in Yiddish letters in Argentina, in contrast to the situation in Vilna, Warsaw, Petersburg, and New York.

The immigrant Jewish generation in Buenos Aires and the provinces, including both workers and officials in more established Jewish societies, became more and more attached to the press: "All initiatives were found in the Yiddish press; every society wrote news about its own [board] meetings, assemblies, banquets, and activities."[31] Quite often the press printed so many minutiae—including petty quarrels, letters to the editor, entire board meetings—that the outsider could obtain a false impression of community life in Buenos Aires if the only frame of reference was the Jewish periodicals: "By evaluating according to the dailies one could be convinced that the Argentine [Jewish] institutions are much larger than what they really are. The Yiddish dailies in Buenos Aires are the magnifying glasses of societal life."[32]

A strong reliance on the press bolstered its cultural influence in the Jewish community. The periodicals printed translations of major works of the time, reproduced articles, novels, and poems by Yiddish writers in Europe and the United States, as well as novels, plays, and other works describing Jewish life in Eastern Europe. The journals sponsored by sociopolitical centers imbued with ideologies such as Bundism, anarchism, communism, Labor Zionism, or general Zionism filled their pages with articles—by and large written in the Northern Hemisphere—advocating the principles of their respective positions.

Of the many journalistic designs during the pioneering period of the Yiddish press in Argentina—from the appearance of the first weekly, *Viderkol* (*Echo*) in 1898 until the beginning of World War I—most enjoyed only a very short existence. *Di Folks Shtime* (*People's Voice*) was the only paper to appear throughout the 1898–1914 period. It had, however, no clear stand. Its editor, Abraham Vermont, was inclined to sensationalism and resorted to blackmail against Jewish officials who would not sponsor his journal. Vermont proved to be well informed about the activities of the Jewish white slave dealers in Buenos Aires, against whom he directed fierce attacks. On the other hand, he defended their female victims. Di *Folks Shtime* came out defending the JCA colonists against the "abuses" of the management; it attacked Zionists—who had control of the first two short-lived Yiddish weeklies in 1898, as well as other journals before 1914—and promoted initiatives of interest for the Jewish communities in Buenos Aires and the colonies.[33]

During the first half of this pioneering period, that is, from 1898 until 1906, Zionists published journals propounding their ideas. They all were short-lived, as were some satirical magazines that appeared in 1899.[34]

During the period 1908–14 a variety of ideological periodicals published by the different parties—Zionist and non-Zionist alike—circulated in Buenos Aires. They are described in chapter 5.

The First World War placed obstacles in the way of transatlantic trips. As a consequence, publications in Yiddish from Europe and the United States did not arrive in Buenos Aires with the assiduity and promptness of prewar years. Moreover, the world war and the developments in Europe were a constant concern in Argentina. Jews, in particular, were eager to be properly informed, especially about the manner the Jewish communities in Europe fared throughout the period. Thus the need for a Yiddish daily that would handle these requisites was strongly felt. In January 1914 Der *Tog* published its first issue. With few intermissions it survived for nearly three years.[35] Di *Yiddishe Zeitung* had better fortune. Begun in November 1914, it soon conquered the Jewish street. In it were reflected the interests of the majority of the Jewish population in the country. It printed news about the developments in the local Jewish institutions, including mutual help organizations, religious societies, and Zionist centers, as well as reliable information about the events in Europe and the Jewish world in general. A few weeks after the revolution in Russia, on January 1, 1918, a new daily, Di *Presse*, was first issued in Buenos Aires. It represented the views of the working masses inclined to secularism and to the struggle for social justice by means of socialism and communism. Both latter dailies constituted an important element in the day-to-day life of large sectors of the Jewish population not only in Buenos Aires but also in the rest of Argentina, as well as in the neighboring countries. They prompted and furthered Jewish culture in its many aspects, such as education, theater, and literature. Classics of Yiddish literature were presented in installments in their columns, and important works by Argentinian authors were translated into the language of the Ashkenazi immigrants. In this way the press helped the immigrants familiarize themselves with Argentinian literature and culture. Moreover, it helped them to keep *au courant* with the political, social, and economic situation of the country in which they now lived by devoting sections of their issues to general local news that the cultural and ideological weeklies and monthlies could not publish.[36]

The Russian Revolution on the one hand and the Balfour Declaration on the other deeply affected the Jewish quarters in Buenos Aires. New centers advocating revised ideologies in accordance with developments in Europe were formed. Loyalties among leftists were divided along the lines of the Second International or the Communist International. During the 1920s many groups within the Jewish population were active in promoting various ideologies. Quite a number of them published journals. The facts that the membership in these centers or sections of parties was Jewish (indeed, there was a Jewish section of the Communist party in Argentina), that the language spoken there was Yiddish, and that their periodicals were in this language testify to the existence of a Jewish sentiment in the midst of this fringe groups of the Jewish community even if this sentiment was only manifest in the will of preserving a cultural or language minority.[37] This sentiment was more strongly felt among those advocating a return to Soviet Russia and the establishment of a Jewish Autonomous Region in the Soviet Far East.[38] Labor Zionism, on the other hand, was strengthened by the Balfour Declaration. Within it new currents were developed, always in accordance to European developments. All the new groups that formed as a result of the ideological division within existing parties published their journals in Yiddish during the 1920s.[39]

Some independent cultural magazines appeared during the 1920s, but most of them for only a short period.[40] The population was more inclined to read the dailies in Yiddish and thus gave them their financial support. Monthlies and weeklies suffered from lack of equal sponsorship. Moreover, the commercial sectors of the Jewish community also published their journals, containing information about the state of business and various markets in the city and the country in general. Special attention was given to those branches of commerce where the Jews were more prominent.[41]

The Yiddish Theater

The soaring East European Jewish population of Buenos Aires provided an audience large enough to maintain Yiddish theaters. The Jews arriving with the first wave of immigration at the end of the nineteenth century felt the need for a Yiddish theater that would represent themes that were dear to their hearts, be they drama or satirical productions. This strong desire for entertainment and spiritual rejoicing in their mother tongue was amply justified because the Spanish theater could not satisfy the Yiddish-speaking immigrants, due first to the language difficulties and second to the incomprehensibility of the themes, which were new and foreign to them.

A group of dramatic art enthusiasts organized performances at the turn of the century in Buenos Aires. The first production was Abraham Goldfaden's satirical comedy *Kuni Lemel* at the Doria (later Marconi) theater at the initiative of the actor Bernardo Weissman.[42] David Hassan, a West European oldtimer Jew in Buenos Aires, evaluating this first *mise-en-scène* in a letter to the *Jewish Chronicle*, wrote the following:[43]

> I enclose a programme in Hebrew type which announces a comic operatta called "Cuhere Lehmmele" [*sic*], The Stammerer, by A. Goldfaden, at the Doria. This place is known as a theatre at popular prices, and a "Platea mit

entrada," as you will see, costs 3s.—(stall with entrance 5s.)|*sic*|. The piece was nicely mounted and, of course, well acted. These people are born actors. The music at times was "National," judging by the chorus of "ay, zai, yei" and the rest "Copy." The house was in a constant roar of laughter the whole time, and although I do not understand a word of "Jargon," I would have been amused at this, to me a novelty, had I not felt depressed at the sight of the audience.

The house was full, but I did not meet a single member of any of our congregations[44] and much less their families. Certainly some not oversensitive showy families were there with their daughters, sons, young children, and even babies . . .

These plays can hardly be defined as refined, but they need not be the motive of a public scandal, and yet I am told the same thing can be seen in some European cities.

The actors performed quite often. A year later, in 1902, the main Spanish newspapers in the capital published notices of the "Compañía Israelita" at the Libertad Theater, as well as a copy of the program of Goldfaden's *Shulamis*.[45]

The Yiddish theater flourished with local actors and with some who came from Europe and the United States. However, it matured at a very slow pace, notwithstanding the constant growth of the number of people enjoying the Yiddish plays through 1930. Some reasons for this are evident even in the above-quoted description of the first steps of this artistic expression. Before the First World War the public preferred "coarse burlesque actors to more refined artists, and the farce to serious drama."[46] The audience was to a large extent controlled by Jewish white slave dealers and their "merchandise."[47] This was detrimental to the attendance of a considerable sector of the general Jewish population, especially families. Before 1930 different groups rose to lead a battle against the *tmeyim* ("impure," as the dealers were called by the rest of the Jewish population) and clean the Jewish theater of their presence. However, the problem was not simple, and only towards the end of the 1920s (and more during the first years of the 1930s) was the "pure" community able to free itself from the negative presence of the dealers. Official authorities in the city, the theater managers, and even some of the actors had vested interests in the presence of this abhored element of the Jewish population. They all, in smaller or larger measure, made a living from the Yiddish shows, and the white slave dealers used this factor for their benefit. They were thus able to impose their will in some aspects of the theaters' policy, such as banning specific plays from the stage.[48]

The popular character of the audiences and the conspicuous presence of the basest element in the community during the performance kept the most educated and intellectual Jews from attending. Moreover, they were quite at home with the Argentinian environment and could better enjoy a more profound play at the national theaters.

The Yiddish theater was not self-sufficient, not even at the peak of its popularity in Buenos Aires during the late 1920s and 1930s. It had no organic plan and no definite program. To a large extent it depended on what a guest actor—mainly from the United States—could offer during two or three months, while profiting from the summer months' intermission in his country, and becoming a "star" in the Buenos Aires season.⁴⁹ Moreover, except for a few isolated cases, the works or plays written by local authors were not performed on the stage. The most fortunate playwrights had their works published in the local dailies and other Yiddish periodicals.⁵⁰

Besides presenting plays by the most popular playwrights in the Yiddish world, such as Goldfaden, Zalman Libin, Jacob Gordon, Leon Kobrin, Joseph Lateiner, Peretz Hirschbein, and Leon (Leib) Malach, some guest actors introduced to the Argentinian public drama from Dumas, Shakespeare, Leon Tolstoy, Strindberg, Mirabeau, and other European authors. The local companies, moreover, tried to introduce some of the most successful plays by Argentinian authors, such as Florencio Sánchez and José González Castillo.⁵¹

The Yiddish theater played a national role among the Jews in Buenos Aires. True that throughout the period ending in 1930 the theaters' policies were, to a large extent, under the influence of the Jewish white slave dealers. Still, the theater grew more and more popular and was slowly evolving into maturity during the late 1920s. As a cultural expression it constituted a powerful tie with the Yiddish language and Jewish creativity in Eastern Europe, which was later transplanted to New York and other American centers. It proved to be one of the few ties with Jewish culture for many Jews who were removed from participation in the Jewish community and were assimilated to the cosmopolitan life of Buenos Aires. It has been affirmed that the Yiddish theater was in the capital "a school of *Yiddishkeit*" and that "in Buenos Aires more Jewish children go to the [Yiddish] theaters than to the Jewish schools."⁵²

The Yiddish theater groups were consolidated during the 1920s. Before then, in 1916, there were already two companies working in Buenos Aires, performing twice weekly.⁵³ In 1926 one of the companies performed daily; by 1927 two did so; and by 1929 three theaters presented Yiddish plays daily in Buenos Aires. According to Rollansky, it was the guest actor Boris Tomashefsky who, in 1926, established the daily Yiddish theater on a stable basis.⁵⁴

Several actors' unions were formed during the period. They were mainly concerned with the improvement of working conditions and increased salaries for the actors, as well as in raising the level of the Yiddish theater in Buenos Aires. Coinciding with the visit of Hersh D. Nomberg in Argentina in 1922, the actors' organization just formed led an aggressive action to bring the Yiddish theater to a higher cultural and artistic rank. The actors fought against managers and people who made commerce out of the theater and who sponsored only low-level plays. They also launched a battle against the *tmeyim*, "those 'Jews' who have nothing to do with Judaism, nor with the Jewish community and its culture, and who became the defenders of the Yiddish theater, and are opposed to the actors' organization."⁵⁵

Amateur theater circles were also formed in various Jewish social clubs and cultural societies in Buenos Aires. They presented short sketches, monologues, and one-act comedies.⁵⁶

Buenos Aires was a center of growing importance in the history of Yiddish theater. In the early 1930s it was placed among the four major areas for

Yiddish performances together with the USSR, Poland, and the United States. Being the only theatrical center in the Southern Hemisphere, Buenos Aires profited from the opposite seasons, thus becoming host to visiting actors from the North.[57]

The First Native Generation—Jewish Culture in Spanish

Mundo Israelita, a Jewish weekly in Spanish, dealt in an editorial with the question of cultural work among youth, apropos of a debate concerning this topic held at the Poale Zionist convention earlier in August 1924. Most speakers pointed out the lack of interest among the Jewish youth in Argentina for Jewish life, culture, and literature, while a few participants spoke in more optimistic terms. The editor, on the other hand, observed that the Jewish youth in Argentina was removed from the main foci of Jewry and Judaism and therefore ignored their language and literature. He blamed the immigrant generation because, to a large degree, it had opted for a religious instruction—when a Jewish education was given at all—that clashed openly with the secular atmosphere in the country. While stating that the case was not one of complete assimilation into another culture but an estrangement of the youth from its people, *Mundo Israelita* advocated the introduction of an Argentinian slant into Jewish literature. Furthermore, due to the language abyss, a major step in the process of reconquering this "estranged" generation would be to promote Jewish culture in their own language, in Spanish.[58]

The issue of a "Jewish" language could have remained unnoticed to the careless observer of Jewish society in Buenos Aires, for Yiddish dailies and periodicals were being published and read, Yiddish plays were performed more frequently, and the Yiddish language was spoken in many Jewish societies and in some sectors of metropolitan commerce. Moreover, during the 1920s the constant flow of new immigrants from Eastern Europe gave added impetus to Yiddish. On the other hand, there was already a substantial number of young men and students born in Argentina, or at least fully educated in the country, whose main language was Spanish. What was their Jewish identity? In what way did they participate in the life and destiny of the still young and growing Jewish community in Argentina? This was the topic of the debate at the convention of Poale Zionists, and the concern of the editors of *Mundo Israelita*. In the following pages we shall describe some of the activities within the Jewish realm of this youth and their attitudes regarding Jewish culture, and attempt to gauge the proportion of the Jewish youth it involved.

The first cultural center of Spanish-speaking Jewish young men in Buenos Aires was created on January 6, 1909. During 1908 the activities of the Jewish white slave dealers had alarmed most sectors of the community, thus inducing a general movement of protest among Jews with the intention of putting an end to this scourge. Many young Jews also cooperated with the general committee formed on the occasion. However, once they realized that their objective was similar to that of the whole community, as well as that of an Argentinian society sponsored under official auspices (Comité Contra la

Trata de Blancas), they opted to found a cultural center with a wider though not yet fully determined scope of activities.[59]

Most, though not all, of the founders and members of the Centro Juventud Israelita Argentina (CJIA) were sons of colonists from settlements sponsored by Baron de Hirsch in various provinces. They migrated to Buenos Aires to pursue university careers or engage in commercial occupations. Their main reason for founding CJIA was the inborn necessity for intercommunication with fellow Jews, though they also manifested a strong desire both to defend the interests of the community against some of its own most vicious elements and to teach the language of the country to the new immigrants.[60]

The constitution of CJIA clearly stated that its aim was to "assist in the moral, physical, and intellectual development of its members and of the community [colectividad]."[61] However, there was no unanimous attitude towards what the cultural aim of CJIA should be. Indeed, there was general agreement in that the center was "to dispense with everything concerning systematic creeds and Jewish patriotism," in spite of the fact that some of the members of the group, including Isaac Nissensohn, its first president, were active Zionists.[62] The crux of the matter was focused on whether this youth center should promote cultural activities of a distinctive and peculiar Jewish character in addition to their lectures, discussions, concerts, and theatrical performances on general and universal subjects—or not.

Most of the members of CJIA had only a minimal knowledge of Judaism and its place in the world. Their Jewish education, at most, consisted of elementary courses at the JCA schools in the colonies. Once in the metropolis they could not pursue their interests in Jewish subjects, due to the lack of publications in Spanish on these themes. They had not experienced the Jewish life of Eastern Europe; moreover, the little knowledge they had about Herzl's message did not stir their souls. Manuel Bronstein, one of the leaders of those who advocated more Jewish culture in the center, weighing the main factors that formed the personalities of those young Argentinian Jews, concluded that "they very soon found themselves freely immersed in the national life of the country and its concatenation with the world's ado. That is to say that when they were acquiring a conscientiousness of their personality, they felt Argentinian before Jewish. They lived their Argentinianism existentially, while their Judaism was a tenuous palpitation about something they knew only vaguely, but which was not felt sufficiently enough as to generate the need to proclaim it and build a will to live it."[63]

The monthly magazine *Juventud*, which appeared during the period 1911–17, clearly mirrored the different factions struggling within CJIA. A well-printed and clearly written journal directed to an educated public and opening its columns to all writers—Jewish or not—who wanted to try their hand at Spanish belle lettres, *Juventud* started out as a periodical of evident Jewish orientation. However, in its fifth issue it changed to a more assimilationist posture. Articles attacking Jewish rituals and advocating the renouncement of Jewish particularism were published, while the amount of space devoted to Jewish concerns was reduced.[64] This provoked the reaction of the rest of the organized

Jewish community in Buenos Aires against CJIA and its magazine, notwithstanding the fact that the views were personal and did not characterize the whole membership.

A crisis was precipitated by this negative attitude of the community. CJIA was split in two groups ideologically irreconcilable. One sector, influenced by the romantic socialism of the time, believed in a universal community without class and without religious or national divisions that would, inter alia, put an end to the persecutions and penury of the Jewish people. The second group, admitting as well the excellence of universal culture, was convinced that the abdication of its Jewish conditon would prove sterile and believed that there was no incompatibility between a social revolution and the persistence of the Jewish people.[65] The two groups clashed in an assembly of the CJIA on April 27, 1913 devoted to a new delineation of objectives. The "assimilationists" proposed that the center shorten its name to Centro Juventud, thus making it void of all national allegiances. They were willing to effect a complete transformation of its character. They advocated an "ample ideal of culture, without blood or race colorings; because we understand that there cannot be an accomodating culture; because we want to bring to our brains the authoritative words of Darwin, Spencer, and Ameghino, the philosophic truth of Montesquieu, Voltaire, and Rousseau; because we want to destroy the religious sentiment, or better, the religious instinct, which crystallizes our activities and kills our enthusiasms."[66] The other group, which advocated a stronger emphasis on things Jewish, manifested its pride of being Jewish and its will to be considered such. Wolf Nijensohn, who, in later decades became a Zionist leader in Argentina, synthesized their position stating "We, the young generation, are morally obligated to defend the community that gave us birth. Those who came to us did so on account of the Jewish name of our Center; if not, in my opinion, they came to the wrong place." He further motioned the following new objectives for the center be added to its constitution: (1) to defend "specific" interests of the Jews and (2) to foster Jewish culture.[67]

After more than five hours of debate it was voted to retain the name CJIA. The supporters of the shortened name *Centro Juventud* presented their resignation. When a motion of the chairman of the assembly asking for the reincorporation of the dissenting members was approved, only one of them did so. The rest left and soon afterwards founded Ariel, a center with an orientation in accordance with their convictions, and published a journal under the same name, both of ephemeral existence.[68] Two months later, in a general assembly, the reform of the constitution of CJIA according to Nijensohn's proposal was discussed and approved. Thus a new and definitive orientation was given to the center.[69]

During the early part of 1915 the CJIA merged with the Asociación Israelita Argentina, of similar character, forming the Asociación Juventud Israelita Argentina (AJIA). As a result of this merger the magazine *Juventud* began a new era with a larger format, and AJIA initiated some new departments, including a music conservatory.[70]

A new cultural center, the Asociación Hebraica, was formed on February

5, 1923 as a result of a crisis at AJIA. This new organization had similar but more ambitious goals. These included the promotion of Jewish and general culture; the advancement of the spirit of intellectual sociability; the creation of a library for Jewish studies and Argentinian works; and the strengthening of the bonds of the Jewish community with cultural circles in the country. Asociación Hebraica further abstained from all participation in political and religious issues.[71] Its formation immediately aroused the interest of a variety of individuals in the community, especially those completely at home with the language and culture of the country, as opposed to the Yiddish-speaking immigrants. In a few months its membership surpassed the 400 mark.[72]

Asociación Hebraica rapidly became the major cultural center of the Jewish community in Buenos Aires. Conferences and concerts attracted large audiences. The library grew rapidly due to acquisitions and donations from abroad. Books of Jewish interest such as two volumes dealing with the modern period in Jewish history from Simon Dubnow's *World History of the Jewish People* were translated and published in 1924 and 1928. In 1925 Albert Einstein was brought by the Asociación Hebraica to Buenos Aires for a series of lectures. This event won sympathies for the institution from most corners of the Jewish population in the country.

The high level of the cultural activities caused, soon afterwards, the dispersion of many members who could not reach that level. The membership, of quite heterogeneous cultural preparation, began to dwindle. A similar crisis was reflected among officials of the institution, some of whom resigned. Almost simultaneously, an analogous crisis was affecting AJIA. The leaders of both groups considered merging into one society. From this union the Sociedad Hebraica Argentina (SHA) was created on May 11, 1926. Fifteen days later the Ateneo Estudiantil Israelita, with its 200 members and library, was incorporated to SHA.[73]

Under the same lines as its original factions—though now in a stronger way—SHA displayed a wide range of cultural, social, and sports activities during the rest of the decade. By 1928 its membership reached 1400. The topics for the cultural gatherings were eminently Jewish, and the library was enlarged with the acquisition of many volumes of Jewish classics.[74] By the end of the decade SHA had a growing influence in the Jewish community. Its membership was largely middle-class Jews and students, in contrast to the Jewish proletariat. Most had received an Argentinian education in Spanish, were quite removed from Judaism, and had never been confronted with the environment of Eastern Europe, unlike the immigrants who arrived after World War I. Moreover, it was quasi-exclusively Ashkenazic. Sephardim had a social and cultural society—Círculo Social Israelita—though its activities and level did not compare with those of SHA.[75]

Many other groups were formed by the Jewish youth in several neighborhoods of Buenos Aires. However, they never attained the popularity and importance of Juventud and SHA. Still, the activities of the Asociación Juventud Cultural Sionista showed a deeper concern for Jewish culture than most other societies, which stressed their social activities. Besides a series of conferences, the members of this Zionist youth group concerned themselves with making Zionist classics available in Spanish. The first book, Herzl's *The Jewish State*, appeared in Buenos Aires just before the end of our period, in 1929. Moreover, in response to the idea of the Ateneo Juvenil Israelita of Rosario of federating all Jewish cultural societies, the Asociación Juventud Cultural Sionista took the lead in calling a congress of these societies for October 1930. The congress, however, was limited to those "Jewish cultural institutions in the country with a national ideology. In other words, to those with activities leading to the ultimate objective of considering the Jewish people as a national entity, with its national culture, history, and traditions." FICHA—Federación de Instituciones Culturales Hebreas Argentinas—which was formed at this congress, did not have an important role in the life of the cultural societies.[76]

The main difference between the Jewish culture of the immigrant and that of the native Jew in Argentina was rooted in the language. Not only was Yiddish an instrument of contemporary Jewish cultural creativity, but it also served as the language that bound the Jew to his community, in Eastern Europe as well as in Buenos Aires. The Jew educated in Argentina, basically in Spanish, was not only limited in his access to Jewish works because of the language but also lacked a special language for Jewish activities. Spanish was for such a Jew both the language of daily occupations and of Jewish interests. This "normalization" of Jewish and more general activities—at least with respect to language—was a major factor for the dilution of such Jews' Jewish culture in the midst of the Argentinian and universal culture.

This factor is evident when comparing the Yiddish press with the Jewish press in the vernacular in Argentina. The Spanish Jewish press had a totally different function in Buenos Aires than its Yiddish counterpart. The latter played a role in daily life for a substantial number of Jews. The Yiddish dailies were the main source of information relating to world, national, and specifically Jewish events. They catered to an immigrant population used to the Yiddish press in Eastern Europe. On the other hand, the Spanish press had to create its market from among the young generation or those immigrants who have been absorbed more rapidly into cultural expressions in Argentina's vernacular. The Sephardic population, furthermore, was a prospective group of readers. All these latter groups read the regular daily press in the country, thus making a daily Jewish press superfluous. Curiously enough, the first attempt of a daily in Spanish came from a Sephardic-sponsored periodical, *Israel*, in 1920.[77]

The lack of Spanish-language journals with leftist ideologies sponsored by Jewish societies—as opposed to Yiddish-language journals—is not necessarily an indication that there were no Argentine-educated Jews involved in such political and social struggles. Indeed, it reveals that those who were active preferred to act in the general arena and not through a circle composed of a national or cultural minority. They did not need a Yiddish-speaking group, for they had full command of Spanish; moreover, they did not participate as Jews in those groups, for they considered themselves either Argentinian or universalist.[78]

Only one of the publications in Spanish during the period terminating in 1930 was directed by members of the Sephardic communities. In March 1917 Samuel de A. Levy and Jacob Levy published *Israel*, which appeared monthly, then weekly, then (for six months in 1920) five times a week. *Israel* did not have a definite line. Notes, interviews, illustrations, articles, and news about the Sephardic communities in Buenos Aires—especially the Moroccan one—as well as in the interior and abroad, were published without an organic structure. Its leanings towards Zionism were quite atypical of Sephardim in Buenos Aires up to 1930. Only in this last year did a new Sephardic journal, *La Luz*, raise the level of Sephardic journalism in Buenos Aires.[79]

It would have been only natural that the periodicals in Spanish should try to attract Sephardic readers, since Spanish was spoken also by many immigrants.[80] However, this was not the general case. Of the nine "Ashkenazic" periodicals issued in Spanish before 1930—with varying fortunes: only one is still published, one barely made it to 1930, and seven closed before that date—only three, those with a Zionist orientation, made an effort to broaden their scope to include Sephardic issues. *El Sionista*, with which the Jewish press in Spanish made its debut in Argentina on June 15, 1904, was devoted to Zionist issues. It was also concerned with the Moroccan Jewish community in Buenos Aires, of which, during those early years of the century, many members were active in Zionist centers.[81] Both *El Macabeo*, which appeared for a short period of time in 1920, and *El Semanario Hebreo*, a weekly that appeared irregularly for nearly a decade starting in 1923, were definitely Zionist-oriented. The latter, especially, wrote about developments in the Sephardic communities, and about Zionist activities among Sephardim.[82]

The most prestigious weekly in Spanish, *Mundo Israelita*, issued since 1923, was during the twenties a constant critic of the Jewish community in Argentina. At first it was considered the spokesman of Asociación Hebraica, though it became independent quite rapidly.[83] It adopted a secularist position, though opposed to extreme leftist groups; it defended all Jewish cultural and relief organizations and raised its voice against antisemitic outbursts or cases of discrimination against Jews. Lukewarm to Zionist aspirations at its most early stage, by the end of the decade it adopted a much more positive attitude in this respect. Its prime concern, as reflected in its columns during the twenties, was that of educating an Argentinian Jewish generation and promoting native leadership in the community. Fully conscious of the differences between the "new" generation born in the country and their parents' generation, as well as of the differences betwen the former and newly arrived immigrants, the combatant editors of *Mundo Israelita*, León Kibrick and Salomón Resnick, saw the future of the Jewish community in a leadership conversant in Spanish.[84] They promoted translations of books from Yiddish and other languages into Spanish, many of which were first published in installments in the weekly. There Mendele, Shalom Aleichem, Shalom Asch, Abraham Reisen, Haim Zhitlowsky, Israel Zangwill, Hermann Cohen, and Simon Dubnow, among others, first appeared in Spanish during that decade.[85] *Mundo Israelita* was one of the main forces struggling for the formation of a Kehilla—organized Jewish community—in Buenos Aires. Opposing all other opinions favoring the formation of an *Alianza*, or organization composed of delegates from all Jewish societies in the city, *Mundo Israelita* advocated the transformation of the Chevra Keduscha into the Kehilla. When other attempts failed, its thesis succeeded, though not until two decades later, in 1949.

Juventud (1911–17), and the literary monthly *Vida Nuestra* (1917–23) published articles by the most distinguished Argentinian authors and works by intellectual Argentinian Jews, as well as translations from leading works by European Jewish writers.[86] Their impact—especially that of *Vida Nuestra*—was powerful among the native Jews. Even of greater importance was their impact among Argentinian intellectuals and politicians. This was especially reflected in an inquiry about their disposition towards Jews and their immigration to the country and their attitude toward the perpetrators of the disturbances of the Semana Trágica in January 1919.[87]

Three short-lived magazines in Spanish were published during the first half of the 1910s. *Israel* (*Organo de los israelitas en la Argentina*) appeared five times in 1911. It was the organ of the Club Israelita, founded on August 23, 1908, with the purpose of fighting against the white slave dealers. Soon the Club Israelita became a social center promoting the naturalization of Jews, stressing their civic and political responsibilities. However, it degenerated into a gambling den, while its leaders profited from selling the votes of the members to the political parties before elections.[88] *El Israelita Argentino*, starting on July 1, 1913, published news about Jewish institutions in Buenos Aires and in the interior of the country. It fought strongly for the formation of a federation of Jewish institutions in 1913, learning from the errors made by the first attempt at such a federation in 1909–10.[89] The weekly *Crónica Semanal*, reporting mainly on social events in the Jewish community, was issued only during the first five months of 1915.[90]

The Argentinizing aspects of the national culture proved to be effective among a generation of Jews, namely those who arrived as youngsters and were educated in Argentina. The numbers of Jews entering the universities and professions was forever growing. During the twenties Jews were invited to teach in many faculties at the national universities, including the University of Buenos Aires. They profited from a new liberalized policy, which, undergoing processes of reformation and counterreformation, especially since the Córdoba Reform in 1918, had permitted sons of immigrants and non-Catholics to lecture at the faculties.[91]

The doors of the most important dailies in Argentina were also opened to Jews. The traditional and influential *La Nación* included Alberto Gerchunoff among its regular columnists and Gregorio Fingermann as its art critic. Enrique Lippschutz wrote for the equally influential *La Prensa*. In 1908 Gerchunoff started publishing in *La Nación* his first sketches about the life of the Jews in the Argentinian Pampas, colonists in the JCA settlements, which were collected in his *Los gauchos judíos*.

Published in commemoration of Argentina's centenary in 1910, *Los gauchos judíos* marked the appearance of the Jewish theme in the Argentine literary scene. This work also represented the beginning of Gerchunoff's career as a short story writer in Spanish, for which he received praise from the most acclaimed writers in Spanish of the time.[92] These short sketches comprise a variety of topics, such as a description of the meeting held by the rabbi and elders of the small town of Tulchin, in Russia, when the first dealings were made with representatives of Baron de Hirsch about the organization of Jewish colonies in Argentina ("Génesis"); the Sabbath in the colonies ("La siesta"); sentimental episodes ("El cantar de los cantares"); intermarriage ("El divorcio"); the Jewish rural physician ("El médico milagroso"). Throughout the stories, moreover, we read about the relations between Jewish colonists and gauchos of the area who worked in the colonies.

On occasion these relations were tragic, as when a gaucho killed a colonist because of a disagreement with respect to which horse to use for thrashing ("La muerte de Rabí Abraham"); or when a gaucho stole a silver candelabrum on a Sabbath, while the owner watched helplessly, unable to interrupt his prayers ("El candelabro de plata"). However, in most of the stories relations between gauchos and Jews were excellent, even reaching, the mixed marriage stage.[93] Not only was Argentina compared to Jerusalem by Gerchunoff, who also illustrated this with quotations from medieval Jewish poets in Spain who thought identically of their native Spanish soil,[94] but he also described how Jews had adopted most customs of the gauchos, including eating habits, singing, and the manner of speaking. The author, completely identified with his adoptive country—Gerchunoff was born in Proskurow, Kamenetz-Podolsk, in Russia—emphasized his total integration with the spirit and atmosphere of Argentina and attempted to dispel all prejudices held against Jews for being unassimilable.[95] The symbiosis of Jewish and creole values is so tightly knit that the book, while being unanimously praised for its literary value, received contrasting criticisms from different sectors of the Argentinian population. Some Jewish sectors reviewed *Los gauchos judíos* as assimilationist, while anti-Jewish sectarians considered it Judaizing.

For the period ending in 1930 the interest of Argentine Jewish writers in Spanish did not rest in Jewish topics. Most wrote about universal themes and about particular problems of Argentine society. Only the exception of the most acclaimed were interested in describing Jewish traditions or values. Samuel Eichelbaum (1894–1967), an outstanding figure in Argentine letters as a playwright and short-story writer who received the Buenos Aires Municipal prize for his *Tormenta de Dios* (1930), only indulged in Jewish themes in *El judío Aarón* (1942) and later in *La buena cosecha*. Samuel Glusberg (1898–)—whose pseudonym Enrique Espinoza was a combination of the names of his two literary heroes, Heinrich Heine and Baruch Spinoza—one of the founders of the Argentine Association of Writers, collected a series of reminiscences of Jewish life in the Buenos Aires ghetto in *La levita gris* (1924). In "Mate amargo" and in "Ruth y Noemí" Glusberg deals with the contrasts between Jewish immigrants in Buenos Aires and the assimilationist tendencies of the latter. César Tiempo (pseudonym for Israel Zeitlin, 1906–), poet and playwright, was nearer to Jewish themes, though his publications before 1930 were obviously limited. In

1930 his collection of poems on Jewish values and life in Buenos Aires, *Libro para la pausa del Sábado*, appeared.

During the first three decades of the century there were many Jews who influenced the cultural life of Argentina. Jews contributed individually, mainly as Argentinians, to the cultural creativity in the country. The Jewish aspect of their personalities was not, by and large, a conspicuous element in their writings. A distinct Jewish influence is far from discernable in Argentine literature of the time. Moreover, definite Jewish activities on the part of Jewish intellectuals in Spanish were only sporadic.[96]

Two decades after 1930 the trend continued along similar lines, though works with a particular Jewish character were produced in a somewhat larger proportion. Louis Nesbit, commenting on Jewish contributions to Argentine literature, expressed in no uncertain terms the imposing influence of Argentina on Jewish writers: "Certainly in no part of the world has Jewish intellectual life become permeated with the native atmosphere as rapidly as in Argentina. From the very beginning the Jewish writer has identified himself with Argentine national aspirations."[97]

Jewish intellectuals in Argentina who were not educated in Eastern Europe quite often did not show a clear understanding of Judaism and the role of the Jewish people in world history. Even Gerchunoff had contradictory ideas and views. In 1906 he wrote that "the Jews do not need to return to Zion. What is urgent is to grant them a place in the universe where they will not be massacred. For that, even Chubut is better than the twenty metres of land of the Sultan, sterile and sad."[98] After the Balfour Declaration he changed his attitude. In September 1918 he wrote about "Jerusalem, a vision of peace," singing to its revival.[99] He also spoke at special celebrations for the departure of the Jewish Legionaries from Buenos Aires (1918) and the foundation of the Hebrew University (1925).[100]

Gerchunoff, in his *El cristianismo precristiano* (Pre-Christian Christianity), 1924, showed a partial understanding of Judaism as a religion by asserting that "Catholicism is an organized Judaism."[101] The Christian concept of the fulfillment of the promises in the Old Testament in the Gospels, widespread, of course, in Argentine Catholic society, influenced some secularized and assimilated Jews. However, it changed the life of Julio Fingerit, a contributor to *Juventud, Vida Nuestra, Mundo Israelita*, and director of *Semanario Hebreo* during the early 1920s. A young man in search of God, Fingerit believed in the promise made to Israel, while he accepted Jesus as Messiah and Son of God. However, he asserted himself as a Jew by race. In a letter sent both to *Mundo Israelita* and to *Criterio*, the main Catholic weekly in Buenos Aires, Fingerit wrote "One cannot give up being Jewish, as one cannot give up being German, or Latin, or Slav; but one can give up the Mosaic or Lutheran creed and become Mohammedan or Buddhist. And when one knows the Truth, one becomes Catholic."[102]

The first generation of Argentinian Jews, which flourished during the early decades of the twentieth century, was far removed from Jewish traditions. On the one hand, those young Jews had not experienced the Jewish life of Eastern Europe or of the Sephardic centers; while on the other hand, in Argentina there was no substantial amount of literature dealing with Jewish subjects in the vernacular. Religious, cultural, and even Zionist leaders in Buenos Aires did not appeal to the native-born Jews. These leaders, also immigrants, appealed mainly to Jews of their own generation who had a similar European background. Thus the Argentinian Jew remained ignorant of Jewish culture and values while they entered head-on into the cultural, economic, and professional life of Argentina. Even the most acute differences betwen Judaism and Christianity were polished in their secular minds. Important efforts were made, nonetheless, by some individuals who founded centers like CJIA, SHA, and other social associations. They published periodicals, which, during the years 1911–23 represented a valuable contribution to the Spanish-speaking Jews. Their goals—as can be seen from collections of *Juventud* and *Vida Nuestra*—included publishing works by Argentinian authors as well as by Jewish authors on general topics, along with translations of Jewish classics. In 1923 a change occurred with the foundation of Asociación Hebraica and *Mundo Israelita*. It was mainly the weekly that made an impact upon the Jewish community of Buenos Aires, for it established the first links between the main Jewish institutions in the city and the Jewish world abroad on the one hand and the Spanish-speaking Jews in Argentina on the other. Still, during the rest of that decade Jewish culture in Spanish was in its embryonic period. Publications of books and journals in Spanish, as well as Jewish cultural activities in that language, were intensified as a result of an increase of native-born Jews and world events which had a direct influence on Jewish life during the 1930s and 1940s.

Spirit of Solidarity: The Fight against Poverty and Evil

The assistance and protection of fellow Jews in need has been a constant characteristic of Jewish life throughout the centuries. The spirit of unity and interdependence of Jews all over the world proved to be a major source of strength for individual Jews in distress, as well as for entire Jewish communities confronted with a sad reality of indigence and persecution. This spirit of responsibility for fellow Jews crystallized in different ways in each Jewish community, depending on the factors demanding aid or relief and on the predisposition and means of the Jewish leadership to help those in distress. In particular, the early Jewish community in Argentina responded in three different levels to the situations created by poverty and intolerance. First, it remained linked to the rest of the Jewish people by responding to needs in some of the communities in the Old World. Second, possessed of a deep sense of historic responsibility as pioneer in Argentinian Jewry, it developed a series of mutual help, relief, and charitable institutions that by 1930 had become pillars of Jewish life there. Finally, it responded energetically to a problem affecting the whole Jewish people but that had touched upon Jews in Buenos Aires much more profoundly: white slave trafficking.

Relief Work for Jews in the Old World

The established Jews in Argentina did not cut themselves off from their old communities or remain aloof from world events and their influence upon

184

fellow Jews abroad. Those who crossed the Atlantic by themselves had either spouses and children or parents and siblings to support or help immigrate to Argentina. Many did not forget their communities of old, and provided for their fellow townsmen in Europe through the tens of *landsmanschaften* associations founded in Buenos Aires and some cities of the interior. Their link to the Jewish people was fortified by the numerous relief campaigns organized to help Jewish victims of World War I and of pogroms both before and after the war in Europe, Asia, and Africa. Relief for Jewish communities in the Old World constituted, right from the inception of organized Jewish life in Argentina, a major preoccupation.

Concern with the deteriorating fate of Russian Jewry was evidenced during the early stages of Jewish life in Buenos Aires. The few hundred West European Jews there in 1881 demonstrated their strong kinship with their Russian brethren not only by raising funds to help their coreligionists escape from Russia and other countries but through the influence of some English Jews— probably Henry Joseph among them—managed to enlist the aid of many Christian Englishmen in Buenos Aires in a relief campaign.[1] The Congregación Israelita (CIRA) continued, through World War I, setting the pace for campaigns of relief for Jews abroad. It was especially suited for this, for its members were among the wealthiest Jews in town and had, through many trips to Europe, established sound contacts with organizations directly involved in relief campaigns, such as the Alliance Israélite Universelle (AIU). When the pogroms in Russia reached their climax in October 1905, immediately after Tsar Nicholas II had been forced to grant a constitution to the Russian people, a Comité de Socorros para las Víctimas Israelitas en Rusia was opened at CIRA. During November and December of that year there was an intensive campaign, with the local Spanish newspapers publishing details of it. Even non-Jews spoke at public protests, including Reverend W. P. McLaughlin of the Methodist church. Moreover, due to business ties many Christians also contributed heavily to the funds sent to Russia from Buenos Aires.[2]

When the Sephardic communities in the Old World suffered from pogroms or particular calamities, CIRA took the initiative in relief work. This was the case when the French Protectorate was established in Morocco in 1912, thus provoking a pogrom in Fez claiming over 100 victims.[3] In 1917 a great fire destroyed most of Salonika leaving some 50,000 Jews homeless. The AIU immediately approached Rabbi S. Halphon of CIRA for help. With the help of Sephardim in Buenos Aires, Halphon led a campaign that gathered 6,890 pesos (18,050 francs), which were mailed to AIU.[4]

The concern for Jewish victims in Europe reached a climax during the war years. Early in 1915, sponsored by leading Zionists in Buenos Aires, the Comité Central Pro–Víctimas Israelitas de la Guerra (Zentral Komite far Yiddishe Milhome Leidnde)—hereafter CC—was formed.[5] This nationwide organization—with over seventy branches in the interior of Argentina and in Uruguay, Paraguay, Brazil, and Chile—by means of monthly payments, sales of "*pro-víctimas*" stamps, concerts, dancing parties, and raffles and by such means as donations of wheat by the Jewish colonists in Entre Ríos and special collections during a week instituted as "Día de la Flor" was able to forward over 500,000 pesos to the American Jewish Joint Distribution Committee (JDC).[6]

Relief work continued after the war. The great number of displaced persons, and especially the postwar pogroms in Poland, kept the Jewish population in Argentina active in sending relief and in organizing protest demonstrations. On July 29, 1919, barely half a year after the assaults against Jews during the Semana Trágica, the Jews in the country filled the streets with billboards denouncing those "barbarian acts" in Poland, hoping that the Argentine public opinion would also repudiate them: "All Jewish stores, factories, workshops, and everything that has something to do with material life of our community shall be closed after 12 noon."[7]

In 1919, especially with the Poale Zionists' unconditional adherence to the CC,[8] a radical turn took place in the policy of this relief organization. The labor forces challenged the "conservative and [general] Zionist elements" and decided to send the money to JDC but earmarked it to the account of the People's Relief Committee.[9] The reason for this new policy, the CC leaders argued, was five years of frustrating experiences with JDC. The latter did not send the CC in Argentina official receipts but only letters of acknowledgment; they also did not inform the CC about the relief work and the way the funds were distributed in Eastern Europe. The complaint was that JDC "ignored us and did not help us enhance our prestige in order to add new dimensions to our work."[10]

The People's Relief Committee was opposed to the "philanthropic character of JDC's work," which only encouraged the proliferation of "mendicants and schnorers." It thus advised the CC to decide in its forthcoming convention to adhere to its own policy of "constructive" help. Considering the possibilities of a complete parting of the People's Relief Committee from JDC in case relief work was to pass to private hands, the former wrote that CC's support "would give us more strength to fight from within if we remain in the JDC, . . . and if we are obligated to work independently, we would need your help even more."[11]

At a CC convention of May 16–18, 1920 a long debate ensued. Jacobo Joselevich, a general Zionist, and president of CC, argued that monies should be sent through JDC, which represents all United States Jews, just as CC represents all Jews of Argentina, and asserted that relief work required immediate and effective help without interference of "utopic plans for reconstruction and class struggles, as is the desire of the Jewish Socialists." Other speakers quoted from a letter sent by Dr. Max (Moshe) Soloveitchik, the Lithuanian minister for Jewish Affairs and Dr. Shimshon Rosenbaum, president of the National Committee (Lithuania), in which they expressed their need not of philanthropy but of means to be able to help themselves. Regalsky (P. Z.) finally described the situation in the United States, stating that the *Yahudim* of JDC were antidemocratic and assimilationist, while the People's Relief adhered to national democratic help and was supported not only by Poale Zion and Bund but also by the Jewish masses. Regalsky's proposal that CC work with People's Relief was approved.[12] By 53 votes to 31 its name was changed to Zentral Komite fun

Yiddisher Folks-Hilf far di Milhome un Pogrom Gelitene (lit., "Central Committee of Jewish People's Relief for War and Pogrom Victims"). Moreover, the resolutions of the convention indicate a total identification with People's Relief Committee's principles.[13]

The policy of CC was a matter of constant debates during the following eighteen months. The "conservative" elements did not agree with the changes made at the convention. Arguments on both sides were voiced in the Jewish press in Buenos Aires and were reflected in the correspondence of CC with the People's Relief Committee in New York. During this period four shipments were made to New York, whence they were forwarded to Russia. Fifty per cent of the goods—clothes, shoes, soap, sugar, foodstuffs, and medicine, the first shipment alone valued at 100,000 dollars—were earmarked for the Ukraine, and the rest for other countries in Eastern Europe. Besides, 30,000 pesos (about 12,000 dollars) was cabled to Paris for the Ukrainian refugees in Bessarabia, and private packages and monies were mailed directly to Eastern Europe.[14] When Soprotimis, founded by the conservative Jewish elements in 1922, started work on behalf of Jewish immigrants, some activities overlapped. Later during that decade both institutions agreed to collaborate in some specific areas.

The continuous stream of support for family and communities in the Old World sent through CC, Soprotimis, and the various resident institutions, both Sephardic and Ashkenazic, were responsible for the maintenance of ties with stronger Jewish communities than those in Argentina. In 1930 these ties were still stronger than Zionism among Jews in Argentina, in spite of the fact that Zionism was, as we have seen, conquering larger sectors of Jewry there.

Protection of Immigrants and Mutual Help

The Jewish population in Argentina grew from about 1,500 in 1888 to nearly 220,000 in 1930. More than half of the latter lived in the capital city. During the period 1890–1930 at least two-thirds of the Jewish population in Buenos Aires was foreign-born.[15] Most of these Jewish immigrants did not, when arriving in Argentina, possess economic means with which to subsist and progress there. Many left their native cities and towns without a profession, and with few personal belongings. Moreover, the fact that they did not speak Spanish proved to be a handicap for the East European Jews searching for jobs vis-à-vis their fellow immigrants from Spain and Italy. Thus, a large proportion of the Ashkenazim who settled in the cities were employed as unskilled workers at first. Some progressed by acquiring personal skills, others advanced in commerce and industry. But still, many did not. They and their families constituted the bulk of indigent Jews in the country, for they were the most vulnerable during seasons of unemployment or in cases when the main supporter of the family fell sick or died. To assist them, the organized community developed mutual help associations, popular kitchens, job bureaus, and various medical services, including a Jewish hospital and several clinics. In 1872 the Jews of CIRA formed a Sociedad Israelita de Beneficencia in order to aid members unable to work due to sickness, as well as to provide for burials in cases of death.[16] With the arrival of immigrants from Eastern Europe, however, new institutions were founded. During the period 1894–1900, the three main institutions providing mutual help and medical aid continuing to our days were founded. The Chevra Keduscha was started at the initiative of CIRA, CIL, Poale Zedek, and Mahzikei Emuna in 1894 with the purpose of caring for burials according to Jewish rites. Three years later, in 1897, most of the Moroccan members joined in their own Gemilat Hassadim, and soon afterwards the most veteran institution was renamed Chevra Keduscha Ashkenasi. As we shall see below, this institution became, during the twenties, the central organization for Ashkenazi Jewry in Buenos Aires, with a mutual aid and philanthropic character.

A group of young Jewish workers founded, in 1896, the Unión Obrera Israelita (UOI), a mutual aid society with the purpose of helping immigrants find jobs. Due to their ignorance of the language, many of the latter were exploited by their bosses. The UOI thus started a night school, where Spanish was taught, and a library. At the beginning it was strictly a mutual aid society for Jewish workers. However, five years later, in view of the still small number of Jewish workers in Buenos Aires, the UOI also opened its doors to professionals, excluding those who were not wage earners. In 1903, moreover, all Jews could become members, though the particular workers' character of the institution was maintained.[17] Finally, in 1905, a new change permitted the entrance of *socios protectores*, or members who were not interested in receiving benefits from the society but desired to strengthen its philanthropic work. In 1907 the name was enlarged to UOI Bikur Joilim as result of the addition of a section to provide for the sick. This latter section rapidly became the main concern of Bikur Joilim. Its membership rose from 900 in 1908 to 1,800 in 1916.[18] During 1929, over 3,200 members were examined at Bikur Joilim's clinics—927 at their homes—and 6,058 prescriptions were filled.[19]

On December 25, 1900, the Sociedad Israelita de Beneficencia "Ezrah" (Ezrah) was founded by members of CIRA and East European Jews. Its purpose was "to aid and protect the poor, sick, helpless, and needy coreligionists."[20] This was accomplished by donations of money, clothing, and food. From its inception Ezrah contemplated the erection of a hospital and thus set aside 25 percent of all income for this end.[21] However, the indigence in many sectors of the Jewish population in Argentina during the first decade of the century proved to be a great obstacle not only for the rapid construction of a Jewish hospital but also of a home for the aged and orphans. Long debates at the board of Ezrah were held about the question of whether to utilize parts of the reserve funds earmarked for the hospital in order to solve more immediate problems of needy Jews at the waiting room of the institution.[22]

A Jewish hospital, nonetheless, was urgently needed even at an early stage of the century. Many Jews were not well cared for at the municipal hospitals due to their different customs and because of their difficulties in explaining their needs and maladies in Spanish. Therefore, a special committee "Pro-Hospital" was formed in 1907, which was also supported by Bikur Joilim.[23]

During the following year it was agreed that such a big enterprise should be sponsored by the entire Jewish community, not only by Ezrah. The Federación Israelita Argentina (FIA), formed late in 1908 and comprised of the main Ashkenazic Jewish societies in Buenos Aires—CIRA, Chevra Keduscha, Ezrah, Bikur Joilim, and Talmud Torah—took over from Ezrah the initiative of building the Jewish hospital.

The representatives of FIA made important contacts, during 1909, with the mayor of Buenos Aires and with the president of the Municipal Council (Concejo Deliberante), Dr. Coll, hoping to obtain from the municipality the donation of a tract of land for the hospital in the Parque Centenario neighborhood.[24] The municipal promise was not fulfilled because of a series of events transpiring in Buenos Aires at the end of 1909 and the beginnings of 1910. In November 1909 a Russian Jew, Simón Radowitzky, had killed the chief of police, Ramón Falcón, creating a hostile atmosphere towards other "Russians."[25] Moreover, a group of Jews with political ambitions had presented a petition similar to FIA's to the municipality in the name of the Club Israelita.[26] Furthermore, the director of the Public Health Department (Asistencia Pública), Dr. José Penna, presented an unfavorable report, considering that the Jewish hospital should be built in a private terrain belonging to the Jewish community, as was the case with all other hospitals sponsored by foreign residents in the city.[27] Penna advised the mayor that the site in Parque Centenario was better suited for an asylum than for a hospital.[28] In view of these difficulties, and the imperious need of a hospital to care for the growing number of indigent Jews in need of medical assistance, as well as for demonstrating the Jewish spirit of friendship and gratitude to Argentina by building such a medical institution, a general assembly of Ezrah decided that Ezrah itself would buy a lot in the Flores section of Buenos Aires in July, 1910.[29]

The first pavillion of the Hospital Israelita was inaugurated in May 1921, nearly eleven years after the decision to buy the land. Over 400,000 pesos was spent on the terrain and building expenses. The second pavillion was inaugurated in 1928. The number of beds was raised from 65 to 189, and the yearly number of patients assisted rose from 15,000 in 1922 to 22,000 in 1925, and to 48,000 in 1930.[30] During the early 1920s there were 11 paid and 21 volunteer physicians. In 1929, due to the severe economic crisis, the physicians were asked to donate their salaries for the next two years. However, they continued serving free of charge until 1943.[31]

A Jewish old age home and an orphan asylum were strongly needed in Buenos Aires at the turn of the century. In spite of many projects before the world war, the actual foundation of such institutions was prompted by a series of fortuitous events, which brought the founders face to face with human tragedy. The painful supplications of some old Jews, sick and defenseless, found in a Christian old age home, were decisive. During 1915 a group of Jews met at the precincts of the Chevra Keduscha and decided upon creating a Jewish old age home (Asilo de Ancianos, or Moshav Zkeinim), which opened on June 18, 1916. Shortly afterwards police officials of the twenty-first district called to the attention of some Jews three abandoned orphans almost dead from hunger and cold. This gave the final impetus to add a male orphan section to the old age home.[32] Furthermore, during 1916 the Sociedad de Socorros de Damas Israelitas, which had been founded eight years earlier at the initiative of Rabbi Halphon and under the auspices of CIRA, was able to inaugurate its first building for an asylum for orphan girls. By 1923, 110 girls were housed here. Their number reached 170 in 1928, after their new premises in the Arévalo street were inaugurated.[33] In the meantime the Asilo Israelita Argentino, formed by the old age home and the male orphan asylum, housed 78 elders and 204 boys in 1928.[34] Both orphan asylums provided the boys and girls, respectively, with secular and Jewish education, as well as professional instruction.[35]

Before proper vaccinations to build the body's resistance to tuberculosis were discovered, this malady constituted a serious threat to the world population. By 1930, more than 20,000 people died of TB in Argentina yearly. Moreover, most of the estimated 200,000 sick with TB at the time were not carefully treated in a country with about 3,000 beds for this purpose.[36] During the twelve-year period 1917–28 about 11.6 percent of Jewish deaths in Buenos Aires were caused by tuberculosis.[37] Alert to this threat, a group of young Jews got together during January 1916 in order to get funds and cooperate in the treatment of the sick, founding the Liga de Socorro a los Tuberculosos Israelitas, soon afterwards called Liga Israelita Argentina Contra la Tuberculosis (Yiddish-Argentinishe Lige Kegn Tuberculozis). For the period 1916–25 their activities were reduced to medical assistance in private clinics and the provision of food. In 1925 a clinic was installed in the new headquarters of the institution (Sarmiento number 2153, in Once), thus initiating a new stage of fruitful work against the malady. Intense prophylaxis campaigns were carried on during the next few years. Tens of thousands of copies of a booklet, *Tuberculosis*, in Yiddish and Spanish, were distributed; conferences were given in various Jewish institutions and broadcasted over the radio; and articles were printed in the main periodicals of the community. A special arrangement was made with the Sanatorio Nacional of Santa María, in the Córdoba mountains—where the climate is convenient for the treatment of TB—by which the institution agreed to place 30 of the Liga's patients yearly.[38] The number of patients treated rose from 1,020 in 1925 to 11,342 in 1930.[39]

Of great concern was the absorption of immigrants in the country. During the first years of mass immigration from Eastern Europe immigrants appealed to all Jewish institutions or to the more veteran Jews in Buenos Aires for assistance in finding jobs and other necessities. But this was not sufficient. Thus in 1904 a group of Jews, mainly from CIRA, and headed by Luis H. Brie, president of CIRA, founded the Asociación Protectora de Inmigrantes Israelitas Schomer Israel. During its two-year existence this society ran a kitchen for immigrants, where meals were served either at token prices or gratis. Over 310 meals a day, on the average, were served. Moreover, Schomer Israel tried to place some of the immigrants in the interior of the country, for which it came into direct contact with Juan Alsina, director of the Immigration Department.[40] During the 1920s the activities of Soprotimis and the Comité Central (see above and ch. 1) were more successful in placing immigrants. For the period

1922–30 Soprotimis found jobs for about 6,700 immigrants of the total of 13,459 who were inscribed at their offices. Most of them were sent to the JCA colonies.[41]

During 1922 the Cocina Popular Israelita (Yiddisher Folks Kich un Ajnoses Orjim)—CPI—was founded. It provided meals daily, gratis, to immigrants for ten days. Moreover, for nonimmigrants or those who had been in the country for some time, the CPI furnished meals at very inexpensive rates. By 1930 it served 300 meals daily, half gratis.[42]

All these Jewish philanthropic institutions—with the exclusion of the Chevra Keduscha—had similar patterns of fund raising. They organized dances, raffles, and special week campaigns, as well as such artistic events as concerts, Yiddish theater performances, and motion pictures. However, the bulk of the budget was covered by membership dues paid by Jews all over the country and special campaigns led in all Jewish communities in Argentina. Ezrah had 4,500 members in 1921 and 10,795 in 1932, of which 2,000 were from the interior. From 1,550 members in Buenos Aires and none in the provinces in 1925, membership at the Liga Israelita Argentina contra la Tuberculosis rose to 3,650 in the capital and 2,950 in the interior in 1929. On the other hand, all these charitable institutions provided services that benefited Jews in the interior as well, who often traveled to Buenos Aires in order to get medical treatment at Ezrah or the Liga or to enter one of the orphanages or the old age home. The medical institutions, moreover, were not limited to the treatment of Jewish patients.[43]

The Chevra Keduscha Aschkenasi grew speedily after large numbers of Jews from Eastern Europe settled in Argentina starting in 1906. With the acquisition of the cemetery in Liniers during 1910 the burial society attracted larger numbers of Jews in Buenos Aires who now relied more on the benefits the Chevra Keduscha could grant. From then until the 1950s this institution—later under the name of Asociación Mutual Israelita Argentina, or AMIA—continued to grow. Table 5 reflects the membership movement.

Once the cemetery in Liniers had been paid for, the officials at the Chevra Keduscha realized that the income from monthly dues, burial rights, gravestones permits, and rights for and upkeeping of marble stones—even if many of these services were completely gratis—far surpassed the expenses in charity and in mutual aid to widows and orphans. Thus, the economic power of the Chevra Keduscha permitted it to display a positive role in other areas of Jewish life in Buenos Aires. During the last half of the twenties this was clearly evident in the welfare area. Grants and subsidies went in growing proportions not only to widows and orphans—the original target of this mutual aid society—but also to the needy coreligionists in the country and to charitable and educational institutions in Argentina and outside of it.

The membership at the Chevra Keduscha was mainly Ashkenazic, though a small number of Sephardim were members, and on occasion a Sephardi was even included in the electoral lists to the Chevra Keduscha's board.[44] This membership, however, was a composite of people of the most diverse political inclinations. Both religious and secular Jews, Zionists of vari-

Table 5

Membership at the Chevra Keduscha Aschkenasi (founded 1894)

Year	Number of Members
1906	140
1907	300 plus
1908	800 plus
1910	1,000
1916	4,200
1923	11,000
1928	14,000

Source: Minutes of Chevra Keduscha; Juventud 6, no. 49 (July 1916); and Memoria y Balance, Chevra Keduscha.

ous ideological standings as well as anti-Zionists, communists, and capitalists, all wanted the Chevra Keduscha to support the institutions and parties of their preference. Moreover, the democratic structure of the Chevra Keduscha imposed that it support opposing goals such as Keren Hayesod (for the support of a Jewish National Home in Palestine) and Procor (which advocated the return of the Jews to the Soviet Far East). Table 6 illustrates the growing influence of the Chevra Keduscha among Jewish institutions in Argentina and overseas.

After 1928 the Chevra Keduscha began sponsoring the Jewish schools in Buenos Aires in a more consistent way. Only during the mid-1930s however, did it consolidate its position as main provider of many of the Talmud Torahs and other Jewish schools. Similarly, during the 1920s, its role among welfare institutions in the Jewish community was constantly growing. Due to its support the CPI was able to survive the crisis in 1929, and Ezrah and the asylums were bolstered by the large donations granted them by the Chevra Keduscha.

During the eight-year period before World War I a large number of Jewish workers arrived in Buenos Aires from Russia. Settling in the Jewish quarters—around Corrientes Avenue to the east and especially west of Callao Avenue—they soon formed small mutual aid societies. Leon Chazanovich, the Poale Zionist activist who arrived in Argentina in 1909, succeeded in uniting various sectors of the Jewish working force in Buenos Aires under one mutual help organization, Unión Obrera Israelita de Socorros Mutuos y Enseñanza (Algemeiner Yiddisher Arbeter Varband in Argentine) on September 19, 1909. It immediately became the most important workers' organization in the Jewish street. It combined mutual help services with cultural ends and provided information about work in the country and abroad. By 1914 the number of sick treated reached 750. Its members numbered 746 at the beginning of that year. However, by the end of 1914 the activities at the Unión Obrera were paralyzed due to the general crisis in the country.[45] Other mutual aid workers' societies

Table 6

Subsidies and Donations Made by the Chevra Keduscha Aschkenasi
(in pesos)

Year[a]	Orphans, widows	Help needy	Ezrah	Asilo Israelita Argentino	Girls' Asylum	Cocina Popular Israelita	Liga Israelita Argentina Contra la Tuberculosis	Ezras Noschim	Keren Hayesod	Palestine Workers' Fund	Procor
1925/26	15,700	13,616	—	7,000	—	—	500	—	5,000	500	1,000
1926/27	21,700	18,469	10,000	13,000	—	—	—	1,800	5,000	500	—
1927/28	20,325	21,808	—	500	—	7,500	—	2,200	5,000	—	—
1928/29	29,650	32,657	10,200	—	5,000	—	—	2,400	20,000[b]	2,000	3,000
1929/30	22,400	31,457	3,000	275	—	823	—	2,600	5,000	—	—
1930/31	19,675	31,965	5,000	400	—	23,954	—	2,000	5,000	500	—

[a]The yearly periods start on October 1 and end on September 30.
[b]15,000 pesos were given to the Emergency Fund for Palestine due to the riots that took place there during 1929.
Sources: Chevra Keduscha, Memoria y Balance, corresponding to the respective periods.

were founded in later periods, but after more or less success all closed before 1930.[46]

Not only did the various Sephardic groups in Buenos Aires organize their mutual help and welfare societies separately from the Ashkenazim, but, indeed, each one of them—Damascene, Aleppine, Turkish (Ladino-speaking), and Moroccan—established its own institutions, thus accentuating its separateness. Each of these communities developed its welfare institutions along very similar lines to the others. The one digression was in the organization of the Turkish Jews, concentrated by and large in Comunidad Israelita Sefaradí (CIS). CIS—which was given the character of Kehilla, or community, for Sephardim of Turkish origin when the two sectors of these Jews, in Villa Crespo and in Centro, united in March 1919—concentrated in one institution their educational, religious, and welfare activities.[47] In 1920 CIS added to its charitable activities, providing the poor with money and essentials for the Jewish Holy Days and medical services for its members.[48]

The Damascene, Aleppine, and Moroccan Jews had burial societies independent from their synagogues and schools, though the members and even officials of their respective institutions overlapped to a large extent. The burial societies had a mutual aid character and provided for widows and orphans with a fixed stipend upon the death of the head of the family. Besides, many *hebrot* were created in their specific neighborhoods, to provide for the poor members in need.[49]

While the distance between Ashkenazic and Sephardic immigrants in Buenos Aires is easily explainable due to their different background, language, traditions, and attitudes, the factors that caused the separateness of the various Sephardic groups from each other are more subtle. There were language differences among the Sephardim themselves. Traditions differed even within these language groups. Between the two Syrian communities there existed a separateness even before coming to Argentina, in their own towns of origin.[50] Their attachment to religion varied from one community to the other, the Syrians being the most fervent believers, while the Moroccans were the most liberal. Furthermore, each group settled in different areas of the city, and most of their members worked in their respective neighborhoods. Their societies, quite understandably, were founded in their specific neighborhoods, thus limiting the possibilities of socializing with members of other Sephardic groups. Finally, the strong localism of these Jews was evident in their Argentine environment. Due to their strong emotional ties with their mother communities they did not consider the benefits of stronger all-Sephardic societies even if they would be limited to mutual help organization around a common burial association with a common cemetery.[51]

The membership characteristics of the Sephardic societies have some resemblance to the so-called *landsmanschaften*, or associations of immigrants from the same town or area. However, their differences outweigh their similarities. The *landsmanschaften*, which rose by the tens in Buenos Aires during the World War I period and the twenties built a social atmosphere for the immigrants from the particular area of origin in Poland, Galitzia, Roumania and

Bessarabia, promoting cultural activities. But their main object was to facilitate the economic absorption of the immigrant. The latter could obtain from their *landsmanschaft* loans with which to begin their activities in the country. Moreover, due to their mutual help structure, the members of the *landsmanschaften* and their families were backed in cases of sickness, death, or unemployment. These funds, as well as others established in many areas of the Jewish neighborhoods, paved the way for the formation of hundreds of credit cooperatives. This expansion started during the twenties and continued during the following four decades. While the Sephardic organizations were built around religious and charitable concerns, the Ashkenazic *landsmanschaften* had a secular orientation, were concerned with Jewish culture, and aided their members along lines of loans that could establish them on firm ground, in opposition to charity.[52]

By 1930 the Jews in Argentina could proudly contemplate the fruits of their efforts in the area of welfare institutions for their indigent and defenseless coreligionists. The Ashkenazim, as well as each of the Sephardic groups, had their burial societies that provided a subsidy to widows and orphans of dead members. Two orphanages and an old age home were functioning for nearly fifteen years and had moved to bigger premises. The Hospital Israelita, as well as other institutions offering medical assistance, provided the sick patients with physicians who understood their language and their specific needs. The Liga Israelita Argentina contra la Tuberculosis was doing an important prophylactic work, as well as treating the tuberculous. Immigrants and indigent could receive meals either free of charge or at low prices at the Cocina Popular Israelita, and were aided in getting jobs by Soprotimis, the *landsmanschaften*, and many other organizations. Many of these institutions also had a special section providing the poor with money and clothing and occasionally with a working tool or machine. Even those who died poor and without family or means of support were the object of posthumous acts of charity when the society Hesed Shel Emeth (Ashkenazic) took care of placing a gravestone on their tombs.[53]

While the accomplishments during the forty-year period (1890–1930) were of weight in the welfare field, Argentine Jewry could have achieved higher goals. Endless disputes between organizations or between factions in a specific institution were forever distracting many of the most dedicated officials. Elections for the boards of most of these societies—especially during the 1920s and in later decades—gave occasion for strongly fought campaigns in the Jewish press and street. Even the annual assemblies at times were scenes of fist fights and scandals. These attitudes on the part of officials willing to work but also wanting to receive the due respect and credit for it prevented many other potential officials from participating in the direction of the societies. Moreover, while the assistance given at the medical centers, orphanages, and old age home was meritorious, the attitude with respect to the disabled and indigent left a lot to be desired. First, there was no interinstitutional control of amounts allocated to the same individual; second, the type of assistance was not constructive. Only at the end of the twenties did some of the institutions adopt the services of a social worker in order to study the individual cases and be able to grant help that would allow the beneficiary to become self-supporting afterwards.[54] At any rate, the basic organizational structure had been built, and the services given were varied and numerous. The number of Jews who were associated with these welfare societies—many contributed to as much as ten or twelve institutions annually—are a clear reflection of the significant role played by the latter for the identification of Jews in Argentina with their fellow Jew.

The Jewish Community Fights White Slavery

During the first months of 1930 Raquel Lieberman filed a complaint against Salomón José Korn to the police in Buenos Aires. Lieberman, who had been forcibly introduced into a brothel on her arrival in Argentina in 1924 and kept as a prostitute for about four years, had made up her mind to leave that profession as soon as possible. With the money she saved, Lieberman started a business in *objets d'art*, and by the late 1920s she had accumulated about 90,000 pesos ($33,000 dollars). It was in her store on Callao Avenue number 515 where she met Korn, who—unbeknowst to her—was a leading trafficker in women in Buenos Aires. They started an intimate relationship, and though Lieberman confided her past history to Korn, the latter promised to marry her in a civil ceremony. Korn opted to have a religious ceremony instead, waiving the civil document required by Argentine law.[1] Lieberman denounced her so-called husband for threatening her with violence, for taking away all her money and belongings, and for forcing her to return to a life of prostitution.

The subsequent investigation by the police led to the discovery that Korn was exploiting other prostitutes. Depositions against Korn brought to light the activities of a net of Jewish white slave dealers. These activities were widely known, but the traffickers had managed to secure impunity by bribing key officials. Now, for the first time in almost half a century, the attempts to denounce and effectively destroy the well-knit organization of Jewish traffickers met with at least partial success. The Jews in Buenos Aires, strongly embarrassed by the bad name the traffickers had given their community, welcomed

197

the process, for it finally removed the unfortunate impression that "dealers," *Polacos* (Poles), and Jews were synonymous terms. This scourge of the Jews of Buenos Aires was not removed immediately. Nevertheless, as we shall see, the derivations of the Lieberman-versus-Korn case, together with the political and social changes in Argentine society during the early 1930s, proved to be a mortal blow to Jewish white slavery in the country.[2]

Studies made at the turn of the century about the rising index of criminality in Buenos Aires, showed demographic growth as the main factor responsible for the rise in crime. It was said to be a "growth sickness." The positivist sociologists following Cesare Lombroso said that it was caused by a "biological degeneration." Others, from a Marxist point of view, asserted that crime was not itself a sickness but was a symptom of capitalistic growth. In a country with few industries and a limited job market those who remained on the fringes of organized society formed a proletariat—or better a *lumpenproletariat*—whence vagabonds, prostitutes, white slave dealers, murderers, and other such types rose. Be it a consequence of immigration, a biological degeneration, or a symptom of the social and economic structure of society, the fact is that crime was reaching alarming proportions.[3]

The Jewish immigrant community in Argentina did not lack its criminal offenders, though in a much lower ratio than other immigrant groups. Few Jews were convicted for crimes of violence such as murder or rape. They became conspicuous, however, in what was termed the "social" evil of prostitution and in the traffic of women for this purpose. In this descriptive analysis we devote particular attention to the reaction of the immigrant Jewish community to this "corrupted" element in its midst and to the way it deal with the fact of the existence of such a Jewish element. Moreover, Jewish participation in white slavery is placed in its appropriate context within the total traffic in Argentina.

The Jewish establishment in Argentina has kept as concealed as possible any reference to Jewish participation in white slavery and prostitution. There are no dispassionate studies of this activity not even apologetic articles. The reason is obvious: the Jews dreaded being singled out for crime because of possible antisemitic repercussions, albeit by avoiding the subject they were also concealing what may be described as one of the major attainments of the Jews in Argentina: their unremitting struggle against evil.[4]

Buenos Aires Attains a Reputation

Throughout the half century between 1880 and 1930 Argentina, especially Buenos Aires, was considered in Europe to be the greatest center for the commerce in women. Belisario Montero, Argentine ambassador in Brussels at the turn of the century, repeatedly protested against what he thought was undeserved criticism of his country's moral standing: "Here in Europe they reproach that our Republic, and especially Buenos Aires, is the most open and lucrative market for the sale of European women. They add that the traffickers, once in our capital city with their human merchandise, can consider themselves safe, enjoying the impunity of their crime."[5] Charges continued to be made and not without basis. The English crusader against white slavery, Sir William Alexander Coote, voiced them at an international conference against white slavery in 1913 in London, while books and articles in the main periodicals in Buenos Aires repeated them quite often.[6] Enrique Feinman, in an important article published in *Atlántida* in 1913, asserted that Argentine law provided no defense against white slavery and that "our capital [Buenos Aires] is known as the world center for this type of import and commerce."[7]

A report of the Special Body of Experts in Traffic in Women and Children of the League of Nations stated that in the mid-1920s there was[8]

> a constant flow of foreign prostitutes from every corner of Europe to the Argentine around all barriers devised to check it. This is the opinion of *souteneurs* and prostitutes in every capital of Europe from Paris to Cairo. The Argentine, and particularly Buenos Aires, is considered by such people everywhere as a sort of Golconda. As one of the owners of several houses of prostitution in Europe expressed it: "They keep on going as if they expected to find gold in the streets. Out of my house alone I lost 15 girls in four months. It must be as good as they say because they do not come back."

Throughout these five decades Buenos Aires—even while changing at a very speedy pace—retained the doubtful privilege of being considered one the world's main centers for traffic in prostitutes. Insufficient legislation was undoubtedly a reason. But the rapid growth of the city from about 180,000 inhabitants in 1890 to 950,891 in 1904, to 1,231,698 in 1909, and to 2,415,142 in 1936 was a major factor. Table 7 shows the high ratios of males in the total and foreign populations of Argentina. Buenos Aires, the main port of entry to the country as well as its largest city, retained most of the foreign population with its very high male ratio. Quite naturally, this immense disparity between men and women created a market for prostitutes from overseas to satisfy the desires of new immigrants who did not possess the means to marry and raise a family.

The social structure of Buenos Aires at the turn of the century had two main divisions: *gente decente* (the upper class composed of those who by ancestry, education and wealth retained influence and power in city and national life) and *gente de pueblo* (the working masses). The rapid increase in population and the substantial urban changes did not alter this structure until World War I and the access to political power by the middle class in 1916.[9] The male was the principal provider and thus established the family status. Among the *gente decente* the woman would remain at home, engage in cultural endeavors or charities, and manage the household and servants. In general, women in late-nineteenth-century *porteño* society did not work outside their homes unless the family's financial position absolutely required it. Working women thus came from the lowest classes and were employed as maids, cooks, washerwomen, and seamstresses.[10]

The dominant role of men and the subordinate position of women in this traditional society had definite implications concerning relations and

Table 7

Ratio of Males in the Total and Foreign Populations of Argentina

Year	Total Population	Foreign Population
1869	106	251
1895	112	173
1914	116	171
1947	105	138

Source: Gino Germani, *Política y sociedad en una época de transición*
(Buenos Aires, 1968), 252.

morals between the sexes. The sexual double-standard and taboos of the time did not allow premarital sex for women, thus encouraging young men to visit prostitutes. Moreover, once married, men continued to attend houses of prostitution for less-restrained sexual contacts.[11] While women had few opportunities for social contacts, men, in addition to their business appointments, would patronize the social and political clubs. It was not uncommon for men to "slip out in the evening for a game of cards or dice at the café around the corner," while "houses of prostitution that catered to a wealthy clientele supplemented their standard offerings with elegant drawing rooms where men could converse and smoke."[12] In addition, the social pressures upon men almost demanded that they visit prostitutes as a sign of virility and masculinity. James Scobie, in a profound analysis of *porteño* society, pointed out that "in urban surroundings there was the expectation that men, in addition to being good fathers and providers, should demonstrate virility by pursuing unattached females, visiting prostitutes, and deprecating love as a deep, emotional feeling."[13] It is therefore not surprising that an observer of manners and morals in South America attributed the growth in the white slave traffic to the "rigorous seclusion of women, alluring, provocative but inaccessible, in communities where polygamous instincts are undeniably strong."[14]

The Jews in International Traffic

Jewish women were recruited from impoverished families in Eastern Europe. The extreme poverty of many of the Jewish communities in the Russian Pale of Settlement at the end of the nineteenth century, constantly deteriorating due to the increase in population and to the lack of jobs or productive means, was worsened even more by the effects of the Russo-Japanese War and World War I on the one hand and the successive pogroms on the other. Hundreds of thousands of families remained in the most pitiful indigence, while many others were deprived of their salary-earning heads, leaving the orphans to the protection of charitable societies or, even worse, to their own fate. This situation became the source of wealth for unscrupulous Jewish white slave traffickers, *maquereaux*, procurers, and brothel owners, who supplied the markets in almost worldwide scales. At the turn of the century the traffic in Jewish women, mainly from Russia and Roumania, had reached, among others, Johannesburg, Cape Town, Pretoria, the Phillipine Islands, Alexandria, Cairo, Constantinople, Damascus, Bombay, Rio de Janeiro, and Buenos Aires.

Although some of the women sold themselves in order to survive, fully aware of what they were doing, most were not knowledgeable. Many stratagems were devised by the suppliers in order to convince their prospective "merchandise" to leave their home towns. The most usual way was to seduce Jewish young women and even girls to travel under their tutelage to distant parts of the world, where they would receive good salaries in businesses they personally owned or managed. They would then pass them on to other traffickers in England—or other West European countries—or travel directly with them to Buenos Aires. Others, richly dressed and arriving with presents in the *shtetls*, proposed marriage to such girls and then traveled with them to their destination. Others tried simpler tricks, soliciting young women traveling by themselves and without relatives and friends in the city, at the time of the arrival of the transatlantic vessels in the port of Buenos Aires. After a short period of friendly association the women would be subtly induced to cooperate, submitting themselves to living in a brothel. At times relatives induced their own kin to prostitution, inviting them to come from Eastern Europe to Argentina. A few months after the ship ticket was mailed to her, the young woman was received in the home of her relatives. Some weeks later, first through gentle suggestions and then by more forceful means of persuasion—which even included raping the woman so she would acquiesce once her virginity was destroyed—her life became doomed to the brothel.[15]

False marriage was a way of entanglement also practiced in Buenos Aires, where the traffickers had formed a tightly knit organization, including their own cemetery and synagogue. Here *stille hupas* (religious wedding ceremonies without the previous civil one as required in many countries, including Argentina), were performed. Women knowing that in Russia there was neither civil marriage nor civil divorce were convinced that in other countries the same law prevailed and thus were drawn into a miserable existence of near slavery.

The international traffic in Jewish women had grown to such considerable proportions that many Jewish communities became alerted. In 1885 the Jewish Association for the Protection of Girls and Women (JAPGW) was founded in London in order to combat the expanding involvement of East European Jews in white slavery and to help their victims. Later on, other communities also established Jewish committees to combat white slavery, and a Jewish International Conference on the Suppression of the Traffic in Girls and Women was held in London in 1910.

A prominent aspect of the work of these committees and conferences was to alert the Jewish leadership in Eastern Europe to the existence of the traffic—its ramifications and its perils—and to stir them from their apathy on the subject. In 1898 the chief rabbi of the British Empire, Dr. Hermann Adler, wrote a letter cosigned by the chief rabbis of France, Berlin, Hamburg, Frankfurt, Vienna, and Rome and addressed to the rabbis and officers of the towns in Russia, Poland, Lithuania, Galicia, and Roumania:[16]

> The sad tidings have come to us that evil men and women go about in your countries from town to town and village to village and induce young maidens, by false representations, to leave their native land and to go, by their advice, to distant countries, telling them that they will find there good and remunerative situations in business houses.
> In some instances these wicked men add to their iniquity by going through the form of religious marriage with the girls. They then take them on board ship to India, Brazil, Argentina or other countries in South America and then sell them there to keepers of houses of evil repute.
> We cannot adequately describe their bitter fate and terrible suffering in a strange country, the language of which they do not know. They turn to the right and there is no one to help them, to the left and there is no one to save them from utter ruin. Woe to the ears that hear this! Shall we allow our dear sisters to become harlots?
> [We implore parents to] make strict enquiries as to the character of the man who wishes to marry their daughter and not to listen to those who would entice girls to leave their parental home, for their intentions are evil and the life of their daughters is at stake.

The aforementioned Jewish International Conference of 1910 voted to notify the leaders of the Jewish communities in Eastern Europe anew by mailing to them a copy of the 1898 letter.

Jewish Traffickers in Buenos Aires

It is generally held that Jewish prostitution had not been a disturbing factor before 1880. Its sources are traced to the recrudescence of persecutions in Russia after the pogroms of 1881, which resulted in economic hardships and massive emigration.[17] Buenos Aires became a major city for the "selling" of Jewish prostitutes quite early. Procurers, traffickers, and brothel owners realized that enormous profits could be made in Argentina and thus an extensive part of their efforts in Eastern Europe were directed to that distant land. The first mention of Jewish traffic in Buenos Aires that I have found dates from 1879, almost two years before the pogroms of 1881 in Russia. Jews had started to migrate westward from Russia somewhat before the pogroms of 1881, though after that date the numbers multiplied quickly. Thus we find a corroboration of the link between migration and the rise of white slave traffic among Jews during the last decades of the nineteenth century, both stemming from their impoverishment and their desire to improve their economic situations.

On November 4, 1879 some of the daily newspapers in Buenos Aires announced the arrival of a group of nine Jewish traffickers in prostitution, giving their names, ages, and nationality.[18] Upon their landing in Buenos Aires, the port authorities detained them. However, their detention did not last long. The *Buenos Aires Herald* commented with sarcasm on November 13, 1879 that they had "received carte blanche to pursue their honorable traffic in this country. Our colleague *La Patria Argentina* expects to hear of one of them running for the Presidency of the Republic soon."[19]

A few months later, during April 1880, a waiter at the Hotel du Midi denounced to the police chief of the first section that a group of eight women were held prisoners at the said hotel "by two Russian men, who were selling them as merchandise." All the women were under twenty years of age, and had been brought from Galicia, Austria. They, as well as their captors, were Jews.[20] The incipient activities of the Jewish *caftens* around 1880 soon constituted a plague for the few Jews living in the city.[21] The traffickers also attempted to recruit women from among the newly arrived immigrants at the port of Buenos Aires. Marcos (Mordechai) Alpersohn, who arrived in Buenos Aires in 1891 with a group of 300 immigrants destined for the Mauricio Colony of the Jewish Colonization Association, described how they were met by well-dressed men who tried to speak to the newly arrived women through the gates. They also gave sweets and chocolates to the children. The newcomers then learned from the representative of the JCA that these were Jewish traffickers and were advised not to speak to them nor "let your wives or daughters go out into the streets."[22]

During the following year, 1892, a correspondent in Buenos Aires described the situation in a letter to the *Jewish Chronicle* in London:[23] "A vile traffic has been long the curse of the city, and many a poor Jewess has been inveigled here by these beasts in human form. The pity is one cannot write in a newspaper of these horrible doings. In a city so permeated with vice it can be easily be understood how difficult it is to make headway after the methods of Colonel [Albert E. W.] Goldsmid." Colonel Goldsmid, who had gone to Argentina to supervise the Jewish Colonization Association's colonies, reported early in 1893 about his experience there to his fellows at the Order of the Ancient Maccabeans in London:[24] "In Buenos Aires there are Jews who are a disgrace to Judaism, and when I think of them, I am an anti-Semite of the most bigoted description. I was shadowed by these people all the way to Moisesville." Women came chiefly from Russia and Roumania (and Poland after World War I). Some did so via Egypt, Constantinople, and North America, and many passed through England, though the majority had embarked at a German or French port. Some were picked up among the Jewish immigrants in England.[25] In 1903 a rough estimate in England stated that "during the last twelve years 65 English girls had gone to Buenos Aires, as against 1,211 from Russia."[26]

The fate of these prostitutes was most dramatic. In 1901 one of them, after being seduced in London, was taken to Buenos Aires and Montevideo to houses of ill fame. When she was rescued by JAPGW, assisted by Scotland Yard, the Home Office, and the British consulate at Montevideo, she reported that "most girls brought to Buenos Aires come induced by false pretenses and have no idea of their fate. They show much sympathy towards one another, many being illiterate and ignorant. They do not know how to act in order to gain their freedom."[27]

Though the figures for 1909 show an extremely high proportion of women from Eastern Europe (about 50 percent), the norm was much lower. In 1909, out of 199 licensed brothels in Buenos Aires, 102 (51 percent) were supervised by Jewesses—wives or mistresses of dealers—and of the 537 authorized prostitutes, 265 (49 percent) were Jewish, of whom 213 came from Russia. Of the newly registered women, 96 did not live in brothels, making it quite clear that the amount of clandestine prostitution was very great, consisting, most probably, of women who were under the age limit, too young to be inscribed for licensed brothels.[28] In 1922 there were 497 houses licensed and recognized by the municipality with 1,152 women, of whom 349 were newcomers that year. Of the latter, 89 were Jewish.[29] Many women, however, disembarked in Rio or Montevideo—regular stops of the vessels with final destination in Buenos Aires—and were then smuggled into Argentina either by rail or by coasting vessels.[30] A large number of them were placed in clandestine houses in direct violation of the laws regulating prostitution. According to the Health Department at Buenos Aires there were only 1,200 registered women in 1924, while the number of clandestine prostitutes was estimated by qualified persons to be anywhere between 5,000 and 10,000.[31]

Table 8 shows that out of a total of 8,486 newly registered prostitutes in Buenos Aires for the years 1910–23, only 1,916 (22 percent) were Argentine, 1,743 (20 percent) were French, and 1,733 (20 percent) came from Eastern Europe (Russia, Austria-Hungary, Poland, Roumania, and the Ukraine); while 1,063 (12.5 percent) came from Spain, 844 (10 percent) from Italy, and 805 (9.5 percent) from Uruguay. If one assumes that the totality of the East European women were Jewish—and this estimate seems to be quite plausible—and again if one assumes that the percentages would hold also for the much larger numbers of clandestine prostitutes, one would conclude that Jewish women constituted about 20 percent of the total in Buenos Aires.

Even if the numbers of Jewish prostitutes were far too large for their presence to be ignored, they still were a minority in the profession. Most conspicuous of all were the French prostitutes in Buenos Aires and all over the country. Albert Londres, a French journalist in a report to the League of Nations about prostitution in Buenos Aires during the mid-1920s confirmed that "the French were the aristocracy: five pesos. The Polish were the first estate: two pesos."[32] Moreover, Londres observed that in Argentina[33] "Iron, machinery, the sharp ends of the helmets, were German. Railroads, suits, and the gherkins in mustard were English. The cars, the shaving blades, and bad behaviour were Yankee. The sweeper was Italian. The waiter Spanish. And the polisher was Syrian. The women were French! *Franchuta!*" The most modest group was formed by the creole pimps who first exploited only one woman each and then formed bands devoted to stealing women from each other and to exploiting clandestine gambling.[34]

Owing to their economic power, the Jewish traffickers managed to influence areas of the cultural and economic life of the Jewish community. A report of the turn of the century described their life-style:[35] "They dress with ostentatious elegance, wear huge diamonds, go to the theater or opera daily; they have their own clubs and organizations where the "wares" are sorted, auc-

Table 8

Nationality of the Newly Registered Prostitutes in Buenos Aires, 1910–23

Argentina	1,916
America exc. Argentina	
Brazil	12
Chile	16
North America	37
Paraguay	36
Uruguay	805
Total	906
Europe	
Austria-Hungry[a]	199
Belgium	76
England	25
France	1,743
Germany	40
Italy	844
Poland[a]	155
Portugal	26
Roumania	48
Russia[a]	1,325
Spain	1,063
Ukraine	6
Total	5,550
Other	
Turkey	59
Egypt	1
Other	54
Grand total	8,486

[a]Up to 1921 the Poles were counted as Russians and in some
   instances as Austro-Hungarians.
Source: Records of the Buenos Aires Municipal Health Department.

tioned and sold. . . . They have their own secret wireless code, are well-organized, and—heavens, in South America everything is possible!—shortly they may send a delegate to the Argentinian congress!"

They felt comfortable in the Jewish street, knowing that many Jews—tailors, dressmakers, grocers, furniture and jewelry dealers—depended on them as customers. They also conspicuously patronized the Yiddish theater, not only because their wealth permitted them to do so but also to display their women among the crowds. On the other hand, they never succeeded in what was probably their major ambition: becoming an accepted part of the organized Jewish community in the country. The traffickers were repeatedly banned from all Jewish institutions except their own.

While the French were the aristocracy in the white slavery business in

Buenos Aires, the Jews were the only ones organized in a sort of guild. Being expelled from all synagogues and societies, and especially from the Chevra Keduscha Aschkenasi, which administered the Ashkenazic cemeteries and denied them burial rights, the Jewish traffickers united around their own society and established synagogues and a cemetery. These institutions were limited to traffickers. In their mutual aid society a strong monopoly was held by the board, in the best interest of the members. The leaders thus controlled the buying and selling of women and the exchange of the latter to different brothels. Moreover, a mutual help society compensated the members who had been left without women. The leaders further greased the appropriate palms for all the membership.[36] Their women were almost exclusively Jewish.[37] Their own synagogue and cemetery—two fundamental aspects of Jewish religion—and their mutual contact in their societies provided the Jewish *maquereaux* the possibility of surviving in the hostile atmosphere created around them by the rest of the Jewish community. Many of them, however, dissimulated their criminal acts by adopting licit professions as a cover.[38]

The traffickers' insistence on identifying as Jews greatly annoyed the rest of the Jews in Buenos Aires. Their congregating around Jewish institutions of their own and outwardly participating in Jewish ritual ceremonies lent them a touch of legitimacy in the eyes of naive observers. The other Jews feared comparisons and confusions and dreaded possible antisemitic eruptions as a result of them. The fight against the *tmeyim* was long and not easy but was carried on until this scourge of the Jews of Buenos Aires became a thing of the past. We shall describe it, highlighting the different emphases during the various periods.

Fighting the White Slave Trade

Early Period, 1890–1914

Around the turn of the century the *tmeyim* gave the still small and relatively poor Jewish population in Buenos Aires an "infamous" reputation. Some individuals, however, took it upon themselves to rectify the honor of the rest of the Jews and to protect their coreligionists in Europe and at home from falling into the hands of the traffickers. During this early period their efforts were directed to various areas of concern. They issued warnings about Jewish white slavery in Europe; they prevented the *tmeyim* from joining and participating in the burgeoning Jewish institutions in Buenos Aires; they started a society to protect and help women victims of white slavery, and finally they used their influence to promote legislation to regulate prostitution.

The first measure taken was warning potential victims of the traffic by describing their intentions and their ways of operating. During the 1890s Abraham Vermont, one of the pioneers in Yiddish journalism in Argentina, wrote about the Jewish involvement in the traffic of women in numerous articles he contributed to *Hamelitz* of Petersbury and *Hayehudi* of London.[39] Moreover, the famed editor of Hamelitz, Alexander Zederbaum, who was opposed to Jewish colonization in Argentina, advocating the resettlement of Palestine instead, mentioned the fact that Jews had opened houses of shame in Argentina as an argument against migrating there in a special supplement to his newspaper in 1893.[40]

It was not long before this reputation caught the ears of Sholem Aleichem, the popular Yiddish story writer. In 1909 he published in one of the literary weeklies in Eastern Europe a short sketch entitled "The Man from Buenos Aires." He presented an ostentatiously dressed Jew from Buenos Aires having a dialogue with a coreligionist while traveling in a train in Eastern Europe. During the conversation the former explained that "he had the police of the whole world in his pocket" and that he gave big donations to houses of Jewish learning in Jerusalem, for which he received beautiful laudatory letters with seals and signatures of great rabbis. The common Jew, intrigued, wanted to know the nature of his fellow traveler's business in Argentina and finally received an answer at the end of the sketch: "What is my business, my friend? Ha, ha. It is not with etrogim, my friend; my business is not with etrogim!"[41]

Though enhancing the bad reputation of Buenos Aires, stories like this one by Sholem Aleichem made more people aware of the viciousness of the traffic in women.

The organized Jewish community suffered most from the presence of this malefic element in its midst. Every society carefully investigated the antecedents and acquaintances of all applicants for membership. Numerous applicants were refused membership due to their involvement in white slavery. The Chevra Keduscha Aschkenasi was the principal goal of the dealers, though they also applied to the Congregacion Israelita, the Ezrah Society controlling the Hospital Israelita, and others. These institutions were always prepared to investigate their own membership to eradicate all traces of white slavery within them and did not hesitate to expel members proven to have some type of connection, even if secondary, with the dealers.[42]

The Jewish community in Argentina not only wanted to ban the entrance of the tmeyim to their institutions; they also succeeded in extending the anathema to other areas. Their main battles were fought in order to deny them burial in all cemeteries of the "pure" community and to eradicate them from the Yiddish theater performances, where they managed to exert considerable influence.

When the Chevra Keduscha tried to bring together different sectors of the Jewish population in Buenos Aires to make arrangements for a private plot for a cemetery, the tmeyim availed themselves of the opportunity to join forces. On May 4, 1898, Rodolfo Ornstein, president of the Chevra Keduscha, informed the board "that a group of people have offered to contribute 5,000 to 6,000 pesos, without becoming members."[43] Indeed, the sum was a considerably large one taking into account that there were just over one hundred members paying one peso monthly at the time. The offer, made with the assertion that the donors had no pretension of becoming members of the society, evidently came from the white slave dealers, who knew perfectly well that they would not be accepted as full members. In line with their religious inclinations, they wanted to be assured of a Jewish funeral and considered that such a donation would pave a way for the Chevra Keduscha to agree to it, without their becoming members.[44]

The minutes of the Chevra Keduscha do not mention further contacts with the *tmeyim* concerning the acquisition of the burial place. The aforementioned proposal of the latter was not considered, which denotes that most probably it was turned down without further ado. There is, however, the testimony of an activist in Jewish life of the time, who described what transpired at a meeting held in 1899:[45]

> Meetings were held at the premises of Poale Zedek at Talcahuano 606, at the Temple of the Congregación, and at private homes, all with the same purpose of gathering means to buy a cemetery. . . . Finally a meeting took place in 1899, at the antechamber of the Libertad 785 Temple [Congregación], which was really the most tragic one I can think of. The group of the then Zionist and national Jews had tried to clear the atmosphere. They demanded that the "tmeyim" be excluded, not to receive their dead, and in general, that no dealings be had with them, so that no "hire of a harlot" be accepted in the purchase of a "sacred field."[46] The Sephardim, all Moroccan, a certain number of "Occidental" [West European] Jews, had supported the tendency of *de mortuis nil nisi bonum*.[47] Besides this, they argued, that the Jewish community was small in number and poor moneywise, that the few contemporary rich Jews had completely assimilated, and that if the "tmeyim" would not participate with their money, it would be impossible to gather the amount necessary to buy the "field."
>
> We, the group of the "Liga Dr. Theodor Herzl," fought against these claims with the main argument that precisely because of the wealth and the great numbers of the "tmeyim," the board of the Chevra Keduscha could very quickly fall into their hands, and that would be a terrible disgrace.
>
> Ornstein took the side of the Sephardim. He also had doubts about the economic competence of the honorable families. He was afraid that they would never be able to gather such a large amount of money among the respectable Jews alone, and was ready to compromise.
>
> The delegates of the "tmeyim" . . . assured that they would not take a place on the board, but wanted to be entitled to become members. . . .
>
> Long and impulsively did we discuss and argue. We triumphed. The separation between purity and impurity was extended even to the dead. The delegates of the "tmeyim" left the meeting, and the Moroccans too. Both immediately showed what they were capable of.
>
> The "tmeyim" bought a cemetery in Barracas al Sud, the present day Avellaneda, . . . And the Moroccans bought from them a piece of land, leaving a one meter wide separation so that the impurity would not, God forbid, enter into their cemetery.

The writer of these memoires, Jacobo S. Liachovitzky, was a very active but controversial figure in the Jewish community of Buenos Aires. His testimony might be biased and tended to harm some of his enemies, as well as to justify his own activities and those of the Zionist organization he sponsored. For this reason, his report, undeniably based on actual events, should be seriously qualified.[48]

The general Jewish population in the capital in 1899 was not affluent and might have considered that the contribution of the *tmeyim* might ease the situation. However, Liachovitzky did not mention the conditions of those advocating a compromise with the *tmeyim*; whether the compromise would mean that all Jews would have the right to be buried in the one and only Jewish cemetery or that part of the field would be allocated to the former and the rest would constitute the burial ground for the clean Jews, be it in a common cemetery or divided according to their origin. Moreover, most of the delegates present at the famous meeting were against the compromise, as is evident from the final decision. Furthermore, both the Congregación and the Chevra Keduscha had many times before 1899 been involved in cases of possible infiltration of *tmeyim* in their midst and had conducted thorough investigations to determine the veracity of accusations against members. When these accusations were confirmed, they did not hesitate to expel the undesired members.[49]

The Moroccan Jews, on the other hand, adopted a policy that might have aroused the indignation of some sectors of the Jewish population. In any case, no condemnation was heard, either from the Chevra Keduscha or from the Congregación. Moreover, as the Sephardim had had their differences with the Ashkenazim with respect to a joint cemetery and represented a small community of Jews, the possibility of buying a section of an existing Jewish cemetery in 1900 solved their burial problems.

Liachovitzky's Zionist group was not the only voice that decried the possibility of a common cemetery for all Jews, including the *tmeyim*. Rabbi Reuben Hacohen Sinai, who had originally settled in Moisesville but by 1897 had moved permanently to Buenos Aires, strove to sway the general opinion against the acceptance of the collaboration of the *tmeyim*. His son remembered that in one of his protest sermons Rabbi Sinai announced that "in case the *tmeyim* were accepted into the sacred field, he would write in his testament that after his death he should be interred in the municipal cemetery. 'I prefer— he said—to lie among honorable gentiles than among our *tmeyim*.'"[50]

These voices of condemnation against those willing to compromise and accept contributions from *tmeyim* were the first signs of a growing sense of responsibility among Jewish leaders in Buenos Aires vis-à-vis their relation to the impure sector in their midst. The cemetery question was the first one that tempted the Jewish community in the capital to accept the collaboration of those elements because of its financial advantages. Nevertheless, the result was a complete separation in this area.

The fight was then extended to the Yiddish theater representations. The audiences, from the very beginnings of Yiddish theater in Buenos Aires, was to a large extent controlled by the white slave dealers. The first production, in 1901, was Abraham Goldfaden's satirical comedy *Kuni Lemel*. An oldtimer Jew in Buenos Aires described the audience to the readers of the *Jewish Chronicle* in the following way:[51] "A very large number of flashy, coarse-looking men that I can 'point at,' and the boxes were mostly filled with beautiful women, very extravagantly dressed and loaded with jewellery. At every 'Yiddish' joke or salley, the shrieks of laughter were loudest and longest from these painted lips. It was painful to hear, yet I stood it out; I had come to see and to enquire into this."

Their presence was detrimental to the attendance of a considerable sector of the general Jewish population, especially families. Throughout the years different groups rose to lead a battle against the *tmeyim* and clean the Jewish theater of their presence. Still, the problem was not simple, and only toward the end of the 1920s and more during the first years of the 1930s was the "pure" community able to free itself from the negative presence of the dealers. Official authorities in the city, the theater managers, and even some of the actors had vested interests in the presence of this abhorred element of the Jewish population. They all, in smaller or larger measure, made a living from the Yiddish shows, and the white slave dealers used this factor to their benefit. They were thus able to impose their will in some aspects of the theater's policy, such as banning specific plays from the stage.

A direct confrontation took place at the premises of the Yiddish theater on October 5, 1908, during the performance of the fourth act of Peretz Hirschbein's *Miriam*. Witnessing the miseries of the heroine at a brothel, the white slave dealers present, uncomfortable at being exposed at a public gathering, walked out of the theater, followed by their women. Now the dealers were at odds with the Yiddish theater and the actors. The Poale Zionist group immediately exhorted the Jewish public to take measures. Though the dealers supported the Yiddish theater, Poale Zion considered the time was ripe to cleanse the atmosphere. They formed a special group, Yugent, which met for the first time on October 25, 1908 and carried out an intensive activity for about half a year. They organized mass meetings with speeches delivered both in Yiddish and in Spanish, decrying the activities of the Jewish dealers, especially their influence in the theater. A special Pro-Boycott Committee identified Jews who had secondary dealing with the *tmeyim* and launched boycotts against them in the Jewish quarters.[52]

Another small group gathered around a Club Israelita in 1908 with the goal of fighting white slave traffic. The program included the petitioning of the appropriate authorities to "deport all white slave traffickers, if they are foreigners, and to imprison them if they are Argentine born or naturalized." Mass meetings and public demonstrations petitioning the government to approve of new laws that would limit white slavery and prostitution were organized. After May 1909, events concerning the workers' movement, which had a direct repercussion in the local Jewish community, diverted the attention of these two groups—as well as that of Centro Juventud, a group of Spanish-speaking Jewish young men formed with the same purposes in mind—to other matters. Club Israelita participated in local political activities, while Yugent suffered from police persecution because of its overall socialist ideology. Centro Juventud devoted all its efforts to cultural endeavors.[53]

Jews still were active in their fight against white slavery through nonsectarian associations. The main activist was Rabbi Samuel Halphon, of the Congregación Israelita, who had a leading role in the Argentine Asociación Nacional Contra la Trata de Blancas. But the fight against dealers in the theater was not won in 1908. The Jewish community was still small, the theater had limited resources and repertoires, and there was a dearth of talented artists. Thus the *tmeyim* remained strong in the Yiddish theater. Even in 1910, when Avangard, a Bundist group in Buenos Aires, called for the formation of a theater committee with representatives of both progressive (Poale Zion, Bund) and established (Congregación, Chevra Keduscha, etc;) societies to take the theater from private companies in order to prevent *tmeyim* from exerting pressure, it failed.[54] The undesirable elements continued to patronize the Yiddish theater and indeed to be the main supporters of it up to the mid-1920s, occupying the boxes and choicest seats.

The traffickers' insistence in identifying as Jews continued to affect the Jews of Buenos Aires, who feared that the decent institutions might be confused with those of the *tmeyim*. In 1905 when both the Congregación Israelita and the traffickers' place of prayer were located on Libertad Street and the daily *El Censor* confused the cantor of the Congregación with that of the *tmeyim*, the leaders of the former protested vehemently.[55] Similarly, when the Sociedad Israelita de Socorros Mutuos, the society in charge of the aforementioned traffickers' cemetery in Avellaneda, moved its premises to the capital in 1909, the board of Chevra Keduscha Aschkenasi was most irritated because the similarity in names might cause people to confuse their institution with that of the white slavers.[56]

Parallel to the warnings issued in Europe, and Jewish societies' denial of membership to the *caftens*, refusal to cooperate with them in the acquisition of private land for a Jewish cemetery, and attempts to cleanse the Yiddish theater, individual Jews realized that the fight had to be worldwide. First contacts were made with the JAPGW in London during the early 1890s notifying them of the extent of Jewish traffic in South America—Buenos Aires, Rio, Montevideo.[57] Concerned individuals from Buenos Aires, when in Europe for business purposes, approached influential Jews involved in the fight against white slavery, including Leopold Rothschild and officers of the Gentlemen's Committee of JAPGW.[58]

These contacts led—through the instrumentality of Mr. F. Perugia, brother of Mrs. Leopold Rothschild—to the founding in 1901 in Buenos Aires of a committee headed by Rabbi Henry Joseph, assisted by Mr. Alfredo Gelpi. Gelpi used his influence and ability to trace missing women and met immigrants at the port. Joseph, who besides being the rabbi was an established and well-connected businessman in Buenos Aires, succeeded in alerting the local police and port authorities and attempted to gain the sympathy of some judges. He also joined the nonsectarian societies engaged in the suppression of the traffic and worked harmoniously with the Argentine National Association against White Slavery.[59] The Buenos Aires branch not only intervened in cases referred to it by JAPGW in London but also established contacts with societies in Europe and other South American cities. Inquiries about specific cases came from the large Jewish centers in Eastern Europe such as Warsaw,

Lodz, and Petersburg, as well as from Central Europe. The Buenos Aires office also centralized inquiries involving cities and towns in the interior including Rosario, Bahía Blanca, Tucumán, Carlos Casares, Médanos, and Palacios, to name a few.[60]

There were enormous difficulties in establishing permanent relations with the port and police authorities, which underscores the ability of the *caftens*, both Jewish and non-Jewish, to divert the attention of the authorities from their own activities. Undoubtedly they knew who to bribe in order to continue their clandestine operations. This is reflected in the ongoing struggle of the branch of JAPGW in Buenos Aires, latter called Ezras Noschim (EN), to secure permits to board the incoming ships before the passengers disembarked. By 1903 Gelpi was allowed to visit all steamers on their arrival in Buenos Aires, just as in England practically every ship leaving for South America, as well as every connecting train, was watched by agents of JAPGW. By 1906, however, difficulties arose, and the authorities ruled that vessels could not be boarded immediately upon arrival. Agents were allowed only at the port premises but not on board, thus complicating the detection of women traveling alone who were met by procurers or brothel owners at the port of Buenos Aires. Efforts to revoke this rule failed for almost a decade, until finally in 1916 permission was obtained for the inspector of JAPGW in Buenos Aires to visit the ships on arrival. Even in later periods difficulties arose, and the Jewish leaders could renew their permits only with enormous efforts.[61] In later years Rabbi Samuel Halphon, who headed the committee in Buenos Aires, was able to obtain permits for the inspector to board ship, thanks to his invaluable connections and influence.[62] Inspection at the ports was an enormous undertaking. In 1908 a total of 454 ocean liners arrived in Buenos Aires, with 232,821 passengers. In addition, there were 1,192 arrivals of local boats from Montevideo. These had to be closely watched because in order to divert the attention of officials, the *caftens* would change vessels in Montevideo to enter the country in local boats. In 1912, 464 ocean liners with 263,166 passengers plus 1,393 local boats entered the port of Buenos Aires.[63]

The dimensions of the traffic in Jewish women to South America continued to worry the leadership of JAPGW in London. In 1913 the secretary of its Gentlemen's Committee, Mr. S. Cohen, traveled to Buenos Aires in order to bolster the organization against the traffic there and to bring a full report to London. The same year Rabbi Joseph died, and Rabbi Halphon, who had been playing a growing role during the preceding years, took over as head of the committee. Both Cohen's visit and Halphon's leadership gave new impetus to the work. Though the committee established under Halphon was independent, it closely cooperated with JAPGW in London, which continued to give an annual grant. Halphon also kept in close touch with the Sociedad de Damas Israelitas (Jewish Women's Society), which did valuable work.[64]

The Jews of Buenos Aires fully endorsed the efforts of Socialist congressman Alfredo L. Palacios to enact legislation that would repress procurement for immoral purposes. There were some abolitionists in Argentina at the time who argued against regulation as being arbitrary and immoral and demanded one moral code for both men and women. They maintained that regulation of prostitution meant sanctioning it.

While it was held that abolition would represent an ideal stage for private and public health, it was widely accepted that it was unthinkable in the still traditional Argentine society.[65] Thus regulation through municipal and police action was the step to take. Before and during 1913 when the issue was debated in Parliament, most Jewish groups endorsed the passing of laws that would repress the traffic. Public debates and conferences were convened, and nonsectarian committees formed, in order to inform the public and press for legislation. As witnesses of the time confirm, the Jews were very visible among the organizing leadership.[66] When Law number 9143 (Ley Palacios) was finally passed, a delegation of representatives of the major Jewish organizations in Buenos Aires visited Dr. Palacios at his residence to thank him for his efforts publicly.

Ley Palacios made procurement for immoral purposes a criminal offense, and those guilty could be sentenced to up to fifteen years in jail, depending on the age of the victim and whether the criminal was a relative of the victim or her guardian. The law, moreover, established that no woman under twenty-two years of age could register as a prostitute. An optimistic report sent to the JAPGW stated that respectable women could now walk unaccompanied about the streets. It further maintained that about 2,000 men and women left the country because of the new regulations. Though this last number may appear exaggerated, it is evidence that the new law had at least some impact upon traffic in Buenos Aires.[67]

The Jewish traffickers who left Argentina went back to Europe. Cohen, who as secretary of JAPGW in London was aware of developments in the trade worldwide, wrote to Halphon early in 1914:[68] "Many of the men who were driven out from Buenos Aires are at the present moment in Paris, although a large number have gone to Russia, and a few are in England. I believe many have gone to the East, and I hope shortly to be going to Constantinople where a great deal needs to be done."

World War I considerably reduced the number of passenger steamers entering Buenos Aires and therefore reduced the work of Halphon's committee proportionately. Halphon himself was able to exert leadership also in the Argentine National Association against White Slavery, to which he was appointed honorary secretary in 1914 and vice-president in 1917. Reports continued to be sent on a monthly basis to London.

After World War I

The reopening of normal transatlantic routes after the war aggravated anew the problem posed by the existence of the traffic in Argentina. Rabbi Halphon and his coworkers at Ezras Noschim realized that European geopolitical developments were in many ways responsible for the recrudescence of white slave traffic between Eastern Europe and South America and in particular between Poland and Argentina.

As a result of the war Poland was reconstituted as a sovereign state. The rebirth of Poland, which its Jews had hoped for, was not peaceful, as Lithuanian, Ukrainian, and Bolshevik armies clashed with the Polish army. Jews were often caught between these warring nations, and were frequently victims of pogroms. Even after the boundary questions were settled Jews suffered greatly from discrimination at all levels, which caused the economic decline of Polish Jewry and accelerated its demographic decline through emigration. During the 1920s, moreover, the United States imposed progressively stricter immigration quotas, thus forcing larger numbers of Polish Jews to opt for other countries to settle in. Argentina—mainly Buenos Aires—was chosen by most.

Among the many Polish immigrants there were also Jewish traffickers and prostitutes to be placed in licensed or clandestine brothels in the country. The fact that many of the women were from Poland brought the Polish government and its representative in Buenos Aires into the picture. In 1925 a Polish senator asked Halphon whether anything could be done regarding the women in the licensed brothels in Buenos Aires. He stated that his government had requested the consul in Buenos Aires to make an inquiry among the women of Polish nationality to determine whether they would be prepared to return to Poland. The reply he received was that all the women were Jewish and that they refused to be repatriated because "economic conditions in Poland are bad," and "anti-semitism is even worse." No matter how bad their fate was in Buenos Aires, for these women to return to Poland was out of the question. They would rather assert they had come to Argentina as prostitutes of their own free will.[69] This type of response by a white slave undoubtedly made prosecution of traffickers more difficult. On the other hand, the response was not unexpected. It linked prostitution to economic privation and physical persecution and provided a vivid description of the wretched existence of a segment of Polish Jewry.

In contrast, the display of wealth by the *tmeyim* did not go unnoticed by newly arrived Polish Jews, inducing some to join them at their trade. Halphon observed, "Many Jewish homes have been ruined by the influence of the traffickers. We reckon that a great many heads of family, having been married only a few years, and having migrated from Poland to our country with the only purpose of working to bring their families to Argentina, have started here, for a variety of reasons, to deal with their *tmeyim* fellow-countrymen, who, unfortunately, are in abundance, and whose permissive life-style they envy. Advised by the latter, they have sent for their wives to exploit them in this vile trade."[70]

The rest of Buenos Aires' Jewry maintained its ban on white slave dealers in all its societies. The dealers were forced to organize their own community life, their own synagogues, schools, and cultural and social institutions. Their two main guilds were Varsovia (of Poles, the largest), and Asquenasum (of Russians and Roumanians). The former, located in Avellaneda, a suburb of the capital, was operating as a mutual aid society under a charter issued by the government of the Province of Buenos Aires in 1906. During the mid-1920s it moved its headquarters and synagogue to 3280 Córdoba Avenue in Buenos Aires. A visiting Yiddish writer described the scene:[71]

The "excommunicated" have been forced to organize a community life of their own. They have their own synagogue—each with the requisite rabbi, *chazan*, *shammes*, "vessels of the Holy House," their own schools, their own social and cultural institutions. One of their congregations recently moved to a new building. There wended through the street the ceremonial procession customary in Jewish communities.

But on this occasion what a mockery! At the head, the rabbi of the panderers, concerning whose *smichas* not too great an examination had been made. Followed in order the *gabbai*, the *shammes*, the *chazan*, the *shul* officers and holy men, all bearing the Scrolls of the Law, the *shul* fixtures, the decorations and ornamentations. And behind them their flock, the pimps, the brothel keepers, the prostitutes.

The organized Jewish community in Buenos Aires was to respond more energetically. After the world war and throughout the 1920s the Jewish population of Argentina had grown considerably, numbering over 200,000. Many Jewish immigrants had improved their economic conditions, and the community as a whole had become progressively more established. Developments during the war and right afterward had impressed upon the Jewish leadership in Buenos Aires the need to confront its problems with maturity and responsibility. Some antisemitic uprisings—including the first major incident against Jews in Buenos Aires, the so-called Semana Trágica of January 1919—had brought Jews of different background and ideology together in order to petition the authorities and to restore order and dignity to the community. Moreover, the Zionist leadership had on several occasions approached President Hipólito Yrigoyen seeking support for the Balfour Declaration and for the British Mandate in Palestine. The mostly positive responses no doubt emboldened many Jews to pursue the internal war against the local *tmeyim* with greater energy.

The archives of Ezras Noschim for the postwar period contain large quantities of communications from all parts of the world—the Middle East, Turkey, Eastern Europe, England, the United States, and Canada. Nonetheless, at this juncture, the Jews in Buenos Aires felt the need to wage war against the *tmeyim* in the streets, at the theater, and also by denouncing their illegal activities to the police. Under the leadership of Rabbi Halphon, Ezras Noschim was reorganized in 1926, allowing the main societies of the community to send delegates to its executive committee. Thus, the Chevra Keduscha, the Congregación Israelita, Ezrah Society, Sociedad de Damas Israelitas, and Soprotimis bolstered the image of Ezras Noschim. The campaign in the Jewish press and in the various societies helped make everyone aware that the leadership of Buenos Aires Jewry was quite adamant. Through these means they explained their work against white slave traffic to the entire community, highlighting the need that every Jew should contribute to the cause, because only a joint effort could succeed in effectively destroying the plague that was ruining the reputation of the Argentine Jewish community.[72]

The Yiddish theater was one of the main areas of concern. Earlier attempts by the respectable elements to close the theaters' doors to the *tmeyim* were met with the resistance of the dealers themselves, and that of some of the theaters managers. Events took a drastic turn in April 1926 when Leon Malach's play *Ibergus* (*Transfusion*) was rejected by the manager of a theater because its theme—prostitution in Rio de Janeiro—would not be to the liking of the "audience." Di *Presse* attacked the manager and his theater for compromising with the dealers, while Di *Yiddishe Zeitung* defended the right of the manager to select the plays. The argument between both newspapers continued in a fiery manner for a few months and divided even the respectable community, who took sides on the issue. Di *Presse* argued that its colleague sided with the dealers, which was obviously far from the truth. However, Di *Presse* continued with its crusade against the vicious social elements, and in its quasi-religious frenzy managed to affect some of the positive institutions in the community, such as two of the Yiddish theater companies and the Society of Jewish Actors, decrying them as nests of ruffianism and vice. Nonetheless, a positive turn was made. The pressure of some Jewish institutions, and of the public began to be felt once it had the backing of some of the Jewish guilds and the press. First one theater surrendered and posted the announcement Entrance Forbidden to Tmeyim. Other theaters followed suit with similar signs.[73]

In 1927 Ezras Noschim denounced to the authorities in Avellaneda that most members of Varsovia had criminal antecedents. However, after some months of investigation, the answer given was that "all members of the society were respectable people" and honorable merchants.[74] Notwithstanding the help and cooperation of such important factions as various judges; the Argentine National Association against White Slavery; the German Pastor Dr. Bussmann; and the British, French, German, Austrian, and Polish consuls—no end could be put to this delinquency.

Julio L. Alsogaray, commissar of the seventh section of the federal police and active in the disentanglement of the net the traffickers had knitted around them to protect themselves and their business, uncovered the main reasons for the perseverance of the trade in Argentina. In what he described as the "trilogy of white slavery"—composed of municipal authorities, including some judges; the police, especially commissars and personnel at the investigation department there; and the traffickers—the road was paved for the criminal activities to remain unchecked. The traffickers provided the money, while some municipal authorities and police officials made sure they remained safe and protected, their brothels and women unraided and untouched.[75]

Halphon nevertheless tried to bring as much pressure as possible on all three parties of the "trilogy" by courting the responsible municipal authorities, judges, and officials at the Police Department. He also got the minister of Poland in Argentina, Ladislao Mazurkiewicz, to help in the work, because most of the women were Polish. Mazurkiewicz visited the offices of Ezras Noschim and had access to its archives and promised to propose to his own government that it issue more stringent emigration laws for women leaving the country by themselves.

Women under twenty-five years of age who desired to emigrate were required by Polish law to obtain an affidavit certified by the Polish consul at the country of emigration, testifying to the honorability of the person issuing the affidavit. Frequently women under twenty-five who could not obtain this certificate would try to appear older. Cases were reported of women who obtained affidavits through so-called "agents" who appeared honest but did so only to facilitate the emigration of women destined to the brothels. Both Halphon and Selig Ganopol, who headed the office of Ezras Noschim as administrator and inspector, repeatedly impressed upon the Polish representative the need for stronger supervision in Poland before issuing passports to single women. It was noted that some women disembarked in Montevideo even without an affidavit certified by the local Polish consul and later entered Argentina illegally.[76]

Moreover, at the meeting of Ezras Noschim on August 30, 1927 Mazurkiewicz said that the Varsovia society was an "offense to Polish national honor, because it has taken the name of the Capital of the Republic of Poland."[77] He promised the Jewish leaders to complain to the Argentine Foreign Ministry, calling their attention to the opprobrium Varsovia represented to the reputation of the Polish nation and indicating that Ezras Noshim had enough data to document the immoral activities of that society. Ezras Noschim, in turn, when it denounced the members of Varsovia, included the words of the Polish representative in its statement. As a result of this combined action between the Polish consulate and Ezras Noschim, the Varsovia society was compelled to change its name and remove its notice boards and name plates from its doors. After August 20, 1929, it was called Zwi Migdal, after the name of one of its presidents.[78]

The beginning of the end of Zwi Migdal occurred in 1930, when Raquel Lieberman, with the backing of Ezras Noschim, denounced Salomón José Korn. Judge Manuel Rodriguez Ocampo led an investigation that reached the headquarters of Zwi Migdal. Ganopol was personally invited by the judge to be present at the time the search of the premises in Córdoba Avenue took place. Warrants were issued against its 424 members, men and women, for their arrest. Of these, 108 were actually arrested, 70 were already dead, and the rest had fled to Europe, to other South American countries, or to the Argentine hinterland. Though Zwi Migdal functioned under the guise of a mutual aid society, regularly chartered as a limited stock corporation by the Province of Buenos Aires, the investigation showed that its members had been carrying an international traffic in women for decades. Testimonies revealed that contracts for the sale and purchase of women were executed before Zwi Migdal officials, as were agreements regarding the shipment of women to the interior. However, a legal technicality prevented their being held on that charge. The court order said that as long as the repugnant activity in which they were engaged was tolerated by Argentine law, nobody could be punished for engaging in it. It could not be proved that any one under arrest was exploiting girls under age or using force or intimidation to control the women working for them. They were, therefore, technically not guilty of violating any law. When formally charged with "illicit association," the traffickers appealed, and through valuable contacts in the police department and at different levels of the Ministry of Justice, they were set free.[79]

The traffickers release from prison provoked a strong reaction by the press and public opinion. Editorials demanded the provisional government—which had taken over on September 6, 1930, through a military coup—to deport the dealers under the suspension of constitutional guarantees accompanying martial law, as it had deported other undesirables. When the Argentine government started deporting them, over one hundred members of Zwi Migdal sought to remain in Uruguay, whence, in spite of the expensive legal talent they had engaged, they were also deported.

Brothels were closed, and campaigns against prostitution, clandestine gambling, and drug traffic were launched. During the first half of the 1930s police repression, the modification of the social and economic structures in Buenos Aires with industrial development, and the raid at Zwi Migdal caused the disbandment of Jewish traffickers. Many willingly left the country around that time, while most others were deported by the government in small groups as undesirable aliens. Several of the latter started habeas corpus proceedings, but a criminal court ruled in September 1934 that the law makes the executive branch of the government the sole judge of a foreigner's desirability as a resident. Thus, foreigners ordered to be deported had no recourse to habeas corpus proceedings. That particular ruling was considered an important victory for the JAPGW, which brought the original charges against the dealers.[80]

During the following years Ezras Noschim's original aims—protection of women and fight against white slavery—were not actual any more, though it still advised the Polish consulate in order to make it difficult for *tmeyim* to obtain migration certificates. Its major areas of concern now were control of weddings to protect women against bigamists, search for men who had abandoned their families in the Old World, help to minors and the aged, and the like. By 1937 the JAPGW headquarters in London, considering that Ezras Noschim did not play the role of previous years any more, decided to stop its financial support. Though the monies for Ezras Noschim came almost exclusively from local institutions and individuals, the decision of JAPGW denoted that the fight against the vicious elements in the midst of the Argentine Jewish community had at long last been won.[81]

Conclusion

For over four decades the immigrant Jews in Argentina, while striving for a better economic situation and building their national, religious, social, and welfare institutions, were confronted with a sector in their midst dealing in white slavery. Their first response consisted of two simultaneous measures: to maintain a thorough separation between the white slave dealers and the rest of the Jews, and to try to provide protection to victims or prospective victims of the traffickers. Thus, while *tmeyim* were kept out of their synagogues, cemeteries, and later also theaters and were avoided in commercial relations, the Jewish institutions cared for the girls and women who were alone in the country or who had been seduced into prostitution. At the moment when the Jewish community felt it was large and powerful enough to combat the *tmeyim* and considered the social and political moment ripe in Argentina, it participated in the fight that brought about the final annihilation of organized Jewish white slavery.

The following questions arise: Why such a thorough separation? Wasn't it normal for every group or community to have its own complement of criminals? Why didn't other immigrant groups, especially the French, the Spanish, and the Italians, fight their conationals involved in traffic in the same way Jews did? And why didn't the Jewish organizations eradicate other criminals or offenders, who obviously were among them as they were among all other groups and institutions?

Apparently both within the Jewish minority, as well as in Argentine society at large, crimes where restitution could be effected were not considered as serious as those impairing the free will of persons or as those where use was made of the victims' bodies to the advantage of the criminals. Offenses against morality and offenses against the person were held to be much more serious than offenses against property.

Jews had a long history of expulsions and resettlements. When they settled in Argentina, they desired above all to meet with the approval of the majority group. Their impulse to be segregated arose from a fear of being identified with, and of being absorbed by, a relatively large number of Jewish traffickers. Once ousted from societies, the *tmeyim* organized seemingly honorable institutions with an outward appearance of respectability. Witnessing their synagogues, their mutual aid and burial societies, and their own parochial cemeteries, one could readily believe that they were a regular Jewish community. Therefore the Jewish leadership contended that the traffickers' tight and exclusively Jewish organization was most injurious to the rest of the Jews. The identification by the host society of the whole Jewish population with this infamous part was not only a remote possibility but an actual fact even during the late nineteenth century. Thus when the Jews felt there was enough backing to push a *razzia* of the *tmeyim*, they willingly joined.

The work of Ezras Noschim succeeded in spite of a number of negative factors in Argentina. One of these factors was Argentina's nonadherence to the Geneva Convention of 1921 of the League of Nations, which had set up an international advisory committee on traffic and urged governments to make annual reports on conditions. At the same time JAPGW in London was appointed assessor for all Jewish committees around the world, which helped set the traffic to Argentina in its international perspective. In spite of Argentina's not having signed the Geneva Convention, Halphon considered that the various laws, decrees, and ordinances issued in Argentina were proof of the government's intentions to limit the infamous trade in women. He also praised the help from different officials at the Immigration and Police departments, as well as various ministries. This help, however, was only partial, because apathy was prevalent, and the traffickers' money could at times be more powerful than the good intentions of others.[82]

Another negative factor was the disbandment of the Argentine National Association against White Slavery in 1928. The causes were "lack of funds and interest, and mainly lack of people of good will to collaborate." Halphon attributed it to the general indifference of the members of the national association to the work. He wrote that "here in America, the great affliction of all collective societies—and this is common to all foreign groups in the country—is the lack of people prepared to sacrifice part of their time for matters other than their own. To this effect, the Jewish community here often gives the best example of the spirit of sacrifice and noble altruism."[83] The dissolution of the national association was a blow to the general work of Ezras Noschim. Buenos Aires was at the time a major import center for women. The laws on traffic were not duly executed, and execution became even weaker when public opinion remained aloof and would not make demands upon members of Parliament. Ezras Noschim thus stood up as the strongest voice against the traffic. Halpon's praise for the local Jewish community was not undeserved, even reckoning that some sectors remained apathetic while others feared antisemitic repercussions.[84]

Other communities with a high index of prostitutes in Buenos Aires were the French, the Spanish, and Italian. These communities were many times larger than the Jewish one; their Romance languages were related to Spanish; they were Catholic; and their countries of origin were familiar in Argentina. Though concerned about the bad reputation criminals might give to the whole group, the leaders of the French, Spanish, and Italian institutions were not as adamant as the Jewish ones, for they had much less at stake.

The deportation of most members of Zwi Migdal during the 1930s did not cause the Jews to feel totally integrated into the country, although it was a great step in that direction. During that decade the Jews raised their voices and demonstrated against Nazi atrocities in Europe and against the racist and antisemitic repercussions in Argentina. At the same time, however, they made every possible attempt to conceal what in their eyes was a black spot in the history of the community, namely the existence of a net of Jewish traffickers in flesh, though it was now a thing of the past. In the context of the rising antisemitism of the 1930s it was to their best interest and safety not to tempt the devil and to keep whatever argument that might lead to anti-Jewish activity as inconspicuous as possible. In our own days, with half a century of perspective, we cannot but emphasize the other side of the same coin. Whether due to humane, moral, or protective reasons, the immigrant marginal Jewish community in Buenos Aires took an attitude, bold enough to emasculate an economically powerful and influential sector of coreligionists because of its immoral commerce.

A Kehilla in the Making: Centralization and Rivalries

The Congregación Israelita (CIRA) was the only Jewish institution in Buenos Aries until 1890. The few hundred Jews there had been gathering at CIRA for almost three decades, where they could enjoy the services it performed. These were mainly circumscribed to religious duties such as prayers, weddings, circumcisions, and burials. Though most of the Jews had arrived from Germany, France, England, and other West European countries, differences in origin were disregarded, and a few Sephardim from Morocco, as well as some East European Jews, had entered CIRA before 1890. However, this year became a turning point in the history of the Jews in Argentina. During 1891 the Jewish Colonization Association opened its offices in the capital, the Jews from Morocco opened their first synagogue—Congregación Israelita Latina—and the Russian Jews founded their first *hebra* Poale Zedek. There was a proliferation of Jewish societies with the arrival of Jewish immigrants who settled in Buenos Aires after 1890. During the following four decades various institutions were initiated in the city, including religious, Zionist, cultural, welfare, and defense organizations. Some of these were discontinued after more or less short periods of existence; others merged with each other in order to strengthen their activities; while still others divided themselves due to internal strifes.

In 1930 there were over 120 Jewish institutions functioning in the Argentine capital. It was therefore justified that numerous attempts were made to centralize Jewish institutional life in order to join forces for the accomplishment of the major needs of the entire Jewish community, and to represent it to the Argentine officialdom as well as to the rest of the Jewish world.

In most institutions there was a powerful group of leaders, some of whom were real *caudillos,* a fact that caused profound divisions among institutions that often had overlapping goals and activities. Thus cooperation between institutions did not reach a desirable level, and great efforts were lost due to personal rifts and aspirations. Individual concerns and the desire for recognition among officials for their own work and for the goals of the institutions they led worked to the detriment of the general progress and consolidation of the growing Jewish community. The important achievements we have described in previous chapters could have been made with less effort had there been more cooperation among leaders.

These achievements, moreover, could easily have been surpassed, and a description of Jewish life in Buenos Aires in 1930 could have shown a much more progressive communal development. The reasons for the poor spiritual, religious, and cultural accomplishments of Argentine Jewry of later decades are linked to the foundations laid during the settlement and early periods or organized Jewish life there. The main concerns were centered, during the early decades of the century, in building welfare and social institutions and in securing the physical survival and economic advancement of individual Jews. Cultural and religious initiatives were relegated, as we have shown, to a secondary place.

A centralization of Jewish institutional life, especially of the welfare institutions, would have spared many efforts that could have been utilized in the development of cultural, national, and religious ideals within the Jewish framework. Indeed, most Jewish immigrants in Argentina had experienced in their countries of origin a control by the central Jewish organizations of religious behavior and of the economic and social life of the individual. There, the judiciary was in the hands of these organizations, and rarely did Jews resort to non-Jewish courts. However, the full freedom and equality Jews enjoyed in Argentina allowed them to slacken their ties with the Jewish organizations. A united community structure was not imperative because of the openness of the general society. Still, Jewish officials in Buenos Aires repeatedly attempted to federate or merge their societies in order to create a representative body for Argentine Jewry. The various attempts at centralization and the reasons for the failures clearly reflect the limited number of organizational personalities active in Arentine Jewry at its period of inception and the feebleness of their endeavors to transcend the primordial welfare phase and propound a program for higher concerns.

The first concrete initiative of a federation of Jewish societies in Buenos Aires was launched at the end of 1908 when a group of observant Jews was disturbed by the conduct of the ritual slaughters and kosher butchers in Argentina. Besides charging exorbitant prices for the meat, it was confirmed that the latter did not prepare it according too the prescribed Jewish ritual. Therefore, at an assembly held at the Talmud Torah Harischono, it was decided that the "community" should be in control of ritual slaughtering and sale of kosher meat "without raising the price, and [thus] creating a source of income for all collective needs."[1] Representatives of the major Jewish institutions were therefore invited to discuss the formation of a federation.

The delegates of the Jewish societies discussed an elaborate Constitution for the future Federación Israelita Argentina (FIA) during three meetings at the beginning of 1909.[2] Among the objectives and attributes of the FIA were the following:[3]

a. To represent the Jewish Community [Colectividad Israelita], . . . to protect its rights, and to promote its moral and social progress.
b. To further the well-being of the Jewish societies.
c. To acquire properties for the creation of new religious and welfare institutions, and for schools to propagate the Jewish spirit and the Argentine patriotic sentiments among the children.
d. To tighten the bonds of union and solidarity among the Jewish societies.
e. To contribute . . . both morally and financially . . . to the development of the confederated societies.
f. To endow the Jewish community of Argentina with a Chief Rabbi who shall be the official representative of the Jewish cult.

During the following months, up to July of that year, various organizations discussed in separate general assemblies whether or not to participate in the FIA. The Chevra Keduscha was interested in participating, for in this way the acquisition of a permanent field for a cemetery could be eased.[4] Analogously, Ezrah, where the idea of a Jewish hospital was born, was anxious to have the rest of the Jewish population participate in this major enterprise.[5] The Talmud Torah, moreover, was the initiating body. It was interested in the creation of a federation that would regulate the slaughtering and selling of kosher meat. At CIRA, however, the decision was not unanimous. It was the oldest Jewish organization, and its leaders were economically among the most powerful Jews in the country. Therefore, many of its members considered that CIRA should continue being the de facto representative body of the Jews in Argentina. However, when the trend to participate in the FIA was also felt at CIRA, its officials tried to avoid an infringement of their independence, for CIRA constituted a small numerical minority. They therefore voted to introduce two additions to FIA's Constitution in order to enter the federation. First, to the abovementioned Article 4, clause f, they desired to add that "CIRA has the right to appoint its Rabbi directly, according to its own Constitution, and the latter shall not be subject to the Chief Rabbi by a dependence tie, except in the case an assembly of its members, especially called for this purpose, should so decide."[6] Moreover, CIRA desired to "retain the right of leaving the FIA in case of any modification of this Constitution, or when she [CIRA] considers it convenient."[7]

At the first official meeting of the FIA, on August 5, 1909, the changes proposed by CIRA were discussed. Henry Joseph, representing CIRA, openly stated that the addenda were proposed in order to "protect the interests of the

English, French, and German Jews of CIRA."[8] It was clear that CIRA represented a minority but a minority that considered itself representative of the whole and that it was afraid of being overrun by the East European majority. Gustavo Weil, also representing CIRA, who was proclaimed president, said that "here there are no German, or French, or Russian, or English Jews. There are only Jews, or if you prefer, Argentine Jews, because even if we are not Argentine, all our sons are and will be Argentine Jews."[9] Eventually, CIRA desisted from her special conditions.

The delegates of the four institutions constituting the FIA met assiduously during the second half of 1909. They were possessed by a feeling of historic mission in setting the basis for future generations of Argentine Jews by establishing a community that they were convinced would grow in numbers and prestige.[10]

The first program of action presented to the delegates was many-sided and embraced all facts of communal life. It included the erection of a Jewish hospital, the surveillance of kosher meat, the establishment of a bureau of information for Jewish immigrants, the organization of Jewish schools for children, the acquisition of a plot for a cemetery, the foundation of an orphanage and a home for the aged, and the sponsorship of a daily newspaper and an official organ of FIA.[11] By the end of 1909 some headway was made in organizing kosher slaughtering. However, when the FIA was finally disbanded in October 1910, it had accomplished nothing.

The failure of FIA was due to a variety of reasons. First, those who saw in its existence a danger to their own interests—the ritual slaughters and butchers—did everything possible to destroy it. They entered into agreements with FIA in order to weaken it from within. They relied on their customers' leniency concerning kosher meat, for most of whom the "kosher" sign was enough; they did not demand full control.[12] Thus the main goal of the Talmud Torah was defeated. Furthermore, as we have seen (ch. 8), FIA was not able to make progress regarding the Jewish hospital. Ezrah thus decided to go on independently with this project. Analogously, the Chevra Keduscha made separate arrangements at the end of 1909 to buy the definite plot of land for the cemetery. Therefore, both the Ezrah and the Chevra Keduscha pursued their main goals independently of FIA. CIRA, which was more interested in promoting religious values and in establishing a representative body for local Jewry, remained the main force within FIA. It was the only partner that fully contributed its monthly dues to FIA.

The fact that both Ezrah and Chevra Keduscha decided to pursue their original endeavors separately and not through the logical FIA channels is a telling example of the spirit of individuality and the atmosphere of petty rivalries among officials and among institutions at the time. Moreover, among the East European officials in both these institutions there was a feeling of mistrust for the West European Jews of CIRA, who were depicted as assimilationists. In 1910 they felt that the French and German Jews would dominate the Russian ones, in spite of all the nice words expressed at the inception of FIA.[13]

The main factor, however, for the failure of FIA was that its leaders did not try to make it as universal as possible for the Jews living in Buenos Aires. It only included Ashkenazic Jews, this being a positive attitude, for in 1910 there was practically no common language—of either words or ideas—between Ashkenazic and Sephardic immigrants in Buenos Aires. However, it was also limiting to many sectors of Ashkenazic Jewry, for it concentrated mainly on religious questions such as *kashrut*, rabbis, and so on, thus excluding the secular Jews. Moreover, Rabbi Samuel Halphon was the "soul of the FIA." His studies at the Ecole Rabbinique in Paris had estranged him from East European orthodoxy, a fact that was accentuated by Halphon's ministration at CIRA, where semiorthodox services were held for traditional but nonobservant Jews. Furthermore, due to its ambivalent position vis-à-vis Zionism, the Zionist group active during the preliminary sessions did not enter FIA when it was officially formed.[14]

Finally, FIA did not deal with problems that affected the entire population at the time, thus failing to avail itself of the possibility of gaining support from larger sectors. In their second meeting the delegates of FIA decided "not to engage themselves in the fight against white slavery."[15] This fight should have concerned FIA, for white slavery constituted the greatest threat from within to normal Jewish life. On the other hand, FIA never even dealt with the situation of Jewish education in Argentina. When Halphon, who had held the FIA together during its last months of life, left for a year in Europe, the federation faded out.

At the end of 1913 and during 1914 another attempt was made to federate the Jewish organizations in Buenos Aires. Representatives of the Chevra Keduscha, Ezrah, Centro Juventud Israelita Argentina, and Federación Sionista Argentina entered this federation. According to its constitution, it would represent the Jewish population in Argentina as a civil body to the country's authorities and would promote all types of initiatives within the Jewish community.[16] In spite of the dissidence of some organizations, the majority enabled the federation to intervene in religious questions.[17] Though it managed to represent the Jewish population for a short time,[18] this Federación Israelita failed after about one year of existence, due to divergent positions regarding religion and Zionism.[19]

During the first Argentine Jewish Congress of February 26–29, 1916, a committee of thirty-six delegates was appointed to study ways to establish a representative body of the community. Though the committee included Zionists, religious, and Sephardic representatives, as well as delegates from communities in the interior of the country, it never produced concrete results.[20]

In response to the events of the Semana Trágica, a Comité de la Colectividad was convened by the leaders of the Federación Sionista Argentina with the participation of CIRA, especially its rabbi, Samuel Halphon. In spite of all the efforts for maintaining this *comité* after the emergency was over, a representative body of Argentine Jewry was still not organized. As we have seen, the enormous rivalry between CIRA and the Zionists concerning the representation of the community was again the main factor working against a unified front.[21]

The proliferation of institutions continued worrying the Jewish leaders in Buenos Aires. In May 1920 the spokesman for a group of individuals interested in forming an Alianza (Alliance) "because of the great number of societies functioning, and to their precarious life due to the lack of official protection" approached the largest Jewish institutions in Buenos Aires.[22] The Chevra Keduscha immediately accepted this proposal and decided to constitute itself the chief promoter of the enterprise.[23] During the rest of the year little progress was made in this direction. Various meetings were held with delegates from all Jewish societies except "international political centers," that is, Bundists, communists, and anarchists.[24] The year 1921 was spent in deliberations about the way of organizing the Alianza, but no effective work was done.

At the end of 1921 the initiating group led by Bernardo Savransky, Natalio Frankel, and Felipe Gamberg, noticing that the Chevra Keduscha had not paid sufficient attention to the Alianza project, founded a Comité Pro Alianza Israeliate Argentina (CPAIA). The underlying rationale was to "conquer" the institutions with officials convinced of the practical value of the Alianza. Their first aim was to propagandize among Jews the list that this *comité* proposed for the elections at the largest Jewish society, the Chevra Keduscha.[25] At the same time, the candidates of CPAIA's list contributed funds to it, thus establishing a strong bond of interdependence between the Chevra Keduscha and CPAIA after March 1922, when this list won the elections.

The new board of Chevra Keduscha again took in its own hands the organization of the Alianza. Under the presidency of Miguel Zabotinsky a project was formalized with the following goals:

a. To unite all philanthropic, cultural, and educational institutions in one central entity.
b. To represent the interests of the Jewish community in Argentina.
c. To watch over the progress of the institutions and to exert a strict control over their development, both moral and material.
d. To found new institutions, . . . or expand those already in existence.
e. The Alianza . . . shall not participate in political struggles.

From this initiative a new committee was formed, called Junta Organizadora de la Alianza o Federación Israelita (JOA).[26] Due to clause a above, the JOA excluded representatives from all synagogues, notably from CIRA. Moreover, there were long debates about the Talmud Torahs. Many delegates considered that the latter reflected a religious outlook and were thus antidemocratic. The opinion favoring the admittance of the Talmud Torahs prevailed due to their positive work in preserving Judaism.[27] CPAIA continued functioning as a propaganda branch and was allowed to send three representatives to JOA.[28] Nonetheless, all delegates at JOA, except those from the Talmud Torahs, represented philanthropic institutions in Buenos Aires. Therefore, the main efforts were geared to a centralization of the philanthropic activities, in spite of the fact that the delegates of JOA were fully aware of the neglected state of Jewish education and culture in the country.[29]

The aim of the JOA was "the fusion of welfare, cultural, and educational societies in one entity ... which would represent the [Jewish] community."[30] Recognizing that the accomplishment of this fusion would not be immediate, it was decided that during the transition period the final organization would be planned, and propaganda would be made at the various institutions. At this stage of the process the goal was to economize in the administration of the welfare institutions and to divide the burden of supporting the institutions more equitably. For that purpose a census of all voluntary contributions and monthly dues was to be arranged. Moreover, the financial situation of every institution, their budgets, and projected expansions were to be studied. When these studies would be completed, the centralization of all collections would be effected by the Alianza, which would assign a monthly sum to each member society. The latter would not be allowed to organize their own separate or additional fund raising. This plan was to be implemented during one year, as a trial, during which all the member institutions would retain complete autonomy and their social properties.[31]

The enthusiasts of the Alianza were encouraged by this accomplishment.[32] However, some of the institutions involved in previous deliberations immediately departed, fearing that they would not be able to met their budgets in this way. The Sociedad de Socorros de Damas Israelites, which supported the girls' orphanage, left the JOA for this reason. The Liga Israelita Argentina contra la Tuberculosis decided to enter only after the actual formation of the Alianza. The Comité Central Pro–Víctimas de la Guerra y Pogroms did not participate because its funds went to help Jews abroad. Soprotimis and Cursos Religiosos, which were in close contact with CIRA, also left JOA. The Cocina Popular did not enter either.[33] The JOA was reduced to the delegations of Chevra Keduscha, Ezrah, Asilo Israelita Argentino, Bikur Joilim, and the Talmud Torahs.

The Ashkenazic community in Buenos Aires was then divided into two sectors: those supporting the Alianza and those against it. The former considered that most of the institutions that left the JOA were "aristocratic," or related to CIRA and its rich membership. This was partially true of Soprotimis, Cursos Religiosos, and Sociedad de Socorros de Damas Israelitas but not of the rest of the list. Notwithstanding the departure of these societies, the *alian-cistas* considered that the "Jewish street"—the masses—were supporting the Alianza. However, this was not altogether correct. Soon an electoral scandal at the Ezrah resulted in this institution's retirement from JOA. The work for the Alianza was thus interrupted for about a year.[34]

When the activities in favor of an Alianza were resumed at the end of 1924 some active leaders of the various Zionist centers became involved.[35] They most probably not only considered that the Alianza was a good instrument for organizing the local community but hoped that its constitution would allow more freedom and less competition for Zionist propaganda and campaigns.

By April 1925 the Alianza had made some progress and had about 3,500 individual supporters. It felt strong enough to launch its platform, including all their principles adopted after 1921. Besides considering itself the highest authority and representative body of the Jewish community in Buenos Aires, embracing all Jewish institutions of a philanthropic, educational, or cultural character, it was to have special departments for mutual aid, social support, education, and culture, and an additional one for elections at the various Jewish institutions, in order to help maintain its control over them.[36]

The deathblow for the Alianza was felt when the candidates it favored at the elections of Chevra Keduscha (January 1926) lost. With lack of support from the largest institution the Alianza only effected symbolic work for another year. With the participation of Ezrah—which had been "reconquered" for the Alianza—the Asilo Israelita Argentino, Bikur Joilim, the Talmud Torahs, and CPAIA to which were incorporated Wolf Nijensohn of the Federación Sionista Argentina and Mordechai Regalsky of Poale Zion, an elaborate Project of Constitution was prepared, printed, and distributed. This project—which consisted of sixty-five articles—clearly defined the goals and methods of the Alianza, in agreement with its previous postures. Nonetheless, the indifference of the Chevra Keduscha was decisive. Though the Chevra Keduscha was not yet strong enough to become the representative body of Argentine Jewry by itself, it was proven that any such body would necessarily have to include the Chevra Keduscha as an integral part of it.

With over half a century of historic perspective, we can see more clearly why the Alianza, along the lines it had set for itself, could not prosper in Buenos Aires during the 1920s. First, the Ashkenazic Jews in Buenos Aires were an amorphous group of immigrants from different areas in Europe. During the twenties, as also during the thirties, the majority of the Jewish population in Argentina was composed of proletarians. As we have seen, only a small portion of them possessed some knowledge of the spiritual and cultural sources of the Jewish people. The leadership therefore rose from among those who had been most successful in building a good economic situation for themselves. However, this leadership was limited in the scope of its influence. While leaders managed to exert their power over the membership of one society, they could not do so for the conglomerate of institutions that sprouted in Buenos Aires.

In the second place, leadership of a large institution represented a source of honor for its bearers. The establishment of the Alianza would not have put an end to president or general secretary chairs at the various societies, for it contemplated allowing a certain degree of autonomy to each of the member societies. However, the very existence of the Alianza with its own executive board would have created posts of greater weight than those at the regular societies. The president of the Alianza would be, with respect to the presidents of the other Jewish institutions, a *primo inter pares*. Thus personal rivalries, as well as rivalries between institutions themselves, dominated over the collective interests of the community at large.[37]

In the third place, the ruling against independent fund-raising caused great concern among officials. Fund-raising was one of the most—if not the most—important concerns of all the organizations, especially the welfare institutions, which were the main partners of the Alianza project. Except for the Chevra Keduscha, which had a permanent income from monthly dues and burial services, all other societies depended heavily on special campaigns in the capital and interior, theater charity performances, balls, and raffles. The Alianza project contemplated the economic fusion of the societies, thus causing justified apprehension among officials who feared that the share of the budget allocated to their institution would not be sufficient.

The way of achieving the Alianza was not realistic. Its proponents considered that by "conquering" the boards of the societies, they could guarantee ultimate union. This method is appropriate when a common ideology can unite the various institutions. In the case of the Alianza there was no such ideology. The goal consisted in merging the societies and establishing a representative body, but there was no underlying ideology here. There was not even a common purpose, such as building an effective defense machinery against a consistent philosophy or organization threatening the Jewish community. On the contrary, the officials included in the electoral lists proposed by the Alianza committees who eventually "conquered" the board of a society were faced with a dilemma, for they were supposed to encourage a fusion that would relegate their own personal standing to a secondary position. Moreover, not all institutions joined simultaneously. By the time the last merged the first might be lost, as indeed happened several times, and ultimately caused the defeat of the Alianza. Finally, the meddling of the Alianza committee in the internal life of each institution, especially in elections, an event of great importance for the contending groups, produced the animadversion of some sectors of the institution's membership to the Alianza.

During the mid and late 1920s some Jewish officials radically opposed the Alianza project and suggested—notably in the columns of Mundo Israelita— a different way of achieving representation of the community and centralization of its activities. In their view the Chevra Keduscha should change its constitution and declare itself the Kehilla, or community. The Chevra Keduscha had the essential quality of a community, for it grouped most Ashkenazic Jews in Buenos Aires, including not only the religiously oriented but also the Zionist, freethinkers, and leftist Jews. The original function of the Chevra Keduscha—Jewish burials—had transcended its purely religious character. Practically all the Jews retained some type of sentimental link with the Jewish people, which was expressed in their desire of a burial at the Jewish graveyard. Thus the Chevra Keduscha constituted the lowest common denominator of most Ashkenazic Jews in Buenos Aires.

The cardinal basis, however, for the Chevra Keduscha's growing ascendancy among Jews in Buenos Aires was that it had a monopoly—not formally but indeed in practice—over the burial services it offered. In Argentina it was not compulsory for a Jew to belong to any type of Jewish society. His attachment to religious, welfare, educational, or Zionist institutions was purely voluntary. He could choose to become a member or not. Accordingly, all Jewish institutions prepared their budgets on the basis of estimates of income from dues or special campaigns, all given willingly by the individual Jews. The

Chevra Keduscha was a voluntary association as well. Nonetheless, an Ashkenazic Jew could only be buried in their cemetery or resort to the municipal ones. Appropriate agreements had been signed with all the smaller Sephardic communities in Buenos Aires, forbidding burials of Ashkenazim in their graveyards, and vice-versa, thus establishing a de facto monopoly in the hands of the Chevra Keduscha.

This circumstance, together with the disproportion between the income of the Chevra Keduscha with its relatively small monetary investment, explains its enormous material power. Its leaders, with the acquiescence of the membership, spread their activities to areas of Jewish concern beyond burial services. The Chevra Keduscha contributed largely to Zionist campaigns, welfare causes, and finally to educational institutions (cf. ch. 8). The Jews of Buenos Aires accepted the expansion of the range of activities of the Chevra Keduscha. They, moreover, got used to the idea of considering it the axis of Jewish organization in the capital.

The Chevra Keduscha Aschkenasi, because of its peculiar development, was, by the end of the 1920s, fulfilling de facto functions of a Kehilla, or community, in Buenos Aires. Active propaganda was carried in *Di Yiddishe Zeitung* and *Mundo Israelita* in order to transform it de jure into the Kehilla. *Di Yiddishe Zeitung* interviewed the past presidents of the Chevra Keduscha and other officials of numerous Jewish societies and illustrated that the general consensus was in favor of changing the character of the Chevra Keduscha and expanding its functions to the representation of the Jewish community.[38] On the other hand, *Mundo Israelita* had been battling against the Alianza and suggesting the transformation of the Chevra Keduscha into a Kehilla ever since 1923.[39]

A group formed by León Kibrick, codirector of *Mundo Israelita*; Dr. Jaime Favelukes, leader at the Hospital Israelita and the Liga Israelita Argentina contra la Tuberculosis; A. L. Schusheim, one of the main columnists of *Di Yiddishe Zeitung*; and members of the board of Chevra Keduscha presented to this institution a project of a new Constitution in 1931. The principal reason for this project was "to legalize the activities which the Chevra Keduscha in fact already performs, and which are not included in its present Constitution, i.e., to represent legally all the Jews, thus preventing that anyone speak in their name, and to intensify and practice systematically social welfare and Jewish instruction."[40] Though the final steps to form the Kehilla took nearly two more decades, the Chevra Keduscha performed many of these functions much earlier.

Antisemitism became strongly felt in Argentina with the rise of nazism in Germany, which influenced nationalist circles in Argentina. Unlike earlier anti-Jewish feelings in Argentina, which were manifest at times with certain strength but did not create a consistent and substantial ideology with the backing of power elements, during the 1930s an extensive organization was established in Argentina by German Nazis, which threatened the spiritual and territorial integrity of Argentina. Moreover, the September 1930 revolution, which deposed the *Radicales* from power, initiated a period of military control of Argentine political life led by people deeply imbued with a strong nationalist ideology that was spread by the communications media and educational programs. Jews were constantly molested, menaced, and attacked. Anti-Jewish feelings had taken root in Argentina and were felt among large sectors of the country's population.

This element—ideologically consistent antisemitism—was what finally provoked the definite formation of a representative body of Jews in Argentina. What started in 1933 as a Comité contra el Antisemitismo y las Persecuciones Judías en Alemania was transformed two years later into the Delegación de Asociaciones Israelitas Argentinas (DAIA), composed of representatives of all sectors of Argentine Jewry, including Sephardim. As in many other opportunities throughout the history of the Jewish people, antisemitism became a relevant factor for unity and identification among Jews in Argentina. This took place in the 1930s. Up to that date this factor had been present with recurrent outbursts in the local daily press and periodical journals and in the thinking of some writers and men of influence, but actual violent demonstrations were isolated, and there was little connection, one with the other. The Jewish response had correspondingly been isolated. Unity among institutions and individuals had been temporary and fragile. When the danger seemed to have evaporated, so did the representative body of the Jews.[41]

The efforts to centralize Jewish life in Argentina made during the first three decades of the twentieth century did not remain without an effect. Indeed, they failed at their time, as we have described. But centralization continued being a permanent goal for Jewish officials. When it was finally achieved, it took forms not altogether conceived by leaders before 1930. The latter had thought of one body, either a federation of institutions—FIA and Alianza projects—or the transformation of one society, namely, the Chevra Keduscha, to constitute a representative body of Argentine Jewry towards the Argentine nation and the Jewish people at large, *as well as* to constitute the Ashkenazic community of Buenos Aires to deal with its internal life. The historical juncture, however, precipitated the formation of separate bodies. DAIA, the "foreign office" of Argentine Jewry, was formed as a response to external perils. On the other hand, the Chevra Keduscha grew into its later role of Ashkenazic community of Buenos Aires. Some of the burial societies of the Sephardic groups grew into central roles in their respective communities as well.[42]

Conclusion: The Jewish Panorama in 1930

The young Jewish community in Buenos Aires, most of which was composed of immigrants, had attained fundamental and lasting achievements by 1930. It had busied itself mainly in providing for the essential and most immediate necessities of the Jewish population. Thus, a Jew could be assisted in cases of sickness, unemployment, or financial difficulties by institutions in which people spoke his own language and better understood his problems. In his old age a Jew could resort to the old age home; orphans were taken care of in appropriate asylums. A new immigrant could apply to societies which would provide for his needs during his first weeks in Argentina and would help him settle and find work either in Buenos Aires, other urban centers, or in the agricultural colonies throughout the country. He could profit from courses in the Spanish language and from orientation for bringing his family, still on the other side of the Atlantic, to join him there.

The tens of Ashkenazic *landsmanschaften* associations, as well as the various Sephardic communities, provided for the Jews in Buenos Aires a microcosm of the Jewish environment they had left behind when sailing to Argentina. Besides furnishing a familiar atmosphere for the immigrant, these residents' societies were deeply concerned with the Jewish problem in their old communities and contributed with whatever means they had to ease the situation of family and fellow townsmen still there. All groups, each with its particular intensity, shared as a vicarious experience the troubles, aspirations, and fates of Eastern Jewries.

Popular cultural centers with a library or an amateur theater group, operated in various areas of Jewish settlement in Buenos Aires. Most of them had a political ideology, such as Labor Zionism, Bundism, anarchism, or communism. There, many young Jewish workers found a place to discuss their political and social views, listen to a lecture, or read a good book or Yiddish newspaper from Eastern Europe, England, or the United States. A large number of the members were bachelors who enjoyed the opportunity for socializing with Yiddish as a common language.

By the end of the 1920s, the Jewish community in Buenos Aires, with few exceptions, was secular. The bulk of immigrants from Eastern Europe rid themselves of religious practices before their arrival in Argentina, or soon afterwards. Lack of a respected religious leadership only accentuated this trend. Among Sephardim, who by and large were much more observant of Jewish ritual law at the time of settlement in Argentina, a slow but indeed noticeable trend of relaxation took place, even among the extremist immigrants from Aleppo. The death of Hachum Shaul Setton Dabbah in 1930, who for nearly two decades kept rigorous control over religious observance among his group, loosened ritual practices even more. The departure of Rabbi Samuel Halphon to Europe during this same year, after a quarter of a century of service at CIRA, deprived Buenos Aires Jewry of a strong spiritual leader and of one of its most prominent communal workers and spokesmen. Both CIRA and the Aleppine community would remain without rabbinic leadership until the eve of World War II.

While there were some leftist groups that ridiculed religious practices of their fellow Jews, the majority of the Jews were indifferent to them. The latter might have required or tolerated religious ceremonies for circumcisions or burials and might have participated in religious services during the Jewish Holy Days, but religion played a meaningful role in daily life for only a very small sector of Buenos Aires' Jewry.

Jewish education, both at the secular schools and at the Talmud Torahs, was deficient in two aspects. First, it only reached a small number of the Jewish population of school age; second, the programs and the general framework of Jewish schools did not compete favorably with the programs of national schools in Argentina. However, by the end of the twenties efforts were initiated to remedy the situation. The first procedures for the modernization and centralization of the various Jewish school systems were made. Moreover, at this time the Chevra Keduscha became involved in educational matters and subsidized all types of Jewish education. The bolstering of the Chevra Keduscha and the persistence of duly alarmed officials resulted in a redefinition of Jewish education after 1930.

The major contact the individual Ashkenazi had with something Jewish was the Jewish street and the Yiddish language. Still in 1930 Jews were concentrated in specific quarters in Buenos Aires, where they constituted either the majority or a conspicuous part of the population. Here Yiddish was spoken freely. Workshops, small factories, and stores were located in these areas, thus facilitating personal contacts among Jews during the day. At night the various Yiddish theaters opened their doors. Other Jews met at the libraries, at the cafés, or at the board meetings of tens of Jewish societies, be they cultural, political, social, religious, or commercial.

In the Jewish street the two Yiddish dailies were avidly read, as were the various weeklies and monthlies in this language and the well-written and combatant *Mundo Israelita* in Spanish. The influence of *Di Yiddishe Zeitung* and *Di Presse* was paramount. They constituted the "Bible" for a large audience, and their main articles and editorials were fervently discussed. Moreover, they promoted the education of their readers with extensive library sections. Their fundamental contribution, however, was in the preservation of the Yiddish language and the Jewish culture built around it among a large number of Jewish immigrants and some of their children, who had learned the language at home and occasionally borrowed the Yiddish dailies from their parents.

While Sephardim had a similar type of "neighborhood" life, they lacked a Jewish press in their own language and promoted by their own communities. With the exception of *Israel* which appeared irregularly and was of low literary standard, Sephardim read *Mundo Israelita* and the general local press. Their lack of a daily and of a periodical of high standards gives evidence to the type of Jewish life in their neighborhoods. They lacked the ebulliency present at the Ashkenazic quarters, where participation in political and social movements within and without the Jewish community were the order of the day. Moreover, the absence of a solid journal witnesses especially their apathy vis-à-vis Zionism.

One area of Jewish concern was having a growing influence among Jews in Argentina. Large numbers of Jews had been affected by years of propaganda from Zionist circles. Zionist activities, which at the turn of the century and even before the Balfour Declaration were displayed mainly by the better-off sector of East European Jews, by 1930 had a more popular character. Zionism had won the sympathy and merited the efforts of some important individuals from the Sephardic communities, the West European Jews of CIRA, and Jews in Argentine political and cultural life, who were of influence in their own circles. It had also spread among the numerous working Jewish population where various Labor Zionist ideologies had taken shape.

On the eve of the European Jewish holocaust, Argentine Jewry was consolidating itself. It had been preoccupied with all manner of material and corporeal necessities of the Jews. However, it had conspicuously neglected one aspect of its growth. It had not seriously faced the question of its spiritual and cultural continuity and had no leadership in these areas. This negligence was reflected in the attitude of the first generation of Ashkenazim educated or born in Argentina. Most received a deficient Jewish education or none at all. The Argentine schools reinforced their assimilation to Argentine values and nationalism. Moreover, they felt the need to assert their Argentinism and thus sought to shed most of their foreign traits. Many had entered, and graduated from, the Argentine universities and were imbued with the spirit of participation in the growth and destiny of the Argentine nation. Definitely estranged from religion, their attitude towards Zionism was ambivalent. They only vaguely understood the Jewish experience in Eastern Europe; and while they understood Yiddish, and even spoke it at times, they preferred their mother tongue, Spanish. From among them rose a group of cultural secularists who initiated a program of social and cultural activities within a Jewish framework. The various centers that constituted the Sociedad Hebraica Argentina in the twenties had laid the cornerstone for Jewish life within the context of the general current of Argentine life.

The lack of religious and, to a large extent, also of educational leadership implied that no such leadership had formed in the country. When required, it had to be imported from the Old World. Each community or group therefore reverted to its own place of origin for this purpose, thus accentuating Argentine Jewry's dependence on the Jewish centers in Eastern Europe, the Balkans, Syria, and North Africa. Jewish centers that were much more vital than the one being formed in Argentina, such as those in the United States and England, played no role in South America. Consequently, the beginning of the end of European Jewry, the progressive weakening of Sephardic communities east of the Atlantic, and the enforcement of immigration restrictions in Argentina after 1930, deprived Argentine Jewry of new blood from Jewish communities with a stronger Jewish identification.

The 1930s presented new problems for Argentine Jewry. The fate of European Jewry and of the Jewish National Home were a constant theme on the international arena, and Jews in far-away Argentina were closely following these issues. Local issues were also affecting Jews in Argentina. There was the growing peril of antisemitism menacing Jewish security; the Jewish community was becoming more Argentine, both in the percentage of locally born Jews and in the time distance of immigrants from the old home. The Jews in Argentina were faced, at that juncture, with two sides of the same coin: they needed to live vicariously the Jewish tragedy in Europe and to respond sympathetically and forcefully to it, while, simultaneously, they had to provide for the internal growth of their own Jewish community. Their success or failure at that goes beyond the limits of this essay.

Abbreviations

AJA	Anglo-Jewish Association
AIA	Alianza Israelita Argentina
AIB	Asociación Israelita de Beneficencia
AIU	Alliance Israélite Universelle
AJHSA	American Jewish Historical Society Archives
AJIA	Asociación Juventud Israelita Argentina
AJYB	*American Jewish Yearbook*
AMIA	Asociación Mutual Israelita Argentina
CC	Comité Central (Pro-Víctimas Israelitas de la Guerra)
CIL	Congregación Israelita Latina
CIRA	Congregación Israelita de la República Argentina
CIS	Comunidad Israelita Sefaradí
CJIA	Centro Juventud Israelita Argentina
CK	Chevra Keduscha Ashkenasi
CPAIA	Comité Pro Alianza Israelita Argentina
CPI	Cocina Popular Israelita
DAIA	Delegación de Asociaciones Israelitas Argentinas
EN	Ezras Noschim
ENAM	Ezras Noschim Archival Material
FIA	Federación Israelita Argentina
FIAC	Federación Israelita Argentina de Cultura
FICHA	Federación de Instituciones Culturales Hebreas Argentinas
FORA	Federación Obrera Regional Argentina
FSA	Federación Sionista Argentina
HIAS	Hebrew Immigrant Aid Society
HICEM	HIAS-JCA-Emigdirect
HSE	Hesed Shel Emeth
IWO	Yiddisher Wisnshaftlecher Institut
JAPGW	Jewish Association for the Protection of Girls and Women
JC	*Jewish Chronicle*
JCA	Jewish Colonization Association
JCA Rapport	JCA, *Rapport de l'Administration Centrale au conseil d'Administration*
JDC	(American Jewish) Joint Distribution Committee
JNF	Jewish National Fund

JOA	Junta Organizadora de la Alianza Israelita Argentina
KH	Keren Hayesod
Liga	Liga Israelita Argentina Contra la Tuberculosis
OSFA	Organización Sionista Femenina de la Argentina
PAF	Palestine Workers' Fund
PZ	Poale Zion
SHA	Sociedad Hebraica Argentina
Soprotimis	Sociedad de Protección a los Immigrantes Israelitas
UOI	Unión Obrera Israelita (Bikur Joilim)
WUSJ	World Union of Sephardic Jews
YZ	*Yiddishe Zeitung*
ZA	Central Zionist Archives
ZO	Zionist Organization
ZZ	Zeire Zion

Notes

Introduction

1. Cf. Simon Weill, *Población israelita en la República Argentina* (Buenos Aires, 1936), p. 28.
2. Cf. Victor A. Mirelman, "A Note on Jewish Settlement in Argentina (1881–1892)," *Jewish Social Studies* 33 (Jan. 1971): 3–12; idem, "Jewish Life in Buenos Aires before the East European Immigration (1860–1890)," *American Jewish Historical Quarterly*, 67, no. 3 (Mar. 1978). 195–207.
3. On the beginnings of the JCA project in Argentina, cf. Haim Avni, *Argentina, the Promised Land; Baron de Hirsch's Colonization Project in the Argentine Republic* (Hebrew) (Jerusalem, 1973).
4. East European Jews presided over CIRA at quite early stages: Rodolfo Ornstein, 1898–99, and Menashe Sigal, 1900–1902.
5. Weill, op. cit., 12.
6. Avni, op. cit. covers the history of the Baron de Hirsch project in Argentina until the death of the Baron in 1896.
7. Sephardic Jews are the Jewish descendants of Spanish and Portuguese Jews of the fifteenth century, who have preserved distinctive customs and traditions even after the expulsion from the Iberian peninsula. However, the word is used popularly to include Arabic-speaking Jews as well, in opposition to Ashkenazic Jews, i.e., East European and Germanic Jews and their descendants. We shall include, when speaking in general about Sephardim, the Spanish-speaking North African Jews; the Ladino-speaking Jews from Turkey, Greece, Yugoslavia, Rhodes, and Bulgaria; and the Arabic-speaking Jews from Syria, Lebanon, Egypt, and Palestine.
8. *Yorbuch 5714 fun der Yiddisher Kehila in Buenos Aires* (Buenos Aires, 1953); *Yorbuch 5715 fun der Yiddisher Kehila in Buenos Aires* (Buenos Aires, 1954); *Pinkas fun der Kehila in Buenos Aires* (Buenos Aires, 1963); *Pinkas fun der Kehila in Buenos Aires* (Buenos Aires, 1969).
9. *Yoblbuch Yiddishe Zeitung* (Buenos Aires, 1940); *Argentine, Futzig Yor Yiddisher Ishev* (Buenos Aires, 1938); *50 años de colonización judía en la Argentina* (Buenos Aires, 1939).
10. *Argentiner IWO Shriftn* (published by IWO Buenos Aires), vols. 1–11 (1941–69).

1. The Jewish Immigration Flow to Argentina

1. There is a very extensive bibliography dealing with the Argentine policy of immigration up to 1930. Some of the most pertinent items are the following: Carl Solberg, *Immigration and Nationalism, Argentina and Chile, 1890–1914* (Austin and London, 1970); Gino Germani, *Política y sociedad en una época de transición* (Buenos Aires, 1968); Nicolás Sánchez Albornoz and José Luis Moreno, *La población de América Latina* (Buenos Aires, 1968); Adolfo Dorfman, *Historia de la industria argentina* (Buenos Aires, 1970); Enrique Dickmann, *Población e inmigración* (Buenos Aires, 1946); Dardo Cúneo, Julio Mafud, Amalia Sánchez Sívori, and Lázaro Schallman, *Inmigración y nacionalidad* (Buenos Aires, 1967); Gladys S. Onega, *La inmigración en la literatura argentina* (1880–1910) (Santa Fe, 1965); A. J. Pérez Amuchástegui, *Mentalidades argentinas* (1860–1930) (Buenos Aires, 1965).

2. Cf. Onega, op. cit., 78ff.

3. *Censo de la Capital Federal del 18 de Setiembre de 1904* (Buenos Aires, 1906), 70; *Censo general de la ciudad de Buenos Aires, Octubre 16–24, 1909* (Buenos Aires, 1910), 88–93; Samuel Halphon, "Enquête sur la Population Israélite en Argentine," in JCA, *Rapport de L'Administration Centrale au Conseil D'Administration pour l'Année 1909* (hereafter JCA Rapport) (Paris, 1910), 302–6. The fact that many Jews did not declare their religion or considered themselves to have no religion is amply documented. See ch. 2 and Ira Rosenswaike, "The Jewish Population of Argentina: Census and Estimates, 1887–1947," *Jewish Social Studies* 22, no. 4 (Oct. 1960). 200–14.

4. Cf. Rosenswaike (op. cit., 200), who concluded that by 1914 the number of Jews in the capital approached 50,000. The figure given by Harry O. Sandberg ("The Jews of Latin America," *American Jewish Yearbook*, 1917/18, pp. 45ff) of 65,000 Jews in Buenos Aires for 1917 appears exaggerated.

5. Cf. *Informe de la Comisión Nacional de Inmigración*, 1896, 56. "45 families abandoned the colonies to return to Russia or to go to the United States, and 230 persons to change residence and work within the country." Many protested against the JCA administration. ibid., 63–67, 199–210. *Voskhod* published strongly worded leading articles in which it called upon the St. Petersburg Central Committee of JCA to tell the public the truth about what occured in its Argentine colonies. Cf. *Jewish Chronicle* (hereafter JC), June 3, 1898, p. 14. Some returned via Constantinople, where they were stranded under great hardships. Cf. JC, Sept. 18, 1896; ibid, Mar. 19, 1897, p. 11 tells about twenty families who left Argentina and were in Constantinople; ibid., Sept. 30, 1892, p. 8, reported that about 120 families returned; ibid. May 27, 1898, p. 14, reported 136 Jews returning.

6. JC, July 24, 1908, p. 10.

7. JCA, Rapport, 1908, p. 15 and 1909, p. 12.

8. Ibid, 1924, pp. 300f.

9. During Jan. 1925, ten Jews were killed while attempting to enter Argentina illegally. Cf. JCA Rapport, 1925, p. 292. During Aug. 1928, two Jewish couples were arrested by the police. They had disembarked in Montevideo because they did not possess all the necessary documentation to land in Buenos Aires. They were taken by an agent to Colonia (Uruguay) and later to Palmira, from where they were brought to the Argentine coast of the Río de la Plata at Punta Chica in a small boat. From there they walked to Tigre, where they took the train to Retiro Station in Buenos Aires. Here they were arrested by the secret police. Cf. *Yiddishe Zeitung* Aug. 23, 1928, pp. 5f.

10. Cf. *Municipalidad de la ciudad de Buenos Aires, Cuarto censo general* (Oct. 22, 1936) (Buenos Aires, 1939), vol. 3, pp. 242f. Rosenswaike (op.cit., 213) explains in detail his method for estimating the number of Jews in those categories. Weill (op. cit., 30) estimated 131,000 Jews in Buenos Aires in 1935, in line with these numbers.

11. The figures for urban and rural distribution of foreigners in 1914 are the following:

Origin	Rural Pop.	Total Pop.	% of Rural Pop.
Spain	219,669	829,701	26.5
France	24,911	79,491	31.3
Italy	292,658	929,863	31.5
Russia	39,996	93,634	42.7

Source: República Argentina, Tercer censo nacional, levantado el 1° de Junio de 1914 (Buenos Aires, 1916), vol, 2, pp. 395f.

12. Pamphlets on Argentina were printed in Yiddish and distributed in Eastern Europe. Cf. also Miron Kreinin, Di Einwanderungs Meglichkeitn kein Dorem Amerike un di Dortige Yiddishe Ishuvim (Berlin, 1928). Max Glucksman, president of both CIRA and Soprotimis, had been present at the Berlin Conference on Jewish immigration in 1928. The conference on the same issue organized in Buenos Aires later that year was a response to the urgent need of new horizons for Jewish settlement after the closing of the doors in the United States. Cf. Yiddishe Zeitung, May 7, 1928, p. 4.
13. Soprotimis, Minutes, May 20, 1922.
14. Ibid., July 1 and 8, 1922. Cf. JCA Rapport, 1921, pp. 122f.; Theodore Bar-Shalom, Hairgun Soprotimis veKlitatam shel Mehagrim Yehudim beArgentina beShanim 1922–1930, M.A. thesis, Hebrew University, Jerusalem, 1971; and Yiddisher Imigranten Shuts-Farain un Tsentral Komite fun Folks-Hilf, 1922–1927 (Buenos Aires, 1928).
15. JCA Rapport, 1922, pp. 144ff.
16. During the period May 1922–July 31, 1923 a total of 4,663 "llamadas" were obtained, but from Aug. 1, 1923 to Mar. 31, 1924 only 122. Cf. Marcos Satanowsky, "La emigración judía y la política emigratoria," Mundo Israelita, May 3, 1924. The printed bulletin of Soprotimis, Yiddisher Imigranten . . . , p. 45, however, does not report a diminution in the number of llamadas.
17. In two months, May 16–June 14, 1923, the JCA offices sent 903 Roumanian Jews to Argentina. Since then and up to the end of 1924, "as a consequence of the restriction to immigration in Argentina," only 131 emigrated from Roumania through JCA. Cf. JCA Rapport, 1924, p. 292.
18. According to A. M. Carr Saunders (World Population [Oxford, 1936]), the following countries absorbed most immigrants during the period 1821–1932:

United States	32,244,000
Argentina (since 1856)	6,405,000
Canada	5,206,000
Brazil	4,431,000
Australia	2,913,000

Source: Germani, op. cit., 264.

19. JCA Rapport, 1925, p. 291.
20. Ibid., pp. 291f.
21. Cf. Ramos's cables of Aug. 8 and Sept. 8, 1924 and JCA's response in Mundo Israelita, Oct. 11, 1924, p. 1.
22. JCA Rapport, 1925, p. 292.
23. Ibid., 1926, p. 313.
24. Ibid., 1930, p. 230.
25. Ibid., 1924, p. 300. This distrustfulness could be due to the existence of a considerable number of Jewish white slave dealers in Argentina and to the fact that the economic possibilities were, in their eyes, much better in the U.S. In any case two-thirds or more of the Jewish immigrants in Argentina during the last half of the 1920s were Polish. Of 7,816 immigrants who solicited help at Soprotimis during

1922–27, 4,757 (61%) were Polish; cf. *Yiddisher Imigranten* . . . , p. 17; the Polish Jews entered in the following numbers:

Year	Total Jewish Immigration	Polish Jewish Immigration	Percentage
1926	7,534	5,884	78
1927	5,584	3,742	67
1928	6,812	4,410	65
1929	5,986	4,264	71
1930	7,805	6,032	77
Total	33,721	24,332	72

Sources: JCA *Rapport*, 1926, 1930; *Four Years of Jewish Immigration*, Report of Activities of the Association for Emigration HIAS, JCA, Emigdirect (Paris, 1931).

26. JCA *Rapport*, 1930, p. 231.
27. Cf. Marcos Regalsky's speech in *Yiddishe Zeitung*, Aug. 28, 1928, p. 4; and Louis Oungre's speech, ibid., Aug. 29, 1928, p. 6.
28. HIAS board meeting of July 24, 1928, as cited by Mark Wischnitzer, *Visas to Freedom: The History of HIAS* (Cleveland and New York, 1956), pp. 128f.
29. Jose M. Bustos's project and the Argentine decree have been dealt with more thoroughly in Victor Mirelman, "A Note on Jewish Settlement in Argentina (1881–1892)," *Jewish Social Studies*, 33, no. 1 (Jan. 1971): 3–12.
30. Cf. Lázaro Schallman, "Proceso histórico de la colonización agrícola en la Argentina," in *Inmigración y nacionalidad* (Buenos Aires, 1967), 166; also Juan Schobinger, *Inmigración y colonización suizas en la República Argentina* (Buenos Aires, 1957), 40ff.
31. The decree, issued on Aug. 6, 1881, was published in *Registro Nacional*, Buenos Aires, Department of Interior, 1881, decree No. 12011. It was also reported in the press. Cf. *La Prensa*, Aug. 20, 1881, p. 1 and *La Nación*, Aug. 20, 1881, p. 1.
32. Cf. Mirelman, op. cit., 5f.
33. *Informe de la Comisión General de Inmigración* (for 1881) (Buenos Aires, 1882). The letter to Bustos was reprinted in Anexo A, pp. 63f.
34. "The Jews in Russia," *JC*, Sept. 23, 1881, p. 7 and Sept. 30, 1881, p. 11; *Archives Israélites*, Sept. 29, 1881, p. 326.
35. "Emigración Israelita," *El Diario*, Dec. 20, 1881, p. 2.
36. Cf. Mirelman, op. cit., 6–9. The subscription for Jews persecuted in Russia was announced by the *Standard and River Plate News* (*Buenos Aires*), July 28, 1882.
37. *Hazefirah*, May 22, 1888.
38. David Viñas, *De los montoneros a los anarquistas* (Buenos Aires, 1971), 160–74; A. J. Perez Amuchástegui, *Mentalidades argentinas* (1860–1930) (Buenos Aires, 1965), 393ff, 427ff.; Ezequiel Martínez Estrada, *Radiografía de la pampa*, 5th ed. (Buenos Aires, 1965), 57f.; Gastón Gori, *Inmigración y colonización en la Argentina* (Buenos Aires, 1964), 83f, 98ff.
39. Excerpts of Hassan's letter, as well as the resolutions of the AJA are found in JC, Jan. 10, 1890, p. 8.
40. Cf. Salo W. Baron, *The Russian Jew under Tsars and Soviets* (New York, 1964), 51–118; Elias Tcherikower, ed., *The Early Jewish Labor Movement in the United States*, translated and revised by Aaron Antonovsky (New York, 1961), 3–74; Lloyd P. Gartner, *The Jewish Immigrant in England, 1870–1914* (Detroit, 1960), 21f; and *Recueil de Matériaux sur la Situation Economique des Israélites de Russie d'Apres l'Enquête de la Jewish Colonization Association* (Paris, 1906).
41. Celia S. Heller, *On the Edge of Destruction: Jews of Poland between the Two World Wars* (New York, 1977), 11, 133–39; Yehuda Bauer, *My Brother's Keeper: A History of the American Jewish Joint Distribution Committee, 1929–1939* (Philadelphia, 1974), 180–209; *American Jewish Yearbook* (1923–24) 25: 352f. and ibid. (1937–38) 39:430.

42. *Hazefirah,* Aug. 1 (13), 1888.
43. S. Kogan, "Alexander Zederbaum's Ongrif Oif der Yiddisher Kolonizatsie in Argentine," *Argentiner* IWO *Shriftn* 5(1952): 83f.
44. Kogan, op. cit., 96–100. Abraham Vermont founded in 1898 Di *Folks Shtime,* a weekly that endured until 1914, when the first Yiddish daily appeared in Buenos Aires. Abraham Vermont was a controvertible personality, who had few scruples and a tendency towards sensationalism. Cf. Lázaro Schallman, "Historia del periodismo judio en la Argentina," in *Comunidades Judías de Latinoamérica* (Buenos Aires, 1970), p. 151; Pinie Katz, Tsu *der Geshichte fun der Yiddisher Journalistik in Argentina* (Buenos Aires, 1929), 41–60; Samuel Rollansky, Dos *Yiddishe Gedrukte Wort un Teater in Argentine* (Buenos Aires, 1941), 46–48.
45. Alexander Zederbaum, *Arba Mamarim* (Petersburg, 1893), passim. The only antisemitic case recorded is an article that appeared in the *Courier de la Plata,* Feb. 2, 1893. This paper appeared in Buenos Aires, and reflected many of the antisemitic sentiments at the time rampant in France.
46. Zederbaum, op. cit., p. 9.
47. Alex Bein, *Theodore Herzl* (Philadelphia, 1941), 120–33.
48. Zederbaum, op. cit., 10.
49. Kogan, op. cit., 86.
50. Some of the more conspicuous correspondents of *Hazefirah* were Abraham Rosenfeld of Mauricio, Province of Buenos Aires; Abraham Horowitz, Moisesville, Santa Fe; Israel Fingerman, Clara, Entre Rios; Jacobo Kahansky, San Antonio, Entre Rios.
51. Jacob Iedvabski and Isidore Hellman, Di *Reise Nach Argentina* (Warsaw, 1891).
52. Propaganda for the country was carried on not only by Jews but also by Argentine immigration agents. The main center for this propaganda in Eastern Europe was Warsaw, where a large amount of material was distributed. Among the latter we find *Argentina, the Way Thither, the Land, Commerce, Agriculture and Industry* (Yiddish) (Warsaw, 1891) and Wilhem Kreuth, *Ams des La Plata Staaten,* translated into Hebrew by Eleazar Finkel (Warsaw, 1891), which say no word about Jews but, due to the languages they were presented in, were evidently meant for Jews in Eastern Europe.
53. JC, May 13, 1887, p. 6.
54. Ibid., Aug. 5, 1887, p. 7.
55. Cf. Oscar E. Cornblit, Ezequiel Gallo(h.), and Alfredo A. O'Connell, "La Generación del 80 y su proyecto: antecedentes y consecuencias," in *Argentina, sociedad de masas* (Buenos Aires, 1965), 18–58.
56. Cf. the letter dated Sept. 4, 1889 sent by Oscar Levy, a French Jew living in Buenos Aires, to Isidor Loeb, secretary of the AIU, Archives of AIU at the American Jewish Archives, microfilm No. 758; David Hassan's letter to his father (JC, Oct. 11, 1889, p. 6); Pedro Palacios, in a letter to the AIU, on Aug. 18, 1890, writes in French the following: "As you shall see, we have signed two documents with the Russian colonists. The first one on August 28, 1889, with the intervention of Rabbi Henry Joseph and Mr. (Simon) Kramer." In a letter to the JC Joseph asserted that the ladies asked among friends for clothes and assistance. Monetary assistance was given by Jews and gentile friends of leading Jewish officials (JC Dec. 20, 1889, p. 8).
57. JC, Dec. 20, 1889, p. 8.
58. JC, Jan. 10, 1890, p. 8
59. JC, Feb. 7, 1890, p. 14.
60. Cf. the attitude of the JC, Jan. 17, 1890, p. 11.
61. CIRA, *Minutes,* Nov. 22, 1891.
62. The Congregación Israelita Latina, founded in 1891 by some of the Moroccan Jews in Buenos Aires, was not the only society of Jews of Moroccan origin at the time. They had a few places of gathering, mainly for prayer, in the area called "Barrio Sud," where most of these immigrants resided, especially in Venezuela street.
63. Chevrah Society, presided by Rodolfo Ornstein, is only mentioned in CIRA, *Minutes,* Nov. 19 and 22, 1891. It is most probably the Sociedad Obrera Israelita (Poale Zedek). Cf. ch. 2.

Notes

64. For more on Sephardic immigration to Argentina see Victor A. Mirelman, "Sephardic Immigration to Argentina Prior to the Nazi Period," in Judith Laikin Elkin and Gilbert W. Merkx (eds.) *The Jewish Presence in Latin America* (Boston, 1987), 13–32.
65. Isaac Benchimol, "La Langue Espagnole au Maroc," *Revue des Ecoles de l'Alliance Israélite* (Paris) no. 2 (July–Sept. 1901): 127 and Robert Ricard, "Notes sur l'Emigration des Israélites Marocaines en Amerique Espagnole et au Bresil," *Revue Africaine* (Algiers) 88, nos. 1 and 2 (1944). 84f.
66. Ricard, op. cit., 84. For Larache cf. Eugene Aubin, *Le Maroc d'Aujourd'hui*, 6th ed. (Paris, 1910), 91, where he asserts, "Parmi les Juifs, quelques negociants et beaucoup d'artisans; un mouvement d'emigration vers l'Amérique du Sud commence a se dessiner dans la communaute qui est pauvre et peu organisée."
67. Cf. *Association des Anciens Eleves de l'AIU, Bulletin Annuel* (Tangiers) no. 8 (1900): 13–17.
68. Ricard, op. cit., 84–86.
69. "Le Circoncisione a Buenos Aires," *Vessillo Israelitico* (Casale Monferrato, Italy), 1883, p. 352. The Benjetrit (maybe Benchetrit, V. M.) family moved to Buenos Aires. Their second son was born there and circumcised after ten days.
70. Interview with his son, Samuel de A. Levy, Mar. 1972. The latter was born in Buenos Aires in 1886, was active in all Sephardic institutions in the city, and by means of his journal *Israel*, founded 1917, kept in contact with the communities in the interior of Argentina and other South American countries, as well as with Jewish institutions in Morocco itself.
71. *Informes de los Consejeros Legales del Poder Ejecutivo* (Buenos Aires, 1890–1902) vol. 8, p. 224. For the marriage question in Argentina and how it affected the Jews, cf. Victor A. Mirelman, "Jewish Life in Buenos Aires before the East European Immigration (1860–1890)," *American Jewish Historical Quarterly* 67, no. 3 (Mar. 1978): 197–202.
72. Benchimol, op. cit., 128. Manuel L. Ortega (*Los hebreos en Marruecos* [Madrid, 1919]), 301f. quotes the same.
73. *Bulletin de l'AIU* 19(1894): 66.
74. As quoted in *Bulletin de l'AIU* 24(1899): 118.
75. Ibid., 119.
76. Ibid., 175–86; ibid. 26(1901): 96–99; ibid. 27(1902): 66: "Les éléves originaires de la Turquie et ceux du Maroc septentional ou l'on parle également l'espagnol—etaient donc tous designés pour les écoles de l'Argentine ou l'espagnol est la langue d'enseignement."
77. Benchimol, op. cit., 133.
78. Benchimol, op. cit., 133.
79. Angel Pulido Fernández, *Españoles sin patria y la raza sefardi* (Madrid, 1905), 643f.
80. Samuel Halphon, "Enquête sur la Population Israélite en Argentine," JCA *Rapport* 1909, pp. 251–310. Cf. also the *Minutes* of the Congregación Israelita Latina of Buenos Aires and those of the Ets Ajaim in Rosario, both of Moroccan Jews. During 1926 the director of *Israel* visited numerous cities and towns in the interior of Argentina and reported in the journal about the Jewish communities there, giving details, especially about Jews of Moroccan origin.
81. Cf. Ricard, op. cit., 86, where, based on data obtained from the French consulate in 1929, the following numbers for emigrants from Morocco to Argentina are given: 1924, 50; 1925, 43; 1926, 36; 1927, 45, indicating that most of them were Jewish.
82. Ricard, op. cit., 87.
83. Ibid.
84. Cf. Isaac Laredo, *Memorias de un viejo tangerino* (Madrid, 1935), 434. Other cases of Jews from Tangiers who moved to Buenos Aires are found on pp. 279 and 461. Bibas had been on the board of the Banco Comercial Israelita in Rosario, and president of the Bene Kedem, a Sephardic Zionist organization founded by the Keren Hayesod delegate, Ariel Bension, in 1927.
85. Abraham Galanté, *Histoire des Juifs de Rhodes, Chio, Cos, etc.* (Istanbul, 1935), 81; idem, *Histoire des Juifs d'Anatolie: Les Juifs d'Izmir (Smyrne)*, vol. 1 (Istanbul, 1937), 161f; idem, *Hisoire des Juifs d'Istambul*, vol. 2 (Istanbul, 1942), 119; David de Sola Pool, "The Lev-

244

antine Jews in the United States," *American Jewish Yearbook*, 1913/14, p. 209. Walter Paul Zenner, (*Syrian Jewish Identification in Israel*, Ph.D. dissertation, Columbia University, 1965, pp. 1–98) describes the economic, social, political, and religious situation of the Jews in Aleppo and Damascus in the later decades of the nineteenth century and the first of the twentieth. Cf. also Philip K. Hitti, *The Syrians in America* (New York, 1924), 48–52.

86. JC, May 13, 1887, p. 6. Juan Bialet-Masse (*El estado de las clases obreras argentinas a comienzos del siglo* [Córdova, 1968; first printed 1904]) mentioned *turcos* and Jews as peddlers in the Chaco (p. 135), and turcos in La Rioja (p. 178), Mendoza (p. 562), and San Juan (p. 595) also as peddlers or petty merchants. The word *turcos* is utilized to designate anyone coming from the Near or Middle East, be it present-day Syria, Egypt, or Turkey. Sephardic Jews are also generically called *turcos*, whatever their country of origin.

87. Cf. *Habima Haivrit* 1, no. 6 (1921): 11–12; Behor Issaev, "La Colectividad Sefardi Bonaerense en el Quinquenio 1958–1962," in *Pinkas fun der Kehila* (Buenos Aires, 1963), Spanish Section, p. 46; Minutes from Hessed Shel Emet (organization formed around the synagogue Es Ajaim, in Calle 25 de Mayo St., no. 696), Aug. 19, 1927.

88. Nissim Teubal, *El inmigrante, de Alepo a Buenos Aires* (Buenos Aires, 1953), pp. 68f, 79f.

89. Alberto Massri, president of Asociacion Union Israelita Sefaradi "Luz Eterna," in a speech commemorating the 50th anniversary of the institution (1970).

90. Sola Pool, op. cit., 209; Zenner, op. cit., 53f; Hitti, op cit., 51. During the First World War many Jews served in the Turkish Army. By the end of the war some of them deserted the army and fled. Zenner, p. 54, tells us of a Syrian Jew who fled to Jeblel-Druze and later to Argentina.

91. Teubal, op. cit., 68.

92. Interview with Jacques Mizrahi, Buenos Aires, Apr. 7, 1972.

93. Robert Foerster, *The Italian Migration of our Times* (Cambridge, Mass., 1924), 261f.

94. Teubal, op. cit., p. 83.

95. Ibid., p. 75.

96. Cf. L. Zitnitzky, "Yiddn in Buenos Aires Loit Der Munitsipaler Tseilung Fun 1936," *Argentiner IWO Shriftn* 3(1945): 16. This article, however, is full of errors based on a poor transcription of the census figures and should not be consulted for those purposes.

97. For example, from among the 4,857 men and 1,960 women who requested the help of Soprotimis to find jobs during the years 1922–27, fully 3,292 were without a profession. Of those with skills 1,012 were agriculturists, 336 seamstresses, 242 tailors, 233 shoemakers, 148 mechanics, 141 bakers, 130 butchers, 112 carpenters, and 106 locksmiths. Cf. *Yiddisher Imigranten Shuts-Farain un Tsentral Komite fun Folks-Hilf*, 1922–1927 (Buenos Aires, 1928), 18f.

98. JC, Sept. 9, 1898, p. 20.

99. *Der Yiddisher Soicher* 1, no. 5 (May 1910): 11f.

100. The first Jews who arrived in Buenos Aires from Aleppo at the turn of the century sold "cotton cloths and fabrics—a line of business which they had practiced in the Orient—, but they had no shops. They were travelling salesmen." Cf. Teubal, op. cit., 69. Similarly the Damascene Jews were engaged in peddling. Out of 568 persons inscribed in the first members book of their main institution, Sociedad Israelita Sefaradí Bené Emeth, over 70 percent were peddlers or small merchants. Cf. their *Primer libro de socios*, 1915–1919. Moreover, in the book sent by the Zionists in Argentina to Herzl in 1903, it is mentioned that among Moroccan Jews a large percentage are peddlers.

101. *El Sionista* 1, no. 4 (Aug. 1, 1904): 1f; Pinie Katz, *Yiddn in Argentina* (Buenos Aires, 1946), 48f.

102. JC, Nov. 3, 1905, p. 26.

103. Halphon, op. cit., 303–7.

104. Arturo Bab, "Die berufliche und soziale Schichtung der Juden in Argentinien," *Der Morgen* 4 (Apr. 1928): 89–92. Cf. also M. Benario, "Di Geshichtliche Antwiklung fun

Yiddishen Handel un Industrie in Buenos Aires," in *Yoblbuch Yiddishe Zeitung* (Buenos Aires, 1940), 267–90.

105. Halphon, op. cit., 306; Bab, op. cit., 84–90.
106. Simon Weill, *Población israelita en la República Argentina* (Buenos Aires, 1936), 16.
107. Bab, op. cit., 92.
108. Benario, op. cit., 286.
109. On March 10, 1910, the Liga de Defensa Comercial Israelita Argentina was founded with the purpose of bettering the economic condition of its members. The Liga had in mind the formation of a cooperative of production, consumption, and loans when its membership would reach the 500 mark. Cf. Article 2 of *Estatutos de la Liga de Defensa Comercial Israelita Argentina* (Buenos Aires, 1910), IWO Archives; and *Broit un Ehre* no. 3 (May 1, 1910): 9. The union was limited to "Jews residing in the capital, who sell merchandise on their own, in weekly or monthly installments, without having an established store" (Art. 3). To its constitution was added an article intended to protect the Liga against the intrusion of the wholesalers denying all rights to those members who established themselves with a wholesale store, especially one selling to peddlers (Art. 15). At the same time a group of peddlers residing in the Boca-Barracas district founded Cooperativa Israelita, later called Tesoro Israelita Argentino, with analogous purposes. Cf. *Estatutos del Tesoro Israelita Argentino*, IWO archives. During 1911 they had their headquarters in Magallanes 420, in the Boca-Barracas area; by 1913 they had moved to Lavalle 1059, in Centro (Cf. IWO archives).
110. Art. 13 of *Estatutos de la Unión Ambulantes Israelitas*, IWO Archives.
111. Cf. *Almanach fun Yiddishn Ambulantn Farain* (1915–1930) (Buenos Aires, 1930), 3–11.
112. An economic history of the Jews in Argentina would reveal important insights that could help us understand some of the processes in community life. Documentation, however, is scant. Some material had been collected at the IWO archives in Buenos Aires. A wealth of information, both as advertisement and as notes, appeared in the daily Yiddish press or in special publications of the various commercial societies. The above paragraphs are based on this documentation. Nonetheless, the sources at hand do not allow more profound conclusions, which could be made only after a much more thorough study of commercial institutions.
113. Cf. M. Smilg, "Dos Yiddishe Bank-Wezen in Buenos Aires," *Yoblbuch Yiddishe Zeitung* (Buenos Aires, 1940), 291–308; *Yiddishe Folks-Bank, Ioblbuch 1921–1951* (Buenos Aires, 1951); *Banco Comercial de Buenos Aires, 1917–1950* (Buenos Aires, 1950); *Banco Popular Israelita, Memoria y Balance* (1933). For the Banco Comercial Israelita, founded in 1921 in Rosario, which opened a branch in Moises Ville in 1925, see *50 Años Creciendo con la Ciudad* (Rosario, 1971).

2. Jew and Gentile in Argentina

1. Nathan Glazer and Daniel Patrick Moynihan, *Beyond the Melting Pot* (Cambridge, Mass., 1963), 139.
2. Moisés Goldman, "Der Antisemitism in Argentine," in *Yoblbuch Yiddishe Zeitung* (Buenos Aires, 1940), 583–85; Silvia Schenkolewsky, "Di Zionistische Bavegung in Argentine fun 1897–1917," in *Pinkas fun der Kehila* (Buenos Aires, 1969), 102f.
3. A more detailed analysis of the 1881 decree and the response of the Jewish community in Buenos Aires to attacks of some groups is found in Victor Mirelman, "A Note on Jewish Settlement in Argentina (1881–1892)," *Jewish Social Studies*, 33, no. 1 (Jan. 1971): 3–12.
4. "L'immigration Juive," *L'Union Française*, Aug. 22, 1881, p. 1.
5. *La Nación*, Aug. 26, 1881, p. 1.
6. "Las calumnias de L'Union Française," *El Nacional*, Aug. 25, 1881, p. 2.

7. Cf. *El National*, Aug. 26, 1881, p. 2; JC, Oct. 28, 1881, p. 11; *Archives Israelites*, 1881, p. 421; and *La Nación*. Aug. 28, 1881, p. 2.

8. *Chevra Keduscha*, *Minutes*, Dec. 21, 1895.

9. Pinie Katz, *Tsu der Geshichte fun der Yiddisher Journalistik in Argentine* (Buenos Aires, 1929), 37.

10. Ibid., 38; JC, Oct. 28, 1898, p. 15.

11. Simon Ostwald, *Sion!*, speech at the Zionist society Liga Dr. Theodor Herzl, on Dec. 25, 1901, p. 6.

12. CIRA, *Minutes*, May 16, 1927.

13. Cf. Oscar E. Cornblit, Ezequiel Gallo (h.), and Alfredo A. O'Connel, "La Generación del 80 y su proyecto: Antecedentes y consecuencias," in *Argentina: sociedad de masas*, ed. Torcuato di Tella, Gino Germani, and Jorge Graciarena (Buenos Aires, 1965), 52–57; Emilio Herrera, "Los prejuicios raciales en la Argentina del 80: Julián Martel y su novela 'La Bolsa'," *Indice* 1 (Apr. 1968): 110–16.

14. José Luis Romero, *A History of Argentine Political Thought* (Stanford, 1963), 194.

15. J. M. Miró, *La Bolsa* (Buenos Aires, Editorial Huemul, 1965), 53.

16. A. J. Pérez Amuchástegui, *Mentalidades argentinas*, 1860–1930 (Buenos Aires, 1965), 36ff.

17. José Luis Romero, *El desarrollo de las ideas en la sociedad argentina del siglo XX* (Mexico, 1965), 17.

18. Pérez Amuchástegui, op. cit., 36–42.

19. Robert F. Byrnes (*Antisemitism in Modern France* [New Brunswick, 1950], 8–9) says "French history has shown that an area can be antisemitic even though it has no Jews."

20. Edouard Drumont, *La France Juive*, 2d. ed. (Paris, 1886). Cf. the above-quoted passage of *La Bolsa* with Drumont's description of Gambetta: "avec son nez d'une courbe si prononcée, se rattachait a la tribu d'Ephraim" (vol. 1, p. 34) and that of Henry Aron: "avec ses yeux striés de filaments rouges, se reclamait de la tribu de Zabulon" (p. 35).

21. Miró, op. cit., 120ff. Throughout the argument Granulillo interrupts Glow in an attempt to defend the Jews.

22. Ibid., 45.

23. Ibid., 123ff. Cf. Drumont, vol. 2, esp. pp. 54–67.

24. Miró, op. cit., 54.

25. Ibid., 124. Rothschild is a common theme in Drumont's work. Cf. Byrnes, op. cit., pp. 119, 202. The House of Rothschild is also mentioned in antisemitic literature in the United States. Cf. Richard Hofstadter, *The Age of Reform* (New York, 1955), 77–81 and sourcenotes thereto.

26. Cf. *Memoria del Departamento General de Inmigración correspondiente al año 1891* (Buenos Aires, 1892), 15; ibid., 1895 (Buenos Aires, 1896), 214.

27. JC, July 12, 1901, p. 11.

28. Juan A. Alsina, *La inmigración en el primer siglo de la independencia* (Buenos Aires, 1910), 7–11.

29. Cf. Carl Solberg, *Immigration and Nationalism, Argentina and Chile, 1890–1914* (Austin, 1970), 135f.

30. Arturo Reynal O'Connor, "Por las colonias," *Revista Nacional* 33(Jan. 1902): 48f.

31. Cf. Gino Germani, *Política y sociedad en una época de transición* (Buenos Aires, 1968), 249 (table 6), 251 (table 7).

32. Cf. José Luis Romero, *El desarrollo de las ideas en la sociedad argentina del siglo XX* (Mexico, 1965), 32f.; Sebastian Marotta, *El movimiento sindical argentino, su génesis y desarrollo*, vol. 1 (Buenos Aires, 1960), 107f; Enrique Dickmann, *Recuerdos de un militante socialista* (Buenos Aires, 1949), 68f.

33. Cf. Carl Solberg, op. cit., 109ff.; Diego Abad de Santillán, *La F.O.R.A., ideologia y trayectoria del movimiento obrero revolucionario en la Argentina*, 2d. rev. ed. (Buenos Aires, 1971), 97–99; Marotta, op. cit., 147.

34. Cf. Solberg, op. cit., 111.

35. Cf. the classification of strikes for the period 1907–30 in Adolfo Dorfman, *Historia de la industria argentina* (Buenos Aires, 1970), 262–67.
36. Santillán, op. cit., 125–42.
37. Ibid., 175–80; Dickmann, op. cit., 158–83.
38. *La Nación*, Nov. 16, 1909, p. 6; *La Prensa*, Nov. 15, 1909, p. 8.
39. Cf. Marotta, op. cit., vol. 2, pp. 69–76; Santillán, op. cit., pp. 189–98, Dickmann, op. cit., 183–88. Attacks on the Jewish quarter are mentioned by Marotta, p. 75, based on the testimonies of the victims published in the *Boletín de la* C.O.R.A. (Confederación Obrera Regional Argentina).
40. The lists of deportees are published in Santillán, op. cit., 198f. and Marotta, op. cit., vol. 2, p. 85.
41. Marotta, op. cit., vol. 2, p. 81.
42. Ibid., 81–84.
43. *Broit un Ehre* no. 2 (Apr. 15, 1910): 1.
44. *Haolam* 4, nos. 21–22 (June 9, 1910): 24.
45. Cf. Pinie Wald, "Yiddishe Sotsialistishe Arbeter-Bavegung in Argentine biz 1910," *Argentiner IWO Shriftn* 2(1942): 101–6.
46. Ernesto A. Bavio, "Las escuelas extranjeras en Entre Ríos," *El Monitor de la Educación Común* 27(Nov. 30, 1908): 597–604 and 28(Jan. 31, 1909): 3–44.
47. Manuel P. Antequeda, *Breve exposición sobre las escuelas ruso-alemanas é israelitas: escuelas nacionales (Ley Lainez) de la provincia de Entre Ríos* (Buenos Aires, 1909), 25f.
48. Ibid., 9.
49. *La Nación*, Dec. 11, 1908, p. 11.
50. *La Nación*, Dec. 14, 1908, p. 6. This article ended with the following remark: "What the Marqués de Santillana said in the fifteenth century is still valid today: 'Al judío datle un palmo é tomará quatro.'" Other articles in this daily are found at Dec. 12, 1908, p. 7 and Dec. 19, 1908, p. 6.
51. *La Prensa*, Nov. 30, 1908, p. 8. Other articles in the same newspaper dealing with the Jewish schools, all in 1908, are Nov. 25, p. 10; Dec. 3, p. 12; Dec. 7, p. 5; Dec. 8, p. 9; Dec. 11, p. 9; Dec. 12, pp. 9, 10; Dec. 15, p. 9; Dec. 16, p. 11; Dec. 20, p. 9; Dec. 26, p. 8; and Dec. 28, p. 9.
52. Published in 1909, we shall quote from Ricardo Rojas, *La restauración nacionalista*, 3d. edition (Buenos Aires, 1971), 127f.
53. Ibid., 128.
54. Ibid., 128.
55. Cf. *Sarmiento*, Apr. 4, 1910, pp. 1, 3; ibid., Apr. 20, 1910, p. 1; *La Razón*, Apr. 9, 1910, p. 7.
56. *Sarmiento*, Apr. 4, 1910, pp. 1, 3; *Der Avangard* 3, no. 3 (Mar. 1910), pp. 23f.
57. Cf., for example, A. Aiberman, "Kinder Ertziung" [Children Education], *Di Yiddishe Hofnung* 2, no. 7 (July 1909): 4f.
58. Cf. Pinie Katz, *Tsu der Geshichte fun der Yiddisher Journalistik in Argentine* (Buenos Aires, 1929), 127ff.
59. *Avangard* 3, no. 3 (Mar. 1910): 23f.; cf. ibid., 1, no. 5 (Dec. 1908): 32.
60. *Broit un Ehre* no. 2(Apr. 15, 1910): 1f.
61. Cf. *Di Yiddishe Hofnung* 2, no. 7 (July 1909): 4f; ibid., 3, no. 1 (Mar. 1910), Spanish Section, article by Jacobo Ben-Joseph [Joselevich]; ibid., 3, nos. 14–15 (Oct. 1, 1910): 10f; ibid., 3, nos. 16–17 (Nov. 1, 1910): 14f.
62. *Federación Israelita Argentina, Minutes*, Nov. 15 and 22, 1909.
63. Cf. Rabbi Halphon's reports to the JCA headquarters in Paris, dated June 24, 1910 and Sept. 16, 1910, JCA (*London*) *Archives*, 432 III.
64. Lugones wrote,

> *Pasaba por el camino el ruso Elías*
> *Con su gabán eslavo y con sus botas*
> *Manso vecino que fielmente guarda*
> *El Sábado y sus raras ceremonias*

Con sencillez y sumisa que todos respetan
Porque es trabajador y a nadie estorba.

Darío sang,

Cantad, judíos de La Pampa,
Mocetones de ruda estampa,
Rubenes de largas guedejas,
dulces Rebecas de ojos francos,
patriarcas de cabellos blancos
y espesos como hípicas crines;
cantad, cantad, Saras viejas,
y adolescentes Benjamines,
con voz de vuestro corazón:
¡Hemos encontrado a Sión!

65. Alberto Gerchunoff, Los gauchos judíos (Buenos Aires, 1910) and many later editions. We shall quote the 1957 edition of Editorial Sudamericana. For a portrayal of Gerchunoff see Manuel Kantor, Alberto Gerchunoff (Buenos Aires, 1969). The above quotations are taken from Kantor, pp. 9 and 10, who took them from Gerchunoff's autobiography written in 1914 and published posthumously as an introduction to his Entre Ríos, mi país (Buenos Aires, 1950). For other examples of comparison of Argentina with Jerusalem or the Promised Land, cf. Los gauchos judíos, pp. 32, 49f., 52f. Also José Liebermann, Tierra soñada (Buenos Aires, 1959), 125–31; Nicolás Rapoport, Desde lejos hasta ayer (Buenos Aires, 1957), 43, 88; Enrique Dickmann, op. cit., 35.
66. Sarmiento, June 16, 1910, p. 1.
67. "Israel en la Tierra Prometida," La Nación, June 19, 1914, p. 11. Cf. quite similar attacks in La Prensa, Sept. 27, 1913, p. 9.
68. Juventud 4, no. 37 (July 1914): 54f.
69. Bericht fun'm Yuddishen Kongress in Argentina (Buenos Aires, 1916), 31ff.
70. Ibid., 33–45.
71. Francisco Stach, "La defensa social y la inmigración," Boletín Mensual del Museo Social Argentino 5, nos. 55–56 (July–Aug. 1916), 361–89; Manuel Bronstein, "La inmigración israelita," Boletín Mensual . . . 5, nos. 59–60 (Nov.–Dec. 1916): 550–67; Natan Gesang, "Los judíos," Revista Argentina de Ciencias Políticas, Derecho Administrativo, Economía Política, Sociología, Historia, y Educación 13(1916):225–47.
72. Stach, op. cit., 384ff.
73. Cf. Bronstein, op. cit., passim.
74. Cf. Gesang, op. cit., passim.
75. Cf. Dorfman (op. cit., 262), who gives the following absolute figures of strikes and strikers:

Year	Strikes	Strikers
1915	65	12,077
1916	80	24,321
1917	138	136,062
1918	196	133,042
1919	367	308,967
1920	206	134,015

76. Maximalista was a term used to identify anarchists, anarchosyndicalists, and communists in Argentina at the time. All historians dealing with the period analyze the Semana Trágica according to their own views of history. The latest work is Julio Godio, La Semana Trágica de Enero de 1919 (Buenos Aires, 1972). The main articles that deal with its impact among Jews are Pedro Wald, "Yiddn in der Tragisher Woch,"

Argentiner IWO Shriftn 4(1947): 5–55 and Nahum Solominsky, *La Semana Trágica* (Buenos Aires, 1971).

77. Cf. Godio, op. cit., 17–22.
78. Ibid., 179–86.
79. Juan E. Carulla, *Al filo del medio siglo* (Paraná, 1945), 156.
80. Juan José de Soiza Reilly, "El Martirio de los Inocentes," *Revista Popular* 2, no. 42 (Feb. 1919): 1–4.
81. Cf. Pedro (Pinie) Wald, *Koshmar* (Buenos Aires, 1929).
82. These three reasons were given respectively by *La Razón*, Jan. 16, 1919, p. 3; *Vanguardia*, Jan. 16, 1919, p. 1; and *La Razón*, Jan. 17, 1919, p. 3.
83. In 1936 in Buenos Aires, out of a total of 31,368 Russians, 23,171 (75%) were Jews. However, 4,137 had no religion or unknown religion. Most of the latter were also Jews. For Poles, the respective numbers were 46,519, 31,172 (67%), and 3,052; and for Roumanians 8,483, 5,175 (61%), and 1,089. See *Municipalidad de la Ciudad de Buenos Aires, Cuarto Censo General* (Oct. 22, 1936) (Buenos Aires, 1939), vol. 3, p. 316f.
84. Cf. "Encuesta sobre la inmigración," *Boletín Mensual del Museo Social Argentino* 8(1919):36.
85. Ibid., 54.
86. Carlos Ibarguren, *La historia que he vivido* (Buenos Aires, 1955), 343.
87. Cf., for example, *La Vanguardia*, Jan. 14, 1919, p. 2.
88. Frederick Jessup Stimson, *My United States* (New York, 1931), 418–21.
89. Katherine S. Dreier, *Five Months in the Argentine; From a Woman's Point of View,* 1918 to 1919 (New York, 1920), 183–84. For this national panic there was, however, some degree of justification. Toward the end of the war the labor movement had been progressively gaining momentum, strength, and prestige. The number of strikes and strikers per annum was steadily increasing due to rising prices and the desire of the workers for a higher standard of living. The labor strikes and manifestations were bolstered to a large extent by the presence of a large proportion of foreign workers. Many had arrived in Argentina after fleeing persecution in their home countries, especially from Spain after the bloody repression of the revolution in Catalonia (1901–20, in particular during 1909) and to a minor degree from Russia when the failure of the 1905 revolution caused many labor leaders and agitators to flee. See Gerald Brenan, *The Spanish Labyrinth* (Cambridge, 1967), 17–77 and Salo Baron, *The Russian Jew under Tsars and Soviets* (New York, 1964), 69–71. During the Semana Trágica many voiced the opinion that immigration from Spain and Russia had been prejudicial because of the above mentioned factors. See, for example, *La Razón*, January 13, 1919, p. 3; moreover, the weekly *Caras y Caretas* devoted a full issue to these events, concluding that the riots were due to undesirable immigrants, who were men without a fatherland, and that the immigration policy should therefore be revised. Cf. *Caras y Caretas* 22, no. 1059 (Jan. 18, 1919).
90. Interview with Gregorio Fingermann, Aug. 1972, Buenos Aires.
91. Cf. *Avangard* 1, no. 5 (Dec. 1908): 32.
92. The text of Rabbi Halphon's letter to Beiró, dated in Buenos Aires June 25, 1917, is found in CIRA, *Minutes* of the same date. *Israel,* Jan. 1919 (pp. 769ff) reproduced it. The above-quoted line is from a note in *La Argentina,* p. 149, where it brings other antisemitic paragraphs from Francisco Latzina, *Diccionario geográfico argentino,* (various editions) and from Colombo y Urien, *La República Argentina en* 1910 (Buenos Aires, 1910). For the protests in 1926, cf. *Semanario Hebreo,* June 11, 1926, p. 1 and the editorials in *Yiddishe Zeitung,* June 3, 1926, p. 6 and June 8, 1926, p. 6.
93. Cf. Hobart Spalding, *La clase trabajadora argentina* (*Documentos para su historia* 1890–1912) (Buenos Aires, 1970), 497–549 ("Movimiento Social Católico"); and Godio, op. cit., 179f.
94. Francisco P. Sagasti, *Monseñor de Andrea y el Arzobispado de Buenos Aires* (Buenos Aires, 1924), 29. Cf. also *Pensamiento Cristiano y Democrático de Monseñor de Andrea,* 2d. edition, Senado de la Nación (Presidencia) (Buenos Aires, 1965), 290–94 for the prelate's antianarchist and anticommunist activities in Argentina.

95. Cf. Di Presse, Dec. 28, 1918, p. 1; Jan. 6, 1919, p. 3; and Jan. 7, 1919, p. 3. See also Sagasti, op. cit., 30.

96. Boletín Mensual del Museo Social Argentino 8(1919): 32.

97. Vida Nuestra 2, no. 8 (Feb. 1919).

98. Cf. the responses of Enrique Barros and Carlos N. Caminos to the questionnaires submitted by Vida Nuestra 2, no. 9 (Mar. 1919) and 2, no. 10 (Apr. 1919), respectively, and Leopoldo Lugones, "Los falsos problemas," Vida Nuestra 2, no. 2 (Aug. 1918): 25f.

99. Critica, Jan. 22, 1919, p. 1. Cf. also Soiza Reilly, op. cit., 1–4.

100. Justo's speech at the 1896 Congress is reproduced in Dickmann, op cit., 84. On pp. 80–100 Dickmann gives his own account of the Congress and its aftermath.

101. Pedro [Pinie] Wald, "Yiddishe Sotsialistishe Arbeter-Bavegung in Argentine biz 1910," Argentiner IWO Shriftn 2(1942): 109f.

102. Enrique Dickmann, "Sionismo y Socialismo," Vida Nuestra 2, no. 4 (Oct. 1918): 73f. Reprinted in his Recuerdos de un militante socialista (Buenos Aires, 1949), pp. 442ff.

103. Di Neie Zeit, Nov. 2, 1919, pp. 2f.

104. Di Neie Zeit, Apr. 9, 1927, p. 5.

105. Palacios wrote many articles praising the Jewish people. Cf. his "La Redención de Israel," Vida Nuestra 1, no. 6 (Dec. 1917): 125–8. He was a welcome guest at the Argentine Jewish Congress of 1916, at the reception for the Argentine legionaries (1918), and at many other Jewish gatherings. The Jewish community expressed its gratitude to the congressman for the law that carried the latter's name, Ley Palacios, against corruption of women. Cf. Juventud 3, no. 29 (Nov. 1913): 30.

106. Bilboard at IWO Archives, Buenos Aires.

107. In 1911 Beilis was accused by the Black Hundreds in Kiev of ritual murder. He was acquitted in 1913.

108. Shtraln 3 (Dec. 1913). Cf. Juventud 3, no. 31 (Jan. 1914): 51, and Rapoport, op. cit., 105.

109. Di Neie Zeit 2, no. 36 (July 29, 1919): 6.

110. Juan B. Justo, "Por qué no me gusta escribir para una hoja que se dice israelita," Vida Nuestra 6, no. 9 (Mar. 1923): 193–97. It was reprinted in Nosotros, Apr. 1923 and in Juan José Sebreli, La cuestión judía en la Argentina (Buenos Aires, 1968), 86–90.

111. Cf. Versiones Taquigráficas del Honorable Concejo Deliberante (Buenos Aires), Dec. 30, 1921; Feb. 21, 1922; Nov. 24, 1924; Sept. 22, 1925; Dec. 16, 1925; Dec. 30, 1925; April 16 and 23, 1926; and May 4, 11, and 28, 1926. The Versiones Taquigráficas are published yearly by the Concejo Deliberante. We quote here the dates of the particular sessions.

112. Ibid., May 4, 1926.

113. Ibid., Apr. 23, 1926.

114. Chevra Keduscha [hereafter CK] Copiador, letter from David Calles to Halphon, May 18, 1926.

115. Versiones Taquigráficas . . . , Dec. 16, 1926.

116. Cf. Israel, 1919, pp. 765ff.

117. Cf. memorandum presented by the Comité de la Colectividad in Diario de Sesiones de la Cámara de Diputados, Jan. 28, 1919, pp. 312ff.

118. Ibid. The memorandum includes the names of 69 Jews either killed or wounded by the police or Guardia Blanca, as well as descriptions of the incidents.

119. See CK, Minutes, Apr. 27, 1919, and May 4, 1919. Also CK Copiador no. 3, letters from its president Israel Muller to Simon Ostwald, who was able to obtain a hearing with President Yrigoyen for the Jewish delegation, dated Apr. 29 and May 6, 1919.

120. Cf. ch. 5 on Zionist activities for the quarrel between CIRA and FSA.

121. Pamphlet of Partido Israelita Argentino, IWO Archives, Buenos Aires, Gebit 36.

122. Cf. Pamphlet of Partido Israelita Argentino, IWO Archives, J. S. Liachovitzky file. At IWO, Gebit 89, there are copies of pamphlets distributed by this party in both languages.

123. According to various persons interviewed, most Jews voted Socialist during the

1910s. There are, however, reasons to believe that many voted Radical. Cf. *El Israelita Argentino*, July 1, 1913, p. 6.
124. Most of the Jewish press—except the journals put out by the Jewish parties—advocated this posture.
125. Cf. Godio, op. cit., 184f. for the main ideas of the Liga Patriótica Argentina and the leading members of it. A more detailed description is found in *La Razón*, Jan. 20, 1919, p. 2.
126. Cf. *Vida Nuestra* 3, no. 1 (July 1919) for the ad of the Liga Israelita Pro-Argentinidad and for the reaction on p. 24.
127. The Liga Patriótica Argentina, founded during the Semana Trágica events was the main civic organization that fought, utilizing violence when deemed necessary, against workers' organizations, attempting to drown its leftist leadership. As result of many class struggles between the Liga and workers, Jews were often accused and attacked by the forces of order. One of the strongest attacks against Jews took place in Villaguay, an urban center in the heart of the JCA colonies of the province of Entre Ríos having a large number of Jews among its inhabitants, in February 1921. The bourgeois press of the area wrote antisemitic charges with titles such as "La judiada se amotina" |The Jewish mob rebels| "La judiada se acerca" |The Jewish mob is approaching|, etc. Cf. *La Vanguardia*, Feb. 15–24, 1921; and *Vida Nuestra* 4, no. 9 (Mar. 1921): 193–209 for the Jewish response.
128. Lucas Ayarragaray, "Inmigración judía en Argentina," in his *Cuestiones y problemas argentinos contempóráneos* (Buenos Aires, 1930), 422–30. Cf. also p. 234.
129. Ayarragaray, op. cit., 427.
130. Luis Abascal, "El Teatro" ("Israel" de Henri Bernstein en el Odeón), *Criterio* 1, no. 19 (July 12, 1928): 57.
131. Luis Barrantes Molina, "La Apostasía Moderna," *Criterio* 3, no. 111 (Apr. 17, 1930): 508f. Cf. Silvio Torre, "Los Príncipes de los judíos y *La Prensa*," pp. 512f. in the same issue and Guillermo Saenz, "Temas Internacionales, El problema árabe-sionista en Palestina," *Criterio* 3, no. 139 (Oct. 30, 1930).
132. Russian Jews encountered several difficulties in being helped in municipal hospitals. Cf. *Ezrah*, *Minutes*, July 2, 1910. This was one of the main reasons for building the Hospital Israelita. For additional cases of antisemitism in hospitals and in the school of medicine at the University of Buenos Aires, cf. *Vida Nuestra* 3, no. 9 (Mar. 1920): 216 and *Semanario Hebreo*, May 23, 1930, p. 2. Moreover, the appointment of Dr. Alejandro Zabotinsky as professor in the school of odontology was contested because of religious and national reasons. Cf. CIRA, *Minutes*, July 26, 1926. With respect to antisemitism in the workers' unions, some incidents have been reported. Cf. *Di Neie Zeit*, Apr. 12, 1918, p. 2.

3. Religious Institutions and Observances

1. A. L. Schusheim, "Letoldot Haishuv Hayehudi be-Argentina," *Sefer Argentina* (Buenos Aries, 1954), 32. Cf. also David Goldman, *Di Juden in Argentine, in der Vergangenheit un in der Gegenwart, in Wort un in Bild* (Buenos Aires, 1914), 100.
2. The leaders of Machzikei Emunah are listed in Goldman, op. cit., 100.
3. Schusheim, op. cit., 37.
4. The first Hebrew (and Yiddish) Linotype arrived in Buenos Aires at the end of 1898. For that reason the statutes of Sociedad "Zion," a Zionist society founded in 1897, were printed in New York in 1898. A copy of these statutes is found at the IWO Archives, Buenos Aires, Gebit 34–35.
5. JC, Apr. 27, 1894, p. 9.
6. CIRA, *Minutes*, Dec. 26, 1894. The issue first arose on Dec. 13, 1894, and on Feb. 3,

1895 a general assembly accepted responsibility for the school, which at the beginning had twenty students and now sixty-five. Cf., *Minutes* up to Dec. 7, 1895.
7. Goldman, op. cit., 101; cf. *La Prensa*, June 24, 1893.
8. *Hazefirah*, 1896, no. 264, p. 1286. Cf. also ibid. 1897, no. 275, pp. 1354f., where the existence of Mikveh Israel synagogue is mentioned.
9. JC, Oct. 28, 1898, p. 15.
10. JC, Oct. 25, 1901. p. 27.
11. Cf. Luis F. Nuñez, *Almario de Buenos Aires: Los cementerios* (Buenos Aires, 1970), 47f. According to Shalom Rosenberg and Daniel Rubinstein-Novick ("Instituciones y tendencias de la vida religiosa judía en la Argentina," in *Pinkas fun der Kehila*, 1963–1968 [Buenos Aires, 1969], p. 134), some Jewish oldtimers in Buenos Aires forbade their grandchildren to play in that plaza for this reason.
12. CK, *Minutes*, Feb. 11, 1894.
13. CK, *Preliminary Minutes*, Sept. 26, 1893.
14. Ibid., Oct. 3, 1893.
15. Cf. CIRA, *Minutes*, Sept. 4–17, 1893.
16. Ibid., Sept. 5, 1894.
17. Ibid., Oct. 31, 1893.
18. A somewhat different interpretation is given by Lázaro Schallman, "Antecedentes históricos y sociales de la fundación de la A.M.I.A.," in *Pinkas fun der Kehila* (Buenos Aires, 1969), 22–24.
19. CK, *Minutes*, Jan. 12, 1895.
20. Ibid., Dec. 21, 1895.
21. Ibid., Feb. 18, 1897.
22. Jacobo Simón Liachovitzky, *Zamlbuch* (Yiddish) (Buenos Aires, 1938), 87ff.
23. JC, Oct. 30, 1874, 491.
24. CIRA, *Minutes*, passim, especially Nov. 28, 1875; July 29, 1886; Sept. 7, 1890; and Nov. 1, 1891.
25. CK, *Minutes*, Jan. 19, 1896 and Feb. 28, 1897.
26. Ibid., Mar. 20, 1898.
27. Ibid., Apr. 26, 1900, states that the "Dissidents' Cemetery had decided not to permit the burial of Israelites in that cemetery any more."
28. Ibid., May 1, 1900.
29. Ibid., Mar. 20, 1898 and May 4, 1898.
30. Ibid., June 12, 1898.
31. Cf. *Hazefira*, 1897, no. 275, pp. 1354f.
32. Ibid., May 4, 1898.
33. Nonmembers were also buried by the CK, though the tariff was of course higher.
34. J. S. Liachovitzky, op. cit., 89f.
35. JC, Oct. 28, 1898, p. 15.
36. JC, Oct. 25, 1901, p. 27.
37. *El Sionista*, Nov. 8, 1905, p. 7.
38. *Di Yiddishe Hofnung*, Sept. 1, 1912, pp. 6–8.
39. Boris Garfunkel, *Narro mi vida* (Buenos Aires, 1960), 178.
40. Marcos Alpersohn, *Kolonie Mauricio, Dreisig-iehrige JCA Kolonizatzie in Argentina* (Buenos Aires, 1922), 60.
41. Walter Paul Zenner, *Syrian Jewish Identification in Israel*, Ph.D. dissertation, Columbia University, 1965, pp. 69–74.
42. For an Aleppine immigrant's experience in Argentina in 1906 see Nissim Teubal, *El inmigrante* (Buenos Aires, 1953), esp. 81. The above data was obtained in an interview with Jacques Mizrahi, Nellm Yacar, and Elías Teubal, Apr. 7, 1972, Buenos Aires.
43. Cf. *Or Torah, Minutes*, Mar. 10, 17, and 24, 1923; Apr. 21, 1923; and Mar. 18, 1926; and *Yesod Hadath, Minutes*, Aug. 9, 1925.
44. *Or Torah, Minutes*, Mar. 24, 1923; Apr. 21, 1923.
45. The decree, Exp. 10177–12/925 of the Consejo Nacional de Educación was pub-

lished in *La Nación*, Oct. 31, 1925. *Israel* reprinted it on Apr. 9–16, 1926, p. 76. Hacham Shaul Setton Dabbah reprinted it in his *Dibber Shaul* (|Hebrew| |Jerusalem, 1928|, 57b) in Judeo-Arabic translation.

46. David de Sola Pool, "The Levantine Jews in the U.S.," *American Jewish Yearbook*, 1913/ 14, p. 216.

47. In 1907 two members of the Moroccan community took an oath at the synagogue, over the Scroll of the Torah, in an inheritance case. This was accepted by the judge when the inheritors of Jacobo Benoliel alleged that being of the Jewish faith, "they could only take an oath according to their rites." *La Prensa*, Aug. 31, 1907, p. 8.

48. *Habima Haivrit* 1, no. 5 (1921): 5.

49. In a letter from the Federación Sionista Argentina (Buenos Aires) to Keren Hayesod (Jerusalem) (Hebrew), Dec. 20, 1926, at Central Zionist Archives, Jerusalem, Z4, 35791.

50. Benjamín Benzaquén, *La colectividad israelita sefaradí de Buenos Aires no debe permitir que se exploten más sus sentimientos religiosos* (Buenos Aires, 1929), 2.

51. Jacobo Kraviez ("Desde el antiguo carpintero hasta el moderno fabricante," *El Industrial Maderero* 5, 44 |July 1944|: 47–54) makes references to this situation from personal experience.

52. JC, Aug. 2, 1907, p. 16.

53. *Juventud* 1, no. 1 (July 1, 1911): 10.

54. Ibid., 3 , no. 26 (Aug. 1913): 5–8.

55. Ibid., 3, no. 36 (June 1914): 45–48.

56. *Vida Nuestra*, Apr. 1918, p. 242.

57. Joseph Aharon Taran, *Zichron Iosef* (Jerusalem, 1924), contains the legal discussions about the wild ducks' controversy. It was written in 1918, though the actual controversy took place at the beginning of the century.

58. Cf. David Goldman, *Di Juden in Argentine, in der Vergangenheit un in der Gegenwart, in Wort un in Bild* (Buenos Aires, 1914), ch. 5.

59. Several times the Asociación Israelita de Beneficencia in Rosario consulted Rabbi Goldman in Moisesville due to the links many Jews in that city had with that colony.

60. Rabbi Goldman arrived with the first group of East European Jews in 1889, even before the formation of the JCA. In 1891 however, the bulk of the group was colonized by JCA. Cf. "Nómina de los inmigrantes llegados en el vapor 'Weser' el 14 de agosto de 1889," in *50 años de colonización judía en la Argentina* (Buenos Aires, 1939), Documents section. Rabbi Tarán settled in the Horace Gunzburg colony in 1894 and later in Zonnenfeld.

61. *Hazefirah*, 1894, no. 238. A biography of Rabbi Sinai (1850–1918) was written by his son Michl Hacohen Sinai, "Harav Reuben Hacohen Sinai," *Argentiner IWO Shriftn* 3(1945): 171–82.

62. *Hazefirah*, 1896, no. 264.

63. Different views with respect to the motivations of Sinai's departure from Moisesville are given by Michl Hacohen Sinai, op. cit. and Noe Cociovich |Katsovich|, *Mosesviler Breishis* (Yiddish) (Buenos Aires, 1947), 153–61.

64. Preaching was not a regular event. In the 1920s ads announcing them were sporadic and emphasized the character of a special occasion. Cf. for example, *Yiddishe Zeitung*, May 18, 1927, p. 5; June 28, 1927, p. 4.

65. CIRA, *Minutes*, Nov. 22, 1882–Jan. 9, 1883.

66. CIRA, *Minutes*, Oct. 20 and 28, 1894.

67. Ibid., Jan. 3, 1895; Nov. 9, 1895.

68. Ibid., Feb. 3 and 18, 1895.

69. Joseph wrongly maintained, for example, that wedding ceremonies at night "were contrary to Jewish law" (CIRA, *Minutes*, Jan. 18, 1904).

70. Ibid., July 13, 1903.

71. A committee was formed to study a financial project that would enable CIRA to keep a rabbi. *Minutes*, Dec. 21 and 24, 1903; Jan. 18, 1904. Conditions stipulated that the candidate be between the ages of 30 and 35, married with no more than two

children, and fluent in French and German and have served as rabbi previously (Ibid., Jan. 18, 1904). Cf. also ibid., Sept. 24, 1905.

72. JCA, *Rapport de l'Administration Centrale au Conseil d'Administration, pour l'Année* 1905 (Paris, 1906), 49. On Rabbi Halphon, see J. Bauer, *L'Ecole Rabbinique de France* (1830–1930) (Paris, 1931). Halphon was born in 1877.

73. CIRA, *Minutes*, May 3 and 13, 1906; JCA *Rapport*, 1907, p. 37.

74. When in 1926 the Chevra Keduscha was having problems in the habilitation of a new plot for cemetery, it turned to Halphon to "intercede before the President of the Republic so that he indicate who is empowered to veto the order and the habilitation of the cemetery." CK, *Copiador de Cartas*, May 18, 1926. The case was lost, and CK sold the field. Cf. ch. 2.

75. From Callao uptown was located the main Jewish quarter in Buenos Aires, limited approximately by Cuyo (today Sarmiento) and Viamonte.

76. Cf. JC, May 13, 1904, p. 29; Boris Garfunkel, op. cit., 349–58. Ostwald was respected at CIRA, where he was given the honor of delivering the inauguration speech at the opening of their new synagogue in 1897. He was also active in Zionist activities at the beginning of the century and in 1903 was suggested by the Zionist Organization in Europe for the unifying head of all Zionists in Argentina.

77. *El Sionista*, Oct. 7, 1904, p. 8.

78. *La Prensa* (Sept. 22, 1903, p. 8; Mar. 15, 1904, p. 8; Mar. 30, 1904, p. 7; Oct. 27, 1904, p. 8; Dec. 7, 1904, p. 8; Apr. 9, 1905, p. 8; June 4, 1905, p. 8; Dec. 2, 1905, p. 8; Feb. 2, 1906, p. 9; Oct. 15, 1907, p. 10; June 16, 1908, p. 10; June 23, 1908, p. 8) published short news about the activities of Hoffmann.

79. In 1905 he solicited help from Ezrah (cf. *Ezrah Minutes*, Feb. 10, 1905). His father-in-law helped him in starting a bookshop with his brother-in-law, which utterly failed. Also the project led by Ostwald to build a new synagogue for the Unión Israelita Argentina in 1905 was dropped in spite of its being in an advanced stage. Hoffmann also was involved in the Talmud Torah Harischono in Buenos Aires and was arbiter in divorce cases. Cf. *Ezrah, Minutes*, Oct. 10, 1907; CIRA, *Minutes*, Mar. 19, 1908.

80. Dated Hamburg, Jan. 7, 1908. Cf. CIRA, *Minutes*, Feb. 13, 1908.

81. Ibid., Feb. 13, 1908.

82. *La Prensa*, June 16, 1908, p. 10 and June 23, 1908, p. 8; *El País*, June 13, 1908, p. 13; June 14, 1908, p. 4; June 15, 1908, p. 4; June 24, 1908, p. 3.

83. He wrote *Babel Bibel Fabel* (Buenos Aires, 1903) and an introduction to a commentary on the Pentateuch of Cabbalistic orientation by Menachem Mendl Hirshorn. Cf. Rosenberg and Rubinstein-Novick, op. cit., 139–41.

84. Cf. the letter by Jacobo Joselevich to the Zionist Organization in Cologne, dated in Buenos Aires between June 18 and 24, 1908, Zionist Archives, Z.B. Koln B. lg 123 fasc. 1.

85. *La Prensa* (June 23, 1908, p. 8) printed a Spanish translation of Hoffmann's last letter in German.

86. Interview with Gregorio Fingermann, August 1971, Buenos Aires. Fingermann asserted that Hoffmann was a cultured person "of a fine, delicate spirit." Moreover, he stated that there were two groups at CIRA, one supporting Halphon and the other Hoffmann, and concluded that "Halphon was responsible for his (Hoffmann's) suicide."

87. CK, *Minutes*, Jan. 22, 1930.

88. Cf. files "Get'n" by Rabbi David Maler at the Superior Rabinato de la Comunidad Israelita de Buenos Aires. D. Glasserman advertized in the Jewish newspapers that he granted divorces. CK *Copiador*, wrote to him on Oct. 10, 1929, asking for "a detailed list of all the divorces you have performed until now."

89. CK, *Minutes*, June 30, 1929.

90. *Ezras Noschim, Informe General*, for the year 1931 (Buenos Aires, 1932), 8–10.

91. CK, *Minutes*, Oct. 25 and Nov. 8, 1925.

92. Cf. AIB, *Minutes*, Dec. 31, 1922; Feb. 3 and 22, 1923; Jan. 24, 1924; Apr. 25, 1929.

93. On Gottlieb in Rosario cf. AIB, *Minutes*, May 2, Aug. 8, Oct. 16, and Nov. 17, 1926;

Aug. 15, Sept. 7, and Dec. 15, 1927; and Jan. 16, 1928. Upon returning to Buenos Aires, Gottlieb was associated with Hebra Mishnaies Shomrei Shabbes. Cf. *Yiddishe Zeitung,* Jan. 10, 1928, p. 5.

94. Cf. *Yiddishe Zeitung,* Mar. 30, 1927, p. 5; Apr. 18, 1928, p. 4.

95. David Goldman, op. cit., 100.

96. Cf., for example, JC, Oct. 28, 1898, p. 25.

97. CIRA, *Minutes,* Oct. 26, 1903.

98. JC, Aug. 2, 1907, p. 16.

99. CK, *Minutes,* Nov. 3 and Dec. 11, 1908; *Ezrah, Minutes,* Nov. 5 and Dec. 2, 1908; CIRA, *Minutes,* Nov. 2 and 9 and Dec. 3, 1908.

100. FIA, *Minutes,* Aug. 5 and 9, 1909.

101. FIA, *Minutes,* Aug. 16, 1909.

102. Cf. "Schecheta Board," JC, July 29, 1910, p. 20; the kosher-meat-from-Argentina ad appeared in ibid., Aug. 19, 1910, p. 3 and was repeated in several issues after that. For reactions in the East End, cf. Aug. 19, 1910, pp. 6 and 23. About the success of the project, see Sept. 9, 1910, p. 11.

103. FIA, *Minutes,* Aug. 23, 1909.

104. Ibid., Sept. 13, 1909.

105. Ibid., Sept.–Oct., 1910. See also *El Israelita Argentino* 1, no. 3 (Aug. 1913): 1–4 and *Di Yiddishe Hofnung,* Mar. 15, 1910, pp. 1–3.

106. *Yiddishe Zeitung,* July 10, 1925, p. 5.

107. Rabbi David Glasserman, in *Yiddishe Zeitung,* Aug. 10, 1925, p. 5.

108. Ibid., Nov. 22, 1925, p. 7.

109. Ibid., Dec. 28, 1925, p. 7.

110. Ibid., Feb. 17, 1927, p. 5; Mar. 10, 1927, p. 5.

111. Ibid., Mar. 25, 1927, p. 6.

112. Ibid., Apr. 12, 1927, p. 5.

113. Ibid., Apr. 14, 1927, p. 5.

114. Hebra Mishnaies Shomrei Shabbes supported the Waisman group (*Yiddishe Zeitung,* Apr. 15, 1927, p. 3); on the other hand, small groups of Machzikei HaDath supporters were formed in various sectors of the city, i.e., Hebra Machzikei HaDath De Boca-Barracas (ibid., May 18, 1927, p. 3 and June 14, 1927, p. 3) and even in Montevideo by Kitaygorodsky personally.

115. Ibid., July 7, 1927, p. 3.

116. For several days Agudat Israel de Buenos Aires printed an ad declaring the meat of D. Yarusky nonkosher and recommended the Jews to look for their seal in the shops. The Permanent Beit Din published their approval of the same *shechita.* Cf. *Yiddishe Zeitung,* Sept. 19, 1927, p. 4; Sept. 21, p. 4; Sept. 23, p. 6.

117. *Yiddishe Zeitung,* Nov. 8, 1927, p. 4; Nov. 9, 1927, p. 5; CK *Minutes,* Nov. 13 and Dec. 18, 1927.

118. *Yiddishe Zeitung,* Nov. 29, 1927, p. 3.

119. Ibid., Jan. 11, 1928, p. 4.

120. Ibid., Feb. 20, 1928, p. 3. Cf. also Feb. 17, 1928, p. 5.

121. Ibid., Feb. 28, 1928, p. 4.

122. Ibid., Apr. 15, 1928, p. 3. Those that left were Waisman, Men, Maler, and Ehrlich.

123. Such was the position of *Mundo Israelita* since it first appeared in June 1923.

124. Cf. *Yiddishe Zeitung,* Jan. 1, 1928, p. 5.

125. *Mundo Israelita,* "La desunión de los rabinos," Apr. 21, 1928, p. 2.

126. CIL, *Minutes,* Mar. 4, 1917; Oct. 12, 1920; and Nov. 9, 1921.

127. *Comunidad Israelita Sefaradí* (CIS), *Minutes,* Asamblea General, Oct. 29, 1922.

128. CIL, *Minutes,* Sept. 19, 1901.

129. Cf., for example, *Minutes* from Sociedad Kahal Kadosh La Hermandad Sefaradí (later, in 1919, Comunidad Israelita Sefaradí), Sept. 29 and Oct. 19, 1918; Feb. 8, 1920.

130. Ibid., Dec. 22, 1918; Jan. 19, July 29, and Aug.–Sept. 1919; when in Mar. 1920, the board decided to consult a rabbi about a conversion, Rabbi Halphon was con-

sulted; while Hacham Shaul Setton, though his name came up in the meeting, was not approached. Cf. *Minutes*, Mar. 18 and May 2, 1920.

131. CIL, *Minutes*, Aug. 12 and Sept. 4, 1923.

132. Ibid., May 22 and June 9 and 16, 1927. Among the institutions that invited Djaen were the following: Club Social Alianza, Centro Sionista Sefaradí, Comunidad Israelita Sefaradí, Círculo Social Israelita, Legión de Voluntarios Kanfé Yoná (Sefardi), CIL, and Revista *Israel*. Cf. the letter signed by officials of all these institutions to the Confederation Universelle des Juifs Sepharadim on June 29, 1927, Sephardic Community Committee Archives, Jerusalem (Vaad Ha'eda HaSepharadit).

133. Letters at the above-mentioned archive.

134. Djaen to Confederation, Jan. 15, 1929 same archive.

135. Copy of this circular in CIL, *Minutes*, Oct. 12, 1928.

136. Cf., for example, *Shebet Ajim*, Minutes (Rosario), June 25, 1929; *Ets Ajaim*, Minutes (Rosario), May 19, 1929.

137. CIL kept Djaen until June 1930, cf. *Minutes*, Mar. 4, 1931. Cf. CIS, *Minutes*, Nov. 9, 1930.

138. CIL, *Minutes*, Mar. 3, 1929.

139. Benjamín Benzaquén, *La colectividad israelita sefaradí de Buenos Aires no debe permitir que se exploten más sus sentimientos religiosos* (Buenos Aires, 1929). Cf. CIL, *Minutes*, Aug. 1929–Jan. 1930.

140. CIS, *Minutes*, Aug. 10 and 24, 1929; Oct. 19, 1930. Cf. "La Actuación del gran rabino D. Sabetay J. Djaen," *Mundo Israelita*, Jan. 24, 1931, p. 1.

141. Interview Yacar, Teubal, and Mizrahi (cf. n. 42).

142. Cf. *Yesod Hadath*, Minutes, Feb. 22 and 27, 1928; Apr. 14, May 13, July 1, and Aug. 19 and 23, 1928; and Mar. 16, 1930. *Yesod Hadath*, General Assemblies, Mar. 25, 1928; Mar. 10, 1929.

143. Or *Torah*, Minutes, Mar. 26, 1928; *Israel*, Mar. 22, 1929, p. 12.

144. For a Responsa prohibiting conversions to Judaism in Argentina from 1928 to "eternity," which we shall analyze in ch. 4, Setton consulted Rabbi Goldman of Moisesville, the only Ashkenazic rabbi who merited his approval at the time. Other interesting questions dealt with in his collection of Responsa refer to *mikvaot* in Rosario and to the problem of a Jew giving a job to a contractor knowing that the latter would work on Sabbaths and Jewish Holy Days. The permissive answer is based on the fact that the Jew acquires the building, when finished, from the gentile contractor, thus neither himself trespassing—nor making other trespass—the Sabbath laws. Cf. Shaul Setton Dabbah, *Dibber Shaul* (Jerusalem, 1928).

145. Another Syrian rabbi in Buenos Aires was Isaac Laniado, who was born in Aleppo and left for the Holy Land and later went to New York, where the First World War prevented him from returning home. In 1916 he arrived in Buenos Aires, where he died in 1918. He was a learned rabbi, and in Buenos Aires he taught a group of advanced students in rabbinical texts at Agudat Ahim, one of the Aleppine synagogues there. Cf. David Zion Laniado, *Lakedoshim Asher BeAra'z* (Aram Zoba, i.e., Aleppo) (Jerusalem, 1952), 111f. One of Rabbi Laniado's sermons in Buenos Aires was reprinted in his posthumous work, *Vaizara Izhak*, (Aleppo, 1928), pp. 122–35.

146. Cf. José Luis Romero, *El desarrollo de las ideas en la sociedad argentina del siglo XX* (Mexico, 1965), 9–46; and Esteban F. Rondanina, *Liberalismo, masonería, y socialismo en la evolución nacional* (Buenos Aires, 1965), 223–58.

147. Seymour Martin Lipset ("The Study of Jewish Communities in a Comparative Context," *Jewish Journal of Sociology* 5 [Dec. 1963]: 158) makes this argument to explain French Jewry's irreligiosity.

148. Joaquín Adúriz, S. J., "Religión," in Jorge A. Paita, ed. *Argentina, 1930–1960* (Buenos Aires, 1961), 424.

149. Joseph H. Fichter, S. J. "The Marginal Catholic: An Institutional Approach," *Social Forces*, 32, no. 2 (Dec. 1953): 169. Cf. James Scobie, *Argentina: A City and a Nation* (New York, 1964), 153f.

4. Mixed Marriages

1. AIB, Minutes, July 28, 1927.
2. Habima Haivrit 1, no. 4 (1921): 1–2.
3. Yiddishe Zeitung, Jan. 1, 1933, p. 3.
4. Cf. Moshe Davis, "Mixed Marriage in Western Jewry: Historical Background to the Jewish Response," Jewish Journal of Sociology 10, no. 2 (Dec. 1968): 177–79.
5. On Mar. 5, 1922, a member was expelled because he married a Christian (CK, Minutes). At ibid., June 28, 1925, the Religious Committee decided that "whoever marries a Christian woman cannot be a member, but in case of death, burial must be granted him." At ibid., July 20, 1930, it was noted that there were many members married to Christians, and the issue was reopened.
6. Cf. n. 5.
7. Luis H. Brie, president of CIRA and for some time also of CK (1894–97), was buried at the CK's cemetery in Liniers in 1917. On Feb. 2, 1922, however, we read the following in CK, Minutes: "Mr. Rubin declares that Mr. A (married to a Catholic) cannot be a member of the institution, taking into account the Statutes which allow a subsidy to the widow and children and because the Cemetery is designed for Jewish members. Mr. Kopiloff observes that there was a previous occasion on which a Jewess married to someone of Christian origin was buried. Mr. Rubin answers that according to the documents presented he was a free-thinker." From these minutes it is evident that the policy then followed was that of burying only Jews who were not married to gentiles. Furthermore, on Sept. 11, 1924 Moises Yivoff (president of CK) wrote to B. Kornblum in the Province of Corrientes, answering a question involving this issue: "This society, according to our rites, does not admit him (an intermarried Jew) as member, and neither does it bury him in our Cemetery after his death" (CK Copiador no. 2, p. 89).
8. CK, Minutes, Aug. 29, 1926, where it is stated that the reason for no uniform policy was "the fact that not all cases come up in the same form and in the same social spheres, and in the light of the correlation which they have with certain and specific families in our Society."
9. CK, Minutes, July 20, 1930.
10. CIS, Minutes, Dec. 18, 1930; Nov. 11 and Dec. 18, 1932. The latter case refers to a case in Posadas, Province of Misiones. Yesod Hadath, Minutes, Aug. 31, 1928; CIL, Minutes, Jan. 23, 1936; AIB (Rosario), Minutes, July 28, 1927; Apr. 25, 1928; July 30, 1929; Schebet Ajim (Rosario), Minutes, June 25, 1929.
11. Cf. Registro de Matrimonios, Nacimientos y Defunciones de la CIRA, pp. 1–3.
12. Cf. ibid., 183f, 238f, 241 for texts of letters written by converts stating their reasons for taking this step and also a record of the conversion ceremonies and weddings that took place right after. For the different reactions at the board of CIRA, cf. Minutes, Nov. 4, 1907; July 17 and Aug. 7, 1912; Jan. 14, 1917; and Oct. 27 and Dec. 15, 1924.
13. Shaul Setton Dabbah, Dibber Shaul (Jerusalem, 1928), 10a–b.
14. Ibid., 11a.
15. A General Assembly of Yesod Hadath approved the following on June 21, 1925: "To be an active member it is required: To be a Sephardi Jew of 18 years of age" (Art. 5a). On Mar. 13, 1927, a General Assembly approved unanimously to add, among other particulars, the requirement of being "a descendant of Jewish parents." Moreover, at the above-mentioned General Assembly of Yesod Hadath (Mar. 13, 1927) it was decided to include in Art. 11, which listed the causes for expulsion from the society, "those that do not practice the Jewish religion any more," evidently having in mind those who married gentiles.
16. CIS, Minutes, Dec. 18, 1930.
17. Ibid., Nov. 27, 1932.

Notes

18. Hiskia Shabetay, *Divrei Hiskiahu*, vol. 2 (Jerusalem, 1952), section Yore Deah, p. 34.
19. *Ascamoth Nesiei Harabanut Harashit Leeretz Israel, Batei-Din-Zedek Shel Edot Ashkenazim, Sepharadim, veHalabim Deir Hakodesh Ierushalaim, B.D.Z. veRabanei Aram Zobah; lekaiem ulehazek ascamat haRav Shaul Setton, z.1., léesor kabalat gerim beArgentina hanidpest besifro "Dibber Shaul"* (Buenos Aires, 1938).
20. CIL, *Minutes*, Jan. 23 and 28, 1936.

5. National and Political Challenges

1. See *Al Galah* (Arabic; *Hagolah* in Hebrew) 1, nos. 13–14 (Dec. 28, 1917).
2. Enrique Dickmann, *Recuerdos de un militante socialista* (Buenos Aires, 1949), 31f.
3. Enrique Dickmann, "Sionismo y Socialismo," *Vida Nuestra* 2, no. 4 (Oct., 1918), 73f.
4. For a resume of literature on the Zionist movement (1897–1917) cf. Silvia Schenkolewski, "Di Zionistishe Bavegung in Argentine fun 1897–1917," in *Pinkas fun der Kehila* (Buenos Aires, 1969), 100–130.
5. Cf. Mendl Meiern-Lazar, "Di Sorkin epoche," in *Pinkas fun der Kehila* (Buenos Aires, 1969), 131–50.
6. Cf. ch. 1.
7. Central Zionist Archives, Jerusalem (hereafter ZA), Z4 1658, letter from FSA, June 14, 1921 (Yiddish).
8. Ibid. and other documents in the same file. Cf. also *Bericht fun'm Yiddishen Kongres in Argentina* (Buenos Aires, 1916).
9. *Bericht*, pp. 2f. Argentine Jewry mobilized itself quite early for this Congress. The FSA held the first meeting of delegates to plan the Congress on Aug. 30, 1915. Cf. CK, *Minutes*, Aug. 28, 1915.
10. *Bericht*, pp. 13f.
11. ZA, Z4 1999, letter from FSA to Zionist Organization (ZO) (London), Feb. 19, 1922 (Hebrew). Cf. ZA, Z4 1868, FSA, *Report of Activities*, presented at the Fifth Land Conference (Argentina), Nov. 1–6, 1919 (Yiddish), p. 5.
12. ZA, Z4 1658, from FSA, June 14, 1921. According to this report the following were represented at the Land Conferences of Zionists in Argentina: the Fourth Land Conference, Feb. 1918 had 40 branches with 50 delegates; the Fifth Land Conference, Nov. 1919 had 110 branches with 140 delegates; and the Sixth Land Conference, Nov. 1920 had even higher numbers. The amount of *shekalim* sold were the following: 445 in 1915; 666 in 1916; 5,544 in 1917; 10,858 in 1918, and circa 14,000 in 1919. The figures indicate with extreme clarity the turning point that occured in 1917. Cf. also ZA, L6 34III, letter from FSA (Joselevich and Nahman Gesang) to ZO (Copenhagen), Mar. 20, 1918 (English); and FSA to Jewish National Fund (JNF) (Haag), Aug. 12, 1918, in which Epstein's work for the Redemption (Geulah) Fund Campaign is described. Cf. also *Di Yiddishe Welt* (Buenos Aires) 1, no. 1 (Sept. 2, 1917): 2f., 7–13.
13. Tower was invited to the Fourth Zionist Land Conference held in Buenos Aires, Feb. 23–26, 1918, at the Teatro Coliseo and was cheered by the participants and spectators. At that conference it was decided to cable the British government for the Balfour Declaration. Cf. ZA, L6 34III, letter from FSA to ZO (Copenhagen), Mar. 20, 1918. Tower was a special guest and participant in central events of Jewish institutions in the country. See, for example, his participation in Tucumán (Israel Blumenfeld, *Historia de la comunidad israelita de Tucumán* [Tucumán, 1971], 77f).
14. Marcos Regalsky, "Politishe Shtremungen un Partaien in Argentiner Ishuv," *Yoblbuch Yiddishe Zeitung* (Buenos Aires, 1940), 550–56; *Report of the Executive of the Zionist Organization Submitted to the XIVth Zionist Congress at Vienna* (London, 1925), 386.
15. Regalsky, op. cit., 552–54.
16. Cf. *Di Presse*, Dec. 24, 1918, p. 3; Dec. 27, 1918, p. 3.

17. Cf. *Jewish Labor Yearbook and Almanach* (PZ Almanach) (New York, 1927), 241.
18. Regalsky, op. cit., 561. Among the delegates for the PAF were A. Juris and Eliahu Golomb.
19. *Di Neie Zeit*, Apr. 2, 1922, p. 7; Mar. 15, 1928, p. 1.
20. *Di Neie Zeit*, Aug. 5, 1927, pp. 1f.
21. Regalsky, op. cit., 548–50.
22. Proclamation of May 1, 1918 is found in ZA, L6 34III.
23. Cf. ibid.
24. I. L. Gorelik, *Be'eretz Nod* (Hebrew) (Buenos Aires, 1943), 155ff.
25. Ibid., 32.
26. ZA, L6 32III, letter from FSA to JNF (Haag), Aug. 12, 1918 (Yiddish).
27. ZA, L6 34III, letter from ZO (Copenhagen) to Zeire Zion (Buenos Aires), Oct. 8, 1918. The letter was reprinted in *Di Presse*, Nov. 29, 1918. FSA protested on the same day.
28. ZA, L6 34III, Zeire Zion to ZO (Copenhagen), Apr. 18, 1919 (Yiddish).
29. Cf. ZA, Z4 1868, FSA to ZO (London), Apr. 18, 1919 (Yiddish).
30. H. H. Ben-Sasson ("The Volunteer Movement among American Jews," in *The Jewish Legion, Fiftieth Anniversary of the Jewish Batallions, 1917–1967,* [Jerusalem, 1967], p. 17) concludes, "This volunteers movement ... was doomed by history not to see the fulfillment of its wish.... They ... were enthusiastic, ... longed for a fight and for creativity, and ... were doomed to emptiness and a search for their lives, for their external and Jewish image, and for their very existence."
31. ZA, L6 34III, Zeire Zion (Buenos Aires) to Poale Zion, Dec. 26, 1919 (Yiddish). The letter quotes an article by Regalsky, the Poale Zion envoy, in *Di Neie Zeit* no. 23, in which the latter wrote, "The Jewish people must now join around the Zionist delegation in Versailles." Zeire Zion concurred with such a position. A declaration was sent to the press accordingly.
32. ZA, Z4 34III, FSA to ZO (London), Dec. 1, 1919 (Yiddish).
33. Hitachdut was a Social-Zionist party formed by the union of the Palestine Workers' party, Hapoel Hatzair, with the majority of the Zeire Zion groups in the Diaspora.
34. Cf. M. Koifman, "El Sionismo y los Problemas Societarios Judíos en Sud América," *La Segunda Convención Sionista Sudamericana* (Buenos Aires, 1950), 171; *Habima Haivrit* 4, no. 2 (Sept. 1924): 15; *Report of the Executive of the Zionist Organization Submitted to the XIVth Zionist Congress* (London, 1925), pp. 381ff. confirms the fruitful results of Hechalutz propaganda in Argentina: "The first group of Halutzim from Argentina, who have had agricultural training on Jewish farms, have already arrived in Palestine and begun their agricultural work." A second group of 8 persons from Hechalutz left Argentina on Aug. 5, 1925, to settle in Palestine, among them three carpenters, three farmers, one baker, and one locksmith, cf. *Yiddishe Zeitung*, Aug. 5, 1925, p. 6. For the period Oct. 1, 1921–Apr. 1, 1923, twelve immigrants from Argentina arrived in Palestine (cf. *Report of the Executive of the Zionist Organization Submitted to the XIIIth Zionist Congress*, p. 196), and for the period April 1923–April 1925, 31 immigrants (cf. *Report of the Executive of the Zionist Organization Submitted to the XIVth Zionist Congress*, p. 232).
35. Koifman, op. cit., 172; Regalsky, op. cit., 562. The Hug Eretzisraeli is also mentioned by Jacob (Akiva) Ettinger in his conversation with Solomon Pazi, Jerusalem, Jan. 21, 1929 (cf. ZA, KH4 4531). According to this report the group consisted of about 60 to 70 young people who came from Israel, most of them with the intention of returning there after having assembled enough capital to establish themselves there. Their occupations were by and large *cuenteniks* (door-to-door salesmen, who sold on installments) and peddlers.
36. ZA, Z4 3659. Several letters from FSA to ZO (London) confirm the creation of the joint committee for JNF during the 1927–30 period (cf. Apr. 5, 1927; June 15, 1928; July 22, 1930). In a report to the ZO (London) about the work of the parties in placing *shekalim*, Jan. 30, 1931, we find the following:

Shekalim	5688 (1927/28)		5689 (1928/29)		5690 (1929/30)		5691 (1930/31)	
	PZ	ZZ	PZ	ZZ	PZ	ZZ	PZ	ZZ
Shekalim received	—	200	1,000	600	900	—	500	150
Shekalim returned	—	—	399	139	500	—	—	—
Shekalim paid	—	—	392	173	—	—	—	—
Shekalim to return	—	200	209	288	400	—	500	150

37. ZA, KH4 453I, Hitachdut (Zeire Zion) in Argentina to Keren Hayesod (Jerusalem), Dec. 20, 1928, includes the former's answer of Dec. 10, 1928, to FSA's invitation of Nov. 30, 1928, to participate in the committee for Keren Hayesod.
38. ZA, KH4 454I, Pazi (Buenos Aires) to Keren Hayesod (Jerusalem), May 15, 1929. Only in the 1930s did the parties enter Keren Hayesod.
39. ZA, Z4 3659, ZO (London) to Ettinger (Buenos Aires), Jan. 16, 1928.
40. Di Neie Zeit, June 1, 1927, pp. 2, 6.
41. During the early 1920s Habima Haivrit appeared irregularly. Hechalutz appeared for about a year, starting in 1922. Similarly Atidenu, in 1926.
42. ZA, L6 34III, report of the Ministry of Information, Norfolk St., Strand, W.C.2, Aug. 30, 1918.
43. ZA, Z4 1868. Foreign Office to N. Sokolow, no. 133423/W/44, Aug. 5, 1918. The London Office of the ZO informed FSA in a letter dated Aug. 13, 1918. Cf. also ZO (London) to FSA, June 24, 1918.
44. M. Podolsky, ed., Los Voluntarios Israelitas, album dedicated to the first group of young men departing for the Jewish Legion in Palestine. (Mostly in Yiddish; also some Russian and Spanish) (Buenos Aires, 1918), 24 for details on German; see pp. 11–15 for the beginnings of the legionaries movement in Argentina. The FSA, on the other hand, claimed the opposite. According to their Report of Activities (Yiddish), presented at the Fifth Land Conference (Nov. 1–6, 1919), 7, the president of FSA, Joselevich, introduced on Apr. 9, 1918 V. German and Joseph Katz to the English ambassador, taking the responsibility for their earnestness and honorability.
45. Vida Nuestra, 2, no. 3 (Sept. 1918), 71, under the heading "Partida de los Voluntarios." The editor affirmed, "We, who have not based our highest aspirations in the triumph of Zionism, are happy that it is so, especially if one takes into account that that triumph—we have clearly said it before—more than a party issue, signifies the acknowledgement by the civilized powers, of the revindication of our race, which in twenty centuries has not lost its will to persist."
46. Cf. Podolsky, op. cit., 13ff., 20. See also "Legionarios Israelitas," in CIRA, Memoria (1919); ZA, L6 34III, Zeire Zion to ZO (Copenhagen), Apr. 18, 1919; and Regalsky, op. cit., 548f.
47. Cf. CIRA, Memoria (1917). For Nordau's letter to Halphon see CIRA, Minutes, Oct. 16, 1917. Cf. also Abraham S. Yahuda, Hahagana al Haishuv bemilhemet haolam harishona: Zichronot meiemei shauti bisfarad (Jerusalem, 1952), passim.
48. CIRA, Minutes, Oct. 7, 1918; and "FSA" in CIRA, Memoria (1918).
49. Halphon was a graduate of the Ecole Rabbinique in Paris and had important connections with JCA and AIU. CIRA was constantly in connection with the French Consistoire.
50. From the text of the invitations to the act, at CIRA's archive.
51. Cf. Podolsky, op. cit., 23–35. Cf. H. H. Ben-Sasson, op. cit., 8–17.
52. Cf. Arturo Capdevilla, "Primera Presidencia de Yrigoyen," in Historia Argentina Contemporánea, vol. 1, sec. 2 (Buenos Aires, 1963), 252f. See also "La CIRA," Crítica, July 8, 1916, where it is written, "In a poll among Israelites, all except a few are favoring

the allies." At CIRA there were some members who sided with the Central Powers, and some incidents took place (Cf. CIRA, Minutes, June 20, 1915; June 25, 1917).
53. See, for example, ZA, Z4 1868, FSA to ZO (London), Apr. 18, 1919.
54. Ibid.
55. FSA, Report of Activities, presented to the Fifth Land Conference (Nov. 1–6, 1919), 6.
56. See ch. 2 for more details.
57. Di Presse, Jan. 15, 1919.
58. Di Yiddishe Zeitung, Jan. 14, 1919; Di Presse, Jan. 15, 1919; Di Yiddishe Welt, Jan. 16, 1919.
59. La Vanguardia, Jan. 14, 1919, p. 2; La Razón, Jan. 14, 1919, p. 4.
60. The full document is photographed in Wald, op. cit., 27 and Solominsky, op. cit. 29 (see ch. 2, n. 76).
61. Cf. Wald, op. cit., 26–30; ZA, L6 34III, FSA to ZO (Copenhagen), Jan. 31, 1919. Of course, the role of FSA was quite exaggerated in their report to headquarters. Nevertheless, FSA was the main activist at the time. For CIRA's attitude and participation see CIRA, Minutes, Jan. 27, 1919.
62. ZA, Z1 405, Enrique Rubinsky and Esteban Crenovich to Vienna, May 5, 1904. Benzaquen was vice-president of CIL in 1903, and Benchetrit was vice-president in 1899, secretary in 1905, and later president of CIL.
63. El Sionista (Buenos Aires) 1, no. 12 (Dec. 1, 1904): 6.
64. ZA, Z.B. Koln B. Ig 123, fasc. 1.
65. ZA, Z.B. Koln B. Ig 123, fasc. 3, J. L. Liachovitzky, A. Crenovich, G. Dabin, and G. Zeitlin, "Report on the History of Zionism in Argentina," Mar. 14, 1907.
66. CIL, Minutes, Oct. 30, 1918.
67. Ibid. Aug. 3, 1924.
68. La Luz 12, no. 8 (Apr. 17, 1942): 184–86.
69. Habima Haivrit 1, no. 6 (Sept.–Oct. 1921): 11–12.
70. The Third Zionist Conference in Argentina tried to encourage Sephardim (cf. Schenkolewski, op. cit., 118), as did the Twelfth Conference (cf. Semanario Hebreo, May 23, 1930, p. 3). In 1921 Moisés Senderey (Habima Haivrit, 1, no. 7 [Dec. 1921]: 11) suggested that the World Zionist Organization in London should concern itself with sending a Sephardic delegate to work within those communities.
71. Cf. summary of report of the World Union of Sephardic Jews for the period Iyar 5684– Elul 5686 (approx. Apr. 1924–Sept. 1926) at ZA, Z4 35791.
72. Cf. ZA, Z4 2412, letters from Bension to the ZO (London), dated Mendoza Sept. 22, 1926 and Buenos Aires Sept. 29, 1926, respectively; also S25 519, Bension to Dr. Leo Hermann (Keren Hayesod, Jerusalem), Nov. 9, 1926.
73. ZA, Z4 35791, FSA to Keren Hayesod (Jerusalem), Dec. 12, 1926.
74. Quotations are from the letters mentioned in nn. 72 and 75. For Hacham Shaul Setton's participation in Agudat Israel see both the letter of n. 73 and ZA, KH4 4531, notes on Ettinger's conversation with Shmuel Pazi and Schwartz, Jerusalem, Jan. 21, 1929. Agudat Israel was founded in Argentina in 1920 at a meeting in the synagogue of Hevra Mishnaies, by Orthodox Jews. The event did not merit publication in the Jewish press. Probably Setton joined this group in some capacity. Cf. Habima Haivrit 1, no. 6 (Sept.–Oct. 1921), 14. In his collection of Responsa, Dibber Shaul (Jerusalem, 1928), Hacham Setton deals with the question whether in Argentina, which has opposite seasons to Eretz Israel, Jews should insert the petition for wind and rain in their prayers—which is done during the winter season in the Northern Hemisphere—according to the climate of Israel or during the actual winter in Argentina. His answer is that Jews should follow the seasons of the place. The Aleppine congregation has continued this practice in Buenos Aires, contrary to the custom accepted in all other synagogues in the country. For Setton's views on Jewish education, see Yesod Hadath, Minutes, Feb. 22, 1928; also Yesod Hadath, Minutes of the General Assemblies, Mar. 25, 1928 and Mar. 10, 1929.
75. ZA, Z4 35791, ZO (Jerusalem) to all Zionist Federations and Organizations in the Diaspora, Dec. 7, 1926.

76. ZA, Z4 3579I, Bension to Zionist Organization, Sept. 21, 1927, quotes Cadoche's words.
77. ZA, Z4 3579III, interview with Dr. Moisés Cadoche of Buenos Aires, president of Bene Kedem of Argentina, Mar. 20, 1928. The interview was published in *New Judea* (London) 4, no. 12 (Apr. 1928).
78. Among the goals of WUSJ, according to *Israel* magazine, Feb. 3, 1928, were "to coordinate, to strengthen, and to unite our forces in the Diaspora, in order to present a single front in Palestine, capable of representing before the proper authorities, our claims and the vindication of our brothers. Besides, we feel the urgent necessity to propagate amongst the Sephardim of the whole world the Zionist ideal, and influence them to take part in the common task."
79. Djaen was learned in secular subjects also. Differences in traditions and customs caused a negative response among Moroccan Jews. Cf. Benjamín Benzaquén, *La colectividad israelita sefaradí de Buenos Aires no debe permitir que se exploten más sus sentimientos religiosos* (Buenos Aires, 1929); CIL, *Minutes*, Oct. 12, 1928; Oct. 21, 1928; Mar. 3, 1929; Aug. 11, 1929; Dec. 7, 1929; Mar. 4, 1931. Contacts with Keren Hayesod in Jerusalem (cf. ZA, KH4 4531, Ettinger [Buenos Aires] to Keren Hayesod, Sept. 27, 1928) and Jerusalem's answer. In his conversation with Pazi (ZA, same file), Jan. 21, 1929, Ettinger confirmed that Djaen worked for Keren Hayesod and WUSJ, though he had put some pressure on Cadoche and other activists of Bene Kedem against contributing to Keren Hayesod.
80. Cf. *Los Sefaradim y el Sionismo* (Buenos Aires, 1926).
81. See Ettinger's conversation with Pazi (ZA, KH4 4531, Jan. 21, 1929); Pazi's letter to ZO (London) (May 15, 1929, ZA, Z4 3659); and interview with Cadoche (see n. 77).
82. Cf. *Report of Activities* presented to the 12th Land Conference (FSA), May 1930 (Yiddish), p. 9. Also ZA, KH4 4541, Nissensohn (FSA) to Weizmann, Sept. 23, 1929 and Pazi to Keren Hayesod (Jerusalem), Sept. 17, 1929.
83. Cf. Hesed Shel Emeth Sefaradit, *Minutes*, Sept. 4, 1929; Yesod Hadath, *Minutes*, Sept. 4, 1929, and Nov. 5, 1929.
84. Cf. Nissensohn to Weizmann, Sept. 23, 1929, ZA, KH4 4541. Also *Allgemeine Tetigkeit Baricht*, Oct. 1928–May 1930 (Yiddish), ZA, KH4 4561.
85. *Los Sefaradim y el Sionismo*, 66–71.
86. Cf. Regalsky, *op. cit.*, 543f.; ZA, Z4 1999, cable from FSA to ZO (London), Aug. 8, 1922. Joselevich's speech and the memorandum presented to Yrigoyen are found in Nahman Gesang, "A Kapitel Argentiner Zionistishe Politik," *Yoblbuch Yiddishe Zeitung* (Buenos Aires, 1940), 615–18.
87. Gesang, op. cit., 618.
88. The Portuguese text of Toledo's cable to his government is dated May 12, 1922; it is found in ZA, Z4 1999.
89. ZA, Z4 1658, FSA to ZO (London), May 29, 1922; and answer of July 6, 1922. Thanks to Wilensky's influence, the governments of Brazil and Chile recognized the British Mandate in Palestine. Uruguay followed their steps. The Chilean Government, to demonstrate its sympathy for the Zionist idea, appointed Wilensky honorary consul of Chile to Jerusalem.
90. Rufino Marín, *Lo que piensa América del problema judío* (Buenos Aires, 1944), 141f.
91. *Report of the Executive of the Zionist Organization Submitted to the XIIth Zionist Congress*, 10, 64, 126f.
92. ZA, KH4 4531.
93. Gorelik (op. cit., 83ff.) described the community in 1914 and asserted that most Jews knew nothing about Zionism and that education is terrible. In speaking with Joselevich, the latter told him, "The basis, the fundamental, upon which all national work is based there, in Russia, that is, national education, is lacking [here]."
94. For Jaffe's personal letters written during his stay in Argentina in 1923 cf. his *Beshlichut Am* (Jerusalem, 1968), 75–103; and his *Tekufot* (Tel Aviv, 1948), 186–89.
95. Idem, *Tekufot*, 188f.

96. The following are the totals of the Keren Hayesod campaigns:

1922/23	(with participation of Leib Jaffe)	176,421.22 pesos
1924		147,927.80 pesos
1925	(with participation of Mossensohn)	163,645.65 pesos
1926		143,719.34 pesos
1927	(with participation of Wilensky)	141,271.30 pesos
1928	(with participation of Ettinger)	138,943.30 pesos

Source: *Report of Activities* presented to the 12th Land Conference, May 1930 (Yiddish). Cf. the tables of receipts at Keren Hayesod during the eight-year period ending in March 1929 in *Report of the Executive of the Zionist Organization Submitted to the XVIth Zionist Congress*, 1929 (London, 1929), 140. Some institutions in Buenos Aires, which received contributions also from the interior, had the following approximate yearly income:

Ezrah (Jewish Hospital)	331,027.54 pesos (1928/29)
Liga Israelita Argentina contra la TB	55,765.65 pesos (1928/29)
Chevra Keduscha Ashkenasi	390,679.51 pesos (1926/27)

97. In August 1922, the FSA had requested the coming of Mossensohn or Vladimir Jabotinsky, among others. Benjamin Jaffe says that the FSA also requested Haim Weizmann or Nahum Sokolow. In November of the same year, when all other candidates were crossed out, FSA finally accepted Jaffe. Cf. ZA, Z4 1999, various cables. Also Jaffe, *Beshlichut Am*, 75.

98. Cf. Gino Germani, *Política y sociedad en une época de transición* (Buenos Aires, 1968), 238–88; and Carl Solberg, *Immigration and Nationalism, Argentina and Chile, 1890–1914* (Austin, 1970), passim.

99. ZA, Z4 2412, FSA to ZO (London), Jan. 1, 1926.

100. ZA, KH4 4531, Schwartz (Jerusalem) to Jaffe (Warsaw), Jan. 21, 1929.

101. Various letters in ZA, KH4 4551.

102. Cf. Regalsky, op. cit., 550–56.

103. ZA, Z4 3659, Zeire Zion (Hitachdut) to ZO (London), August 15, 1928, wrote, "However, the lack of special *shlichim* from the columns of 'Hapoel Hazair' and 'Hitachdut' is strongly felt, and it is clear that if someone of the leaders of the world [movement] 'Hitachdut' will come here, he will win many of the opponents . . . , and will also strengthen Zionist loyalties within our camp."

104. For the delegates at the Zionist Congresses, cf. the respective *Protokoll des Zionisten Kongresses*. Gesang's speech is found in the *Protokoll* to the 14th Zionist Congress in Vienna (London, 1926), 269–72. For the resolutions of the Ninth Land Conference in Argentina, cf. ZA, Z4 1999. An excellent treatment of the conflict of ideologies in the establishment of the Jewish Agency is found in Ben Halpern, *The Idea of the Jewish State* (Cambridge, Mass., 1961), 188–98.

105. ZA, KH4 4551, Gesang to Leib Jaffe, Oct. 4, 1929 and Nissensohn to Weizmann, Dec. 31, 1929.

106. ZA, KH4 4551, Sokolow (Warsaw) to Jaffe, Feb. 11, 1930. Cf. also Jaffe's letter to Keren Hayesod (Jerusalem), Feb. 2, 1930.

107. ZA, KH4 4551, Gesang to Keren Hayesod (Jerusalem), Feb. 12, 1930.

108. ZA, KH4 4571, Leo Hermann to Pazi (Buenos Aires), Sept. 10, 1930 and Jaffe's cable to Gesang, Nov. 10, 1930. Gesang replied calling off Sokolow's trip both by cable (Nov. 17, 1930) and in a letter to Jaffe, Nov. 20, 1930.

109. ZA, KH4 4571, cable from Actions Committee to FSA, Jan. 19, 1931. Gesang answered positively to this appeal in a cable to London, Jan. 21, 1931.

110. Cf. ZA, KH4 4571, Jaffe to Gesang, Dec. 11, 1930. Jaffe told Gesang, after the latter's decision to cancel Sokolow's trip, that precisely now Sokolow had to go because of the economic crisis, for only he could start a successful campaign for Keren Hayesod.

111. Cf. Jaffe's letter of Feb. 2, 1930 at ZA, KH4 455I. See also the collection of letters from his trip in 1923 in *Beshlichut Am*, 75–103 and *Tekufot*, 186–89.
112. Cf. the articles by Guillermo Sáenz in *Criterio* (Buenos Aires): "La actualidad de Palestina," *Criterio* 2, no. 79 (Sept. 5, 1929): 13; "La legislación y la religión en Palestina," *Criterio* 2, no. 83 (Oct. 3, 1929): 147f.; and "Polémica de familias y razas," *Criterio* 3, no. 110 (Apr. 10, 1930): 475.
113. The resolution is found in ZA KH4 454I.
114. *Report of Activities* (Yiddish), presented to the Twelfth Land Conference (FSA), May 1930, p. 9 gives the following sums for the emergency fund:

Capital (Buenos Aires)	
Several	86,128.69 pesos
Societies	29,690.00 pesos
Sephardim	35,661.00 pesos
Yiddishe Zeitung	42,920.00 pesos
Total Capital (Buenos Aires)	194,399.69 pesos
Province Buenos Aires	18,453.20 pesos
Province Entre Ríos	35,400.15 pesos
Province Santa Fe	37,650.75 pesos
Total	313,377.04 pesos

Cf. also in ZA, KH4 454I, letter from Nissensohn (president, FSA) to Weizmann (London), Sept. 23, 1929; and from Pazi to Keren Hayesod (Jerusalem), Sept. 17, 1929.
115. Various articles in the collection of *Juventud*, a monthly put out by the organization of the same name during 1911–17. Cf., for example, 1, no. 2 (Aug. 1911): 3; and 2, no. 12 (June 1912): 9–10.
116. Cf. *Minutes* from SHA, corresponding to Aug. 27 and 28, 1929, and Sept. 4, 11, and 20, 1929. The weekly *Mundo Israelita* was edited by mainly the same group that led SHA during the first years and represented the view of that institution. In the 1920s *Mundo Israelita* was non-Zionist, and on several opportunities criticized FSA and emphasized the Argentine idiosyncrasy of most Jews in the country. On June 21, 1924 (p. 1), the editor wrote, "In Argentina, for example, the Jewish youth, which has no reason to hide a vague sympathy towards Zionism, has followed, however, a different road . . . it has searched for a way to express its national sentiments, and has ended, by and large, in the field of culture." On the other hand, occasionally, *Mundo Israelita* expressed certain sympathy to the Jewish national movement; cf. "La Campaña pro Eretz Israel," June 12, 1926, p. 1. Around the time of the Palestine assaults, *Mundo Israelita* underwent a change in its position with respect to Zionism. Cf. its position against SHA because the latter did not take a more positive stand to help the Jewish victims in Palestine, editorials of their issues of Sept. and Oct., 1929.
117. Hebrew education was criticized several times by *Habima Haivrit*, cf. 1, no. 2 (1921): 1–2 and 3, no. 2 (1923): 5–8. In the same periodical, every issue brought some news of various Tarbut groups, (which had the intention of maintaining the Hebrew language) in all corners of the country. Already in 1923 leaders of FSA were seriously thinking about commerce with Palestine. Cf. Wolf Nijensohn, "Our Effective Work for Eretz Israel," *Habima Haivrit*, 3, no. 2 (1923): 3–4. In 1929 the Argentina-Palestina Society, which had been trading with Palestine for some time, organized an exposition of Palestinian products (cf. *Mundo Isaelita*, Apr. 13, 1929, p. 1). In a letter from Buenos Aires, M. Graiver informs Jaffe that due to the economic crisis, business with Palestine was maintained at a low level (cf. ZA, KH4 457I, Dec. 1, 1930). Among the articles imported from Palestine were biscuits, wines (Carmel Mizrachi), cocoa, halva, marmelade, chocolate, almonds, oil, preserved fruits, and artistic objects. The head of the Sociedad de Comercio Argentina-Palestina was Dr. Isaac Nissensohn, and the directors were Michael Graiver and Joseph Galili.
118. Cf. Germani, op. cit., passim.; Solberg, op. cit., passim.
119. Jaffe, *Bishlichut Am*, 80.

120. Cf. Mordechai Maidanik, "Al Hatnua Haivrit be-Argentina," in *Sefer Argentina* (Hebrew), edited by Maidanik (Buenos Aires, 1954), 158.
121. Cf. *Der Avangard*, 2d. epoch, 1, no. 1 (Jan. 1916): 1–5.
122. Cf. *Der Avangard*, 2d. epoch, 2, no. 13 (Jan. 1917): 39ff.
123. *Oifgang* 1, no. 6 (Aug. 1927): 13f.
124. Jorge Abelardo Ramos, *El partido comunista en la política Argentina, su historia y su crítica* (Buenos Aires, 1962), 28; *Mundo Israelita*, Nov. 22, 1924, 1f.
125. Ibid., 30f.
126. *Der Roiter Shtern*, Mar. 1, 1924, p. 1.
127. *Roite Hilf*, Aug. 1930, p. 6; cf. also *Nodl Arbeter* 1, no. 1 (Aug. 1922), 5f.
128. *Yiddisher Proletarisher Hilfs Aktsie fur Soviet Russland in Argentine*, Memorial 1921–23, passim.
129. On the Birobidzhan project see Salo Baron, *The Russian Jew under Tsars and Soviets* (New York, 1964), 230–36. Procor was thoroughly discussed by the local Jewish press. Cf. also the report published by the delegation from Argentina visiting the USSR in 1929, *Baricht fun der Procor Delegatzie* (Buenos Aires, n.d.).
130. *Procor, Bulletin* no. 2 (Aug. 1927), Spanish section, pp. 41–38.
131. *Mundo Israelita*, July 7, 1928, p. 1.
132. Pinie Katz, *Yidden in Argentina* (Buenos Aires, 1946), 173–75.
133. *Der Yiddisher Poier* started publication in 1929.
134. Cf. *Yiddishe Zeitung*, Apr. 13, 1925, p. 7; CK. *Minutes*, July 14 and Aug. 8 and 15, 1926; and *Mundo Israelita*, Sept. 22, 1928, p. 3.
135. *Semanario Hebreo*, Oct. 4, 1929, p. 1.
136. *Unzer Gedank* (Zeire Zion-Hitachdut), Jan. 1930, p. 4.
137. *Mundo Israelita*, Apr. 19, 1930, p. 1 and May 3, 1930, p. 1.
138. *Unzer Shul* 4, no. 1 (June 1932): 3.
139. Samuel Rollansky, *Dos Yiddishe Gedrukte Wort un Teater in Argentine* (Buenos Aires, 1941), 100ff.

6. Concern for Jewish Education

1. Cf. the many requests of colonists in Santa Fé and Entre Ríos for establishing schools in the JCA colonies during the 1890's in *Hazefirah* of Warsaw, esp. no. 84 (1894): 369; no. 255 (1894): 110lf.; no. 61 (1895); 282f,: and no. 93 (1895): 429. See also Haim Avni, *Argentina, the Promised Land: Baron de Hirsch's Colonization Project in the Argentine Republic* (Hebrew) (Jerusalem, 1973), 174–177.
2. Cf. Gregorio Weinberg, ed., *Debate Parlamentario sobre la Ley 1420* (1883–84) (Buenos Aires, 1956); and Carlos Alberto Campobassi, *La enseñanza privada en la América Latina y en la Argentina* (Buenos Aires, 1965). According to Art. 4 of the Ley de Educación Común, the school obligations could be fulfilled in private schools as well.
3. Cf. Walter P. Zenner, *Syrian Jewish Identification in Israel*, Ph.D. dissertation, Columbia University, 1965, pp. 73–76; Nissim Teubal, *El inmigrante, De Alepo a Buenos Aires* (Buenos Aires, 1953), 50–54; André Chouraqui, *Cent ans d'histoire: L'Alliance Israelite Universelle et la renaissance juive contemporaine* (1860–1960) (Paris, 1965), 161–200. On p. 161 Chouraqui describes the rapid growth of the alliance's educational work in the Orient: "De 1860 á 1880, l'Alliance fondá 14 écoles; de 1880 á 1890, 11 écoles. En 1900, 100 écoles de l'Alliance Israélite Universelle scolarisent 26,000 enfants. A la veille de la premiére guerre mondiale, l'Alliance possede 188 écoles qui scolarisent 48,000 élèves, avec une budget superieur a 2,000,000 de francs-or."
4. For the school situation in the colonies, cf. Jedidia Efrón, "La obra escolar en las colonias judías," in *50 años de colonización judía en la Argentina* (Buenos Aires, 1939), 239–62; Máxico Yagupsky, "Di Yiddishe Dertsiung in di Kolonies un Provintsen," in *Yoblbuch Yiddishe Zeitung* (Buenos Aires, 1940), 445–58; and M. Meiern Laser, *Dos Yiddishe Shulvezn in Argentine* (Buenos Aires, 1948), 15–34.

5. Cf. Laser, op. cit., 41.
6. Cf. *Talmud Torah Harischono, Minutes*, July 12, 1903.
7. Cf. Clippings from newspapers in Spanish in file J. S. Liachovitzky, IWO Archives, Buenos Aires; *Di Yiddishe Hofnung*, nos. 14–15 (Oct. 1, 1910): 10f; and Laser, op. cit., 43.
8. T. T. Dr. *Herzl, Minutes*, Oct. 12, 1915. Laser, op. cit., 41 says wrongly that there were 220 students in 1914.
9. Ibid., Apr. 25, 1922; Jan. 3, 1924.
10. Ibid., July 28, 1925; Nov. 16, 1926.
11. T. T. *Harischono, Minutes*, Nov. 14, 1927.
12. T. T. *Harischono, General Assemblies Minutes*, Dec. 27, 1928; T. T. *Harischono, Minutes*, Feb. 19, 1928.
13. Cf. Halphon, op. cit. and Efrón, op. cit., 249f.
14. Cf. the Comunicado del Directorio General de la JCA a la Colectividad Israelita de la Argentina, signed by Louis Oungre, director general, in *Semanario Hebreo*, Mar. 14, 1930, p. 3.
15. Cf. JCA *Rapport* (Paris, for the period). In general the number of schools do not differ notably. On the other hand, the number of students is sometimes 20% and even 30% lower than that which appears in table 4. Laser, (op. cit., 58, 60) makes this observation.
16. Cf. *Di Presse*, Feb. 5, 1920, p. 3 and May 25, 1920, pp. 4f; *Hechalutz* no. 9 (1923): 17f.
17. *Di Presse*, Feb. 5, 1920, p.3.
18. *Di Presse*, May 25, 1920, pp. 4f; July 5, 1920, p. 2; and July 7, 1920, pp. 4f, Cf. also Laser, op. cit., 62.
19. *Di Presse*, July 21, 1920, p. 5. Other Jewish professional organizations adopted similar positions. Cultural organizations of Jewish workers likewise sided with the striking teachers. Cf., for example, the position of solidarity of Kultur Verein I. L. Peretz (*Di Presse*, July 28, 1920, p. 5).
20. Cf. *Programa analítico de la enseñanza hebrea en la República Argentina*. (JCA); T. T. *Harischono, Minutes*, Nov. 14, 1927; *Yiddishe Zeitung*, Nov. 7, 1927, p. 6; and *Haolam*, Dec. 30, 1920, pp. 7f., letter from I. L. Gorelik from Argentina.
21. A. Aiberman, "Kinder Erziung," *Di Yiddishe Hofnung* 2, 7 (July 1909): 4f.
22. Ricardo Rojas, *La restauración nacionalista*, 1st edition (Buenos Aires, 1909). We quote the 3d edition (1971). Cf. especially ch. 3, "Bases para un renacimiento nacionalista," (pp. 139–238).
23. Robert F. Foerster, *The Italian Migration of Our Times* (Cambridge, Mass., 1924), 272.
24. *Congregación Israelita Latina* (CIL), *Minutes*, June 24, 1917.
25. T. T. (CIL), *Minutes*, Apr. 16, 1922; July 31, and Oct. 27, 1923.
26. CIL, *Minutes*, May 13, 1928; Nov. 17, 1929; T. T. (CIL), *Minutes*, July 25, 1925.
27. Laser, op. cit., 194.
28. *Boletín del Comité Central de Educación Israelita en la República Argentina* no. 1 (1916–1917): 4; Laser, (op. cit., 194) wrongly dated it 1919.
29. *Habima Haivrit*, 1, no. 6 (*Sept.–Oct.* 1921) 11f.
30. *Yesod Hadath, Minutes*, Feb. 22 and 27 and Apr. 14, 1928; *Yesod Hadath, General Assemblies*, Mar. 25, 1928; Mar. 10, 1929; Mar. 26, 1930. Cf. also *Habima Haivrit* 6, no. 3 (Mar. 1929): 19.
31. *Or Torah, Minutes*, Nov. 10, 1921; *Yesod Hadath, Minutes*, May 13, 1928; Apr. 22, 1930.
32. *Or Torah, Memoria Y Balance* 1921/22, and 1929/30; cf. *Minutes*, Mar. 19, 1924. Laser, (op. cit., 189) wrongly says 100 for 1929.
33. *Habima Haivrit* 1, no. 5 (1921): 6f; ibid., 3, no. 5 (1924): 15; *Yesod Hadath, General Assemblies*, Mar. 2, 1932.
34. *Habima Haivrit*, 6, nos. 5–6 (May–June 1929): 17.
35. Cf., for example, *Or Torah, Minutes*, Feb. 20, 1922; May 26, 1923; and *Yesod Hadath, Minutes*, Sept. 5 and 12, 1926.
36. Zenner, op. cit., 72.
37. *Boletín del Comité Central de Educación Israelita en la República Argentina*, no. 2 (1917–18); 8.

38. Efrón, op. cit., 257f.
39. CK, Minutes, Dec. 26, 1926; Jan. 9, 1927; Jan. 15, 1928; Jan. 13 and 20, Feb. 10, June 2, Sept. 29, 1929; Jan. 19 and 26, 1930.
40. Such was the case, for example, of the T. T. of Parque Patricios in Buenos Aires. Cf. CK, Minutes, Jan. 15, 1928.
41. Boletín del Comité Central de Educación Israelita en la República Argentina, no. 2 (1917–18), 11.
42. Junta Organizadora de la Alianza Israellita Argentina, Minutes, Feb. 5, 1923.
43. Cf., the Statutes of the Jewish Workers Federation in Der Avangard, 3, no. 3 (Mar. 1910): pp. 24ff. Article 2 mentions among the goals of the federation offering rational (i.e. secular) education for that of children.
44. Cf. Laser, op. cit., 77.
45. Pinie Katz, Yiddn in Argentine (Buenos Aires, 1946), 129.
46. Cf. Di Presse, 10th anniversary volume (1928), 196.
47. Cf. Laser, op. cit., 79.
48. Cf. Pinie Wald, "Yiddish-Weltliche Shul-Bavegung in Argentine, " Arbeter Ring Shul Almanach (Philadelphia, 1935), 320–29.
49. Cf. Wald, op. cit., 322; Laser, op. cit., 84; Katz, op. cit., 169; Di Presse, 10th anniversary volume, 196.
50. Unzer Shul (Yiddish Journal for parents, edited by the Central Parents Committee of the Workers' Schools) no. 1 (Sept. 1929): 21.
51. Laser, op. cit., 82.
52. I. Adamsky, "Der Birgerleche un Proletarishe Shul Wezn," Unzer Shul no. 1 (Sept. 1929): 5ff.
53. Katz, op. cit., 168f.
54. Ibid., 169; cf. Unzer Shul no. 1 (Sept. 1929): 21.
55. Cf. Wald, op. cit., 324; Katz, op. cit., 169.
56. Cf. for example, CK, Minutes, Oct. 2, 1927; Aug. 19, 1928. Keren Hayesod, or Foundation Fund, was a fund for colonization and immigration in Palestine, envisaged by Zionist leadership. Procor was linked to Gezerd, an organization for Jewish colonization in Soviet Russia.
57. Cf. CK, Minutes, Jan. 19, 1930.
58. Cf. Di Yiddishe Hofnung 2, no. 7 (July 1909): 4f; Wald, op. cit., 324f; Mundo Israelita, (June 14, 1930, p. 1) wrote with respect to a Jewish education program: "The only way of correcting the defect is to create schools where an integral and not captious Jewish education will be imparted. Everything Jewish in spirit—languages, ethics, history, literature, philosophy, and other cultural expressions of our people—should be focussed with a rigorous spirit of impartiality."
59. Cf. Unzer Shul no. 1 (Sept. 1929): 6; Di Yiddishe Hofnung: 2, no. 7 (July 1909) 4f; Leib Jaffe, Bishlichut Am (Jerusalem, 1968), 80.
60. Leib Jaffe, op. cit., 78.
61. Laser, op. cit., 57f.
62. Cf. S. Freilaj, "Der Matvez fun di Hige Yiddisher Shuln," Di Presse, 10th anniversary volume (1928), 25, 27.
63. José Mendelson, "A Pashuter Shumes iber a Vichtige Frage," Yiddishe Zeitung, Nov. 30, 1926, p. 7. We have considered the Ashkenazic population in Buenos Aires to be-between 65,000 and 85,000 souls. About 15,000 were Sephardim.

7. Jewish Cultural Expressions in an Acculturating Community

1. A group of Russified Jews settled in Buenos Aires during the first decade of the twentieth century and developed a center where Russian was spoken while Yiddish was fought. Cf. Pinie Wald, "Yiddishe Sotsialistishe Arbeter-Bavegung in Argentine biz 1910," Argentiner IWO Shriftn, 2(1942): 101–5.

2. Cf., for example, Nissim Teubal, *El Inmigrante, de Alepo a Buenos Aires* (Buenos Aires, 1953), 50–54.
3. Cf., for example, the commentaries in *Dorem Amerike*, Mar. 1926, p. 28; May–June, 1926, pp. 49–51; and *Atideinu* no. 1 (Jan. 1926), p. 1.
4. For some details on the contributions of the above-mentioned rabbis in the field of Responsa cf. chs. 3 and 4. Iekutiel Grinwald (*Hashochet Veashechita Besifrut Harabanut* [New York, 1955], p. 15) mentions that in 1904 Rabbi Haim Asher Anshel Hoffman of Buenos Aires wrote to his father about the way the ritual slaughtering was done in Buenos Aires. Cf. Moshe Grinwald, *Arugat Habosem* (New York, 1927), Iore Deah, Responsa no. 3.
5. Cf. Mordechai Maidanik, "Al Hatenua Haivrit Beargentina," in *Sefer Argentina* (Buenos Aires, 1954), 154f. During the 1890s a large number of letters from Argentina were printed in *Hazefirah*. Among the most assiduous correspondents of this newspaper were Israel Fingerman of Colonia Clara (Entre Ríos), Abraham Isaac Horowitz of Moisesville (Sante Fe), Jacobo Joshua Kahansky of San Antonio (Entre Ríos), and Abraham Rosenfeld of Colonia Mauricio (Buenos Aires). Jacobo Joselevich wrote letters to *Haolam* of Vilna; cf. 4, nos. 21–22 (June 10, 1910): 23f.; no. 35 (Sept. 5, 1910): 13f.; no. 36 (Sept. 22, 1910): 12f.; 5, no. 5 (Feb. 15, 1911): 15f.; no. 6 (Feb. 22, 1911): 14f.; no. 11 (Mar. 29, 1911): 17f.; and no. 20 (June 8, 1911): 13f. From 1897 onwards, *Hayehudi* of London also published letters from Argentina, especially ones written by Abraham Vermont, Jacobo S. Liachovitzky, and Michl Hacohen Sinai.
6. Cf. Maidanik, op. cit., 155; and David Goldman, *Di Juden in Argentine, in der Vergangenheit un in der Gegenwart, in Wort un in Bild* (Buenos Aires, 1914), ch. 17.
7. Ezequiel Rinkevich, "Prakim Letoldot Hachinuch Hayehudi Beargentina," in *Sefer Argentina* (Buenos Aires, 1954), 120f.
8. *Habima Haivrit* 1 no. 1 (April 1921), 1.
9. *Atideinu* no. 1 (Jan. 1926). 1. Cf. *Hechalutz* 1, no. 1 (Dec. 1922): 1, where Gorelik asserts that he left *Habima Haivrit* only to fight with greater vigor from *Hechalutz* for similar goals.
10. *Habima Haivrit* 1, no. 1 (April 1921): 2. Cf. also *Atideinu* no. 1 (Jan. 1926): 1f.
11. *Hechalutz* 1, no. 1 (1922): 10f.; *Habima Haivrit* 1, no. 7 (Dec. 1921): 10f and 5 (1925): 37.
12. Cf. *Habima Haivrit* 2, no. 3, p. 15; no. 4, pp. 1, 16; no. 5, p. 19; no. 6, pp. 13, 16; 3, no. 1, p. 16; no. 2, p. 20; no. 5, p. 15; 4, no. 1, pp. 15f; no. 2, p. 15.
13. Cf. José Horn, "Dos Yiddishe Kultur-Leben in Argentine," in *Yoblbuch Yiddishe Zeitung* (Buenos Aires, 1940), 470. Goldman's book, even if not a fairly balanced appraisal of Argentine Jewry up to his time because of the various omissions and commissions due to pressures from insititutions and Jewish officials of the time, represents a valuable historic document for the history of the period. Alpersohn, though quite partial in his appreciations of the role of the JCA administration in some of the Jewish colonies, brings interesting insights to Jewish life in Argentina. Another contribution to the history of the Jewish community in Argentina published before 1930 is Pinie Katz's, *Tsu der Geshichte fun der Yiddisher Journalistik in Argentine* (Buenos Aires, 1929).
14. Cf. Horn, op. cit., 471.
15. Ibid., 472. Among the most prominent Yiddish writers who visited Argentina—some more than once—are Peretz Hirschbein, Hersh David Nomberg, Jacob Zerubavel, Zalman Rejsen, S. Niger, H. Leivick, and Leib Malach.
16. Pinie Wald, "Yiddish-Weltliche Kultur-Bavegung in Argentine (1895–1920)," *Argentiner IWO Shriftn* 6(1955): 46, 56.
17. Progreso, formed in 1912 by the fusion of Unión Obrera Israelita and what was left of Biblioteca Rusa, had 5,000 volumes in 1916, most of them in Yiddish and some in Russian. Cf. *Juventud* 6, no. 49 (July 1916): 95–99.
18. Cf. *Di Presse*, 10th anniversary volume (1928), 194ff. for the main centers in 1928.
19. *Juventud* 6, no. 49 (July 1916): 49f.
20. Cf. *Avangard*, 2d epoch, 1, no. 1 (Jan. 1916): 27–29; *Juventud* 6, no. 49 (July 1916): 106.

21. *Avangard*, 2d epoch, 1, no. 1 (Jan. 1916): 4–6; *Juventud* 6, no. 49 (July 1916): 80; *Bulletin FIAC* 1, no. 2 (1916): 6.
22. Bulletin FIAC 1, no. 2 (1916): 1.
23. Ibid., 3. Cf. *Di Yiddishe Zeitung*, May 29, 1916.
24. *Juventud* 6, no. 50 (May 1, 1917): 11; *Bulletin FIAC* 2, no. 4 (May 1917): passim.
25. *Bulletin FIAC* 2, no. 4 (May 1917): passim.
26. At the IWO archives in Buenos Aires there are many samples of pamphlets of political propaganda in Yiddish. The large amount of these pamphlets raised the curiosity of *La Razón* (cf. "Qué Dirán?" *La Razón*, Aug. 26, 1930, p. 1). According to the 1936 census 66,572, or 7.6% of the total 870,722 foreign-born persons living in Buenos Aires, were naturalized. Only 3,689, or 5.0%, of the 73,588 foreign-born Jews were naturalized. Cf. *Municipalidad de la Ciudad de Buenos Aires, Cuarto Censo General*, vol. 3, pp. 310f.
27. Cf. Samuel Rollansky, *Dos Yiddishe Gedrukte Wort un Teater in Argentine* (Buenos Aires, 1941), 57f; and Horn, op. cit., 468.
28. Besides the above-mentioned work by Rollansky, the following works are of importance for the study of Yiddish journalism in Argentina: Jacob Botoshansky, "Dos Gedrukte Yiddishe Wort in Argentine," in *Argentine, Fufzig Yor Yiddisher Ishev* (Buenos Aires, 1938); Lázaro Schallman, "Historia del periodismo judío en la Argentina," in *Comunidades judías de Latino América* (Buenos Aires, 1970), 149–73; and Pinie Katz, *Tsu der Geshichte fun der Yiddisher Journalistik in Argentine* (Buenos Aires, 1929).
29. Cf. Rollansky, op. cit., 62.
30. The Constitution of the Zion Society, for example, was printed in New York in 1897. A copy of it is found in the IWO archives in Buenos Aires. Cf. Rollansky, op. cit., 21.
31. Horn, op. cit., 468.
32. Rollansky, op. cit., 24.
33. Cf. Katz, op. cit., 47–52; Michl Hacohen Sinai, "Di Erste Hige Yiddishe Shreiber," in *Yorbuch*, 5714 (Buenos Aires, 1953), 133ff. *Di Folks Shtime* was the only regular periodical in the Jewish community at the time. This may have been an important reason for its endurance. Fear of Vermont's blackmailing may also have gathered support among the more established Jews in Buenos Aires.
34. The *Viderkol*, edited by Michl Hacohen Sinai, first appeared in March 1898. Sinai had to engrave the text of the notes by hand in stone plates due to the lack of a Yiddish printing press in Buenos Aires. Only three issues came out. *Der Yiddisher Fonograf (The Jewish Phonograph)* was edited by Fabián Halevy, a man with a deep culture in Jewish classics. It lasted for six months. Both these weeklies had a Zionist orientation. In 1904 Jacobo S. Liachovitzky started publishing *Der Zionist* in Yiddish and *El Sionista* in Spanish. Liachovitzky was one of the main pillars in Yiddish journalism in Buenos Aires during the pioneering period (cf. Katz, op. cit., 109–22). During the upper year 1899 two magazines appeared having the main goal to lampoon the editor of *Di Folks Shtime*, Vermont. *Der Pauk (The Drum)* came out thirty-one times until it closed in 1901. *Di Blum (The Flower)*, on the other hand, only appeared sixteen times.
35. J. S. Liachovitzky was the first director of *Der Tog*, though he left it after a short time. He was also the first director of *Di Yiddishe Zeitung*, though for only eight months.
36. *Di Presse* was directed by Pinie Katz. At *Di Yiddishe Zeitung*, after Liachovitzky's departure, Leon Maas took control until 1922. Then José Mendelson directed it until 1929, when Matías Stoliar became its director.
37. See ch. 5.
38. *Der Yiddisher Poier* was the organ of Procor, the organization associated with Gezerd, campaigning for a Jewish settlement in Birobidzhan. A *Bulletin* of Procor was published from 1927.
39. The main official organs of the various Labor Zionist groups were the following. *Di Neie Zeit* of the Poale Zionist first appeared in 1918. It remained with the rightist Poale Zionists after the division. *Dos Arbeter Wort*, of the leftist Poale Zionist, was first published in 1922. *Unzer Gedank*, of Zeire Zion Hitachdut, saw the light of day in Sept. 1924.

40. *Peinimer un Peinimlech* (1923–35), *Zeglen* (1924), *Oifgang* (1927), and *Der Karikatur* (1924).
41. *Der Yiddisher Soicher*, directed by Jacobo Liachovitzky, was published in 1910; *Di Yiddishe Handels-Woch* was first printed in 1924.
42. Cf. Rollansky, op. cit., 230f.
43. JC, Oct. 25, 1901, p. 27. According to this letter this was the third performance of the kind, the last being *The Witch*, also by Goldfaden.
44. Hassan is here referring to the Congregación Israelita and the Congregación Israelita Latina.
45. Cf. JC, Oct. 17, 1902, p. 13.
46. *Juventud* 6, no. 49 (July 1916): 66.
47. Pinie Wald ("Yiddish-Weltliche Kultur-Bavegung in Argentine [1895–1920]," *Argentiner IWO Shriftn* 6 [1955]: 50f.) asserts that workers went only sporadically to the Yiddish theater and that when they went, they got the least-expensive seats: "The real supporters of Yiddish theater were the *chevreleit* and the *nekeives* [the dealers and their women]."
48. As a consequence of the scandal promoted by the public at the presentation of Peretz Hirschbein's *Miriam* on Oct. 5, 1908 a group, *Yugent*, was formed to battle against the Jewish white slave dealers and remove them from the Yiddish theater atmosphere. Cf. *Lebn un Freiheit* no. 2 (Oct. 1908): 14–17, 21f.; *Der Avangard* 1, no. 5 (Dec. 1908): 29–32. In 1926 a case with similar characteristics arose when Leon Malach's play *Ibergus (Transfusion)* was rejected by the manager of a Yiddish theater because the theme—prostitution in Río de Janeiro—would not be of the liking of the "audience." *Di Presse* attacked the manager and his theater for compromising with the dealers. *Di Yiddishe Zeitung* defended the right of the manager to select the plays. The argument between both dailies continued in a fiery manner for a few months, *Di Presse* arguing that its colleague sided with the dealers, obviously far from the truth. Commenting on the public at the theaters, Rollansky (op. cit., 203), wrote that "the fate of the Yiddish theater in Buenos Aires was placed in the auditorium, with the public, more than on the stage, among the actors."
49. Cf. Rollansky, op. cit., 195f. Among the most famous guest actors and actresses were the following: Sigmund Feinman, Fanny Epstein, Maurice Moscovitch, Samuel Goldenburg, Boris Tomashefsky, Regina Zucker-Zimbalist, and Menashe Skulnick.
50. Hundreds of manuscripts of plays in Yiddish lie in oblivion at the IWO archives in Buenos Aires. Pinie Wald wrote in 1935 that "to perform a play of an Argentinian Jewish writer is even today an event in the Argentinian Yiddish theater world" (cf. Rollansky, op. cit., 218). Some of the few exceptions were Aaron Brodsky's *Kinder fun Folk* (1910); Mordechai Alpersohn's drama *Galut*, performed in 1926; and S. Glasserman's *Zisie Goi*, performed in 1931. Cf. also *Juventud* 6, no. 49 (July 1916): 51f.
51. *Juventud* 6, no. 49 (July 1916): 68; Pinie Katz, *Yiddn in Argentine* (Buenos Aires, 1946), 56, 71f.
52. Rollansky, op. cit., 214ff.
53. *Juventud* 6, no. 49 (July 1916): 68. Goldenberg directed the group at the Olimpo theater, while Guttentag headed the one at the Battaglia.
54. Cf. Rollansky, op. cit., 100, 211.
55. *Nodl Arbeter* no. 1 (Aug. 1922), 2. Cf. the issue with the U.S. actor David Baratz also in Katz, op cit., 163ff.
56. Some of these were Sociedad Jacob Gordin, Artistishe Winkele, La Musa, Asociación Drámatica Cultural "Freiheit," La Joven Argentina (Yung Argentine).
57. Cf. Leon Malach, "Lemazav Ha-Teiatron Ha-Yehudi Be-Markezei Ha-golah," *Bama* (Tel Aviv), 5–6 (Dec. 1934). 66ff.
58. *Mundo Israelita*, Aug. 16, 1924, p. 1.
59. Cf. *Juventud* 6, 49 (July 1916): 100f.
60. Cf. Manuel Bronstein "Orígenes de la Sociedad Hebraica Argentina," *Davar* no. 119 (Oct.–Dec. 1968): 63ff. A few years before, in 1906, a group of young men, noticing the helplessness of certain groups of Russian immigrants destined for the Jewish agricultural colonies because of their ignorance of the Spanish language, decided

to teach it to them at the precincts of the Talmud Torah, in Buenos Aires, together with some elementary concepts about the country (cf. Gregorio Verbitsky, *Rivera, afán de medio siglo* [Buenos Aires, 1955], p. 95; Nicolás Rapoport, *Desde lejos hasta ayer* [Buenos Aires, 1957], pp. 82f.). The Jewish youth in the colonies perhaps was more involved in Jewish life than that of the capital, due to their school years experience in a more Jewish society. A comparison in attitudes and activities within the Jewish community could be of value for later periods.

61. Samuel E. Bermann, president of CJIA, in a speech on July 15, 1911 (cf. *Juventud* 1, no. 2 (Aug. 1, 1911): 3.

62. Zionist leaders were frequently invited to speak at CJIA. Jacobo Joselevich, the leader of the Federación Sionista Argentina, lectured there, and wrote for their magazine (cf. *Juventud* 5, no. 48 (Apr. 1916): 42 and 3, no. 23 (May 1913): 15). Baer Epstein, the first overseas emissary to come to Argentina to promote Zionism, spoke at CJIA too. Cf. *Juventud* 6, no. 50 (May 1917): 8. See also Bronstein, op. cit., 67, 80. There was no ambiguity, however, with respect to religion.

63. Bronstein, op. cit., 71.

64. Cf., for example, German Berlitzky, "El problema judío," *Juventud* 2, no. 12 (June 1912): 9f., where he defends those Jews inclined to assimilation; Simón Scheimberg, "Asimilación es vida," *Juventud* 2, no. 14 (Aug.1912): 10; Ohermes, "Bris Milah," *Juventud* 2, no. 15 (Sept. 1912): 8f., where circumcision is attacked as being antinatural. On the other hand, Miguel Frumkin ("La asimilación es un ideal?" *Juventud* 2, no. 13 [July 1912]: 10ff. and "Del cosmopolitismo y nacionalismo," *Juventud* 2, no. 15 [Sept. 1912]: 6ff.) wrote against assimilation and for the preservation of differences.

65. Cf. Bronstein, op. cit., 75.

66. *Juventud* 3, no. 23 (May 1913): 17.

67. Ibid., 16f.

68. Cf. Bronstein, op. cit., 77. The name of this center, as of its journal, clearly reflects the influence of José E. Rodó (1872–1917), the Uruguayan author who with his short book *Ariel*, influenced a whole generation of Latin American youth.

69. *Juventud* 3, no. 26 (Aug. 1913): 27f.; cf. also the articles by Gregorio Fingermann and Manuel Bronstein on this new orientation in *Juventud* 3, no. 24 (June 1913): 2–7.

70. *Juventud* 4, no. 41 (Feb. 1915): 43 and 6, no. 49 (July 1916): 102f.

71. *Asociación Hebraica, Minutes*, Feb. 5, 1923.

72. Ibid., June 2, 1923.

73. SHA, *Minutes*, May 26, 1926. The name for SHA was given by Alberto Gerchunoff, the most reknown Jewish writer in Spanish in Argentina.

74. Cf. SHA, *Memoria y Balance* (1927/28) (Buenos Aires, 1928), 14ff. Donations for the library came from, among others, the chief rabbi of France, Julien Weill, whose brother Simon was head of JCA in Buenos Aires and member of SHA; the Hochschule fur die Wissenschaft des Judentums in Berlin; the Alliance Israélite Universelle; the JCA; and the Jewish Community of Frankfurt am Mein (cf. *Mundo Israelita*, Oct. 15, 1927, p. 2). The "Jewish" character of SHA did not remain invariable. During 1929 its attitude with respect to the campaign in favor of the Jewish hungry in Bessarabia was qualified as "shameful" by *Mundo Israelita*. This weekly also attacked SHA for not adopting a positive attitude to the special campaign to help the "*ishuv*" in Palestine after the 1929 riots. Furthermore, many conferences during the previous year were assimilationist, some even "apologetic of Christianity" (cf. *Mundo Israelita*, Oct. 12, 1929, p. 1).

75. Cf. *Mundo Israelita*, Jan. 26, 1924, p. 2; and Feb. 2, 1924, pp. 2f. Isaac Chaufan, president of the Círculo Social Israelita, proposed, in view of the many Ashkenazic members of his society, that it and SHA should have closer ties.

76. Other cultural centers in Buenos Aires during the latter half of the 1920s were Ateneo Juventud Hebraica Sefaradí, Círculo Juventud Israelita, Agrupación Juvenil Socialista Poale Sión, Círculo Cultural Ruso-Israelita, Asociación Israelita de Jóvenes, and Macabi.

77. For more on *Israel* see below. From Jan. 2 until July 13, 1920 *Israel* appeared from Monday though Friday (nos. 75–206).
78. Many Jews voted for the Socialist party in elections. Some were among the leaders of this party. Enrique Dickmann, many times congressman from the socialists, also directed their official organ, *La Vanguardia*. His brother Adolfo was also a socialist congressman. The researcher of Jewish participation in the general leftist movements in Buenos Aires before 1930 is presented with obvious obstacles.
79. *Israel* (Mundo Hebraico Argentino) had correspondents in 11 provinces. They were immigrants of Moroccan origin.
80. Arabic-speaking Jews put out, in 1917, the monthly *Al Gala*, of which only one number was available, no. 13–14 (Dec. 28, 1917).
81. *El Sionista* was directed by J. S. Liachovitzky. Only 47 numbers of this fortnightly saw the light of day.
82. Especially at the end of 1926 and during 1929–30 *Semanario Hebreo* published news about Sephardim in Buenos Aires, coinciding with visits of important Sephardic emissaries from Zionist centers in Jerusalem.
83. Cf. *Asociación Hebraica*, Minutes, Nov. 27, 1924. In SHA, *Minutes*, May 29, 1928, there is a long debate about the position of *Mundo Israelita* vis-à-vis SHA. The periodical was written in the premises of the society, and had views similar to those of SHA leadership.
84. Cf. the editorial in *Mundo Israelita*, June 22, 1923, p. 1.
85. The main translators were Resnick himself and León Dujovne.
86. Among the Argentinian personalities were Alfredo L. Palacios, Carlos Ibarguren, Ricardo Rojas, Leopoldo Lugones, Enrique Dickmann, *interalia*. The Jewish contributors included Kibrick himself, Jacobo Joselevich, Pinie Katz, Salomón Resnick, Enrique Feinmann, and Marcos Regalsky.
87. Cf. *Vida Nuestra* 2, nos. 7–9 (Jan.–Mar. 1919).
88. Cf. *Israel* 1, no. 2 (Oct. 5, 1911): 5f., 13. All Jewish societies raised their voices against the Club Israelita and against Liachovitzky personally. It was finally closed by the police in 1912. Cf. *Juventud* 1, no. 5 (Nov. 1911): 3f., 11; 1, no. 6 (Dec. 1911): 7, 13; 2, no. 9 (Mar. 1912): 13; 2, no. 10 (Apr. 1912): 1f.; 2, no. 11 (May 1912): 1f.; CIRA, *Minutes*, July 3, 1912; *Federación Israelita Argentina*, Minutes, Sept. 6, 1909, and Feb. 28, 1910; *Chevra Keduscha*, Minutes, Sept. 26, 1911, and Mar. 3, 1912; *Ezrah*, Minutes, Nov. 5, 1908, and Jan. 27, 1909; *Di Yiddishe Hofnung* 2, nos. 11–12 (Nov.–Dec. 1909): 1f. (Spanish); 3, no. 3 (Apr. 1, 1910): 2f. (Spanish). Cf. also IWO Archives, Gebit 36 and Liachovitsky file.
89. Cf. *El Israelita Argentino*, directed by Alejandro Gerstein and Enrique Schuster 1, no. 3 (Aug. 1, 1913): 1–4; 1, no. 2 (July 15, 1913): 1–6.
90. Directed by David Danemann (cf. *Juventud* 6, no. 49 [July 1916]: 62).
91. For the reform movement and its aftermath at the University of Córdoba, and others in Argentina, especially the University of Buenos Aires, cf. Alberto Ciria and Horacio Sanguinetti, *Los Reformistas* (Buenos Aires, 1968), esp. 13–66.
92. Among others we find Roberto Payró, Rubén Darío, and Miguel de Unamuno. Cf. Manuel Kantor, *Alberto Gerchunoff* (Buenos Aires, 1969), 29ff. Gerchunoff belonged to the group of Argentine writers who during the first decades of the century standardized the main exponents of national belles-lettres, and who met periodically in certain *cafés* in Buenos Aires. They included, among others, Payró, Ricardo Rojas, Leopoldo Lugones, Mario Bravo, and Luis Grandmontaigne.
93. Alberto Gerchunoff, *Los gauchos judíos* (Buenos Aires, 1957), cf. 46f. and "El episodio de Miryam."
94. Cf. ibid., 32f., 86f.
95. The Balfour Declaration (1917) and Semana Trágica (1919), the 1930s reaction in Argentina, and especially World War II made Gerchunoff return to Jewish topics and to active work for the Jewish people, mainly for Zionist causes.
96. Cf. Isaac Goldberg, "Jewish Writers in South America," *The Menorah Journal* 11, no. 5 (Oct. 1925): 475f.

97. Louis Nesbit, "The Jewish Contribution to Argentine Literature," *Hispania* 33, no. 4 (Nov. 1950): 319.
98. "Los Judíos," in *El pino y la palmera* (Buenos Aires, 1952), 13.
99. Ibid., 19.
100. Kantor, op. cit., 38.
101. Alberto Gerchunoff, *El cristianismo pre-cristiano* (Buenos Aires, 1924), 31.
102. *Criterio*, June 13, 1929, p. 213. Cf. *Mundo Israelita*, June 15, 1929, p. 2 and, for the editor's reaction, ibid., 1.

8. Spirit of Solidarity: The Fight against Poverty and Evil

1. *Standard and River Plate News* (Buenos Aires), July 28, 1882, announced that "a subscription is now being raised in this city for the Jews now so barbarously persecuted in Russia. Lists will be sent to all houses. . . . When others require their aid, the Jews, especially in England, are always amongst the first to put their hands in their pockets."
2. Cf. billboard of Comité de Socorros para las Víctimas Israelitas de Rusia, placed at all Jewish institutions, dated Nov. 1905, CIRA Archives; and *La Prensa*, Nov. 11–27, 1905 and at intervals in Dec. for information about events organized by this committee, including public acts, movies, functions, and a Hanuka gathering organized by the Federación Sionista Argentina. *La Nación*, Nov. 17, 1905 brings a list of main donations: CIRA gave 1,000 pesos and Chevra Keduscha 2,000; several Jewish business concerns gave sums of 500, 200, and 100 pesos each; non-Jews gave sums up to 500 pesos (Ernesto Tornquist y Cia.); and there were various donations of 200 pesos each. By Nov. 22, 10,637 pesos had been raised. The Moroccan Jews in Buenos Aires collected 1,796.45 pesos for this purpose (cf. CIL, *Minutes*, Dec. a, 1905).
3. Also in 1907 a committee for relief among Jews in Morocco was formed in Buenos Aires (cf. *La Prensa*, Oct. 12, 1907, p. 10 and the billboard of Comité Pro-Víctimas de Marruecos; a los Israelitas, May 1912, CIRA Archives).
4. CIRA, *Memoria*, 1918.
5. Among the promoters of the CC, besides the Zionists, were members of CIRA (including Rabbi Halphon), of Juventud (M. Bronstein), Ezrah (Alejandro Zabotinsky), etc. Cf. billboard at CIRA Archives.
6. CC remitted to JDC the following sums:

between Feb. 24, 1915 and Nov. 30, 1917	172,476.27 pesos
between Dec. 1, 1917 and Nov. 30, 1918	207,524.98 pesos
between Dec. 1, 1918 and Nov. 30, 1919	150,100.00 pesos
Total	530,101.25 pesos

The biggest effort was made in 1918, when the machinery was more effective. When the war ended, many branches closed, but when the pogroms in Poland hit the newspapers, they were reopened (cf. *Balance General del* CC, 1917–18, pp. 2f, 13 and 1918–19, 3f).
7. Billboard in Yiddish and Spanish of the Comité Israelita de Protesta contra los Pogroms de Polonia (Jewish Committee of Protest Against the Pogroms in Poland), IWO Archives.
8. *Balance del* CC, 1918–19, p. 3.
9. In 1915 the People's Relief Committee joined JDC, which was formed in 1914 to distribute the funds collected by the American Jewish Relief Committee and the Central Relief Committee. Cf., for the passage quoted, the letter of Marcos Regalsky (CC) to Baruch Zuckerman (People's Relief Committee), Mar. 22, 1921, American Jewish Historical Society Archives (AJHSA).
10. CC to People's Relief Committee, Dec. 16, 1919, AJHSA.

11. General manager of People's Relief Committee to José Koriman, secretary of CC, Mar. 23, 1920, AJHSA.
12. *Yiddishe Folks-Hilf far di Milhome un Pogrom Gelitene* [Minutes of the first Relief Conference in Argentina], May 1920, pp. 6–12. See also Ezra Mendelsohn, *The Jews of East Central Europe between the World Wars* (Bloomington, 1983), 219–31.
13. Among the resolutions were the following: "The first Jewish convention for relief work in Argentina greets the People's Relief Committee of North America in its battle for national-democratic, and constructive principles in their relief work. . . . As an organization we join in the People's Relief Committee. . . . In case constructive help is given to private hands we recommend that the People's Relief Committee step out from JDC. Cf. *Yiddishe Folks-Hilf far di Milhome un Pogrom Gelitene*, 6, 10, 17, 18.
14. Cf. the letters from CC to People's Relief Committee dated Nov. 14 and Dec. 17, 1920 and Aug. 1, 1921 and the cable of Jan. 13, 1921, AJHSA.
15. The following are the results of the municipal censuses of Buenos Aires. While the number of Jews are to be raised, the proportions for foreigners are probably accurate.

Year of Census	Total Jews	Foreigners	% of Total
1904	6,065	4,099	67.5
1909	16,589	13,294	80.0
1936	120,195	73,588	61.2

Due to the small number of Jewish immigrants who entered Argentina during 1931–36, we can safely assert that in 1930 foreign-born Jews were more than 67% of the total Jewish population in Buenos Aires.
16. Cf. *Sociedad Israelita de Beneficencia, Estatutos* (Buenos Aires, 1872), esp. Art. 13–17.
17. UOI, *Estatutos* (Buenos Aires, 1903). Art. 26 says, ". . . to maintain cordial relations with all workers' societies in the country." Art. 80 states "The name UOI can never be changed."
18. *Lebn un Freiheit* 1, no. 2 (Sept. 1908): 20f.; *Juventud* 6, no., 49 (July 1916): 89–91.
19. *Yiddishe Zeitung*, Mar. 24, 1930, p. 4.
20. *Ezrah, Estatutos* (Buenos Aires, 1901), Art. 3.
21. Ibid., Art. 17.
22. Such a situation prompted the resignation of the president of Ezrah, Simon Ostwald, in 1904. Cf. *Memoria de la Sociedad Israelita de Beneficencia Ezrah en el día de la Inauguración del Hospital Israelita, 29 de Mayo de 1921* (Buenos Aires, 1921), p. 16. In 1905 Ezrah again decided to use parts of the Hospital funds "due to the enormous flow of [needy] people," hoping that a circular letter to the members explaining the situation would reimburse this special fund. Cf. *Ezrah, Minutes*, Mar. 2, 1905.
23. *Ezrah, Minutes*, Aug. 15, 1907; Dec. 17, 1907.
24. FIA, *Minutes*, Nov. 2, 1909; Nov. 15, 1909.
25. Cf. ch. 2. Most Russians in Argentina were Jewish, and Jews were thus called Rusos.
26. This club was presided over by Jacobo S. Liachowitzky. Cf. FIA, *Minutes*, Feb. 28,1910; Apr. 10, 1910; *Ezrah, Minutes*, July 2, 1910.
27. The Spanish, Italian, British, and German residents in Argentina built their respective hospitals.
28. FIA, *Minutes*, Feb. 28, 1910.
29. *Ezrah, Minutes*, July 2, 1910.
30. *Ezrah, Memoria y Balance* for the respective years.
31. Cf. "Régimen de trabajo y remuneraciones del personal médico del Hospital Israelita," *Archivos del Hospital Israelita* (*Revista de la Asociación de Médicos del Hospital Israelita*) 6 (1949):126.

32. Enrique Cohen, "Para el sexto aniversario de los Asilos de Ancianos y Huérfanos," *Boletín, Asilo Israelita Argentino* no. 4 (June 18, 1922), Spanish section, pp. 7ff.
33. The Sociedad de Socorros de Damas Israelitas had the purpose of "assisting the needy Jewish parturients and newly-born, furnishing, according to the needs, midwives, physicians, medicine, clothes, food, and attention" (Cf. *Estatutos*, approved Sept. 17, 1908, Art. 1. See CIRA, *Minutes*, June 1, July 31, and Aug. 31, 1916; CIRA, *Memoria y Balance*, 1916–1923; CIRA, *Minutes*, May 16, 1927 and Nov. 27, 1928).
34. *Di Presse*, 10th anniversary volume (1928) 196.
35. In 1928, 32 boys were learning the printing profession at the printing press of the Asilo Israelita Argentino. Other professions were also taught, and some pursued university studies. Girls were trained as dressmakers, milliners, nurses, and bookkeepers. Jobs were found by the asylum authorities.
36. *Liga Israelita Argentina Contra la Tuberculosis Memoria y Balance*, 1929–1930, p. 8. This organization is hereafter referred to as Liga.
37. Cf. Jaime Favelukes, *Mortalidad entre los israelitas de la ciudad de Buenos Aires*, 1917–1928 (Buenos Aires, 1938), esp. pp. 38f. Favelukes did not cover all Jewish deaths in Buenos Aires, but his numbers are accurate for about 85–90% of Jewish deaths.
38. *Liga . . . Memoria y Balance*, 1925/26, pp. 7f; 1928/29, pp. 9f.; and *Liga . . . Boletín informativo*, 40th anniversary, Jan. 1956, pp. 5–9.
39. The number of prescriptions filled rose from 971 in 1925 to 7,898 in 1930. (cf. *Liga . . . Memoria y Balance*, 1925/26–1930/31).
40. Cf. IWO Archives, Buenos Aires, Gebit 50; *Schomer Israel Memoria*, read at the General Assembly on July 30, 1905. There were then 225 members of the institution. During Apr. 24–July 15, 1905, 26,035 meals were served, averaging 313 daily.
41. Theodore Bar-Shalom, *Hairgun Soprotimis veKlitatam shel mehagrim Yehudim beArgentina beshanim 1922–1930*, M.A. thesis, Hebrew University, Jerusalem, 1971, pp. 99f.
42. Cf. *Di Presse*, 10th anniversary volume (1928), 194. José Liebermann, *Los judíos en la Argentina* (Buenos Aires, 1966), 236. The budget for the period Mar. 1931–July 1932 reached 37,132.45 pesos (cf. CPI, *Memoria y Balance*, 1931/32).
43. Cf. the annual reports of all these institutions, where contributions from every city, town, or colony are detailed.
44. Jacobo Karmona, of Turkish origin, was a member of the board of the Chevra Keduscha Ashkenasi in 1924. He proposed several times a rapprochement between Sephardim and Ashkenazim but to no avail. On another occasion he insisted that the board members abide by Art. 3 of the society's constitution, which confirms that the official language is Spanish. He was answered that "everything possible will be done . . . but because the majority of the members can make themselves understood better in "jargón" (Yiddish) than in Spanish . . . , when they will not be able to explain themselves in Spanish, he will get a translation" (CK, *Minutes*, Aug. 3, 1924; cf. also ibid., July 13 and 27, 1924).
45. Pinie Wald, "Yiddishe Sotsialistishe Arbeter Bavegung in Argentine biz 1910," *Argentiner IWO Shriftn* 2(1942): 109f.; *Algemeiner Yiddishe Arbeter Varband in Argentine, Bulletin* 2, no. 11 (Aug. 1913): 4–13; *Juventud* 6, no. 49 (July 1916): 95; *Avangard* 3, no. 3 (Mar. 1910): 54ff.
46. The Sociedad Obrera Israelita de Beneficencia [Yiddisher Arbeiter Hilfs Verein], founded Nov. 1, 1914, had its constitution approved at a general assembly on Oct. 17, 1915. Its goals were to assist the Jewish workers and to raise their cultural level. Cf. *Estatutos* (1915), Art. 2, 3, IWO Archives, Buenos Aires. The Yiddisher Arbeiter Verband fur Gegenzeitiger Hilf, founded in 1920, was active until the end of the decade (cf. its *Bulletin*, May 1926, pp. 9f., IWO Archives, Buenos Aires).
47. Both original groups had their own burial societies, called Hesed Shel Emeth (HSE, with variants in spelling), and synagogues. The basic and most important achievement of their unification was the union of these burial societies, for the synagogues continued existing afterwards. HSE of Centro, founded in 1916, met at the Es Ajaim synagogue in 25 de Mayo 696; HSE of Villa Crespo was part of Kahal Kadosh and Talmud Torah La Hermandad Sefaradí, founded in 1914 (cf. *Hermandad Sefaradí*,

Minutes, Feb. 9 and Mar. 2, 13, and 16, 1919; and HSE [*Centro*], *Minutes*, Mar. 9, 1919).

48. CIS, *Memoria*, Oct. 17, 1920.
49. Cf. the *Estatutos* of Bene Emeth (Damascene burial society, founded on Oct. 17, 1913) of 1922, Art. 67; and *Estatutos* of HSE Sefaradit (Aleppine burial society, founded Aug. 5, 1923) of 1925, Art. 3 and *Reglamento General* of same date, Articles 3–6. Among Moroccan Jews, besides Gemilut Hassadim, their burial society, there were other aid institutions such as Hessed Laalafim, Kissé Eliyahu, Hesed Veemet, etc. Among Aleppine there were Ahaba Vehajaba and Ahavat Sedek.
50. Cf. Walter Paul Zenner, *Syrian Jewish Identification in Israel*, Ph.D. dissertation, Columbia University, 1965, p. 17.
51. In 1905 the Moroccan Jews were the only group with a cemetery of their own. However, they would not admit other Jews in it. Their burial society decided, in order to exclude the Ladino-speaking Jews, that "all members who are not descendant from South European [i.e., from Spain and especially Gibraltar, to which many Moroccan Jews had migrated] or North African parents shall enjoy all rights from the Reglamento except that of burial" (cf. *Hesed Veemet*, *Minutes*, July 31, 1905).
52. On *Landsmanschaften* see L. Zitnitsky, "Landsmanschaften in Argentine," *Argentiner IWO Shriftn* 3(1945): 155–61; Pinie Katz, *Yiddn in Argentina* (Buenos Aires, 1946): 142ff.; *Poilishe Yiddn in Dorem Amerika* (Buenos Aires, 1941); and *Galitziener Yiddn, Yoblbuch*, 1925–65 (Buenos Aires, 1966).
53. *Hesed Shel Emet*, lit. "loving-kindness of truth," an act for which the performer receives no recognition from the beneficiary. Cf., for the activities of this society, CK, *Minutes*, Mar. 6 and Oct. 16, 1927, etc.
54. On the proliferation of institutions and its negaative consequence for the normal development of the Jewish community, see the editorials in *Mundo Israelita*, esp. Dec. 10, 1927, p. 1 and Nov. 6, 1926, p. 1. A strong criticism of the welfare institutions within the Jewish community, especially concerning their work against indigence, was made in 1930 by Dr. Jaime Favelukes, who was active especially in the Hospital Israelita and the Liga Israelita Argentina contra la Tuberculosis. It first appeared in installments in *Mundo Israelita*. Cf. J. Favelukes, "La Asistencia Social en Nuestra Colectividad," *Mundo Israelita*, Oct. 4, 1930, p. 6; Oct. 11, 1930, p. 5; Oct. 18, 1930, p. 4; Oct. 25, 1930, p. 4; Nov. 1, 1930, p. 3; Nov. 8, 1930, p. 4.

9. The Jewish Community Fights White Slavery

1. The Law of Civil Marriage, established in Argentina in 1888, sanctions as legal a marriage performed by the authorities of the civil registry. Only *after* the civil ceremony could a religious one take place.
2. *Report of the Jewish Association for the Protection of Girls and Women for the year* 1930 (hereafter *Report* JAPGW, 1930) (London, 1931), 32–36. See also the "Confidential Report" sent by Mrs. Aslan, vice-president in charge of Ezras Noschim in Buenos Aires to Samuel Cohen, general secretary of JAPGW in London, April 15, 1930, Ezras Noschim Archival Material (hereafter ENAM).
3. Cf. Juan José Sebreli, *Buenos Aires, vida cotidiana y alienación* (Buenos Aires, 1965), 126f.
4. Edward Bristow, *Prostitution and Prejudice: The Jewish Fight against White Slavery* (Oxford, 1982) describes the international dimensions of Jewish involvement in white slavery.
5. Belisario Montero, *Estudios sociales* (Brussels, 1905), 131.
6. Cf. Enrique Feinman, "La mujer esclava: Historia social de la moralidad," *Atlántida* 11, no. 32 (1913): 161–92.
7. Ibid., 180.
8. League of Nations, *Report of the Special Body of Experts in Traffic in Women and Children* (Geneva, 1927), pt. 2, p. 13.
9. James Scobie, *Buenos Aires: From Plaza to Suburb, 1870–1910* (New York, 1974), 210.

10. Ibid., 216.
11. Marion Kaplan, *The Jewish Feminist Movement in Germany: The Campaigns of the Jüdischer Frauenbund 1904–1938* (Westport, Conn., 1979), 104 and Sebreli, op. cit., 82.
12. Scobie, op cit., 48.
13. Ibid., 229.
14. John O. P. Bland, *Men, Manners, and Morals in South America* (London, 1920), 75.
15. These were the general characteristics of most cases involving Argentina presented in the annual *Report JAPGW* from 1885 on, as well as cases mentioned in the Jewish press in Buenos Aires and the hundreds of cases dealt with in documents at ENAM.
16. The text of the circular, signed also by rabbis Zadoc Kahn of France, Moritz Güdemann of Vienna, Israel Hildesheimer of Berlin, M. Hirsch of Hamburg, M. Horovitz of Frankfurt, and M. Ehrenreich of Rome, is found in the *Report of the Jewish International Conference on the Suppression of the Traffic in Girls and Women* (London, 1910), 156f.
17. Kaplan, op. cit., 108.
18. *Buenos Ayres Herald*, Nov. 4, 1879, p. 3; *La Prensa*, Nov. 4, 1879, p. 2. Earlier in September the *Buenos Ayres Herald* published a note about Jews involved in prostitution in Rio and made the remark that a similar traffic existed in Buenos Aires. See *Buenos Ayres Herald*, Sept. 18, 1879, p. 3.
19. *Buenos Ayres Herald*, Nov. 13, 1879, p. 1.
20. *La Paz*, Apr. 6, 1880, p. 2.
21. *El Diario*, Jan. 13, 1882, p. 2; JC, Aug. 5, 1887, p. 7.
22. Marcos Alpersohn, *Kolonie Mauricio: Dreisig-lehrige JCA Kolonizatzie in Argentine* (Yiddish) (Buenos Aires, 1922), 18–20.
23. JC, Nov. 4, 1892, p. 11.
24. Ibid., Jan. 16, 1893, p. 8.
25. *Report JAPGW*, 1913, p. 39.
26. JC, Feb. 27, 1903, "Supplement," p. vi.
27. *Report JAPGW*, 1901, pp. 23–26.
28. Cf. *Report of the Jewish International Conference on the Suppression of Traffic in Girls and Women* (London, 1910), 33f.
29. *Report JAPGW*, 1923–24, p. 25.
30. Montevideo was linked to Buenos Aires by several overnight trips daily. On board these vessels a trafficker could disguise his "overseas" character and look more like a neighbor visiting his neighbor. The police did not bother much. The Jewish committee against the traffic watched these ships too.
31. League of Nations, op. cit., 16f.
32. Albert Londres, *El camino a Buenos Aires* (Buenos Aires, n.d. [Ediciones Aga-Taura]), 115.
33. Ibid., 66. *Franchuta* is slang for "French."
34. Sebreli, op. cit., 122f; Londres, op cit., 161ff. One of the most famous gang leaders was Ruggierito. Cf. Norberto Folino, *Barceló, Ruggierito y el populismo oligárquico* (Buenos Aires, 1966), esp. 75–94.
35. Quoted by Kaplan, op cit., 109 from a report edited in Germany in 1903.
36. Julio L Alsogaray, *Trilogía de la trata de blancas, rufianes, policía, municipalidad* (Buenos Aires, 1933), 126.
37. Londres, op. cit., 115.
38. Alsogaray, op. cit., 247; *Mundo Israelita*, May 24, 1930, pp. 1f.
39. Especially during the years 1898–1902. For example, in *Hayehudi* of June 2, 1898, p. 3, Vermont wrote that on board a ship crossing the Atlantic he found "a white slave dealer going to Europe to get women to sell here [Buenos Aires]."
40. Alexander Zederbaum, *Arba Maamarim* [Four Articles] (Petersburg, 1893), 9.
41. *Der Yid*, 1909. Reprinted in *Alle Werk fun Sholem Aleichem*, (New York, 1942), vol. 5, sec. 5, pp. 69–88. A translation is Sholem Aleichem, "The Man from Buenos Aires," in his *Tevye's Daughters* (New York, 1949), 128–40. This edition translates the lines quoted in our text as follows: "'What do I deal in?' (He burst out laughing.) 'Not in prayer books, my friend, not in prayer books.'"

42. Among the hundreds of examples in the *Minutes* of the Chevra Keduscha, the following (though corresponding to a somewhat later period), are particularly interesting. On Oct. 28, 1923 a delegation of the Tailors' Association asked for reconsideration of the resolution adopted by the board of the Chevra Keduscha expelling one of its members. The president of the Tailors' Association mentioned that "he assumes the responsibility for the morality of the expelled, and moreover declares that this gentleman has promised to leave in five or six months the few clients of fragile reputation that he now has." The board decided to reincorporate the member. Another case of interest took place on Sept. 7, 1925, when the Chevra Keduscha wrote to two members imposing a fine on them because they had been the witnesses in the death of the daughter of a person "not pleasing to this society." They were warned that the next time they did something of the kind they would be expelled. Cf. CK, *Copiador de Cartas* 4, 191ff. Thus one sees that the Chevra Keduscha, as well as other major Jewish societies, did not tolerate even indirect contact with the traffickers.
43. CK, *Minutes*, May 4, 1898.
44. Nonmembers were also buried by the Chevra Keduscha, though the tariff was of course higher.
45. Jacobo S. Liachovitzky, *Zamlbuch* (Yiddish) (Buenos Aires, 1938), 89ff.
46. A parable of Deut. 23:19, "You shall not bring the hire of a harlot, or the wages of a dog, into the house of the Lord your God, in payment for any vow; for both of these are an abomination to the Lord your God."
47. A Hebrew bon mot meaning, "Of the dead say nothing but good," whose origin is in the titles of three consecutive weekly portions of the Torah in the Book of Leviticus.
48. Liachovitzky was a founder of the first Zionist Society in Buenos Aires in 1897. He later founded Liga Dr. Herzl in 1899, which was recognized by the World Zionist Organization as representative of Argentine Zionists. In 1909, after a hard-fought battle, this recognition passed to Tiferet Israel, Liachovitzky was discredited. His political activities were also denounced in 1909 by the main Jewish institutions in Buenos Aires. He founded many Jewish periodicals both in Yiddish and in Spanish, including the daily Di *Yiddishe Zeitung* in 1914.
49. Cf. *Congregación Israelita*, Minutes, Feb. 13, 1897; Aug. and Sept. 1893; and CK, *Minutes*, Feb. 15, 1897.
50. Michel Hacohen Sinai, "Harav Reuben Hacohen Sinai," *Argentiner* IWO *Shriftn*, 3(1945): 180
51. JC, Oct. 25, 1901, p. 27.
52. Cf. *Lebn un Freiheit* 2(Oct. 1908): 15–17, 21f.; *Der Avangard* 1, no. 5 (Dec. 1908): 29–32; and *Yugent Society Minutes*, (Yiddish), Oct. 25, 1908–Apr. 20, 1909, IWO Archives, Buenos Aires.
53. *Israel* 1, no. 2 (Oct. 5, 1911): 5.
54. *Der Avangard* 3, no. 4 (Apr. 1910): 11ff.
55. *El Censor*, Aug. 16 and 18, 1905; *Congregación Israelita*, Minutes, Aug. 27, 1905.
56. CK, *Minutes*, Oct. 5, 1909.
57. *Report* JAPGW, 1901, p. 40.
58. *Hayehudi*, Sept. 22, 1898, pp. 3f; *Report* JAPGW, 1900, p. 25
59. *Report* JAPGW, 1901, pp. 14, 40f.
60. As becomes evident from many documents at ENAM.
61. *Report* JAPGW, 1906, p. 26; ibid., 1912, p. 44; ibid., 1913, p. 41.
62. Various letters at ENAM for the years 1914–15. Halphon worked in close contact with several other societies, notably the National Vigilance Association, of the British colony in Buenos Aires. Cf. Cohen to Halphon, May 27, 1914, ENAM.
63. Cf. the respective *Report* JAPGW.
64. *Report* JAPGW, 1914, p. 26.
65. Feinman, "La mujer esclava," 185f.
66. Manuel Galvez, *Amigos y maestros de mi juventud* (Buenos Aires, 1961), 158–65.
67. *Report* JAPGW, 1914, p. 26.

68. Cohen to Halphon, Feb. 3, 1914, ENAM *Copiador de Cartas*.
69. Cohen to Halphon, Jan. 10, 1925, ENAM.
70. Halphon to Cohen, July 1, 1926, ENAM.
71. Leon Malach, "Two Generations in the Argentine," *Menorah Journal* 13(1927): 414f.
72. Halphon to Cohen, Dec. 30, 1926, ENAM.
73. Malach, op. cit., 415, and the Jewish press of the time, especially *Di Yiddishe Zeitung*, *Di Presse*, *Mundo Israelita*, and *Semanario Israelita*.
74. Halphon to Cohen, Aug. 31, 1931, ENAM; *Report* JAPGW, 1930, p. 31.
75. Alsogaray, op. cit., passim.
76. Halphon to Cohen, Aug. 31, 1927 and *Ezras Noschim*, Minutes, June 29, 1930, ENAM.
77. The minutes of that meeting are transcribed in several documents at ENAM.
78. *Report* JAPGW, 1930, pp. 32–36. Also documentation at ENAM.
79. Cf. the general Argentine press and Alsogaray, op. cit., 199.
80. Cf., for example, the comments in *New York Times*, Sept. 20, 1934, p. 10.
81. *Ezras Noschim, Informe General* for the years 1934 and following.
82. Halphon to Cohen, Dec. 20, 1928, ENAM.
83. Halphon to Cohen, Dec. 12, 1928, pp. 1–2, ENAM.
84. Cohen to Halphon, Jan. 18, 1929, ENAM.

10. Kehilla in the Making: Centralization and Rivalries

1. *El Israelita Argentino* 1 No. 3 (Aug. 1, 1913), 2.
2. The sittings were held on Jan. 31 and Feb. 2 and 21, 1909. Cf. FIA *Minutes*, Aug. 5, 1909.
3. Cf. *Estatutos* of FIA, CIRA Archives (Art. 4) and FIA *Minutes*, Aug. 5, 1909.
4. The General Assembly of the Chevra Keduscha voted to enter the FIA unanimously. Cf. CK, *Minutes*, July 12, 1909.
5. Cf. ch. 8.
6. Cf. text at CIRA Archives.
7. Ibid.
8. FIA, *Minutes*, Aug. 5, 1909.
9. Cf. FIA, *Minutes* Aug. 9, 1909.
10. The heading of FIA's minutebook reads "It is the unanimous desire of this Board that the future Jewish generations learn their original history and pursue with eagerness the work in favor of the Union, Culture, and Aggrandizement of the large Jewish family in this great country of liberties. Buenos Aires—Aug. 5, 1909—Ab 18, 5669." Cf. also FIA, *Minutes*, Sept. 20, 1909, when it was decided to write extensive minutes in order to leave "written evidence to posterity . . . of how . . . the FIA, and therefore *Argentine Judaism* [italics mine] has been formed and developed."
11. Cf. FIA, *Minutes*, Aug. 9, 1909.
12. Cf. FIA, *Minutes*, Sept. 6, 13, and 20, 1909; Oct. 25, 1909.
13. Cf. *El Israelita Argentino* 1 no. 3 (Aug. 1, 1913); 2.
14. Cf. FIA, *Minutes*, Oct. 11, 1909; CK, *Minutes*, July 12, 1909; CIRA, *Minutes*, July 25, 1909.
15. FIA, *Minutes*, Aug. 9, 1909.
16. Cf. *Juventud* 3, no. 33 (Mar. 1914); 5 ff.
17. Cf. *Juventud* 3, no. 36 (June 1914); 5 ff.
18. When the Argentine president Roque Sáenz Peña died, the Chevra Keduscha asked the Federación Israelita to express the Jewish community's sorrow (cf. CK, *Minutes*, Aug. 9, 1914).
19. Cf. *El Israelita Argentino* 1, no. 12 (Dec. 15, 1913); 1ff.
20. Cf. *Bericht fun'm Yiddishen Kongress in Argentina* (Buenos Aires, 1916), 29–42. See also *Juventud* 6, no. 49 (July 1916); 77–88.
21. Cf. ch. 5.
22. CK, *Minutes*, May 19, 1920.

23. Ibid.; see also Mordechai Regalsky, "Der Durchfal wos hot sich Farendikt mit a Groisn Nitsochn (Tsu der Geschichte fun der 'Alianz' Bavegung)," in *Yorbuch fun der Yiddisher Kehila in Buenos Aires* (5715) (Buenos Aires, 1954), 21–35.

24. CK, *Minutes*, June 13, 1920; Oct. 2 and 21, 1920; Dec. 5 and 19, 1920.

25. Cf. CPAIA, *Minutes*, Dec. 21, 1921; Jan. 12, 1922.

26. JOA, *Minutes*, Dec. 17, 1922.

27. JOA, *Minutes*, Feb. 5, 1923.

28. CPAIA, *Minutes*, June 25 and Nov. 22, 1922.

29. Cf. Miguel Zabotinsky's speech when taking over the presidency of JOA. JOA, *Minutes*, Dec. 17, 1922.

30. JOA, *Minutes*, Mar. 8, 1923.

31. JOA, *Minutes*, Apr. 26 and May 10 and 17, 1923; see also *Mundo Israelita*, June 15, 1923, pp. 5f.

32. *Mundo Israelita*, July 27, 1923, p. 5.

33. Cf. JOA, *Minutes*, July 16 and 23, 1923.

34. Cf. CPAIA, *Minutes*, Feb. 28, 1924; JOA, *Minutes*, June 3, 1924.

35. Wolf Nijensohn was active at the Federación Sionista Argentina; Mordechai Regalsky at Poale Zion (Right); David Lomonosov and Hilel Malimovka were leaders of Zeire Zion Hitachdut.

36. Cf. Regalsky, op. cit., 27.

37. Cf. the critique of Jewish leadership in Buenos Aires made by H. Sajak, *Di Yiddishe Zeitung*, Mar. 26, 1929, p. 7.

38. Among others, the interviewed included the Chevra Keduscha's past presidents Moisés Edelman, Miguel Zabotinsky, Moisés Yivoff, and Naúm Enquin. Cf. *Yiddishe Zeitung*, issues corresponding to the months of Jan. and Feb. 1929.

39. Cf. *Mundo Israelita*, Aug. 4, 1923, p. 2; Nov. 24, 1923, p. 1; Dec. 20, 1924, p. 1; Mar. 14, 1925, p. 1; Dec. 18, 1926, p. 2; June 28, 1930, p. 1; and Dec. 6, 1930, p. 1, among others.

40. The project consisting of 68 articles is included in CK, *Minutes*, Nov. 11, 1931. Cf. Jaime Favelukes, "La Organización de Nuestra Colectividad," *Mundo Israelita*, Oct. 24, 1931, p. 4; Oct. 31, 1931, p. 5; and Nov. 7, 1931, p. 4.

41. Cf. Moisés Goldman, "Der Antisemitism in Argentine," in *Yoblbuch Yiddishe Zeitung* (Buenos Aires, 1940), 581–600; Julio Adin, "Nationalism and Neo-Nazism in Argentina," *In the Dispersion* 5–6 (Spring 1966), 139–60; Juan C. de Mendoza, *La Argentina y la swástica* (Buenos Aires, 1941).

42. This is true of both the Arabic-speaking communities, the Aleppine and Damascene. Among Ladino-speaking communities the burial society is part of the community structure. Among the Jews of Moroccan origin, the syngagogue (CIL) is separate from the burial society, though their membership is practically the same (cf. Behor Issaev, "Los Sefaraditas de Buenos Aires," in *Yorbuch* 5715 [Buenos Aires, 1954], Spanish section, 13–18).

Bibliography

Archives

Yiddisher Wisenschaftlecher Institut (IWO) Archives, Buenos Aires.
Congregación Israelita de la República Argentina (CIRA) Archives, Buenos Aires.
Central Zionist Archives, Jerusalem.
Chevra Keduscha Ashchkenasi Archives, Buenos Aires.
Sephardic Community Committee (Vaad Ha'Eda HaSepharadit) Archives, Jerusalem.

Organizations and Institutions
Ashkenazim

Congregación Israelita de la República Argentina
    Minutes (1873–1930)
    Memoria y Balance (1874–1930)
    Copiador de Cartas
    Registro de Matrimonios, Nacimientos y Defunciones de la CIRA
Chevra Keduscha Aschkenasi
    Preliminary Minutes (1893–1894)
    Minutes (1894–1930)
    Memoria y Balance (1894–1930)
    Copiador de Cartas
    "Get'n" (Divorce) files (1924–30), by Rabbi David Maler
Sociedad Israelita de Beneficencia "Ezrah"
    Minutes (1900–1930)
    Memoria y Balance (1900–1930)
Sociedad de Protección a los Inmigrantes Israelitas (Soprotimis)
    Minutes (1922–30)
Ezras Noschim, Buenos Aires
    Archival Material
    Informe General (1931)
Liga Israelita Argentina contra la Tuberculosis
    Memoria y Balance (1925–30)

Talmud Torah Harischono
    Minutes (1900–27)
Talud Torah Dr. Herzl
    Minutes (1908–27)
Sociedad Hebraica Argentina
    Asociación Hebraica *Minutes* (1923–26)
    SHA *Minutes* (1926–30)
    Memoria y Balance (1927–30)
Federación Israelita Argentina
    Minutes (1908–10)
Alianza Israelita Argentina
    Comité Pro-AIA *Minutes* (1921–24)
    Junta Organizadora de la AIA *Minutes* (1922–27)
    AIA Board *Minutes* (1924–26)

Sephardim

Moroccan Group
    Congregación Israelita Latina *Minutes* (1899–1930)
    Hozer Dalim *Minutes* (1916–25)
    Hebra Hesed Veemet *Minutes* (1905–30)
    Talmud Torah *Minutes* (1922–30)
Ladino-Speaking Group
    Kahal Kadosh y Talmud Torah La Hermandad Sefaradí *Minutes* (1914–19)
    Hesed Shel Emeth (Centro) *Minutes* (1916–19)
    Comunidad Israelita Sefaradí *Minutes* (1919–30)
Aleppine Group
    Yesod Hadath *Minutes* (1925–30)
    Yesod Hadath General Assemblies *Minutes* (1920–30)
    Hesed Shel Emeth Sefaradit *Minutes* (1928–30)
Damascene Group
    Asociación Unión Israelita Sefaradí Or Torah *Minutes* (1920–30)
    Or Torah *Memoria y Balance* (1924–30)
    Asociación Israelita Sefaradí Bene Emeth *Primer Libro de Socios*
    Bene Emeth *Libro de Defunciones*

Provinces

Asociación Israelita de Beneficencia (Rosario) *Minutes* (1920–30)
Etz Ajaim (Rosario) *Minutes* (1920–30)
Schebet Ajim (Rosario) *Minutes* (1924–30)

Official Documents

República Argentina. *Tercer Censo Nacional, Levantado el 1° de Junio de 1914.* Buenos Aires, 1916–19.
———. *Censo General de Población, Edificación Comercio, e Industrias de la Ciudad de Buenos Aires, Capital Federal de la República Argentina.* Setiembre 18, 1904. Buenos Aires. 1906.
———. *Censo General de Población, Edificación, Comerico, e Industrias de la Ciudad de Buenos Aires, Capital Federal de la República Argentina,* Octubre 16–24, 1909. Buenos Aires, 1910.
———. *Municipalidad de la Ciudad de Buenos Aires, Cuarto Censo General,* Octubre 22, 1936. Buenos Aires, 1939.
———. *Registro Nacional.* Buenos Aires, Departamento del Interior, 1881.
———. *Congreso Nacional. Diario de Sesiones de la Cámara de Diputados* 1919.
———. *Municipalidad de la Ciudad de Buenos Aires. Versiones Taquigráficas del Honorable Concejo Deliberante.* 1918–30.
———. *Dirección General de Estadística de la Nación.* 1928–36.

———. *Informe de la Comisión Nacional de Inmigración.* 1881.
———. *Informe de la Comisión Nacional de Inmigración.* 1896
———. *Informes de los Consejeros Legales del Poder Ejecutivo.* 10 vols. Buenos Aires, 1890–1902.

Major Periodicals

European Jewish Press
    Hamelitz. St. Petersburg, Odessa. Hebrew.
    Haolam. Berlin, Vilna, Odessa, London. Hebrew.
    Hayehudi. London. Hebrew.
    Hazefirah. Warsaw. Hebrew.
    Jewish Chronicle. London.
General Argentine Press (Buenos Aires)
    Buenos Ayres Herald
    Caras y Caretas
    El Censor
    Criterio
    La Crítica
    El Diario
    La Nación
    El Nacional
    La Paz
    La Prensa
    La Razón
    Sarmiento
    Standard and River Plate News
    L'Union Française
    La Vanguardia
Argentine Jewish Press (Buenos Aires)
    Al Galah. Arabic (1917).
    Atideinu. Hebrew (1926).
    Der Avangard. Yiddish. Bundist (1908–20).
    Broit un Ehre. Yiddish. Poale Zionist (1910).
    Dorem Amerika. Yiddish. Literary (1926).
    Habima Haivrit. Hebrew (1921–30, irregular).
    Hechalutz. Hebrew (1922).
    Israel. Spanish. Club Israelita (1911).
    Israel. Spanish. Sephardic (1917–).
    El Israelita Argentino. Spanish (1913).
    Juventud. Spanish (1911–17).
    Lebn un Freiheit. Yiddish. Anarchist (1908).
    Mundo Israelita. Spanish (1923–).
    Di Neie Zeit. Yiddish. Poale Zionist (1918–30).
    Nodl Arbeter. Yiddish. Needle Workers (1922).
    Di Presse. Yiddish. Leftist Daily (1918–).
    Roite Hilf. Yiddish. Journal of the Jewish subcommittee of the International Red Relief (MOPR) and Polish subcommittee in the Argentine section (1928).
    Der Roiter Shtern. Yiddish. Jewish section of the Communist party in Argentina (1923–26).
    Semanario Hebreo. Spanish. Zionist (1923–30).
    Shtraln. Yiddish. Literary (1913).
    El Sionista. Spanish. Zionist (1904–06).
    Unzer Gedank. Yiddish. Zeire Zion Hitachdut (1924–30).
    Unzer Shul. Yiddish. Central Parents' Committee of the Workers' Schools (1929).
    Vida Nuestra. Spanish (1917–23).
    Di Yiddishe Handels-Woch. Yiddish. Commerce (1924–28).

Di Yiddishe Hofnung. Yiddish. Zionist (1908–17).
Di Yiddishe Welt. Zionist (1917–30).
Di Yiddishe Zeitung. Yiddish. Daily representing the views of the Ashkenazic establishment (1914–).
Der Yiddisher Poier. Yiddish. Procor (1928–33).
Der Yiddisher Soicher. Yiddish. Commerce (1910).

Special Reports

Almanach fun Yiddishn Ambulantn Farain (1915–30). Buenos Aires, 1930.
Ascamoth Nesiei Harabanut Harashit Le'eretz Israel, Batei-Din-Zedek Shel Edot Ashkenazim, Spharadim, veHalabim Deir Hakodesh Yerushalaim, B.D.Z. veRabanei Aram Zobah; (lekaiem ulehazek ascamat haRav Shaul Setton, z.l., le'esor kabalat gerim beArgentina hanidpeset besifro "Dibber Shaul" [Agreements of the Presidents of the Chief Rabbinate in Eretz Israel, Courts of Justice of the Ashkenazic, Sephardic, and Aleppine communities in the Holy City of Jerusalem, and the Court of Justice and Rabbinate in Aleppo; to confirm and to strengthen the regulation of Rabbi Shaul Setton, of blessed memory, to forbid conversions in Argentina, published in his book Dibber Shaul]. Buenos Aires, 1938.
Asilo Israelita Argentino. Boletín no. 4. Buenos Aires, June 18, 1922.
Association des Anciens Elèves de l'AIU. Bulletin Annuel Tangiers. No. 8.
Baricht fun der Procor Delegatzie [Report of the Procor Delegation]. Buenos Aires, n.d.
Bericht fun'm Yiddishen Kongress in Argentina [Report of the Argentine Jewish Congress]. Buenos Aires, 1916.
Boletín del Comité Central de Educación Israelita en la República Argentina. Buenos Aires. 1916–17, 1917–18.
Bulletin de l'Alliance Israélite Universelle. Paris, 1876–.
Federación Israelita Argentina de Cultura. Bulletin (Yiddish). 1916.
Four Years of Jewish Immigration. Report of activities of the Association for Emigration HIAS, JCA, Emigdirect. Paris, 1931.
Jewish Association for the Protection of Girls and Women. Annual Report. London, 1896–1931.
Jewish Colonization Association. Rapport de l'Administration Centrale au Conseil d'Administration. Paris, 1898–1931.
Jewish Labor Yearbook and Almanach. New York, 1927.
Liga Israelita Argentina contra la Tuberculosis. Boletín Informativo (40 Aniversario, 1916–56). Buenos Aires, 1956.
Memoria de la Sociedad Israelita de Beneficencia Ezrah en el día de la Inauguración del Hospital Israelita, 29 de Mayo de 1921. Buenos Aires, 1921.
Report of the Executive of the Zionist Organization Submitted to the Zionist Congress (12th to 16th Congresses), London, 1921–1929.
Report of the Jewish International Conference on the Suppression of the Traffic in Girls and Women. London, April 5–7, 1910.
Report of the World Union of Sephardic Jews. May 1924–Sept. 1926.
Yiddishe Folks Hilf far di Milhome un Pogrom Gelitene. Minutes of the first Relief Convention in Argentina, May 16–18, 1920. Buenos Aires, 1920.
Yiddisher Immigranten Shuts-Farain un Tsentral Komite fun Folks-Hilf (1922–1927) (Soprotimis y Comité Central de Ayuda Popular). Buenos Aires, 1928.
Yiddisher Proletarisher Hilfs Aktsie fur Soviet Russland in Argentina [Jewish Proletarian Relief for Soviet Russia in Argentina]. Memorial. Buenos Aires. 1921–23.

Printed Books and Articles

Abad de Santillán, Diego. La FORA, ideología y trayectoria del movimiento obrero revolucionario en la Argentina. 2d revised edition. Buenos Aires, 1971.
Adin, Julio. "Nationalism and Neo-Nazism in Argentina." In the Dispersion 5–6 (Spring 1966): 139–60.

Bibliography

Adúriz, S. J., Joaquín. "Religión." In Jorge A. Paita, ed., *Argentina, 1930–1960*. Buenos Aires, 1961: 423–30.

Alpersohn, Marcos (Mordechai). *Kolonie Mauricio: Dreisig-lehrige JCA Kolonizatzie in Argentina* |Mauricio Colony: Thirty Years of Jewish Colonization in Argentina|. Buenos Aires, 1922.

Alsina, Juan A. *La inmigración en el primer siglo de la independencia*. Buenos Aires, 1910.

Alsogaray, Julio L. *Trilogía de la trata de blancas*. Buenos Aires, 1933.

Antequeda, Manuel P. *Breve exposición sobre las escuelas ruso-alemanas e israelitas; escuela nacional (Ley Lainez) de la provincia de Entre Ríos*. Buenos Aires, 1909.

Argentina: The Way Thither, the Land, Commerce, Agriculture, and Industry. (Yiddish). Warsaw, 1891.

Aubin, Eugéne. *Le Maroc d'Aujourd'hui*. 6th edition, Paris, 1910.

Avni, Haim. *Argentina, the Promised Land: Baron de Hirsch's Colonization Project in the Argentine Republic* (Hebrew). Jerusalem, 1973.

Ayarragaray, Lucas. *Cuestiones y problemas argentinos contemporáneos*. Buenos Aires, 1930.

Bab, Arturo. "Die berufliche und soziale Schichtung der Juden in Argentinien." *Der Morgen* 4 (April 1928): 84–92.

Banco Comercial de Buenos Aires, 1917–1950. Buenos Aires, 1950.

Banco Comercial Israelita de Rosario. *50 Años Creciendo con la Ciudad*. Rosario, 1971.

Baron, Salo W. *The Russian Jew under Tsars and Soviets*. New York, 1964.

Bar Shalom, Theodore. *Halrgun Soprotimis veKlitatam shel mehagrim Yehudim beArgentina beshanim 1922–1930* |Soprotimis and the Absorption of Jewish Immigrants in Argentina during 1922–1930|. M.A. thesis. Hebrew University, Jerusalem, 1971.

Bauer, J. *L'Ecole Rabbinique de France (1830–1930)*. Paris, 1931.

Bauer, Yehuda. *My Brother's Keeper. A History of the American Jewish Joint Distribution Committee, 1929–1939*. Philadelphia, 1974.

Bavio, Ernesto A. "Las escuelas extranjeras en Entre Ríos," *El Monitor de la Educación Común* 27–28 (1908–9): 597–604, 3–44.

Bein, Alex. *Theodore Herzl*. Philadelphia, 1941.

Benario, M. "Di Geschichtliche Antwiklung fun Yiddishen Handel un Industrie in Buenos Aires" |The Historical Development of Jewish Commerce and Industry in Buenos Aires|. In Hirsch Triwaks, ed. *Yoblbuch Yiddishe Zeitung*, 267–90. Buenos Aires, 1940.

Benchimol, Isaac. "La Langue Espagnole au Maroc." *Revue des Ecoles de l'Alliance Israélite* (Paris) no. 2(July–September 1901): 126–33.

Ben-Sasson, H. H. "The Volunteer Movement among American Jews." In *The Jewish Legion, Fiftieth Anniversary of the Jewish Batallions, 1917–1967*. Jerusalem, 1967.

Benzaquén, Benjamín. *La colectividad israelita sefaradí de Buenos Aires no debe permitir que se exploten más sus sentimientos religiosos*. Buenos Aires, 1929.

Bialet-Massé, Juan. *El Estado de las Clases Obreras Argentinas a Comienzos del Siglo*. Córdoba, 1968.

Bland, John O. P. *Men, Manners, and Morals in South America*. London, 1920.

Blumenfeld, Israel. *Historia de la Comunidad Israelita de Tucumán*. Tucumán, 1971.

Botoshansky, Jacob. "Dos Gedrukte Yiddishe Wort in Argentine." |The Printed Jewish Word in Argentina|. In *Argentine, Fufzig Yor Yiddisher Ishev*, 64–86. Buenos Aires, 1938.

Brenan, Gerald. *The Spanish Labyrinth*. Cambridge, 1967.

Bristow, Edward. *Prostitution and Prejudice: The Jewish Fight against White Slavery*. Oxford, 1982.

Bronstein, Manuel. "La inmigración israelita." *Boletín Mensual del Museo Social Argentino* 5, nos. 59–60 (November–December 1916): 550–67.

———. "Orígenes de la Sociedad Hebraica Argentina." *Davar* No. 119 (October—December 1968): 61–100.

Byrnes, Robert F. *Antisemitism in Modern France*. New Brunswick, 1950.

Campobassi, Carlos Alberto. *La enseñanza privada en la América Latina y en la Argentina*. Buenos Aires, 1965.

Capdevila, Arturo. "Primera Presidencia de Yrigoyen." In *Historia Argentina Contemporánea*, vol. 1, 247–69. Buenos Aires, 1963.

Carr, Saunders, A. M. *World Population*. Oxford, 1936.

Carulla, Juan E. *Al filo del medio siglo*. Paraná, 1945.
Chouraqui, André. *Cent ans d'histoire. L'Alliance Israélite Universelle et la renaissance juive contemporaine* (1860–1960). Paris, 1965.
Ciria, Alberto, and Horacio Sanguinetti. *Los reformistas*. Buenos Aires, 1968.
Cociovich |Katsovich|, Noe. *Moisesviler Breishis* |The Genesis of Moisesville|. Buenos Aires, 1947.
Cornblit, Oscar E., Ezequiel Gallo, Jr., and Alfredo A. O'Connell, "La Generación del 80 y su Proyecto: Antecedentes y Consecuencias." In *Argentina, Sociedad de Masas*, edited by Torcuato Di Tella, Gino Germani, and Jorge Graciarena. Buenos Aires, 1965.
Cúneo, Dardo, Julio Mafud, Amalia Sánchez Sívori, and Lázaro Schallman. *Inmigración y nacionalidad*. Buenos Aires, 1967.
Davis, Moshe. "Mixed Marriages in Western Jewry: Historical Background to the Jewish Response." *Jewish Journal of Sociology*, 10, no. 2 (December 1968): 177–220.
Dickmann, Enrique. *Población e inmigración*. Buenos Aires, 1946.
———. *Recuerdos de un militante socialista*. Buenos Aires, 1949.
Dorfman, Adolfo. *Historia de la industria argentina*. Buenos Aires, 1970.
Dreier, Katherine S. *Five Months in the Argentine; From a Woman's Point of View, 1918 to 1919*. New York, 1920.
Drumont, Edouard. *La France Juive*. 2d edition. Paris, 1886.
Efrón, Jedidia. "La obra escolar en las colonias judías." In *50 Años de Colonización en la Argentina*. 239–62. Buenos Aires, 1939.
Favelukes, Jaime. *Mortalidad entre los israelitas de la cuidad de Buenos Aires, 1917–1928*. Buenos Aires, 1938.
Fichter, Joseph H., S. J. "The Marginal Catholic: An Institutional Approach." *Social Forces* 32, no. 2 (December 1953): 167–73.
Foerster, Robert. *The Italian Migration of Our Times*. Cambridge, Mass., 1924.
Folino, Norberto. *Barceló, Ruggierito y el populismo obligárquico*. Buenos Aires, 1966.
Galanté, Abraham. *Histoire des Juifs de Rhodes, Chio, Cos, etc*. Istanbul, 1935.
———. *Histoire des Juifs d'Anatolie: Les Juifs d'Izmir*. Vol. 1, Istanbul, 1937.
———. *Histoire des Juifs d'Istambul*. Vol. 2. Istanbul, 1942.
Galitziener Yiddn, Yoblbuch 1925–1965 |Galician Jews, Jubilee Book, 1925–1965|. Buenos Aires, 1966.
Gálvez, Manuel. *El diario de Gabriel Quiroga*. Buenos Aires, 1910.
———. *Amigos y maestros de mi juventud*. Buenos Aires, 1961.
Garfunkel, Boris. *Narro mi vida*. Buenos Aires, 1960.
Gartner, Lloyd P. *The Jewish Immigrant in England, 1870–1914*. Detroit, 1960.
Gerchunoff, Alberto. *Los gauchos judíos*. Buenos Aires, 1957 |first published in 1910|.
———. *El cristianismo pre-cristiano*. Buenos Aires, 1924.
———. *Entre Ríos, mi país*. Buenos Aires, 1950.
———. *El pino y la palmera*. Buenos Aires, 1952.
Germani, Gino. *Política y sociedad en una época de transición*. Buenos Aires, 1968
Gesang, Natan |Nahman|. "Los judíos." *Revista Argentina de Ciencias Políticas, Derecho Administrativo, Economía Política, Sociología, Historia y Educación* 13(1916): 225–47.
———. "A Kapitel Argentiner Zionistishe Politik" |A Chapter of Argentine Zionist Politics|. In Hirsch Triwaks, ed. *Yoblbuch Yiddishe Zeitung*, 609–20. Buenos Aires, 1940.
Glazer, Nathan, and Daniel Patrick Moynihan. *Beyond the Melting Pot*. Cambridge, Mass., 1963.
Godio, Julio. *La Semana Trágica de Enero de 1919*. Buenos Aires, 1972.
Goldberg, Isaac. "Jewish Writers in South America." *Menorah Journal* 11, no. 5 (October 1925): 473–85.
Goldman, David. *Di Juden in Argentine, in der Vergangenheit un in der Gegenwart, in Wort un in Bild* |The Jews in Argentina, in the Past and in the Present, in Word and in Picture| (Yiddish). Buenos Aires, 1914.
Goldman, Moisés. "Der Antisemitism in Argentine." |Antisemitism in Argentina|. In Hirsch Triwaks, ed. *Yoblbuch Yiddishe Zeitung*, 581–600. Buenos Aires, 1940.
Gorelik, I. L. *Be'eretz Nod* |In the Land of Nod|. Buenos Aires, 1943.

Bibliography

Gori, Gastón. *Inmigración y colonización en la Argentina*. Buenos Aires, 1964.

Grinwald, Iekutiel. *Hashochet Veaschechita Besifrut Harabanut* |Slaughter and Slaughtering in Rabbinic Literature|. New York, 1955.

Grinwald, Moshe. *Arugat Habosem* |Garden of Perfume|. New York, 1927.

Hacohen Sinai, Michl. "Harav Reuben Hacohen Sinai" |Rabbi Reuben Hacohen Sinai|. *Argentiner IWO Shriftn* 3(1945): 171–82.

———. "Di Erste Hige Yiddishe Shreiber" |The First Local Jewish Writers|. In *Yorbuch* 5714, 133–41. Buenos Aires, 1953.

Halpern, Ben. *The Idea of the Jewish State*. Cambridge, Mass., 1961.

Halphon, Samuel. "Enquête sur la population israélite en Argentine," JCA, *Rapport de l'Administration Centrale au Conseil d'Administration pour l'Année* 1909, 251–308. Paris, 1910.

Heller, Celia S. *On the Edge of Destruction: Jews of Poland between the Two World Wars*. New York, 1977.

Herrera, Emilio. "Los prejuicios raciales en la Argentina del 80: Julián Martel y su novela 'La Bolsa'." *Indice* 1(April 1968). 102–31.

Hitti, Phillip K. *The Syrians in America*. New York, 1924.

Hofstadter, Richard. *The Age of Reform*. New York, 1955.

Horn, José. "Dos Yiddishe Kultur-Leben in Argentine." |Jewish Cultural Life in Argentina|. In *Yoblbuch Yiddishe Zeitung*, 459–78. Buenos Aires, 1940.

Ibarguren, Carlos. *La historia que he vivido*. Buenos Aires, 1955.

Iedvabski, Jacob, and Isidore Hellman. *Di Reise nach Argentina* |The Trip to Argentina|. Warsaw, 1891.

Issaev, Behor. "Los sefaraditas de Buenos Aires." In *Yorbuch* 5715, 575–82. Buenos Aires, 1954.

Issaev, Behor. "La colectividad sefardí bonaerense en el quinquenio 1958–1962." In Isaac Janasowicz, ed. *Pinkas fun der Kehila*, 668–71. Buenos Aires, 1963.

Jaffe, Leib. *Tekufot* |Periods|. Tel Aviv, 1948.

———. *Bishlichut Am* |On a Mission for the People|. Jerusalem, 1968.

Kantor, Manuel. *Alberto Gerchunoff*. Buenos Aires, 1969.

Kaplan, Marion. *The Jewish Feminist Movement in Germany: The Campaigns of the Jüdischer Frauenbund 1904–1938*. Westport, Conn., 1979.

Katz, Pinie. *Tsu der Geschichte fun der Yiddisher Journalistik in Argentine* |On the History of Jewish Journalism in Argentina|. Buenos Aires, 1929.

———. *Yiddn in Argentina* |Jews in Argentina|. Buenos Aires, 1946.

Kogan, S. "Alexander Zederbaums Ongrif Oif der Yiddisher Kolonizatsie in Argentine" |Alexander Zederbaum's assault on the Jewish Colonization in Argentina|. *Argentiner IWO Shriftn* 5(1952): 81–108.

Koifman, M. "El sionismo y los problemas societarios judíos en Sud América." In *La Segunda Convención Sionista Sudamericana*, 167–75. Buenos Aires, 1950.

Kraviez, Jacobo. "Desde el antiguo carpintero hasta el moderno fabricante." *El Industrial Maderero* 5, no. 44 (July 1944): 47–54.

Kreinin, Miron. *Di Einwanderungs Meglichkeitn kein Dorem Amerika un di dortige Yiddishe Ishuvim* |The Immigration Possibilities to South America and the Local Jewish Communities|. Berlin, 1928.

Kreuth, Wilhelm. *Ams de la Plata Staaten* (Hebrew). Translated by Eleazar Finkel. Warsaw, 1891.

Laniado, David Zion. *Lakedoshim Asher BeAra'z* |To the Saints in Aleppo| (Hebrew). Jerusalem, 1952.

Laniado, Isaac. *Vaizara Izhak* |And Isaac Sowed| (Hebrew). Aleppo, 1928.

Laredo, Isaac. *Memorias de un viejo tangerino*. Madrid, 1935.

Liachovitzky, Jacobo Simon. *Zamlbuch* |In Memoriam|. Buenos Aires, 1938.

Liebermann, José. *Tierra soñada*. Buenos Aires, 1959.

———. *Los judíos en la Argentina*. Buenos Aires, 1966.

Lipset, Seymour Martin. "The Study of Jewish Communities in a Comparative Context." *Jewish Journal of Sociology* 5(December 1963): 157–66.

Londres, Albert. *El camino a Buenos Aires*. Editorial AGA-TAURA. Buenos Aires, n.d.

Bibliography

Maidanik, Mordechai. "Al Hatenua Haivrit BeArgentina" |On the Hebrew Movement in Argentina|. In Mordechai Maidanik, ed. *Sefer Argentina*, 154–62. Buenos Aires, 1954.

Malach, Leon. "Lemazav HaTeiatron Hayehudi Bemerkezei Hagolah" |State of the Jewish Theater in the Centers in the Diaspora|. *Bama* (Tel Aviv) nos. 5–6(December 1934): 66–68.

Marín, Rufino. *Lo que piensa América del problema judío*. Buenos Aires, 1944.

Marotta, Sebastián. *El movimiento sindical argentino, su génesis y desarrollo*. 3 vols. Buenos Aires, 1960–70.

Martínez Estrada, Ezequiel. *Radiografía de la pampa*. 5th edition. Buenos Aires, 1965.

Meiern, Laser, Mendl. *Dos Yiddishe Shulvezn in Argentine* |The Jewish Schools in Argentina|. Buenos Aires, 1948.

————. "Di Sorkin epoche" |The Sorkin epoch|. In Isaac Janasowicz, ed. *Pinkas fun der Kehila*, 131–50. Buenos Aires, 1969.

Mendelsohn, Ezra. *The Jews of East Central Europe between the World Wars*. Bloomington, 1983.

Mendoza, Juan C. de. *La Argentina y la swástica*. Buenos Aires, 1941.

Mirelman, Victor. *The Early History of the Jewish Community of Buenos Aires, 1860–1892*. Masters thesis. Columbia University, 1969.

————. "A Note on Jewish Settlement in Argentina (1880–1892)." *Jewish Social Studies* 33, no. 1 (January 1971): 3–12.

————. "Jewish Life in Buenos Aires before the East European Immigration (1860–1890)." *American Jewish Historical Quarterly* 67, no. 3 (March 1978): 195–207.

————. "The Jewish Community versus Crime; The Case of White Slavery in Buenos Aires." *Jewish Social Studies* 46, no. 2 (Spring 1984): 145–68.

————. "Sephardic Immigration to Argentina Prior to the Nazi Period". In Judith Laikin Elkin and Gilbert W. Merckx, eds. *The Jewish Presence in Latin America*. Boston, 1987: 13–32.

Miró, José María. *La Bolsa*. Various editions.

Nesbit, Louis. "The Jewish Contribution to Argentine Literature." *Hispania* 33, no. 4 (November 1950): 313–20.

"Nómina de los inmigrantes llegados en el vapor 'Weser' el 14 de Agosto de 1889." In *50 Años de Colonización Judía en la Argentina*. Buenos Aires, 1939.

Nuñez, Luis F. *Almario de Buenos Airs, Los cementerios*. Buenos Aires, 1970.

Onega, Gladys S. *La inmigración en la literatura argentina (1880–1910)*. Santa Fe, 1965.

Ortega, Manuel L. *Los Hebreos en Marruecos*. Madrid, 1919.

Ostwald, Simon. "Sion!" |Speech at the Zionist Society Liga Dr. Theodor Herzl on Dec. 25, 1901|. Buenos Aires, 1902.

Pensamiento Cristiano y Democrático de Monseñor de Andrea. 2d edition. Senado de la Nación (Presidencia). Buenos Aires, 1965.

Perez Amuchastegui, A. J. *Mentalidades Argentinas (1860–1930)*. Buenos Aires, 1965.

Podolsky, M., ed. *Los Voluntarios Israelitas*. Album dedicated to the first group of men leaving for the Jewish Legion in Palestine (Mostly in Yiddish; also some Russian and Spanish). Buenos Aires, 1918.

Poilishe Yiddn in Dorem Amerika |Polish Jews in South America|. Buenos Aires, 1941.

Pulido Fernández, Ángel. *Españoles sin patria y la raza sefardí*. Madrid, 1905.

Ramos, Jorge Abelardo. *El partido comunista en la política argentina, su historia y su crítica*. Buenos Aires, 1962.

Rapoport, Nicolás. *Desde lejos hasta ayer*. Buenos Aires, 1957.

Recueil de Matériaux sur la Situation Economique des Israélites de Russie d'Après l'Enquête de la JCA. Paris, 1906.

Regalsky, Mordechai |Marcos|. "Politishe Shtremungen un Partaien in Argentiner Ishuv" |Jewish Political Parties in Argentina|. In *Yoblbuch Yiddishe Zeitung*. 537–62. Buenos Aires, 1940.

————. "Der Durchfal wos hot sich Farendikt mit a Groisn Nitsochn: Tsu der Geshichte fun der 'Alianz' Bavegung" |The Failure that ended in a great triumph: On the history of the Alianza movement|. In *Yorbuch 5715*, 15–19. Buenos Aires, 1954.

Reynal O'Connor, Arturo. "Por las colonias." *Revista Nacional* 33 (January 1902): 41–49.

Ricard, Robert. "Notes sur l'Emigration des Israélites Marocaines en Amerique Espagnole et au Bresil." *Revue Africaine* (Algiers) 88, nos. 1–2 (1944): 83–88.
Rinkevich, Ezequiel. "Prakim Letoldot Hachinuch Hayehudi Beargentina" [Chapters on the history of Jewish education in Argentina]. In Mordechai Maidanik, ed., *Sefer Argentina*. 105–53. Buenos Aires, 1954.
Rojas, Ricardo. *La restauración nacionalista*. 3d edition. Buenos Aires, 1971.
Rollansky, Samuel. *Dos Yiddishe Gedrukte Wort un Teater in Argentine*. [The Jewish printed word and theater in Argentina]. Buenos Airs, 1941.
Romero, José Luis. *A HIstory of Argentine Political Thought*. Stanford, 1963.
———. *El desarrollo de las ideas en la sociedad argentina del siglo XX*. Mexico, 1965.
Rondanina, Esteban. *Liberalismo, masonería y socialismo en la evolución nacional*. Buenos Aires, 1965.
Rosenberg, Shalom, and Daniel Rubinstein-Novick. "Instituciones y tendencias en la vida religiosa judía en la Argentina." In Isaac Janasowicz, ed. *Pinkas fun der Kehila*, 111–54. Buenos Aires, 1969.
Rosenswaike, Ira. "The Jewish Populations of Argentina: Census and Estimates, 1887–1947." *Jewish Social Studies* 22, no. 4 (October 1960): 195–214.
Sagasti, Francisco P. *Monseñor de Andrea y el Arzobispado de Buenos Aires*. Buenos Aires, 1924.
Sánchez Albornoz, Nicolás, and José Luis Moreno. *La población de América Latina*. Buenos Aires, 1968.
Sandberg, Harry O. "The Jews of Latin America." *American Jewish Yearbook*, 35–105. 1917-18.
Schallman, Lázaro. "Proceso histórico de la colonización agrícola en la Argentina." In D. Cúneo, et al., eds. *Inmigración y nacionalidad*. Buenos Aires, 1967.
———. "Antecedents históricos y sociales de la fundación de la AMIA." In Isaac Janasowicz, ed. 19–34. Buenos Aires, 1969.
———. "Historia del periodismo judío en la Argentina." In *Comunidades Judías de Latinoamerica*. 149–73. Buenos Aires, 1970.
Schenkolewski, Silvia. "Di Zionistishe Bavegung in Argentine fun 1897–1917." [The Zionist movement in Argentina during 1897–1917]. In Isaac Janasowicz, ed. *Pinkas fun der Kehila*. 101–30. Buenos Aires, 1969.
Schobinger, Juan. *Inmigración y colonización suizas en la República Argentina*. Buenos Aires, 1957.
Schusheim, A. "LeToldot Haishuv Hayehudi beArgentina" [On the history of the Jewish community in Argentina]. In Mordechai Maidanik, ed. *Sefer Argentina*, 27–65. Buenos Aires, 1954.
Scobie, James. *Argentina: A City and a Nation*. New York, 1964.
———. *Buenos Aires: From Plaza to Suburb, 1870–1910*. New York, 1974.
Sebreli, Juan José. *Buenos Aires: Vida cotidiana y alienación*. Buenos Aires, 1965.
———. *La cuestión judía en la Argentina*. Buenos Aires, 1968.
Los sefaradim y el sionismo. Buenos Aires, 1926.
Setton Dabbah, Shaul. *Dibber Shaul* [Shaul spoke]. Jerusalem, 1928.
Shabetay, Hizkia. *Divrei Hizkiahu*. Vol. 2. Jerusalem, 1952.
Sholem Aleichem. *Alle Werk fun Sholem Aleichem*. New York, 1942.
———. "The Man from Buenos Aires." In his *Tevye's Daughters*. New York, 1949.
Smilg, M. "Dos Yidishe Bank-Wezen in Buenos Aires." [Jewish Banking in Buenos Aires]. *Yoblbuch Yiddishe Zeitung*, 291–308. Buenos Aires, 1940.
Soiza Reilly, Juan José de, "El martirio de los inocentes." *Revista Popular*, no. 42 (February 1919): 1–4.
Sola Pool, David de, "The Levantine Jews in the United States," *American Jewish Yearbook* (1913/14), pp. 207–20.
Solberg, Carl. *Immigration and Nationalism, Argentina and Chile, 1890–1914*. Austin, 1970.
Solominsky, Nahum. *La Semana Trágica*. Buenos Aires, 1971.
Spalding, Hobart. *La clase trabajadora argentina (Documentos para su historia, 1890–1912)*. Buenos Aires, 1970.
Stach, Francisco. "La defensa social y la inmigración." *Boletín Mensual del Museo Social Argentino* 5, no. 55–56 (July–August 1916): 360–89.

Stimson, Frederick Jessup. *My United States*. New York, 1931.

Taran, Joseph Aharon. *Zichron Iosef* [Joseph's Recollection]. Jerusalem, 1924.

Tcherikower, Elias, ed. *The Early Jewish Labor Movement in the United States*. Translated and revised by Aaron Antonovsky. New York, 1961.

Teubal, Nissim. *El inmigrante, de Alepo a Buenos Aires*. Buenos Aires, 1953.

Verbitzky, Gregorio. *Rivera, afán de medio siglo*. Buenos Aires, 1955.

Viñas, David. *De los montoneros a los anarquistas*. Buenos Aires, 1971.

Wald, Pinie [Pedro]. *Koshmar* [Nightmares]. Buenos Aires, 1929.

————. "Yiddish-Weltliche Shul Bavegung in Argentine" [Jewish Secular School Movement in Argentina]. *Arbeter Ring Shul Almanach*, 220–29. Philadelphia, 1935.

————. "Yiddishe Sotsialistishe Arbeter Bavegung in Argentine biz 1910" (The Jewish Socialist Workers movement in Argentina until 1910). *Argentiner IWO Shriftn* 2(1942): 92–126.

————. "Yiddn in der Tragisher Woch" [Jews in the Tragic Week]. *Argentiner IWO Shriftn* 4(1947): 5–55.

————. "Yiddish-Weltliche Kultur-Bavegung in Argentine (1895–1920)" [The Jewish secular cultural movement in Argentina (1895–1920)]. *Argentiner IWO Shriftn* 6(1955): 45–78.

Weill, Simón. *Población israelita en la República Argentina*. Buenos Aires, 1936.

Weinberg, Gregorio, ed. *Debate parlamentario sobre la Ley 1420*, (1883–84). Buenos Aires, 1956.

Wilensky, Yehuda L. *Prakim M'Chaiai Hatziburiim* [Chapters on my public life]. Jerusalem, 1968.

Wischnitzer, Mark. *Visas to Freedom: The History of HIAS*. Cleveland and New York, 1956.

Yagupsky, Máximo. "Di Yiddishe Dertsiung in di Kolonies un Provintsen" [Jewish Education in the colonies and provinces]. *Yoblbuch Yiddishe Zeitung*. 445–58. Buenos Aires, 1940.

Yahuda, Abraham S. *Hahagana al Haishuv Bemilhemet Haolam Harishona: Zichronot meiemei shauti bisfarad* [The defense of the community during World War I: Memoires of my days in Spain]. Jerusalem, 1952.

Yiddishe Folks Bank, Yoblbuch, 1921–1951 [Banco Popular Israelita, Jubilee volume, 1921–1951]. Buenos Aires, 1951.

Zederbaum, Alexander. *Arba Maamarim* [Four Articles]. Petersburg, 1893.

Zenner Walter Paul. *Syrian Jewish Identification in Israel*. Ph.D. dissertation. Columbia University, 1965.

Zitnitsky, L. "Yiddn in Buenos Aires Loit der Munitsipaler Tseilung fun 1936" [Jews in Buenos Aires according to the municipal census of 1936]. *Argentiner IWO Shriftn* 3(1945): 5–22.

————. "Landsmanschaftn in Argentine." *Argentiner IWO Shriftn* 3(1945): 155–61.

Index

Index

Rabbinic culture, 162–63
Rabbis, 86–99, 154. *See also under rabbis'*
names
Radical Party, 14, 62, 72–73, 75, 121, 136,
230
Radowitzky, Simon, 54, 189
Ramos, Juan P., 24
Red scare, 50, 64–65, 250n.89
Regalsky, Marcos (Mordechai), 68, 114,
134, 186, 228
Resnick, Salomon, 179
Revista Argentina de Ciencias Políticas, 60–61
Revista Nacional, 52–53
Reynal O'Connor, Arturo, 52–53
Rio de Janeiro, 32, 99, 128, 212
Roca, Julio A., 27, 53, 99
Rodriguez Ocampo, Manuel, 217
Roite Hilf, 143
Der Roiter Shtern, 143, 146
Rojas, Ricardo, 57, 59, 138, 153
Rollansky, Samuel, 103, 173
Romanoff, 55
Rosario, 36, 91, 103, 128, 129, 157, 165,
167, 178, 212
Rosenbaum, Shimshon, 186
Rosenzwit, Ephraim, 92
Rothschild, Leopold, 211
Rothschild, stereotype of, 51, 115
Roumania: emigration from, 23, 26,
241n.17; white slave dealers from,
214
Russia: antisemitism in, 27–30, 48–49,
185; emigration from, 26, 29–33, 139–
40; reemigration to, 22
Russian Jews in Buenos Aires, occupa-
tions of, 40–45
Russian Revolution, 61, 64–65, 114, 142,
168, 170

Salant, Samuel, 86
Salonika, 185
San Remo, 131–32
Sarmiento, Domingo F., 48
Savransky, Bernardo, 226
Schapira, A., 140
Schomer Israel, 190
Schools: accused of anti-Argentine edu-
cation, 56–58; Arbeter Shuln, 143,
158–59; Borochov Shuln, 114, 146,
157–59; Folks Shuln, 114, 157–59; sec-
ular, 156–59; Sephardic, 153–55, 160;
Talmud Torah Harischono, 92, 149,
153, 189, 222–24; Talmud Torahs, 57–
58, 149–56, 159, 227–28. *See also* Cur-
sos Religiosos Israelitas

Schoua, Moises, 128
Schusheim, A. L., 230
Scobie, James, 200
Semanario Hebreo, 145, 179, 182
Semana Trágica, 61–68, 117, 131, 180,
186; aftermath of, 71–73, 215; Zionists
during, 123–25
Sephardim, 15, 74, 164–65, 232, 239n.7;
and intermarriage, 103–8; localism of,
in Buenos Aires, 31, 77, 130, 164, 177,
194–95, 230, 232, 234; occupations of,
42–43; religious practices of, 84–85,
96–99; Zionism among, 125–31, 137,
139, 179. *See also* Aleppine, Dama-
scene, Moroccan, and Turkish Jews in
Buenos Aires; Ashkenazim and Se-
phardim
Setton, Jacobo, 98–99
Setton Dabbah, Shaul, 86, 93, 98–99, 163,
233; ban on conversions, 105–8,
257n.144; and Jewish education, 154–
55; and Zionism, 126, 128, 262n.74
Shabetay, Hiskia, 96, 107
Shochetim, 92–95, 154
Sholem Aleichem, 167, 179, 207
Shtraln, 68–69
Sinai, Michl Hacohen, 269n.5, 270n.34
Sinai, Reuben Hacohen, 87, 90, 209
El Sionista, 83, 89, 125, 179, 270n.34
Smyrna (Izmir), 35–36, 154
Socialista Argentino Party, 68
Socialista Party, 54, 67–68, 72, 110, 115,
141; and Jewish cemetery, 70–71; and
Jewish socialists, 67–70, 141, 273n.78
Socialists, 53–55, 62, 67–71, 140–42; Jew-
ish, 186. *See also Der Avangard*; Bund;
Poale Zion
Sociedad de Damas Israelitas, 89, 190,
212, 215, 227, 276n.33
Sociedad Hebraica Argentina (SHA), 137,
177, 183, 235, 272n.74; and Zionism,
137–39
Sociedad Sportiva Argentina, 54
Soiza Reilly, Juan José de, 63
Sokolow, Nahum, 120, 127, 130, 135–36
Solá, Ricardo, 60
Soloveitchik, Max (Moshe), 186
Soprotimis, 23–24, 75, 187, 190–91, 195,
215, 227
Sorel, Georges, 62
Sorkin, Zalman, 54, 112
Spain, 121
Spanish, Jewish press and culture in,
175–83
Spektor Elhanan, 87

299

Victor A. Mirelman is the rabbi at the West Suburban Temple Har Zion in River Forest, Illinois. He holds the M.S. degree from the University of Buenos Aires and the M.A. and Ph.D. degrees from Columbia University. His rabbinic ordination is from the Jewish Theological Seminary in New York. Dr. Mirelman has taught at the Hebrew University of Jerusalem and at the Jewish Theological Seminary. He has published numerous articles in scholarly journals.

The manuscript was edited by Michael Lane. The book was designed by Don Ross. The typeface for the text is Novarese Book. The display face is Tiffany Heavy and Helvetica Bold. The book is printed on 60-lb Finch Opaque paper and is bound in Joanna Kennett cloth.

Manufactured in the United States of America.